3/20/21

BRIAN

MW00344594

CHURCHILL'S SPY FILES

Courtesy of Nicola Loud

CHURCHILL'S
SPY
FILES

MI5'S TOP-SECRET
WARTIME REPORTS

NIGEL WEST

The
History
Press

First published 2018

The History Press
The Mill, Brimscombe Port
Stroud, Gloucestershire, GL5 2QG
www.thehistorypress.co.uk

British Library Cataloguing in Publication Data.
A catalogue record for this book is available from the British Library.

ISBN 978 0 7509 8549 9

Typesetting and origination by The History Press
Printed and bound in Great Britain by TJ Internationa Ltd

CONTENTS

FOREWORD

Within Whitehall the Security Service enjoys a unique position, and the Director-General, although answerable to the Home Secretary, has direct access to the Prime Minister. The Service is not an instrument of political power but it operates within a political environment. The delicate balance between the political world and the political neutrality of the Security Service in defending national security depends to a large degree on the relationship between the D-G and the government of the day, including the Prime Minister.

Despite the programme of declassification initiated by my predecessor Sir Stephen Lander, very little is known about how the first D-G, Sir Vernon Kell, coped with successive Prime Ministers until he was dismissed by Winston Churchill in June 1940.

It fell to Sir David Petrie to restore confidence in MI5, which was then almost overwhelmed by the pressures of an unexpected war, and to satisfy the coalition government that the Security Service, long regarded with some suspicion by the incoming Home Secretary Herbert Morrison, was up to the challenge of countering Axis espionage and sabotage, as well as acting professionally and without partisan prejudice in a counter-subversion role.

This was the historical background to the decision to provide regular briefings to the PM, and though the practice was discontinued when Clement Attlee took up residence in No. 10, it was subsequently re-introduced, particularly in the post-Cold War era, when the Service had become the front line in combating terrorist threats. The nature of the threat meant that, especially after 9/11, a much closer relationship developed between Thames House and Downing Street.

During my six years as D-G it fell to me to brief Tony Blair, Gordon Brown and David Cameron on a range of sensitive operations and, based on that experience, I can appreciate the delicacy of Petrie's task: how much to impart without compromising the operational independence of the Service, enshrined in law, and how much detail the Prime Minister needed to know in order to understand the threat facing the country, without burdening him or her with unnecessary detail.

Now, for the first time, we have the chance to see the papers put before Churchill and, with the benefit of hindsight, we can come to acknowledge the fine judgement exercised by Petrie and his supremely able subordinate, Guy Liddell.

The reports to Churchill (and to him alone) demonstrate MI5's global reach, its links with Allied agencies, its skilful and imaginative exploitation of precarious sources of information, and the sheer quality of personnel engaged in a struggle with a very determined adversary operating world-wide. In many ways, it might seem that not much has changed.

Lord Evans of Weardale
Former Director-General of MI5
2018

ACKNOWLEDGEMENTS

The author is indebted to those wartime MI5 agents who assisted his research, among them Dusan Popov (TRICYCLE), Ivo Popov (DREADNOUGHT), Elvira de Chaudoir (BRONX), Harry Williamson (TATE), Eugn Sostaric (METEOR), the Marquis deBona (FREAK), Ib Riis (COBWEB), Juan Pujol (GARBO), Eddie Chapman (ZIGZAG), Roman Garby-Czerniawski (BRUTUS), John Moe (MUTT), Tor Glad (JEFF) and the MI5 officers Tommy Robertson, Ian Wilson, Jack Bingham, Norman Himsworth, Cyril Mills, Dick White, Herbert Hart, the Hon. Hugh Astor, Anthony Blunt, Victor Rothschild, Len Burt, John Maude, Peter Hope, Peter Ramsbotham, Gerald Glover, Sir Rupert Speir, Richard Darwall and Russell Lee.

I am also grateful for the help given by Sigismund Best, Francois Grosjean, E.P.C. Greene; Rui Arajo, Mark Scoble, Douglas Wheeler, Etienne Verhoeyen, Ben de Jong, Gunter Peis, Joan Bright Astley, Margaret Blyth, Ed Lawler from OSS, and five SIS officers, Philip Johns, Cecil Gledhill, John Codrington, Ken Benton and Desmond Bristow, who were based in Iberia during the war; and Peter Falk, who was in Sweden.

ABBREVIATIONS

@	Alias
ACIC	Allied Counter-Intelligence Centre, Iceland
ADB1	Assistant Director, MI5's B1 section
AEM	Alto Estado Mayor
AFHQ	Allied Forces Headquarters
ARP	Air Raid Precautions
ASDIC	Anti-Submarine Detection
ATS	Auxiliary Territorial Service
BSC	British Security Coordination
BUF	British Union of Fascists
C	Chief of the Secret Intelligence Service
CICI	Combined Intelligence Centre Iraq
COHQ	Combined Operations Headquarters
CPGB	Communist Party of Great Britain
CSDIC	Combined Services Detailed Interrogation Centre
Devlag	German-Flemish Working Group
DF	Direction-Finding
DOR	Defence of the Realm Act
DSO	Defence Security Officer
FFI	French Forces of the Interior
FSP	Field Security Police
FUSAG	First United States Army Group
GC&CS	Government Code and Cipher School, Bletchley Park
GOC	General Officer Commanding
IH	Eins Heer
IL	Eins Luft
IM	Eins Marine
ISK	Intelligence Service Knox

ISOS	Intelligence Service Oliver Strachey
JIC	Joint Intelligence Committee
KO	Kriegsorganisation
LRC	London Reception Centre
NKVD	Soviet Intelligence Service
OB	Ossewa Brandweg
OD	Orde Dienst
OGPU	Soviet intelligence service
OKW	Oberkommando der Wehrmacht
OSS	Office of Strategic Services
PLUTO	Pipe Line Under The Ocean
PoW	Prisoner of War
P-Plane	V-1 flying bomb
PRU	Photographic Reconnaissance Unit
PWE	Political Warfare Executive
RASC	Royal Army Service Corps
RCMP	Royal Canadian Mounted Police
RDF	Radio Direction-Finding
RHSA	Reich Security Agency
RIS	Radio Intelligence Section
RSLO	Regional Security Liaison Officer
RSS	Radio Security Service
R/T	Radio-Telephony
SCI	Special Counter-Intelligence Unit
SCO	Security Control Officer
SD	Sicherheitsdienst
SHAEF	Supreme Headquarters Allied Expeditionary Force
SIE	Servicio Informazione Extere
SIGINT	Signals Intelligence
SIM	Servicio Informazione Militare
SIME	Security Intelligence Middle East
Sipo	Sicherheitspolizei
SIS	Secret Intelligence Service
W/T	Wireless Telegraphy
X-2	OSS Counter-intelligence branch
XX	Double-Cross

Code Names

BIGOT	Indoctrinated into invasion plans
CROSSBOW	German V-1 flying-bomb campaign
OVERLORD	D-Day invasion of Normandy
PHOENIX	D-Day harbour caissons
TORCH	Allied invasion of North Africa

INTRODUCTION

When in June 1942 Alfred Duff Cooper was given ministerial responsibility in the Cabinet for the British Security Service, MI5, he was not surprised by the secrecy surrounding the organisation and its operations, which hitherto had been largely undertaken under the aegis of the Permanent Under-Secretary at the Home Office, but he was intrigued to learn about its activities and offered to share some of this information with the Prime Minister.

Churchill had a long history of interest in, bordering on fascination with, secret intelligence, dating back to his period as Home Secretary in 1910 when he had introduced the first communications warrants to allow the interception of a suspect's mail. He was enchanted by Cooper's suggestion, as the newly appointed Chairman of the Home Defence Security Executive, replacing Lord Swinton, to have MI5's Director-General, Sir David Petrie, prepare summary reports on what the country's principal counter-espionage and counter-intelligence authority had been working on. As Petrie explained, this was an innovation as hitherto MI5 had not been keen to advertise its existence, let alone its clandestine role, but he recognised that support from 10 Downing Street was essential. Cooper wrote:

My Dear Petrie,
I had a talk with the Prime Minister on Sunday afternoon, in the course of which I told him about some of our recent activities and described some of the more interesting cases which have come under our control, such as the case of Chapman and Woerman. I also told him about the present we had recently received from the north of Scotland and the evidence that we had about the head of the Ossewa Brandweg. He was very much interested and I subsequently suggested to him that it would be a useful thing for him

to receive a Monthly report on the activities of the Security Service. He entirely agreed. I think the furnishing of such a report would not only be useful from his point of view, in order that he night keep in touch with what is going on, but might also encourage those who are engaged in the work to feel that its importance is properly estimated, and the fact of it reached the highest authorities:

If you agree, perhaps you would inform those concerned in order that such a report might be prepared to cover the present month. It is most important that it should not be a voluminous document as the Prime Minister is naturally overwhelmed with reading material and has very little time to devote to it. It should not consist, in my opinion, of more than two or three pages and should be confined to incidents of exceptional interest.

Perhaps you will let me know what you think.

The four cases referred to that Cooper thought would interest Churchill were those of Eddie Chapman, code-named ZIGZAG, who was one of the most remarkable double-agents of the war; the ultra-nationalist, pro-Nazi Ossewa Brandweg movement in South Africa; the defector 'Woerman', who was actually Major Richard Wurmann, formerly head of the Algiers Abstelle, code-named HARLEQUIN and alias Count Heinrich Stenboch; and the vague allusion to recent events in northern Scotland was a Luftwaffe parachute drop near Aberdeen of sabotage equipment for a pair of Norwegian double-agents, MUTT and JEFF.

The day after Cooper wrote this, the matter was mentioned by Guy Liddell, the Director of MI5's B Division, in charge of counter-espionage, in his diary:

The Director-General has had a letter from Duff Cooper who, after consultation with the Prime Minister, has suggested that we should furnish the Prime Minister with a monthly report. It should not be too long and should only include items of major importance. It is suggested there should be contributions from Herbert Hart, Buster Milmo, T.A. Robertson, the London Reception Centre, Roger Hollis and occasionally items of interest received from Defence Security Officer points abroad. Dick White is going to get out a rough draft which we will then discuss. There are obvious advantages in selling ourselves to the Prime Minister who at the moment knows nothing about the activities of the department. On the other hand he may, on seeing some particular item, go off the deep end and want to take action, which will be disastrous to the work in hand.

Clearly Liddell was worried by Churchill's reputation for spontaneity and meddling, but a few days later, on 16 March, he discussed the matter with his senior subordinates, two from B Division and Hollis, in charge of the counter-subversion branch, F Division:

> I had a talk with Dick White, T.A. Robertson, and Roger Hollis about the monthly report for the Prime Minister. They were all a little apprehensive about Hollis' contribution. The Prime Minister might speak to the Home Secretary about it and if the latter was not also informed we should find ourselves in trouble. We eventually decided to draft something and see what it looked like. Dick will be editor of the B Division material.

What makes this material so remarkable is that it was prepared for the sole consumption of the Prime Minister, and not any of his staff, including his private secretaries, military advisers nor even Desmond Morton, his intelligence aide, seconded from the Secret Intelligence Service. Not even the Cabinet Secretary was a party to these reports, and no copies were retained within the Cabinet Office as every document was delivered to Churchill by hand by Petrie, who waited to offer a verbal briefing if required and then took the file back to his headquarters in St James's Street. No one else, in an era when the word declassification had not been invented, was ever intended to have sight of the contents, thus allowing the authors to be both selective and candid.

The task of assembling the report was given by Liddell to his assistant, Dick White, and on 26 March he produced a covering memorandum explaining that the editorial work had been undertaken by Anthony Blunt:

> The attached paper has been prepared as the first report for Mr Duff Cooper to hand to the PM. The 2½ pages represent condensation from the original script turned into one by various sections amounting to something like 16 pages. These 16 pages were reduced in the first place, by Blunt merely as a precis exercise and then he and I discussed the preparation of this final draft.
>
> As a matter of policy we have not produced any sketch of the work of this office in retrospect as we considered that this would look too much as though we were out to advertise the office. It is surely up to Mr Duff Cooper to let the PM know what sort of things we do in general. The items we have included in this report have been chosen both because they may be expected to interest him in themselves and because they illustrate the type of work we do, at any rate in B Division. We have not had any contributions from

E Division and indeed have not asked for them while I understand it is not considered advisable for Hollis to make any contribution at all.

May I suggest that the procedure should be for Mr Duff Cooper to hand a report of this type to the PM. in a special file marked 'personal for the PM only' or some such wording and that it should be returned to Mr Duff Cooper after the PM has read it.

On 29 March Liddell considered the matter further, and minuted his revised views about the wisdom of mentioning the activities of F Division, for fear that Churchill might raise a matter with Herbert Morrison regarding the Communist Party, about which the Home Secretary had not been briefed. The topics of security and intelligence were regarded with great suspicion by the Labour Party, many members of whom either had been close to the Communist Party of Great Britain, or held views shaped by the events surrounding the defeat of Ramsay MacDonald's administration in October 1924 following publication of the notorious Zinoviev letter. In these circumstances Liddell exercised characteristic caution so as to avoid political controversy:

I enclose a draft report for the Prime Minister in accordance with Mr Duff Cooper's letter. I do not know what you feel about contributions from other Divisions. Personally I think there are difficulties in putting forward anything from F Division since, if the Prime Minister were to discuss the subject with the Home Secretary, the latter would be extremely annoyed that he had not received prior notification on a matter for which he was primarily responsible, and this would place us in bad odour with the Home Office.

It is perhaps for consideration whether we should send a copy of our report to C. I am not anxious to do so if it can be avoided. On the other hand CSS is constantly seeing the Prime Minister, who might well discuss the contents of our report with him where it indirectly impinges upon SIS work.

Lastly, I think it would be better if instead of leaving this report with the Prime Minister, Mr. Duff Cooper showed it to him personally and then took it away. It would not take more than 5 minutes to read, and if there were any supplementary questions or queries they could either be dealt with on the spot or conveyed to Mr. Duff Cooper who could refer them back to ourselves.

You may wish to have a talk about these various problems with the officers concerned before submitting the draft to Mr. Duff Cooper.

By 2 April the first MI5 report, one of twenty-five drawn up before the end of the conflict, had been drafted, as Liddell recorded:

> I saw Duff Cooper and took him the report for the Prime Minister. He seemed quite satisfied with its form and contents. I impressed upon him the degree of secrecy which should be attached to it and the necessity therefore of ensuring that it was seen by the Prime Minister only. At first he had thought of sending it to Desmond Morton. I said I thought it would be far preferable if he handed it to the Prime Minister himself. He would then be able to answer any supplementary questions and ascertain the Prime Minister's reactions. From what he said I do not think that he intends to leave the report with the Prime Minister. In any case he will ask for its return. I told him that if it went to Desmond Morton it was highly probable that he would take a copy and send it to C. While there was no real objection to this it might possibly cause a certain amount of trouble.

Although Liddell appears to have welcomed the principle of winning the Prime Minister's ear, if only briefly, he was obviously very anxious to exclude Morton from access, as he undoubtedly would have informed Stewart Menzies, who in turn would have been bound to confide in Section V, the SIS branch that dealt with MI5 daily on the most sensitive of issues, such as the ISOS intercepts and the management of double-agents. Section V's notoriously prickly chief, Felix Cowgill, was already highly proprietorial about sharing his section's gold dust, and would have been horrified at the prospect of Churchill being entrusted with such delicate secrets as the true identities of agents.

The ticklish task of selecting cases for submission to Churchill was assigned by Liddell to his trusted assistant, Anthony Blunt, who must have relished the prospect of being given a pretext to range far and wide across the Security Service, and elsewhere, to assemble the appropriate material for the Prime Minister. Few spies in history could ever have been presented with such a spectacular opportunity to call for files, question colleagues and demand briefings on topics that would otherwise be completely outside the ambit of his duties. Quite simply, Blunt, who had been a Soviet agent since 1936, was granted a licence to delve into just about any operational issue that caught his interest. As Liddell's personal assistant he enjoyed a lofty viewpoint anyway, and his role in directing the TRIPLEX project[1] provided him with access to some of the organisation's most delicate sources, but his added responsibility, of drafting the monthly reports, must have seemed heaven-sent. His MI5 colleagues already accepted that he routinely acted in Liddell's name, and this additional responsibility must have greatly added to his already exalted status.

The purpose in reproducing all the Prime Minister's monthly MI5 reports here is to give a comprehensive picture of what the Security Service shared with Churchill, and when. As we shall see, Petrie and his subordinate Liddell exercised considerable discretion in what went to Downing Street, and to give the bigger view each report is accompanied by a commentary to reveal the background to some of the events, operations and individuals which are referenced. Very often, particular agents and defectors were not identified by their true name, so this annotated version is intended to leave the reader rather better informed than Churchill.

A few of the cases selected for the Prime Minister's attention will be familiar to *aficionados* of wartime espionage, but the majority will be entirely new to historians. They shed fascinating light on the global aspect of MI5's wartime activities, demonstrating the value of some hitherto relatively unknown officers, such as Colonel Henderson, the Defence Security Officer in Trinidad who, operating from Bretton Hall in Port of Spain's Victoria Avenue, interdicted numerous Axis spies en route to and from South America. These spies underwent a preliminary interrogation before being passed to HMS *Benbow*, the Royal Navy's shore establishment, for a voyage to England and incarceration at Camp 020.

By convention, the identities of MI5 personnel were not disclosed in reports likely to be circulated outside headquarters, so Churchill had little way of knowing that, for example, the officer sent to the United States in April 1943 to advise on American port security arrangements was George Denham, or that the head of MI5's counter-sabotage branch mentioned in several reports was Lord Rothschild. By filling in the gaps, and drawing pen-portraits of such remarkable men as HARLEQUIN and COLOMBINE, not to mention the rather lesser-known double-agents as FIDO, HAMLET and METEOR, it is hoped that more light will be shed on the somewhat misunderstood, murky relationship between the First Secretary of the Treasury and the Security Service.

THE MONTHLY REPORTS

I

FIRST REPORT, 2 APRIL 1943

Entitled *Report on Activities of the Security Service*, the document, with a paragraph redacted, covered several topics and established a standard format of arrested spies and imminent espionage cases, and introduced the concept of controlled enemy agents:

Spies arrested since September 1939
It is believed that while the many Germans who returned to their country when on the outbreak of war took with them a most exact knowledge of the state of our re-armament and the potential output of our factories they left no live spy organisation behind them. Being without up-to-date information, after their defeat in the Battle of Britain, the Germans again resorted to their former system of individual spying. Since September, 1940, attempts at penetration have been persistent. In all 126 spies have fallen into our hands. Of these eighteen gave themselves up voluntarily, twenty-four have been found amenable and are now being used as double-cross agents. Twenty-eight have been detained at overseas stations, and eight were arrested on the high seas. In addition twelve real, and seven imaginary persons have been foisted upon the enemy as double-cross spies. Thirteen spies have been executed, and a fourteenth is under trial.

NEW ARRESTS.
(1) MENEZES
This spy was a clerk in the Portuguese Embassy, London. He was working for the German and Italian Secret Services, to whom he sent reports written in secret ink in private letters sent through the Portuguese diplomatic bag. For a period during which we were able to assure ourselves that the reports

which he was sending were harmless, we watched his operations and finally on an occasion when he had obtained an interesting item of news which duly showed up in a letter, his career as a spy had to be ended. Through the wholehearted collaboration of the Portuguese Ambassador Menezes was arrested and made a full confession. The Portuguese Government having waived his diplomatic privilege, he has now been committed for trial.

(2) DE GRAAF
This Canadian traitor, of Dutch parentage, was detected by our interrogation staff on entering this country. He confessed to having worked for the German Secret Service for more than two years, during which he had insinuated himself into an Allied escape organisation for our prisoners of war which he is believed to have betrayed to the enemy. He was in addition a well trained saboteur.

(3) BATICON, LASKI, PACHECO Y CUESTA
The existence of these three spies on ships bound for South America was revealed by material supplied from special sources. They were successfully identified at our Trinidad control, and are being sent to this country for interrogation.

C. Agents Expected
Similar material reveals German plans for despatching two new spies to this country and two saboteurs to be landed by submarine on the coast of Palestine. Suitable arrangements have been made for their reception.

D. Controlled German Spies ('Double-Cross Spies')
(1) Through a double-cross spy in this country a deal was concluded with the German Secret Service in Madrid, by which £2,500 were paid to the spy here and 250,000 pesetas were put at our disposal in Madrid. This deal was arranged through the unconscious help of the Spanish Assistant Military Attaché in London, who took with him in the diplomatic bag a letter of introduction to the principals in Madrid, on the back of which was a message to the German Secret Service in secret ink.

(2) 'ZIGZAG', an Englishman was dropped as a spy by parachute in October 1942 near Thetford. Extensive information was already in our possession before his arrival, so that his confession on giving himself up could be immediately checked. It was found possible to collaborate with this spy in

deceiving his former masters, who were persuaded to believe that he did in fact perform the mission for which he was sent here, namely to sabotage the de Havilland Mosquito factory at Hatfield. The agent has now been sent back to the Germans via Lisbon, and it is expected that he will be given another similar mission in British or Allied territory.

(3) On the night of 20 March 1943 a wireless set of new design, £200 in notes, and sabotage equipment were dropped by parachute in Aberdeenshire for MUTT and JEFF, who are double-cross spies of Norwegian nationality. The German aircraft flew low over the exact spot indicated by us to the German Secret Service.

(4) On 10 March 1943 one of our agents who has been recruited by the German Sabotage Service in Spain had a faked explosion arranged for him in Gibraltar. The German Sabotage Service gave him some SOE equipment with which to carry out this act of sabotage. As in a previous case where an act of sabotage was staged for another of our Gibraltar agents, this apparently successful enterprise has caused extreme satisfaction in German and Italian circles.

[XXX]*

Important new information about the organisation and methods of the German Secret Service has been obtained from two of its former members. Both these individuals have been induced to collaborate, and as one of them, an officer of the German General Staff, had been chief of an enemy Secret Service base, his revelations were particularly sensational. As a 'book of reference', it is believed his services will continue to prove of great value.

C. General Security Measures

(1) The Security Service has prepared a memorandum, running to sixty-eight printed pages, including diagrams, on the technical counter-measures to be taken against possible enemy sabotage. This memorandum has been circulated to our Defence Security Officers in the most important posts in the Empire. A special section dealing with the defence of shipping against sabotage has been further circulated to all ports in which we have representatives, both in England and overseas.

---

*   Indicates redacted material here and throughout.

(2) On the strength of information about TORCH supplied by the Security Service, the Director of Military Intelligence has issued a strong warning against careless talk about future operations. This warning was based on Security Service investigations which showed that a disturbing amount of loose talk had taken place before the invasion of North Africa.

(3) On the return of a special adviser who had been sent to the Middle East to survey the security position there, the Security Service are implementing his recommendations by sending three officers to the area, two of whom will plan and direct the examination of aliens, who arrive in that area from occupied Europe at the rate of about 900 a month, and the collection of intelligence from them. A third officer will supervise the investigation of Axis espionage. The existing organisation in Middle East requires strengthening on both these sides of the work.

(4) By arrangement with the Director of Military Intelligence the Security Service is supplying certain of its officers who have recently been put through special training courses in preparation for their future work, which will be to act as advisers on general security measures and on the technical aspect of counter-espionage and counter-sabotage work, both to the GHQ Ib staff of future expeditionary forces and to the staff of the Chief Civil Affairs Officer in the area behind the lines. The Director General considers that, with diminishing risks at home, these officers should be released for the purposes stated.

On the following day, Liddell was pleased with Churchill's reaction, which had been scrawled on the bottom of the third and final page:

Duff Cooper has returned our report for the Prime Minister with a letter saying that the Prime Minister would like to have further details about Wurmann. The Prime Minister has minuted the report in his distinctive red ink: 'Seen. Deeply interesting. W.S.C.' Duff seems to think it has been a great success.

The Prime Minister's interest in Richard Wurmann was entirely justified, as he was one of the most unusual cases dealt with by MI5 during the conflict, and a special summary was prepared (see Chapter 27).

This first report was MI5's opportunity to educate Churchill about the breadth of the organisation's activities, demonstrate its competence, and compete with SIS's daily briefings and deliveries of decrypts, usually juicy diplomatic telegrams, carefully selected by Menzies for his consumption. In terms of double-agents, four cases were mentioned by name, being the Norwegians MUTT and JEFF, and the safe-cracker Eddie Chapman, code-named ZIGZAG, then on his first mission to England, having arrived by parachute in December (not October, as stated) 1942. Unnamed is the double-agent who extracted £2,500 from his Abwehr controller in Madrid. This was surely a reference to GARBO, although his case would not be introduced for another three months, and to a scheme known as Plan DREAM that involved the Spanish assistant military attaché conspiring to circumvent the Bank of England's currency regulations with a syndicate of London fruit merchants. Simply, Leonardo Muñoz wanted to send money to Spain, but was willing to pay a nominee in London if he was paid the same sum, plus a generous commission, in Spain. The concept had been inspired by Cyril Mills, in November 1942, as Guy Liddell had noted in his diary:

> Cyril Mills talked to me about a plan he had on foot for getting money for GARBO. Apparently some fruit merchant here who is known to Muñoz, the Spanish assistant military attaché, wishes to transfer money from this country to Spain. It is suggested therefore that this money should be handed over to GARBO and that the German secret service should credit the fruit merchant with pesetas. Quite a large sum of money is likely to be involved. This is known as Plan DREAM.

By the end of January 1943, after complicated negotiations, DREAM had started to look like a practical proposition, as Liddell recorded on 1 February:

> Muñoz, the Spanish military attaché, is returning to Spain on Monday, and for the purpose of Plan DREAM we have arranged for him to take with him a letter of introduction. GARBO is to send a letter giving a new address at which Muñoz can be contacted and the money is to be deposited with Charles Russell & Company. Muñoz will then send a telegram to his contact in London to say that one has received the pesetas and that the sterling may now be released to the notional Mr Wills, in other words Cyril Mills. On the back of Muñoz's letter there will be a message in secret ink about which he will know nothing. The Germans will be notified about the existence of this message.

This transaction, supposedly brokered by the City solicitors Charles Russell & Co., where Richard Butler had worked before joining MI5, was completed without a hitch, and ten days later MI5 received the £2,500, an impressive coup that obviously merited inclusion in the report to Churchill. Indeed, the operation was so successful that it would be repeated again several times to fund GARBO's burgeoning network and expenses.

As if to emphasise MI5's remit across the Empire, Petrie described the three spies seized in Trinidad, Baticon, Laski and Pacheco, who would reappear in the third report, and the anticipated arrival of a pair of agents to be landed by a U-boat in Palestine. In the event, neither turned up, and the subject was not mentioned again. [1]

Such discretion, drawing a veil over an operation that had gone awry, and concentrating on proven success stories, would become a feature of the reports. The de Graaf case is an early example, as Guy Liddell had recorded on 23 January 1943, and there were some aspects to it, such as his temporary employment at the British embassy in Madrid, which had been omitted from the version submitted to Churchill:

> Buster Milmo reported at the Wednesday meeting that there had been a large influx at Camp 020. The main increase is in spies going to South America. He mentioned the case of Johannes de Graaf, a Belgian who had come down an escape route and had been temporarily employed at the British embassy in Madrid. De Graaf admitted that he had been in contact with the Abwehr but said that he had done so in order to escape. He was carrying pyramidon and tooth-picks. He was caught through a clever link-up on the information index at the Royal Victoria Patriotic School which showed that he had been put on the escape route by someone known already to be working for the Abwehr. He is now beginning to come clean. He was highly trained both in espionage and sabotage and appears to have corresponded with German occupied territory after his arrival in Madrid.

The de Graaf case was unusual in many respects. He was born in Saskatchewan in November 1918 to Dutch parents – farmers who returned to Amsterdam in 1928 – and he acquired a British passport in 1933. When the Germans occupied the Netherlands he was employed as a bookkeeper, and in June he was interned at Schoorl because of his dual citizenship. After ten days in detention de Graaf applied for his release, on the grounds that he was more Dutch than British, and he was interviewed by the Sicherheitsdienst in The Hague. Threatened with incarceration at a concentration camp, and anxious to support his elderly parents, de Graaf agreed to his recruitment and underwent a lengthy training course in sabotage and clandestine communications. In 1941 he made contact with an underground escape line that assisted his travel via Toulouse, where he spent six weeks, to the Spanish frontier in February 1942. He stayed in Barcelona for two months, supported by the British consul. Upon his arrival in Madrid he presented himself at the British embassy, where he was employed by Sir Peter Norton Griffiths for eight months as an accountant in the office of the military attaché, Brigadier W. W. T. Torr.

In December 1942 he sailed from Gibraltar for Gurock on the *Llanstephan Castle* and was arrested upon arrival when a search revealed the ingredients for secret writing. He was transferred to Brixton and then moved to Camp 020 where, during his sixth interview, he confessed to his role as a German spy, and admitted having sent three letters to his German controllers, one from Chalon and two from Toulouse.

A detailed interrogation was conducted by Helenus Milmo, who reported on 12 February 1943 that:

> ... since de Graaf's arrival at Camp 020 very substantial progress has been made and we are now in a position to say that this man is an infinitely more important enemy agent than we had originally thought. We are still a long way from obtaining the full truth from him and the extraction is proving a laborious process but from the admissions so far obtained de Graaf has shown himself to be one of the best trained enemy agents who have so far fallen into our hands. Thus he has admitted to having received instruction in political propaganda work, secret ink writing, wireless telegraphy, codes, sabotage, and the use of firearms. Moreover he has confessed to having been in contact with an interesting and important variety of German Secret Service personnel and to have written no less than three letters to the Germans at a time when he was employed on highly confidential work in the British Embassy at Madrid whilst awaiting repatriation to this country.

De Graaf's admission to an espionage role, and having attended some forty classes on radio technique, opened the possibility of a prosecution under the 1940 Treachery Act, and a death sentence, but there was a complication, as the 020 commandant, Robin Stephens, warned on 27 February:

> The position has been reached where a case could be put forward for prosecution under the Treachery Act. The prosecution, however, is much complicated by the astonishing action taken by the British Embassy in

employing this German spy for eight months in the Embassy with access to information on the escape routes. De Graaf relies upon a satisfactory recommendation from the Embassy to bear out his defence that he never intended to work against the Allies. At the same time it must be borne in mind that de Graaf has admitted possession of Pyramidon which was handed to him by the German Secret Service for purposes of secret writing.

Thus, having conceded that he had been sent on a sabotage mission, de Graaf's embarrassing defence was that he had never intended to spy, even though there was evidence from MI9 that he had compromised a major British escape network, having gained access to the information while employed by Brigadier Torr:

> Whilst employed at the British embassy in Madrid, this man was responsible for passing to the enemy information about an escape route from occupied territory and was directly responsible for the arrest by the Germans of probably the most important British agent operating this route who was responsible for the very marked success which it had achieved over the course of the last year.

De Graaf's assertion was that his sabotage mission had been to South Africa, and once it became clear to him that he could not obtain further instructions from his contact in Lisbon, as he had been directed, he had abandoned all thought of espionage. This may or may not have been true, but MI9 certainly did not want to acknowledge that a German spy had been working for them in Lisbon undetected for eight months. The issue was put before the Director of Public Prosecutions in March 1943 by Edward Hinchley-Cooke, and the decision was taken not to proceed with a prosecution. Accordingly, de Graaf's future was referred to the Home Office, with a recommendation from Petrie that he should be isolated at Dartmoor:

> The case against de Graaf has become a more serious and formidable one than was originally suspected, and admissions have been obtained from him which prove beyond question that he is one of the best and most extensively trained enemy agents who have fallen into our hands since the beginning of the war. Thus he has received a very thorough training as a saboteur and is conversant with the most up-to-date German sabotage methods and equipment. He has been fully instructed in the use of secret ink and developers, codes and cyphers, firearms, political propaganda and

has achieved a considerable proficiency as a wireless operator. In short he is an extremely dangerous man.

We had hoped that it would have been possible to prosecute De Graaf under the Treachery Act, but although we do not entertain the slightest doubt that de Graaf's association with the German Secret Service is incapable of any innocent construction, the Director of Public Prosecutions has advised against criminal proceedings because he feels that the evidence available for use in a Criminal Court – and this of course excludes the confessions extracted at Camp 020 – might not be strong enough to satisfy a jury that de Graaf's excuse for undertaking to work for the enemy is necessarily a bogus one. I may say that the excuse in question is the time-honoured one which the Germans instruct their agents to put forward if caught, namely; that he never intended to work for the enemy and only undertook his espionage assignments in order to escape to this country. In these circumstances the DPP has ruled against a prosecution. De Graaf, being technically a British subject and being detained under DOR 18(b), cannot remain indefinitely at Camp 020, but, as in the case of Boyd,[2] we would be strongly averse to his spending the rest of the war with the disaffected British subjects whom he would meet in any ordinary place of detention for 18(b) cases. It is, in our view, wholly undesirable that proved enemy agents, whether they be British subjects or aliens, should be allowed to mix freely or at all with ordinary internees and detainees. The chances of leakage are considerable and no proper safe-guards against such leakages can be maintained. Further, as I think I have stressed on previous occasions, it would not, in our view, be in the public interest that it should become generally known how very difficult it is to establish a strong enough case for prosecution against a spy, or that there are in this country in detention a very large number of spies who are not and cannot be dealt with under the Treachery Act.

We are therefore of the opinion that de Graaf should be moved to Dartmoor and should remain there for the duration.

At the end of April 1943 de Graaf was driven to Paddington Green police station for a final interview, and then escorted onto the Cornish Riviera Express at Paddington station for the rail journey to Exeter, and Dartmoor prison, where he remained for the rest of the war.

Although a highly abbreviated version of the de Graaf case was given to Churchill, he was never informed that, probably unwittingly, de Graaf had succeeded in penetrating MI9 in Madrid, and had betrayed an important British agent. When challenged about his employment, the Foreign Office's security branch, headed by William Codrington, insisted that Norton-Griffiths had disregarded procedures by taking him on without the approval of the embassy's security officer, Alan Hillgarth, and that the Passport Control Officer had known of the situation. Wherever the blame properly lay, de Graaf survived the experience and, having been refused a return to Canada, was repatriated to the Netherlands at the end of the war.

Whereas it had been almost impossible to prosecute de Graaf under the Treachery Act, MI5 encountered no such difficulties with Regeiro de Menezes, even though he was a fully accredited foreign diplomat whose espionage had been detected by that most secret of sources, TRIPLEX. Having arrived in London in July 1942 to work at the Portuguese legation with a junior rank, de Menezes had begun writing letters to his sister in Lisbon, enclosing another note using secret ink addressed to a man named Mendez. His mail had been included in the Portuguese diplomatic bag, which was surreptitiously opened and examined by MI5 as part of a joint SIS operation code-named TRIPLEX and supervised by Anthony Blunt. Although the precise nature of TRIPLEX was not explained in explicit terms, it is probable that Churchill either knew or guessed the sensitivities involved. That Blunt should have selected the de Menezes investigation to put before the Prime Minister is interesting as it illustrated at least six distinct MI5 techniques, including ISOS, the introduction of a woman *agent provocateur*, the penetration of the embassy by an agent code-named DUCK, physical and technical surveillance, and the exploitation of TRIPLEX.

As Blunt would have known, the de Menezes case had involved a high-level discussion about the wisdom of revealing evidence to the Portuguese ambassador that might put TRIPLEX at risk. The proposal, discussed in January 1943, had been vetoed instantly by SIS's David Boyle. Despite this reticence, TRIPLEX continued to supply the spy's correspondence that, under ultra-violet light, revealed secret writing describing London's air defences.

De Menezes's mission as a Sicherheitsdienst spy had been betrayed by an ISOS intercept even before he had landed, and he was watched inside the legation by an MI5 agent, and outside by MI5 surveillance teams. According to Jack Bingham, an MI5 officer who befriended him, he seemed particularly interested in anti-aircraft defences. In February 1943 the evidence was presented to Ambassador Monteiro, who was reminded that three other Portuguese, Gastao de Freitas,[3] Manoel dos Santos[4] and Ernesto Simoes,[5] had been caught spying and, after he had consulted Lisbon, he agreed to withdraw de Menezes' immunity. When arrested, Menezes claimed that he had spied under duress because he had relatives in Germany who were under threat.

In his confession he identified Mendez as a man named Marcello who worked for Umerte, an Italian intelligence officer. He claimed to have been introduced to them by a Portuguese air force officer, Colonel Miranda, and also mentioned Ramos, a cipher clerk in the Portuguese foreign ministry. Nevertheless, he was convicted under the Treachery Act in April 1943, sentenced to death, and reprieved after a plea for clemency from his ambassador. He was imprisoned at Dartmoor and, on the instructions of the Lord Chief Justice, no public statement was made concerning the trial or the reprieve.

As a result of the case the Policía de Vigilância e Defesa do Estado in Lisbon arrested twenty-three members of the Abwehr's local organisation, including Kuno Weltzien, a figure who had long posed a threat to British intelligence operations in the Peninsula. De Menezes was freed and deported back to Portugal in December 1949.

★ ★ ★

Petrie's choice of ZIGZAG, MUTT and JEFF as the three most suitable examples with which to introduce the Prime Minister to the concept of double-agents is quite curious. The two Norwegians, John Moe and Tor Glad, had paddled ashore in Banffshire in April 1941. Their participation in an operation code-named OATMEAL, involving the Luftwaffe dropping them a wireless transmitter and £400 in cash, was ample proof that both men had been completely accepted by their Abwehr masters in Oslo, who demonstrably believed them to be at liberty and active on their behalf. Churchill would later hear more of them, and about BUNBURY, a daring act of sabotage. As would later emerge, OATMEAL had an unexpected aspect, as Liddell confided to his diary on 24 March:

A piece of the parachute by means of which MUTT and JEFF's wireless set was dropped some weeks ago has been picked up by a farmer near Loch Strathbeg. It only reached us quite fortuitously through an officer in AI-1 (g) having given it to Room 055. The general instructions are that objects of this kind should be handed over to the air force by the police. I am going into this matter with RC. The officer's suspicions had been aroused because of a report he had read of an interrogation of a German airman who claimed to have landed an agent here in November 1939 in a Dornier 18 off the Yorkshire coast, not far from Scarborough. This agent was equipped with a short-wave wireless set. At the end of April 1940 he picked up the same man from a bay just to the North of Flamborough Head. This spy was said to

have given the Germans immensely valuable information at the beginning
of the Norwegian campaign and also about a raid carried out in April 1940,
on which advance information was given. There was a raid on 18 April
from which five Hampdens and two Wellingtons failed to return from a
flight to southern Norway. The signal for picking up a spy was to be the
dropping of a bomb and as a bomb had been dropped in connection with
the MUTT and JEFF enterprise the air force officer who brought in the bit
of parachute thought it might have some significance from an MI5 point
of view. The prisoner of war also spoke of another agent that he had landed
at the beginning of the French campaign. This man wore civilian clothes
and was provided with a squadron-leader uniform and a small transmitter.
Landings from aircraft and also descents by parachutes had later gone out of
fashion as they were thought to be too dangerous.

Nothing more was ever heard of these alleged airborne infiltrations, so it is
likely that the Luftwaffe PoW had fabricated the stories, perhaps in the hope
of enhancing his own status with his captors.

★ ★ ★

As for ZIGZAG, he had departed on an Ellerman Line cargo vessel, the
City of Lancaster, for Lisbon on 15 March, and the only way of monitoring his
progress, first in Portugal and then in Norway, was through the interception
of ISOS traffic, which occasionally mentioned his continued survival as a spy
code-named FRITZCHEN. He would not be seen again until his triumphant
return in June 1944, which would earn him further mention.

SECOND REPORT, 2 MAY 1943

The second report, dated 2 May 1943, is very domestic, covering two espionage cases, Frank Steiner and the Portuguese diplomat Rogeiro de Menezes; three double-agents, ZIGZAG, HAMLET and METEOR; and the problem of sabotage in Gibraltar. The final draft was approved by Richard Butler, head of the Director-General's secretariat, on 2 May.

Also described is BUNBURY, an act of sabotage to be carried out by MUTT and JEFF using material captured by the Germans from SOE networks in France. BUNBURY involved an explosion in August 1943 at the electricity power plant at Prospect Row in Bury St Edmunds, which was reported in detail by the *East Anglian Daily Times*, and resulted in claims broadcast on Nazi radio describing the incident and the deaths of 150 workmen. A week later the supposedly independent, Berlin-based Trans-Ocean News Service, which was controlled by Dr Goebbels' propaganda ministry, repeated the story on its North America wireless system.

Supposedly, a bomb placed beside a condenser had detonated causing widespread damage, and another device had been discovered and defused before it could explode. In reality, of course, the entire episode was an elaborate charade intended to build up the status of the two Norwegians.

On 5 August Guy Liddell indoctrinated Sir Frank Newsam, the Permanent Under-Secretary at the Home Office:

I saw Frank Newsam and explained to him Plan BUNBURY. He thought it possible that Watts, head of the explosives department, might be brought in. I said that if and when he was, we might consider whether it would be better to inform him of the true position in case he discovered that the

whole business was a hoax and gave the show away. Newsam was I think
pleased at having been brought into this matter.

The scheme, supervised by Victor Rothschild and Len Burt, had been code-
named BUNBURY in deference to the fictional character in Oscar Wilde's
The Importance of Being Earnest, and took place on 6 August, as Liddell recorded
in his diary the following day:

> Len Burt is going down to investigate Plan BUNBURY which took place
> last night. I have not yet heard any details. Burt thinks that he may be able
> to help a bit on the press side since both the Ministry of Information and
> Frank Newsam think that they could not give the story to the press without
> arousing considerable suspicion. The Chief Constable is giving it to the local
> press and I have suggested that he should explain when doing so that he has
> approval from Censorship, as it is thought that the public need to be made
> aware that something is going on in their midst. It is hoped that this will
> stimulate security.

However, the following week, on 12 August, Liddell noted that the local police
were becoming a little too enthusiastic about the investigation:

> Victor Rothschild and Len Burt came to see me about Plan BUNBURY.
> Burt thinks it desirable to ease up the police a little, who are suspecting
> the Irish and the Poles. There is great activity in the eastern counties and
> I understand that guards at utility undertaking have been doubled. The local
> press have got the story but do not think it worthwhile sending to London,
> as they feel it would not be passed by censorship. We are doing our best to
> grease the wheels but cannot do this too obviously.

Two days later BUNBURY came again, unexpectedly, when Rothschild
referred to the operation during a conference at Oxford attended by MI5's
Regional Security Liaison Officers (RSLO), as Liddell confided to his diary:

> Victor Rothschild has been talking to the RSLOs before lunch and had
> outlined to them Plan BUNBURY. He had written a circular letter which
> he had sent off to all his utility undertakings in which he had drawn attention
> to the incident at the electricity power station at Bury St Edmunds. He said
> quite definitely that we regarded this as an act of enemy sabotage, and had
> made some reference to spies being at large. RSLOs felt that the electricity

undertakings would undoubtedly take this letter to the Chief Constable and ask him for his views. The Chief Constable would then go to the RSLO and ask why it had been thought desirable to communicate the information to utility undertakings which had not been given to the Chief Constables. They would want to know whether it was true. Was the RSLO to lie or take the Chief Constable into his confidence? The general opinion at that stage seemed to be that it might be a wise move to take the Chief Constable into our confidence if he approached the RSLO but not otherwise. The matter however was left in abeyance.

However, the issue did not fade away, as probably everyone hoped, and was brought to the attention of Petrie, who was unamused by Rothschild's initiative. By telling the RSLOs about the true nature of the operation, he had placed them in an invidious position as they acted as MI5's official link to the police. If that relationship was to be based on a lie, implying that the Chief Constables were not fully trusted, then they were in danger of being undermined, thereby potentially compromising future cooperation:

I had a meeting with the Director-General, Jasper Harker, Victor Rothschild, Alan McIver and T.A. Robertson about Plan BUNBURY. The Chief Constables are to be told if they approach the RSLOs that the incident is a special exercise. They are to be asked to keep up the deception with the utility undertakings. I am to visit Colin Robertson, the Chief Constable of Suffolk, and explain the position. There is to be no publication in the *Police Bulletin*. The D–G was rather annoyed about the letter to the utility undertakings being sent out without prior reference to himself. The fact is, however, that the normal way is for a utility undertaking to report to the Central Electricity Board who immediately send teleprinter messages to all their power stations in the country. Moreover, if we are out for publicity which we have so far not been able to get, there is bound to be a reproach by Chief Constables to RSLOs. The only unfortunate thing about the letter to my mind is that there is something about spies being at large, and it is perhaps a little too positive.

Nevertheless, despite the internal friction caused by BUNBURY, MI5 remained keen to exploit the situation and generate some media interest, as Liddell noted on 18 August when Len Burt was authorised to adopt unorthodox tactics to attract the newspapers:

I had a talk with Len Burt about BUNBURY. There is to be publicity in today's press. Burt pretended to get tight in a pub and had leaked to one of his more disreputable contacts and he has now protested to this contact that he has been let down. In the light of this publicity the Director-General has agreed to reverse instructions to RSLOs, provided they have not already been approached. Jasper Harker subsequently ascertained that the field was clear. RSLOs were told that if the Chief Constable approached them they were to say that equipment known to have been used by the enemy was employed and that the matter was still under investigation. If they referred to the letter to utility undertakings they are to be told that this was 'toned up' a bit to make the undertakings more security-minded.

This led Liddell and Rothschild to visit the Chief Constable, and make a clean breast of the situation:

I went down to see Chief Constable Colin Robertson with Victor Rothschild and I explained to him all the various phases of BUNBURY and our difficulties. He told me that in spite of this morning's publicity in every paper, not one question had been put to him about BUNBURY at a Chief Constable's meeting he had attended. He expected everybody to come up and say 'Now give us the lowdown about the sabotage at Bury' but not a word. He was I think pleased we had paid him a visit. He was in thorough agreement with the policy of saying nothing to Chief Constables, and entirely agreed with Len Burt's view that quite a number of them on receiving the information would hold a mother's meeting. He was quite prepared to face his own superintendent if he ever found out. He explained to me how difficult it would be to get the searchers to find the unexploded bomb. He pretty well had to push their noses right into it before it was discovered. It looked just like a part of the old unused generator.

Although the two MI5 officers succeeded in mollifying the Chief Constable, the issue was raised the next day at Scotland Yard, where Special Branch detectives expressed their well-founded suspicions:

When visiting Special Branch, Langdon was confronted by Albert Foster, Charles Gill, and four inspectors with the announcement of Plan BUNBURY. They said 'Whatever your views are about this case, we have come to the conclusion that it is either SOE or Lord Rothschild.' I am afraid Langdon did not put up a very good show. Although he did not commit himself positively, I think he left them with very little doubt about the origin of the outrage. Amongst other things he is reported to have told them to keep it to themselves, which is of course a complete admission of guilt.

This scenario, in which MI5 sought to deceive Special Branch, was exacerbated on 20 August by Len Burt, himself a former Scotland Yard detective, though never a member of Special Branch. Apparently he had no compunction in assuring Foster that the sabotage had been genuine:

Len Burt has seen Albert Foster and considerably shaken him on the question of the genuineness of BUNBURY. Burt gave it as his opinion it was a true bill.

Having committed itself to perpetuating the lie, it began to spread, and the following day another RSLO, Peter Hope, sought Liddell's guidance:

Peter Hope has got a reaction from the Assistant Superintendent in Newcastle about Plan BUNBURY. He has been told to stick to the line given to him for communication to the Chief Constable.

On 24 August Liddell was obliged to address the dilemma yet again:

Alan McIver came to see me about an enquiry about Plan BUNBURY that Hughes had received from the local Security Control Officer. I said that I thought Hughes should tell the SCO exactly what he had told the Chief Constable, otherwise he was putting the SCO *vis-à-vis* his subordinates in the same difficulty as the Chief Constable would be placed. This meant a further spreading of the information.

There the matter rested until early in September when the question arose about how the Home Office should refer to BUNBURY in the monthly *Police Bulletin*, which was circulated routinely to all the regional police forces:

Wells has raised the question of putting something in the monthly Home Office police report on the subject of Plan BUNBURY. He is reluctant to do this because he feels it wrong that the Home Office should mislead the police in an official document. I pointed out to him that we had faced up to this question long ago and made up our minds that in spite of the difficulties the question of the possible leakage of the truth had to be the first consideration. I discussed this matter with T.A. Robertson and Victor Rothschild. We eventually decided that provided Hughes did not think that the Suffolk police would be astonished not to read of the incident in the bulletin we should leave it out, and give a directive to RSLOs to the effect that they should if asked, explain to Chief Constables that the item had not been put in owing to the inconclusive nature of the investigation. Wells said that the Executive did not always put cases into the *Bulletin* and that they could therefore defend themselves in this particular case. He also said that the *Bulletin* was generally read by the head clerk who took an intelligence interest in a matter of this sort and would almost certainly bring it to the notice of the Chief Constables. Hughes telephoned later to say that he did not think that the omission of the BUNBURY item in the *Bulletin* would cause comment from the local police. It was therefore agreed that with the Director-General's approval this line should be adopted and RSLOs if approached should say that the case had been omitted owing to its inconclusive nature.

A month later the *Sunday Chronicle* published an innocuous story about BUNBURY, and that was the final word on the matter which, to everyone's relief, could now be laid to rest.

★ ★ ★

Perhaps the most remarkable item in Petrie's report is the reference to Violet Trefusis, who was Virginia Woolf's lesbian lover and a well-known figure in London's literary circles. Evidently she had engaged in an illicit correspondence with a well-connected French friend in German-occupied Paris, and this had come to MI5's notice through ISOS and a letter intercepted by Postal Censorship. The contact was allowed to continue, as Liddell mentioned in his diary:

A letter has been thrown up by Censorship from the son of General Louis de la Pellouse in Occupied France, to a Mrs Trefusis in London, inviting her to come to Portugal for discussions and giving her a cover address for her reply. It was clear that this letter was written on the instructions of the German secret service, the whole matter being reflected in ISOS. It was possible that this was some form of peace feeler. Mrs Trefusis is known to be pro-Vichy in her sentiments. The letter has been allowed to go on and arrangements made to intercept her reply. The cover address used is a well-known German collecting centre.

There was no further mention of this contact, either by Liddell or Petrie, so presumably Mrs Trefusis did not take up the suggestion of a visit to Lisbon.

SECOND REPORT
A. Spies Detained
(1) <u>STEINER</u>

Frank Steiner, a well-trained Belgian agent of the German Secret Service arrived in this country on 5 April 1943. The Security Service was already in possession of considerable information about him from Most Secret Sources, but he made our task easier by voluntarily disclosing his connection with the enemy to the British authorities in Lisbon. Since his arrival in this country he had enthusiastically supplied the large quantity of valuable and detailed counter-espionage information in his possession. He was moreover given by the Germans a new means of receiving further instructions, namely code messages sent over the Calais broadcasting station. The possibility of using him for double-cross purposes is being investigated.

(2) MENEZES

The Portuguese Government has put in a strong plea that the death sentence pronounced against Menezes should be commuted. The Security Service do not wish to stand in the way of such commutation, but it is assumed that the Portuguese Government would in return be ready to follow up actively the information supplied to them partly as a result of the Menezes case, and round up the circle of German and Italian agents still thriving in Lisbon.

B. Double-cross Spies and Saboteurs
(1) <u>ZIGZAG</u>

The double-cross saboteur ZIGZAG returned to his German Secret Service station via Lisbon, travelling as steward on a British ship. On arrival he was given by the local head of the German Sabotage Service a high explosive bomb camouflaged as a piece of coal with instructions to place it in the ship's bunkers in order to sabotage the ship. ZIGZAG accepted the bomb, but immediately informed the master of the ship, who kept the bomb in a place of safety.

(2) HAMLET

An Austrian subject, who has been in contact with the German Secret Service in Lisbon, was sent to this country with our knowledge on April 4th. Under our direction he had been working for Koessler, a German Jew who is a member of the German Secret Service in Lisbon but who has in fact been double-crossing his German masters. In addition to Fanto, Koessler is supposed to have another agent in this country, who is notional and whose letters will be written by us, and, further, five agents in America, all of whom are also notional. Fanto is a very close personal friend of General von Falkenhausen, and he reports that the General and his staff are convinced that Germany will lose.

(3) METEOR

This Yugoslav was asked by the Germans to work for them in the UK and was given a novel type of instructions. He was told to inform the British authorities in Madrid that he was being sent to England as a spy and that he was prepared to work for the British in double-crossing the Germans. For a period he was to follow exactly the orders given him by the British, but at a later stage he was to receive new instructions from the Germans together with a proper mission, new cover addresses and another secret ink by which he could communicate with the Germans without our knowledge. He has, however, told the whole story to the British authorities.

C. Sabotage

(1) German sabotage plans for Gibraltar

We have now arranged for one of our own agents to be appointed head of the German Sabotage Service operating against Gibraltar. It is hoped that he will be able to persuade the Germans to let him report direct to the German Secret Service station at Algeciras, which would provide us with an independent check on the activities of that station as they are revealed to us in Most Secret Sources. It is believed that the whole of the German Sabotage organisation operating against Gibraltar is now on our side, though still paid for their faked explosions by the Germans.

(2) German Sabotage Equipment

Photographs are attached of two specimens of the type of camouflaged bomb which the Germans attempt to introduce into such places as Gibraltar or smuggle on to our merchant ships in Spanish ports. The first shows a Thermos flask in which the genuine thermos only occupies the top few inches, the rest being filled with an incendiary bomb containing a time clock capable of being set up to twenty-one days. The second shows what appears to be a can of oil, which is, however, in reality filled with Thermit with a timeclock housed in the filler cap.

(3) PLAN BUNBURY

There is in being a plan to build up the two Norwegian agents who were sent here in 1941 as saboteurs. They are been instructed by the enemy to try and sabotage electricity miles, and the undertaking at Basingstoke has been chosen by us as the least important in the area in which they are operating. Having announced to the Germans that they would try and damage this, they were told that in due course proper materials for sabotage would be sent to them by parachute, and in view of the importance which appears to be placed on the project, the possibility of doing a bogus act of sabotage in the power station is being investigated. If this is not practicable, the Germans will be told that the attempt has also failed.

D. Possible Peace Feelers

Most Secret Sources together with a Censorship intercept reveal that the German Secret Service in Paris has arranged for correspondence to be set up between a person in France, probably the son of a General Vicomte Louis de la Panouse, and Mrs. Denys Trefusis in London. A letter was later intercepted to Mrs Trefusis inviting her to meet the writer in Lisbon to discuss matter affecting the best interests of Britain and France. The phraseology of the letter suggests that the subject to be discussed may be some form of Peace feeler. The letter has been allowed to go on to Mrs. Trefusis, and arrangements have been made for intercepting her reply.

E. Political Cases

(1) CRAVEN

On 14 March 1943 William Frederick Craven, an ex-British Union detainee, wrote a letter to the German legation in Dublin, in which be declared that his sympathies were with the Germans and that he hoped for a German victory. He also sent his best wishes to his friends in Germany, particularly to Herr Reinhardt, a former German Consul in Liverpool who was removed from his post on account of his espionage activities. Craven was charged and convicted under the Defence Regulations on two charges, getting the maximum penalty on each, namely Penal Servitude for life on one, and 14 years on the other. He has appealed, but his appeal has not yet been heard.

(2) Ben Greene

The action brought by Ben Greene against Sir John Anderson, claiming damages for wrongful imprisonment on the ground that the order for his detention was made in bad faith, ended on the 9th April, 1943, by the plaintiff abandoning the action and unreservedly withdrawing the charge of bad faith.

During the earlier proceedings before the Advisory Committee, MI5 were pressed, contrary to well established principle, to disclose the names of two of their agents on whose testimony the grounds for Ben Greene's detention largely rested. Later, one of these agents was inveigled into the office of Greene's solicitor, to whom, on being questioned, he denied the truth of the charges against Ben Greene which depended on his information which he had given, so as to avoid admitting by implication he was an MI5 agent. A further hearing of Greene's case took place before the Advisory Committee, who, failing to appreciate the agent's real reason for retraction, submitted him to a most severe cross-examination and finally wrote him down as utterly unreliable. As a result Ben Greene was released and the charges against him which rested on this agent's testimony were formally withdrawn by the Home Secretary.

In the suit just mentioned Ben Greene's Counsel were so unwise as to call this agent, who, under examination by the Attorney-General, convincingly explained his motive for having lied to the solicitor, and was clearly doing so to affirm that his original evidence was true. At the commencement of the fifth day's hearing and before the agent could go on to tell the jury all he knew about traitorous conversations, leading Counsel for the plaintiff intimated that the action would be withdrawn, thereafter judgement was given for Sir John Anderson with costs.

The ignominious collapse of this case has been very satisfactory to MI5 since the reliability to their agent who had been so fiercely assailed and disparaged was vindicated in open court. The immense trouble and expense of the proceedings have also pointedly confirmed the unwisdom of any departure from the established and till now inviolable practice of never disclosing the names of their agents.

I. Security of Services and other wireless signals

As a result of information obtained by the Security Service from a German spy who recently came over here with the intention of working for the English, it has been discovered that the Germans rely to a very large extent for their intelligence on the interception of wireless messages sent in this country. A strong recommendation has therefore been put up to the Chiefs of Staffs that a thorough investigation should be immediately made into the security of wireless communications used both by the Services and by such bodies as the Police and Post Office.

1st May 1943

★ ★ ★

The Prime Minister's reaction to this report was described by Petrie to Dick White on the afternoon of 5 May:

> Mr Duff Cooper sent for me at 4 p.m. this afternoon and returned to me the second report on MI5 activities, which he showed to the Prime Minister to-day. He told me that the PM showed a deep interest in the matters summarised in the report and mentioned one or two specific comments as follows:
>
> 1. Re: Menezes – 'why don't you shoot him?' On being advised that there were reasons why we wanted to retain the goodwill of the Portuguese Government who had taken action against Axis agents in Portugal and were probably taking further action, he said 'well drive a hard bargain'.
> 2. He was impressed by our success in nominating the head of the German Sabotage Organisation, work against Gibraltar.
> 3. Re. Ben Greene – 'Why don't you lock him up?' query had to be dealt with tact.
> 4. He specially noted that we had advised energetic action to compete with the lack of signals security in the Service departments and other official W/T users.
> 5. Both Mr Duff Cooper and the Prime Minister are most anxious to know when the first word is heard from ZIGZAG.

Although Frank Steiner was, according to the report, assessed for his likely value as a double-agent, it seems that the idea was stillborn. Steiner's MI5 file, headed Frank Domien Steiner, alias Jacob Steinbach, reveals his unsavoury background, which dated back to his arrival in England during the First World War and his resettlement in Croydon as a refugee. On his return to Belgium he had worked as a journalist, a language tutor, a salesman selling cosmetics, electrical appliances and Kleen-Ezi brushes. He had also acted as a tout for some Ostend brothels and traded on the black market. In April 1940 he entered into a marriage of convenience with a German Jew, Gertrude Schneider, with whom he had been living for the past two years. Previously she had been engaged to a Swiss journalist, a director of Radio Geneva, by whom she had an illegitimate child.

Soon afterwards Steiner was sent to work as a translator in a German optical instrument factory, the Steinheil works in Munich, but in September 1941 he was approached by an Abwehr officer, Joseph Köchling, who was impressed by his fluency in English and by the fact that his maternal uncle was the former Deputy Chief Constable of Blackpool, Ben Hannan. Köchling recruited Steiner as an agent, using as leverage an implied threat against his wife, who was moved to Freiburg, and against his parents in Antwerp.

According his version of events, Steiner had set out for Portugal, hoping to reach the Congo, but had been detained in Spain at the Miranda del Ebro prison until September 1942, when he had returned to the Netherlands. On his second attempt he turned up in Lisbon in March 1943 and contacted the British for a passage to England. During his interview at the Passport Control Office with an SIS officer he divulged enough of his role as an Abwehr spy to ensure he attracted attention and gained a priority visa for air travel to Poole in April. Upon arrival he was escorted to Latchmere House and interrogated by the commandant, Robin Stephens, who recommended caution. MI5 knew from an ISOS intercept referring to a source code-named JACQUES that the day Steiner had received his entry permit, 4 April 1943, he had telephoned the news to Richard Schubert, his German contact in Lisbon, but he took a week to volunteer this vital information. In fact MI5 was well informed about Steiner long before his arrival, a report having been sent by the Defence Security Officer in Gibraltar, Tito Medlam, warning that two of his sources, one a Czech volunteer, the other a Belgian Sueté agent, had denounced Steiner when he had been a fellow inmate at the Miranda camp. According to Medlam's information, passed to London in August 1942, Steiner was a Nazi spy who intended to travel to England.

Even though Steiner identified another spy, Lucien Rombaut, as a fellow Abwehr recruit, he was considered too unreliable to be run as a double-agent, and spent the rest of the war in detention. He provided an enormous amount of detail concerning Abwehr personalities, premises and procedures, which turned out to be accurate, but he was never entirely trusted and made a poor impression on those that interviewed him. After the war he was flown back to Belgium where he faced collaboration charges and was sentenced to death, but he was reprieved and given a life term.

Because his name was associated with several other cases of interest, MI5 tried to find Steiner's Abwehr contact, Joseph Köchling, after the German surrender, but it seemed that he had been caught by the Soviets and had died in captivity.

★ ★ ★

The case of William Craven may also have been of interest to the Prime Minister, although it was one that had almost entirely escaped MI5's attention until it appeared in court. Craven apparently had known Walter Reinhardt, the German consul in Liverpool, who had been withdrawn in June 1939 after he had been implicated in an attempt in April to recruit William Patrick Kelly as a spy. Employed at the huge Royal Ordnance munitions factory at Chorley as a bricklayer, 30-year-old Kelly had stolen plans of the plant and then approached Reinhardt who, with some reluctance, had passed on his offer to sell the information to the Abwehr. He then had been seen to meet Abwehr representatives in Cologne, and was arrested as soon as he returned to England. Kelly had pleaded guilty to breaches of the Official Secrets Act and was sentenced to ten years' imprisonment. A former BUF member, Craven was a 28-year-old farm labourer in Gloucestershire who had been detained for a month in September 1939 under the 18B regulations, and then again in June 1940 and April 1941. Naturally, all mail addressed to the German legation in Dublin was subject to interception, and Craven's offer had landed him in jail. However, MI5 had played absolutely no part in the investigation or prosecution, and had been completely unaware of the matter until it reached the courts. However, as Liddell pointed out, it was the Home Office's decision, opposed by MI5, that had freed Craven and given him the opportunity to land himself in even greater trouble:

> Craven's release was strongly opposed by ourselves, and Sir Alexander Maxwell minuted the file to the effect that it was a pity that MI5 took such an unbalanced view, and had not got a liberal outlook. The effect on Craven of the Home Office's liberal outlook has been to get him a life sentence instead of merely internment for the duration of the war.

★ ★ ★

The detention of Ben Greene, of the famous Berkhamsted family, proved infinitely more complicated, and a matter of some embarrassment for MI5,

especially when Greene, who had been imprisoned for eighteen months as
a Nazi sympathiser on the word of an unscrupulous informer, Harald Kurtz,
took his case to the House of Lords and won. The version delivered by Petrie
to Churchill is a somewhat partisan view of litigation brought by a pacifist and
Quaker who had been entrapped by Kurtz and his companion, Friedl Gärtner,
a fellow Austrian.

Having examined the evidence, the Home Office had released Greene,
but the failure of his subsequent legal action for libel and false imprisonment
did not reflect on the monstrous injustice he had suffered. When cornered by
Greene's solicitor, Kurtz had admitted that he had been paid by MI5 for every
suspect he denounced. To have told Churchill that MI5 had felt vindicated is
quite a misrepresentation of what had really happened.

★ ★ ★

Of the three double-agents mentioned, ZIGZAG had made an appearance
in the first report, and the brief account of his adventure aboard the
City of Lancaster's voyage from Liverpool did not reveal anything like the full
story, which received much attention from Guy Liddell. The version given
to Churchill omitted to mention that ZIGZAG, who was supposed to desert
his ship in Lisbon, had not told MI5 about a bomb he had placed aboard the
vessel in Lisbon, and had only confided in the master, leaving MI5 to learn
about the scheme from ISOS, as Liddell recalled on 21 March:

> Ewen Montagu has informed J.C. Masterman about a Lisbon–Berlin
> message in which it is suggested that an agent should put explosive or
> incendiary coal on board a ship on which he is serving as steward. The
> agent is clearly ZIGZAG since the message implies that he is identical
> with the individual who did the Mosquito job and that he cannot go back
> to England. He is to slip away as soon as the job is done and go on to
> Paris. This all fits with ZIGZAG's set-up. The difficulty is to know what
> appropriate action should be taken and I am trying to ascertain when
> the *City of Lancaster* is likely to leave Lisbon, since if there is sufficient
> time we might send an officer out. I have also asked Gergie to put a rush
> on the Berlin–Lisbon service in order that we might get a reply at the
> earliest possible moment. The message to Berlin was dated 19 March. Later
> I heard from Ferguson that he was proposing to send a wire to Ralph Jarvis
> informing him that Abt. III were proposing that ZIGZAG should sabotage
> his ship, and asking him whether ZIGZAG had informed the ship's captain.

If not, without indicating the slightest knowledge of the enterprise, it was suggested that the captain should be told to ask ZIGZAG (1) if, and when he was going to desert (2) whether he had contacted the Germans yet and if so with what result, and (3) had he any messages for the captain to take back to England. At that moment I was discussing the whole problem with Ewen Montagu, Ronnie Reed, J.C. Masterman and Ian Wilson. At first we thought that a telegram might be sent to Jarvis explaining to him the position and suggesting that he should arrange discreetly for the master to meet him at a suitable rendezvous for a purpose of arranging a still more discreet meeting between Jarvis and ZIGZAG, bearing in mind that the latter was probably being followed. Ralph Jarvis should show ZIGZAG the signal from Frank Foley and say that he came with other instructions from Reed to ascertain whether ZIGZAG has successfully contact the Germans and if so, what instructions he had had at Lisbon. On no account was ZIGZAG to be asked questions about sabotage. If he failed to come clean about the plan to sabotage his ship, he would be placed in irons by the captain and brought back here. On further reflection we thought that it would be better to send Reed who had the advantage of knowing the whole case and of knowing ZIGZAG personally. This would avoid the difficulty of Jarvis or any of his people, who must be known to the Germans, making contact with ZIGZAG and would have the additional advantage of giving ZIGZAG no way out. If he were approached by anyone else he might not feel under obligation to tell them a story which he thought he had already dealt with in his own way. On the other hand, however, if he failed to disclose what had happened to Reed we should have to assume that he was definitely wrong. In any case we felt that Reed's presence in Lisbon could not be otherwise than a help to Jarvis.

Ferguson, in consultation with Frank Foley, seems to have some doubts about the necessity or indeed the advisability of Ronnie Reed going out but promised to let me have their decision in the morning. Meanwhile, the German reply dated 17.35 on 20 March 1943 had come in saying that the plan devised by the Abwehr in Lisbon had been approved by headquarters. We also learned from the Ministry of War Transport that the ship is not likely to be unloaded before 27 March.

I spoke to Ferguson again at about 7 o'clock, [XXX] suggesting that he should send off a wire to confirm the time of departure of the ship and ensure that as soon as ZIGZAG deserted the matter should be reported. I had in mind that if he deserted in the immediate future we should have to take a more sinister view of his part in the suggested enterprise.

Thus MI5 was confronted with the prospect of having been duped by ZIGZAG, and the consequences of his sabotage of a cargo vessel as it sailed for its next destination, Gibraltar. Accordingly, Liddell was determined that ZIGZAG should be confronted, and the next day persuaded SIS to send Ronnie Reed to Lisbon:

> I was not able to get hold of Felix Cowgill at all till 3 o'clock. He was at first rather reluctant to agree to Ronnie Reed going to Lisbon and thought the telegram would do just as well. I pointed out to him that unless ZIGZAG was confronted with Ronnie Reed we should never be quite certain whether he was right or wrong. If he saw Reed he could have no possible excuse for not telling him about the suggested sabotage incident. I said I thought that no harm could possibly be done by sending Reed who knew the case and the man intimately. He and Jarvis could work out the best method of approach after his arrival. Cowgill eventually agreed. I then rang Herbert Hart and succeeded in getting a place for Reed on tomorrow morning's plane.

Reed's task was to find ZIGZAG and give him an opportunity to disclose his sabotage role without compromising ISOS. With this in mind he flew to Lisbon, but by the time he had arrived ISOS had shown that ZIGZAG had left for Hendaye and Paris. In his absence Reed went straight to the docks, as Liddell reported:

> Two telegrams have at last arrived from Ronnie Reed. He has seen the captain who stated that he had been approached by ZIGZAG, but that in view of his instructions he would not have said anything to anyone except Reed. The sabotage project was suggested to the Germans by ZIGZAG. He had obtained a bomb which the captain had in his safe. Reed would bring it back by air. He suggests that we should stage some sabotage incident when the boat gets back to Liverpool. Victor Rothschild, in conjunction with SOE, is trying to devise some means of doing this without causing damage to the ship.

Three days later, Reed was back in England, and reported by telephone to Liddell:

> Ronnie Reed has rung up to say that he is in Bristol. He says that the captain of the ship had been interrogated four times by the shipping office and had denied that he knew anything about the ZIGZAG affair. He affected

to be extremely annoyed that an agent had been put on his boat without his knowledge. He was in fact acting on strict instructions that he was not to divulge the fact of ZIGZAG's connection with British Intelligence. He was much relieved to see Reed. The piece of coal has been sent round via Gibraltar as Ralph Jarvis was nervous about its being taken on the aircraft in case it had some delay mechanism.

With the immediate drama over, and the bomb safely in the ands of SIS, Liddell gathered his senior staff together on 28 March to discuss the episode:

> I saw Dick White, Victor Rothschild, T.A. Robertson and Ronnie Reed about the ZIGZAG case. It seems that the captain has played his part well and he even instructed ZIGZAG to cause trouble on the ship. ZIGZAG threatened to attack one of the other stewards with a knife, and the incident ended in a brawl, and the steward was laid out. We discussed whether a fake explosion should take place at Gibraltar or Liverpool. There is an advantage in doing it at Gibraltar since the information could easily leak back to the Germans. On the other hand, this is a disadvantage in that since certain people, members of the crew and possibly others, might have to be in the know, the fact that the explosion was a fake might get back too easily to the Germans. We eventually decided to take no action in Gibraltar and work some scheme which can be put into operation as soon as the ship reaches Liverpool. The piece of coal was notionally placed on some spot where it would not be thrown into the boilers until the ship was well out to sea. ZIGZAG has explained this to the Germans. Our methods of communication with him now are by code advertisements in *The Times* and through practice messages which he hopes to be able to send from Paris to Nantes.

★ ★ ★

The other two double-agents introduced in Petrie's second report were HAMLET and METEOR.

HAMLET was Dr Johann Koessler, a wealthy Jewish businessman and former cavalry officer in the Austrian Army who joined the air force in 1916. He then obtained a law degree from Vienna University and married an immensely wealthy Jewish woman of Russian origin. However, anti-Semitism and the confiscation of assets forced him to move first to Milan and then to Brussels, where he rebuilt his commercial activities by exploiting his inventions, including lemonade powder marketed as Limonesco, before his Abwehr-sponsored departure to Portugal.

Koessler was also a double-agent who in 1941 had asked a British insurance broker, Ronald Thornton, code-named MULLET, to approach the British on his behalf. A third member of the network was PUPPET, an executive at Palmolive named Hans Fanto, who was supposedly Koessler's source in England, but in fact relied upon MI5 to supply him with plausible information. Both MULLET and PUPPET operated through HAMLET, based at a villa in Estoril with his wife, but were controlled by an Abwehr officer, Julius Hagemann, in Brussels where Koessler was known as KOLBERG and A-1416, and Fanto was code-named FAMULUS. Born in Belgium and the owner pre-war of a travel agency in Aachen, Hagemann had become a naturalised German and would be arrested and interrogated at Camp 020 in May 1945.[1]

The HAMLET case would turn out to be one of the most complex challenges ever confronted by MI5, not least because Koessler remained at the Palacio Hotel in Estoril while his agent, Thornton, was established in an MI5 flat in Nell Gwynne House in Chelsea. As it turned out, joint management by two intelligence organisations of complicated double-agents was far from an ideal scenario, and Petrie's summary prepared for the Prime Minister was neither comprehensive nor accurate, for Koessler was never formally a member of the Abwehr. As he would indignantly remind SIS, he had not undergone any Abwehr training, and had never visited an Abwehr office.

A 46-year-old inventor and the owner of a number of valuable chemical patents who was keen to market his special non-stretchable bandages and a degrading process, Koessler had been incarcerated by the Nazis in 1938 for three weeks during the Anschluss, but had been allowed to travel to Portugal in November 1941. There he had encountered Thornton, an insurance broker travelling with his wife, their three children and his mother-in-law, and intending to travel to England. Koessler had represented himself as a well-connected anti-Nazi with peace proposals, and had persuaded Thornton to approach the British authorities on his behalf. He was also asked to deliver some gold items to HAMLET's children.

Koessler, who professed to be Roman Catholic and anti-Semitic, had a son and daughter in England, both naturalised citizens, one of whom had tried to join the RAF, the other having married a German Jewish refugee and become a nurse. MI5's Christopher Harmer had interviewed MULLET upon his arrival in January 1942 and taken a favourable view of the opportunity presented, even if he had some doubts about Koessler's bona fides. Section V's study of the ISOS traffic revealed that Koessler's commercial enterprise was known to the Brussels Abwehr, and its sponsoring *stelle* in Cologne, as the KOLBERG organisation, but was constantly the subject of a jealous interest from the Madrid KO and the local Abwehr staff in Lisbon.

In August 1942 MULLET returned to Lisbon, ostensibly to negotiate a manufacturing licence from Koessler for one of his products, fatless soap, and spent two weeks with him. In reality it was arranged that Koessler would act as an intermediary, passing Fanto's reports, written in secret writing on his impregnated business letterheading, to the Abwehr. Upon his return to London, MULLET submitted a detailed report of his visit:

> The German Intelligence Service had four different categories of agents, of which the highest category worked direct to Canaris. He said, that since Mullet's last visit to Lisbon he had become an agent of the German Intelligence and that he was in the highest category and that he was using his cover as an agent to develop his business activities and also to try in his own way to bring the war to an end as quickly as possible. Since he was a first-class agent, his authority depended exclusively on Berlin and that nobody in the Legation in Lisbon had any sort of control over him, but they were at his disposal to help him, and that the Commercial Attaché was his link for using the diplomatic bag for his reports and correspondence.

In December 1942 SIS thought the situation sufficiently promising to send Frank Foley, C's representative on the XX Committee, to fly out to Lisbon and assess Koessler. His report, partially redacted, was enthusiastic:

> The impression or assumption that HAMLET represented a Peace Party or group of German and others who were weakening in their determination to continue the war and were thinking of sounding us about a compromise on an anti-Nazi basis, is wrong.

> 2. HAMLET asserted, and his statements were confirmed independently by PUPPET, that General von Falkenhausen and many officers on the Governor's staff and in the armed forces of the Reich, are convinced that Germany lost this war when she failed to invade England: but these men did not send HAMLET to Lisbon to negotiate.

> 3. The truth is that he is not in direct touch with General von Falkenhausen or Colonel von Harbou. The General is most exclusive and does not receive a Jew. He does not automatically receive even German officers. Until fairly

recently the General and his entourage openly criticised the Party and the Führer's conduct of operations. The dismissal of high officers in the Reich and the appointment of a Nazi official to the Governor's staff had a sudden sobering effect. They have harnessed their tongues. I think it can be assumed that officers and politicians throughout the Reich have also become more discreet and that if there is any inclination in the army to plot against Hitler, it will be done without running lines to anyone outside, unless they are very sure in advance of the contacts that are to be met. They will not send a man out on to neutral highways to look for them.

4. HAMLET is the representative of the Abwehrstelle at Brussels and in particular Major Bergman alias Berkhaus who works under Oberst Servase, the Abwehr chief in the rue Royale. The office is labeled: Ausbildungsstab D. Bergman the Chief of I-H. HAMLET came to Lisbon to establish under genuine business cover, the 'organisation HAMLET' espionage service directed against England and the Western Hemisphere. He works independently of Lisbon and in direct touch with Brussels through the diplomatic bag. The Commercial Secretary is the intermediary.

It interested me to know whether Bergman had approached HAMLET or HAMLET Bergman, and in either case what had determined Bergman to back HAMLET, to trust him and to press for permission to employ him in spite of the prohibition against the ban on Jews without the explicit sanction of Himmler. HAMLET is not a small agent controlled by an immediate chief but the controlling person in an organisation outside Germany. Both questions are closely connected with the personalities of the two men.

5. HAMLET is a typical example of the extremely clever and well educated merchant banker who flourished in Central Europe and who made large fortunes at home and larger ones when they emigrated to Western Europe and the Western Hemisphere. They had great contempt for the brains of the aristocratic officer class. He studied law; so did his father, grandfather and great grandfather. He is proud that four generations of HAMLETs have been doctors of law. He has always been rich. The Nazis broke him and dispersed his family. He went to Brussels, the Nazis caught up. He has, according to his statement, been in prison twice, but not in a concentration camp. He was an officer in the air arm of the Austrian Army in the last war. He was Austrian Intelligence officer at Trieste for six months. In Brussels he was trapped again. HAMLET developed an all absolving desire to revenge himself, or as he understated it, to settle his account with the Nazis.

6. He found that Major Bergman who was a businessman serving during the war in intelligence, was in Brussels. Bergman had been wealthy but had lost money on horses, used the old technique and gave him shares in his companies. When the partnership was well established, HAMLET suggested that he should be given facilities to go to Lisbon to establish an organisation for Bergman. Bergman fell into the trap. It was fairly easy to obtain permission and ample funds as Berlin was dissatisfied with Lisbon's work and the Germans wanted to establish a line through Lisbon under Portuguese commercial cover in case diplomatic cover became unworkable for war reasons. I need not point out the advantages of the arrangement both to HAMLET and to Bergman who is interested too in the Portuguese company, an investment which is attractive to a German who had experienced German inflation after the last war, and who sees no hope of Gemany winning this one.

7. HAMLET's plan of attack and revenge was based on his knowledge of the state of the German military mind which thought defeat inevitable. He would further depress their minds and weaken their fighting spirit by emphasising to them the actual and potential strength of the allied nations. He felt he was clever enough to serve up acceptable reports received theoretically, from agents, but in fact gathered from open sources such as newspapers etc. It must not be forgotten that he has the greatest contempt for their intelligence.

8. It is known from the file how he met MULLET. He did not hide his true sentiments. He has not tried to run an objective service. He has passed to Brussels everything we have supplied. He has asked me to use him for strategical deception to hasten the end. That is a new development.

9. Now PUPPET, an Austro-German [XXX] comes into the picture. He is the son of [XXX]. From our point of view the important fact is that PUPPET was a school and art friend of General von Falkenhausen.

10. [XXX]

11. He met HAMLET in the business field and thought he could obtain supplies of oil for PUPPET from Portugal. When HAMLET heard of the father's friendship with von Falkenhausen he naturally suggested to him to obtain a letter of introduction. He did so but PUPPET's father died

before the letter of introduction was presented. General von Falkenhausen liked the pleasant young man and he became a poker friend – a small and exclusive circle.

12. HAMLET's next step was to take PUPPET into his confidence as he found they had common ideals. With PUPPET's knowledge HAMLET persuaded Major Bergman to send PUPPET to Lisbon as the 100% reliable Aryan to make certain that he HAMLET played straight it would obviously strengthen his position enormously in the eyes of the Abwehrstelle. PUPPET is due to be called up for service. He says he will desert and risk being interned in Portugal.

13. HAMLET had suggested to Major Bergman that he thought he could obtain a visa for a visit to the UK. I did not agree that it would be a practical proposition. He did not press the matter. He wanted to obtain from us more support for his plan under cover of spying for the Germans.

14. I did not feel that HAMLET would be of much use if he confined his work in Lisbon to serving up to the Germans open information obtained locally as information emanating from secret sources. I told him that his work would have little effect on the conduct of the war and he would inevitably be found wanting. I said I thought he should, if he really wished to destroy the Nazis, consider whether their destruction could be effected unless the German Army were defeated in the field. When he accepted that proposition I approached the question of his running an active espionage service for us under his Abwehr cover. I argued that knowledge of the enemy was an essential preliminary to his defeat. He was in a position to double the power of the instrument of revenge he had forged. I am inclined to distrust a man who lightly accepts a request to do espionage work. I was pleased HAMLET hesitated. I closed a very long session.

15. My next meeting was with PUPPET. I repeated my arguments to him. I suggested he should return to Brussels and become the spearhead of HAMLET's espionage service, and his courier. It would have been an ideal arrangement as it gave perfect cover and excellent contacts and potential sources of information. He informed me that if he returned to Brussels he would be called to the colours. The Abwehr would not be able to secure his release.

16. As an alternative, I thought it wise to build up HAMLET's organisation by making the Germans think that he had succeeded in placing a first class agent in England. The more they valued his work the easier it would be for him to double back on them in our interest and PUPPET thought they could invent a plan which the Germans would swallow, provided the Ministry approved in principle of PUPPET's coming here. This has now been done.

17. This is only a summary of the very long conversations which took place. I cannot say how successful Koessler will be in giving us information, but I am convinced of his good faith. In any case, I have a great hold on him as I am in possession of the original letters from Bergman to him and of copies of his replies. There are his children too, of course.

18. Most secret sources make it certain that both have told us the truth.

19. This is the ideal type of doublecross agent as it avoids the flaw in the French system when the agent was allowed access to both countries. HAMLET can only give the Germans what we give him through PUPPET. Revenge is the best motive.

20. The Germans will pay for the whole service.

Koessler eventually established two notional agents, Alois Falk, code-named ALOIS, and Georg Budniewicz, code-named BUDNY, who were supposedly attached to the Polish forces in eastern England. Later, this network would expand to include a further four non-existent agents deployed in the United States and Canada. His commercial mission, to negotiate with the Ministry of Supply, was actually cover for his espionage role, as already disclosed by Thornton and, after some hesitation and debate regarding some ambiguous ISOS messages, he was enrolled as a double-agent. Koessler's 36-year-old assistant Hans Fanto was an Austrian aristocrat whose father had been a student with the German military governor of Belgium, General Alexander von Falkenhausen. It was an entrée that had been exploited by Fanto, who was a regular attendee of his poker parties held in his quarters at the Plaza Hotel and the Château de Seneffe.

According to Koessler, his organisation received nearly a hundred messages from London written in secret writing by Fanto, who mailed them to his secretary, Ida Spitz, at her home address in Lisbon at 13 rua Basilio Teres 20.

Madame Spitz was described by MULLET as an anti-Nazi Viennese Jewess whose
son was in the Australian Army. Koessler then employed a retired Portuguese
International Police officer, formerly the chief in Caldas da Rainha, named
Aguiar as a courier to deliver them either to a café in Madrid or to the Spanish
frontier. There they were received by an Abwehr officer, Werner Unversagt, who
in August 1945 would be interrogated at Camp 020.[2]

In July 1943 SIS's Frank Foley travelled to Portugal to see Koessler at his
villa in Estoril and, having met him half a dozen times, was persuaded of his
authenticity and suitability as a double-agent, although MI5 expressed some
misgivings about the lack of control exercised over Koessler's activities and
the security of his contact with the SIS station in Lisbon.

In the months that followed HAMLET's status grew as PUPPET in London
supplied him with increasingly valuable information, including advance
warning of Operaton HUSKY, the Allied invasion of Sicily in August 1943.
Berlin was so impressed by Fanto's accuracy, even if it had been received
too late to act upon, that steps were taken to improve the Abwehr's link
with Koessler. This reaction, of course, was monitored through MI5's study
of ISOS. However, MI5 expressed concern about the uncontrolled nature
of HAMLET's reports to Brussels, which could not be checked through
ISOS, and the fact that PUPPET had not received any funds since Foley had
delivered him $1,000 from Koessler. Another anxiety was that Koessler had
insisted that his commercial activities meant his network was self-financing,
whereas ISOS revealed that he had received payments from the Abwehr that
he had not passed on to Fanto, who had been promised £100 a month. These
and other events developed into a crisis in October 1943 when John Marriott
conducted a review of the case and came to some scathing conclusions:

> This case is regarded by you [Marriott's MI5 superior T.A. Robertson] with
> a good deal of uneasiness, as is evidenced by the note which you yourself
> wrote not long ago. As I share your feelings about it, I have conducted as
> careful an investigation into its merits as its extremely complicated nature
> permits. Before stating my views I should say first that I have no criticism of
> the way in which it has been handled by the Case Officer who has obviously
> put an enormous amount of most careful work into it, and secondly that a
> really complete investigation would involve much more time than I have yet
> been able to give to it; merely to read every document on the files would,
> I think, take about a week without any outside interruptions, while a much
> longer period would be necessary before anybody starting from scratch
> could say that he had a really clear grasp of all the details. I am not at all sure

incidentally that this fact alone is not the worst feature of the case, for its bulk and complexity add immeasurably to the normal obscurity which surrounds even a straightforward B1(a) case. It is, however, possible, and in my opinion reasonable, to decide this case's merits without going into all its ramifications, and indeed my considered view is that it is only by disregarding most of the papers and by applying first principles that we are ever likely to arrive at a correct estimate of its value.

In my submission before we decide to continue this case we must be able to give a satisfactory answer to two questions, namely:-
What are HAMLET's motives and objectives? What are our objectives?
So far as (a) is concerned it seems to be assumed, mainly on the authority of Major Foley, that HAMLET is a man who genuinely desires the overthrow of the present German Government, and that he wishes this to be secured by a military victory on the part of the Allies. So convinced is Foley that this is a correct interpretation of HAMLET's outlook that we are, in his opinion, safe in trusting him completely. With regard to (b), I am not at all clear that this question has ever been answered, except to the extent that it has been decided, and rightly in my view, that we cannot as matters stand use the case for military deception. I suspect, however, that in the back of the minds of some people there is an idea that in spite of HAMLET's own later assertions to the contrary, and in spite of what I regard as the inherent improbability of HAMLET being in any such position, he may somehow or other be used either as a channel for obtaining some sort of peace approach or as a lever for widening breaches between the Nazi Party and the Army. Neither objective is a matter for M15 and if either is proposed to be pursued then I think we should first obtain a pretty clear instruction from the Foreign Office or PWE to proceed on their behalf accordingly. Alternatively we may be hoping that by maintaining HAMLET in position we shall in effect be able to use him as a straight agent. The position is, therefore, that we have answered one question and have partially answered the other. How far are our answers correct and satisfactory?

In the case of (a) we are dealing with what is admittedly only a matter of opinion and, with respect, only Major Foley's opinion at that, but there are certain facts about HAMLET which cannot be ignored. These are:-
(i) He is a traitor to his own country.
(ii) He is a Continental-Jewish financier and big business man.
(iii) He has a genuine financial interest in the Portuguese business which extends beyond the mere maintenance of cover for his espionage activities.
(iv) He is completely and absolutely uncontrolled.

It is of course by virtue of the last fact that HAMLET's motives become a fundamental issue in the case. I recognise that Major Foley is the only officer who has had the advantage of meeting HAMLET in person, and I also recognise that Major Foley, by virtue of his long residence in Germany is entitled to be heard with great attention when he expresses an opinion about the character of a German.

At the same time, however, I am not myself without experience of persons of HAMLET's type, and since my experience has been gained in the way of a profession, which gives one a pretty clear insight into the way in which people behave, and which moreover brings one into a peculiarly close contact with the real character of persons, I venture to claim that in this particular case my opinion is just as good as that of Major Foley. I say, therefore, without any hesitation that I would in no circumstances whatsoever trust a man like HAMLET an inch further than I could see him, and only then if he was absolutely under my control and if I was satisfied his interest was identical with mine. I have too often in the past been led up the garden by gentry like HAMLET ever again to allow myself to be deceived by anything that they may say or do. It is furthermore, in my experience, a universal characteristic of such persons that they invariably so order their every act, even the most fundamentally dishonest, that they can be interpreted in more than one way. Thus, at the moment, although I am satisfied that HAMLET is, because he must be, playing a double game with us, I do not in the least expect that that fact would necessarily be apparent from his actions at this stage. He and his class are much too downy to give any specific indications of their dishonesty.

I should not think it particularly relevant to express my views so strongly were it not for the fact that hitherto we have all, whether we like it or not, really been working upon the basis of a contrary view. In actual fact, however, I think that the argument for not trusting HAMLET should be put in rather a different way. It seems to me that if the experience and policy of this office over a period of many years is anything to go on, we are not entitled to rely absolutely upon the loyalty of any person other than a British subject. Indeed it seems to me that to use the word 'loyalty' in the case of a German is, in relation to British interests, an almost ludicrous misuse of words. That HAMLET may be an Austrian and a Jew, and even an anti-Nazi, does not in my submission alter the argument. If he can betray the Germans how much more likely is he to betray us? In

HAMLET's case, moreover, we have the additional difficulty that his own financial interest enters into the question. This interest may at any time run counter to ours, and I very much doubt whether our grip upon what is going on is ever likely to be such that we should, at a sufficiently early stage, be able to recognise that this financial interest was diverging on to other lines. Lastly, and I suppose, incidentally, I see no reason why we should put ourselves in a great deal of trouble in order to enable HAMLET to do what without our help he could not do, namely build up a successful business, unless in return we see that we ourselves are going to obtain a great advantage.

It is therefore of great importance that we should have the clearest possible idea of what our objectives are. As the matter stands at the moment the only part of this case which we control is the secret correspondence of PUPPET. But much the most important part of the KOLBERG reports consists of the reports which HAMLET makes himself, and which we only influence to the extent of providing HAMLET with an excellent newspaper clipping service. This service, by reason of the fact that it covers many newspapers which are not available in Lisbon, is an improvement on anything which the Germans could maintain for themselves. It is true that the cuttings are submitted to our approving authorities, but in their final form they closely resemble the sort of information which all over the world the Germans for a long time thought, and still think, it worth their while to collect. In other words the information may be harmless, but it is of a type valued by the Germans.

Furthermore, we have absolutely no idea of what use HAMLET makes of this information, nor do we ever see the very numerous reports which he turns in to the Germans. Serious consideration is now being given by LCS and others to the abolition of OSTRO on the grounds that his information, though apparently guesswork, is nevertheless likely to compromise other activities.[3] It seems to me that on that basis we all ought to regard HAMLET as at least as dangerous as OSTRO.

I do not know what others think but I do not myself seriously regard the possibility of using HAMLET either as a person who might be used to exploit breaches between the Army and the Nazis, for the reason that, as we now know; he has no important contacts with the Army, or as a possible channel for peace overtures, for the reason that, as already stated above, I do not trust HAMLET.

The only objective therefore which I can see for continuing the HAMLET case is to use him as a straight agent. It is now ten months since Major Foley first met HAMLET and if, therefore, he were likely to be or become a useful source, we by now ought to have obtained from him a considerable quantity of valuable information. It is possible that not all the information given by HAMLET has been made available to MI5 but if it has been it strikes me for the most part as being of singularly little value, (or possibly even a plant) and now that we have a much better source in ARTIST I should have thought that to be deprived of HAMLET's information in the future would scarcely be regarded as a loss.

I hope I have made it clear from the foregoing that my own inclination would be to close down altogether, but I quite appreciate that after all the work which has been put into the case it may be thought that it would be a pity to abandon it completely. Upon what conditions then can it be run? In my opinion it can be run only upon the condition that complete and effective control can be, and is, exercised over HAMLET. As to this I should draw your attention to the decision taken as far back as 17 July 1943, when it was agreed by you, J.C. Masterman and A.H. Robertson that the maximum degree of control over HAMLET's activities and independent reporting should be established. This decision, although in a slightly different form, was confirmed on 20 July 1943 at a meeting at which Foley was present. On 31 July 1943 at a meeting attended by, amongst others, Foley, it was agreed that Charles de Salis should get into touch with HAMLET and should vet his traffic. By 30 September 1943 it was apparent from an SIS letter that de Salis was not in touch with HAMLET, but that somebody else was, albeit that the first contact had only taken place on 20 Sepyember 1943, i.e. nearly two months after everybody had agreed that effective control must be established. So far as I am aware this contact, such as it is, has produced no sensible result, and in particular we still have no idea of what HAMLET's own reports contain. The present state of affairs must therefore be remedied. This can be done, and in my view can only be done either by removing HAMLET to England, which I should regard, as the correct procedure, or by sending to, and maintaining in Lisbon a HAMLET Case Officer with a personality sufficiently strong to impose his wishes on HAMLET. Whether such an officer is available or not I do not know, but as he would require to be somebody like Cyril Mills I should doubt it. Failing this I agree with Robertson's suggestion that the presence in Lisbon of MULLET himself would be an improvement on the present arrangements. I do not consider that the fact that HAMLET's children are in this country amounts to effective control over HAMLET since, in common I should have thought with every other German, he must be quite well aware that we should never dream of exercising pressure on a man's children, and I am certain therefore that their presence in England has no other effect on HAMLET than to inspire him with a feeling of confidence that no matter what happens they are in safe keeping.

I have considered this case only upon the footing that it is regarded with confidence by the Germans. In actual fact, however, as appears in A.H. Robertson's note of 27 October 1943, there are good grounds for suspecting that it may be blown. Moreover, we know that HAMLET is disliked by most of the Germans with whom he deals and is in particular the object of a good deal of jealousy and suspicion within the Abwehr. This circumstance makes it even more essential to get our ideas straight about this case.

Finally, in view of the singularly nerveless way in which SIS have played their part, I think that Colonel Cowgill himself should be invited to give his candid opinion as to the value of the whole enterprise. There seems to me to be no point in carrying on if the majority opinion in both MI5 and SIS is against it.

Soon after Marriott, a peacetime solicitor, had expressed his views so forcefully, one of the major issues in the payments to HAMLET was explained. ISOS had revealed that he had received money from the Abwehr for PUPPET, but very little had actually reached Fanto. In these circumstances, when it was unlikely that PUPPET would continue his espionage without pay, Fanto had complained direct to the Germans in one of his letters, an event which led HAMLET to explain that he had told the Germans that he had been sending money to London. Furthermore, he claimed that he had already told SIS, presumably either Foley or his local Section V officer, Charles de Salis, about these notional payments. This episode highlighted the difficulties in running a case in which one part of the network was managed in Lisbon by SIS, whereas the other two agents were supervised in London by MI5.

A week after D-Day Ian Wilson undertook a final review of the HAMLET case:

The last general survey of this case by Mr. Robertson was made on 21 April 1944, at which date HAMLET was in contact with WERNER in

Madrid but no report of his meeting had reached us. The main events which
have taken place since then are that HAMLET gave a brief written report
of his meeting with WERNER on 25 April 1944, and on 16 May 1944 put
in a further written report, the first two paragraphs of which again referred
to his meetings with WERNER in April, while the remainder of his report
dealt with discussions he had had with various people in Lisbon, which may
be of some value to SIS but are unintelligible to us and in any event do not
appear to arise out of his Abwehr connections.

In the meantime PUPPET has continued to write secret letters to the
Abwehr, the most important part of which consist of putting over Plan
PREMIUM, which was completed in a letter dated April 25th, notionally
sent through the Ministry of Supply bag. Owing to the ban on air mail,
PUPPET's correspondence has decreased in volume so he can only
communicate by air when it so happens that MULLET is sending a business
letter to HAMLET through the Ministry of Supply bag, and naturally the
frequency with which this occurs is outside PUPPET's control.

Since Plan PREMIUM was completed by PUPPET on 25th April, he
has written a further letter through the bag on May 17th, and has also
written sea mail letters on May 10th and May 25th, the first of which
contained no secret text.

In his report of 16 May 1944 HAMLET summed up the situation, explaining
the perceived relationship between Major Joseph Brinkhaus, alias Bergman of
the Brussels Abstelle, and his direct superior, Colonel Carl Servaes:

In spite of the fact that WERNER was excessively pleasant to me and
repeatedly expressed to me his recognition of my services, it appeared
to me that the opinion exists that I am handling this affair from personal
friendship for Bergman, but do not myself earn the confidence that is placed
in (PUPPET). If, in spite of this, they are sticking to me, this is only because
I appear to them to be irreplaceable, and because they believe they need
(PUPPET's) reports most urgently.

Wilson's review of the case continued, expressing some professional scepticism:

I have little doubt that HAMLET's judgement of the situation as it existed
in April is correct, and that, at least at that time, the Abwehr did regard
PUPPET as being of value and were consequently prepared to find foreign
exchange so that he could be kept active on their behalf, and for the same

reason were prepared to keep in contact with HAMLET not because they liked or trusted HAMLET but because they had no other way of getting reports from PUPPET. Apart from HAMLET's evidence on this point, there was earlier evidence from ARTIST that WERNER was trying to find someone else in the Peninsula who could maintain the contact with PUPPET in substitution for HAMLET.

It is a matter of conjecture whether the Abwehr will in the future continue to place any reliance on PUPPET, and, if so, for how long.

As long as they are prepared to believe in threats to the Pas de Calais and Norway we obviously do not wish to take any step which might, in the eyes of the Abwehr, throw additional doubt on PUPPET, but in my opinion PUPPET has committed himself more deeply to the cover plan for OVERLORD than other B1(a) agents, and therefore has less chance of survival if the time comes when the enemy convince themselves that threats to the Pas de Calais and Norway were deliberately exaggerated. I should myself hesitate to make any great use of PUPPET in this distinct field of deception for fear that he has failed to survive fresh investigations of agents which one may reasonably expect at any time now, both because of the subjection of the Abwehr to RSHA and because the Abwehr may justifiably be accused of having failed in their task of providing accurate forecasts of our invasion intentions.

I submit therefore that it is right that PUPPET should continue to send information of a not particularly deceptive character for such period as, in the opinion of SHAEF, it is desirable so as to keep alive any effect that may have already have been obtained from Plan PREMIUM, but that, in the absence of further evidence in the future, PUPPET is not a good channel for continued deception.

It would seem that the Abwehr are incapable of providing another channel of communication for PUPPET, and I can see no particular advantage in our endeavouring to provide another channel for them. HAMLET may not be the perfect post-box in Lisbon but there is no reason to think that he does not pass on communications from PUPPET to the Abwehr undeveloped, with reasonable despatch.

Apart from his function as post-box for PUPPET I can see no advantages, and several possible disadvantages, in the maintenance of contact between HAMLET and the Abwehr. HAMLET's only direct contact with the Abwehr for a very long time past has been with Sonderfuehrer WERNER. WERNER does not seem to be a man of any great importance, and I cannot see that any information that HAMLET has obtained from WERNER is of any value, whereas some at least of the stories coming from WERNER which he has passed on have been held to be inaccurate and possible plant. It is clear beyond doubt that KO Portugal have no confidence whatever in HAMLET, and they never give him any information. There is no likelihood of his ever being given any position in any German stay-behind organisation in Portugal from which we could derive advantage. I am not sure that it has been previously reported, as it has not been carded in this office, that on 12 August 1943 KO Portugal were expressely forbidden by Eins Heer Berlin to have any contact with HAMLET, although Brussels had requested them to get in contact with him.

It was at one time suggested that HAMLET might be of some use as a channel for getting in touch with General von Falkenhausen. I cannot myself see any such channel operating. There is no reason to think that WERNER is in touch with the General, HAMLET is no longer in direct touch with Bergman, and, in any case, reports that Bergman is probably retiring or moving from Brussels. Even if Bergman continues to be concerned with the affairs previously run through Eins Heer Brussels, we would seem justified in expecting his office to be moved back into Germany proper. It seems not unlikely that even when Bergman was in Brussels his contacts with the General were only of the most formal character.

Bergman's superior, Servaes, appears to have been on more intimate terms with the General, but HAMLET states that Servaes has retired, which is probably true as there have been no references to him on Most Secret Sources over a long period.

It will be remembered that last autumn stories appeared in the English press to the effect that a member of the General's staff had been in Lisbon with a view to peace negotiations with the Allies. KO Portugal were asked to investigate the source of these stories, and, rightly or wrongly, KO Portugal advised Berlin on 7 October 1943 that HAMLET had been spreading these stories. (This was not carded in this office, although carded at Ryder Street, and may not previously have come to notice).

Whether or not there are any grounds for the accusation that HAMLET started these rumours, the mere fact that the accusation has been made would seem hopelessly to compromise any slight chance that might previously have existed of HAMLET's being a suitable channel of communication to the General.

It strikes me as being possibly a little more than a coincidence that at an earlier date HAMLET had reported to us a story about an aerial attack on Gestapo Headquarters in Brussels, which story subsequently found its way into the press through the Belgian News Agency in Lisbon, but on enquiry in this country was found to be totally untrue. It seems therefore at least possible that HAMLET deliberately circulates false rumours in Lisbon.

I do not for a moment suspect HAMLET of working with the present German Government against us. On the other hand, I do not see why we should expect HAMLET to give greater weight to our interests than to his personal business interests, or such political views as he may hold. As a business man he is probably very disappointed that no commerical business has resulted from MULLET's activities here, HAMLET is an ex-army officer and, although a Jew, probably has some of the prejudices of the German officer class. He was no doubt sincere when, at the beginning of his case, he recommended the policy of trying to persuade the German generals that Allied production was so enormous that a compromise peace was desirable. Fortunately the German generals are now receiving more direct evidence of the volume of Allied production, and I strongly suspect that HAMLET would like to see the interests of the German officer class, and of the German industrialists, preserved to a greater extent than we in this country would approve. This, if correct, might not matter greatly if there were full and complete control over HAMLET's activities, but in fact, except on the rare occasions when Major Foley visits Lisbon, there seems to be no effective attempt to direct HAMLET's activities.

While I see no very great danger in HAMLET's continuing to act for the time being as a cover address for PUPPET, and he may at the same time be able to provide SIS with useful information from non-Abwehr contacts in Lisbon, I cannot see that he offers the prospect of any more ambitious exploitation.

Finally it ought perhaps to be considered whether PUPPET could serve any useful purpose other than the implementation of deception. The view has sometimes been expressed that in some way use could be made of PUPPET's personal friendship with von Falkenhausen.

I confess I do not see how this could be brought about. PUPPET has considerable social claim, and his father was a friend of the General's, but this, while it no doubt accounts for PUPPET attending poker parties given by the General, does not necessarily mean that he could influence the General in taking a line independent of the Nazi Government. The fact that PUPPET writes letters to the Abwehr does not seem to me to make it any easier for him to get in touch with the General than for anyone else to do so. If we wish to try putting anyone else in touch with the General, the General's nephew, who is now in this country, may be a more suitable man than PUPPET.

It would seem out of the question to use PUPPET's secret ink letters with this object in view, particularly now when reports through Abwehr channels, if they reach the top at all, go to Kaltenbrunner or Himmler, rather than to the OKW.

If PUPPET's use for deceptive purposes has come to an end, the case is not likely to develop in fresh directions, such as taking a political turn, because thanks to the fact that the enemy can communicate with PUPPET only through HAMLET, who is persona non grata with the Abwehr and will be even less popular with the RSHA on racial grounds, they are unlikely to seek to give delicate political instructions to PUPPET.

My recommendation therefore is that PUPPET should continue to write not too frequently for such period as SHAEF consider desirable in order to support his past letters putting across Plan PREMIUM, and that, as soon as this period is over, serious consideration should be given to closing the case.

The HAMLET–PUPPET–MULLET case finally petered out in September 1944 when it proved impossible to perpetuate the Ministry of Supply's artificial interest in Koessler's inventions, and the final chapter proved to be the interrogation of Abwehr personnel in Brussels, who expressed their reservations about Koessler but were never entirely certain he had remained loyal to the Reich.

★ ★ ★

METEOR was Eugn Sostaric, a Croatian naval pilot and aide-de-camp to the King of Yugoslavia, who had been in contact with his friend Dusan Popov from November 1943. He had been the King of Yugoslavia's ADC, but had been imprisoned after attempting to escape the German occupation via Salonika. On that occasion Sostaric, who had intended to offer his services to the RAF, had been betrayed and sentenced to death. The intervention of Ivo Popov had saved his life, having persuaded Johnnie Jebsen that Sostaric, who was a strongly anti-Communist Croatian, would make an ideal agent. Eventually the Abwehr authorised Sostaric's release and his travel across Europe to Madrid, where he was received at the British embassy. Further delays were experienced while Sostaric waited in Gibraltar for transport to England and then, upon his arrival, while he underwent a security screening at the Royal Victoria Patriotic School in Wandsworth. Finally, in April 1943, the airman was enrolled into Popov's network as METEOR, but there was an unexpected twist to his case. When Sostaric was introduced to

MI5 he cheerfully revealed that he had been instructed by the Abwehr to confess his espionage to the British authorities at the first opportunity. He was to admit that he had been provided with a cover address in Portugal to which he was supposed to send apparently innocuous letters, in which messages were to be written in secret ink. Furthermore, the Germans had told him that, having admitted all this, he was to pretend to cooperate with MI5, and then proceed to correspond with another postbox, this time in Madrid, in a secret ink made from another formula that was to be withheld from the British. The Abwehr's clear intention was to run Sostaric as a triple-cross. Sostaric neatly sabotaged the scheme by disclosing it in its entirety, and it was left to MI5's Ian Wilson, who was appointed his case officer, to devise two separate texts for enemy consumption. The first was to contain material that the Germans would perceive to be false, while the second would contain what the Abwehr were calculating on being an authentic report that they could rely upon. Astonishingly, this charade was maintained without a hitch until May 1944 when Sostaric was posted to the Mediterranean theatre as a liaison officer to the Allied Commander-in-Chief's staff.

THIRD REPORT, I JUNE 1943

The Director-General's third report included mention of eight individuals, and an update on the fate of Rogeiro de Menezes, the Portuguese diplomat caught by MI5 and prosecuted.

The eight consisted of Jean Huysmans, who had been bundled aboard a flight to England for interrogation at Camp 020, quickly followed by his wife, who was accommodated at Holloway prison. He had been identified as an agent referred to in ISOS traffic as 'Jean Legrand' and 'Jean Latour', and promptly confessed when confronted with the weight of evidence against him. He would remain at Ham for the rest of the war, acting as a stool pigeon.

Three were interdicted at Trinidad while en route to South America, and redirected to Camp 020. Of this arrest, Liddell gave more details in his diary:

> The Spanish vessel *Cabo de Buena Esperanza* has just left Bilbao for South America carrying two German agents. One is a member of the crew, a Spaniard named Joachim Baticon, who has already acted on several occasions as courier for the Germans, and wrote a letter which was found on the agent Andrés Blay, introducing him to a contact in South America. The other, Hans Laski, was travelling on a Spanish temporary passport in the guise of a German-Jewish refugee. Arrangements have been made to have both of these men arrested at Trinidad.

Thus Baticon had betrayed himself by writing a letter of introduction for Dr Andrés Pigrau Blay, an important Abwehr Einz Marine agent arrested in Trinidad in October 1942. Blay had been the Paraguayan consul in Barcelona but had been recruited by an Abwehr acquaintance, his German counterpart Horst Müller. When Blay was interrogated at Latchmere House he made a detailed statement and explained how his recruitment had been conducted by Müller and his colleague Friedrich Ruggeburg, and how he had been handed a letter signed by Baticon, which he was to produce to the Spanish consul-general in Buenos Aires. Utterly compromised, he was transferred to Camp 020R for the remainder of the war.

Hans Laski was travelling on a Spanish temporary passport in the guise of a German–Jewish refugee, but he had been compromised by ISOS, and was arrested in Trinidad. As for Pacheco, he too was arrested in Trinidad, together with his wife who, he claimed, knew nothing about his mission for the Abwehr.

Sibart, a former French commando, arrived in London from Lisbon, but was tripped up during routine interviews conducted at the London Reception Centre, a refugee examination facility housed in the Oratory School in the Brompton Road, Knightsbridge.

★ ★ ★

THIRD REPORT
A Spies arrested.
(1) Huysmans.
Johannes Huysmans, a Belgian national employed by the German Secret Service arrived in this country on 17 March 1943. He had been ordered to obtain information about economic matters; he was to communicate in secret ink and to receive instructions twice monthly by wireless in code. Huysmans is an important agent and had been working for the enemy in the Low Countries since 1941. His contacts in the German Secret Service are extensive and he has proved a most useful source of information. Most Secret Sources indicate that he would be accompanied by his wife, but she panicked at the last moment in Lisbon and the pair decided to call the journey off. The Belgian Intelligence in Lisbon, therefore, acting on our instructions, resorted to a ruse and virtually 'Shangaied' him using the Portuguese International Police as their unconscious instrument. They subsequently did the same thing to Madame Huysmans who arrived here on 29 May 1943 and now awaits examination.

(2) BATICON, LASKI, PACHECO and Wife.
These spies who were arrested in Trinidad and brought here by us for examination have not confessed.

Baticon, a Spaniard, was to join a German organisation in Buenos Aires which specialises in obtaining Spanish seamen's papers to be used by certain

Naval and Marine personnel stranded in South America, to enable them to escape home.

Pacheco and his wife are a well-known Cuban dancing couple. They had an espionage mission in the Western Hemisphere, as had Laski, who is a Jew, and served in the German Army in the last war. A fifth spy, Lipkau Balleta, was also arrested in Trinidad and has just reached England.

3) SIBART

This French Commando was captured by the Germans in June 1941 during a raid on Crete and later escaped to this country. He was marked down as a suspect by our examiners. Under interrogation he admitted contact in Paris with prominent members of the German Secret Service Sabotage Organisation. He stated that he escaped from his German escort in the Paris Underground.

This story might have excited admiration if it had not been one of the standard and threadbare stories with which the Germans furnish prisoners who they have succeeded in 'turning round'.

(4) VICHY SPIES

Two men, a Frenchman and an Englishman, have arrived in this country who were sent by Vichy to spy against us. Knowing they wished to go to England the French Authorities guaranteed a safe passage from France to Lisbon as an inducement to accept the mission. Neither man really intended to act as a spy and both confessed their whole stories on arrival. Their training was extremely rudimentary, but while part of their questionnaire would have been of use to Vichy France, other items on the military defences of Britain would seem to show that the Germans had a hand in the affair.

(5) MENEZES

The death sentence on this German spy, formerly employed in the Portuguese Embassy in London, has been commuted by the Home Secretary to one of penal servitude for life. In return for this act of clemency our own Foreign Office should be in a position to drive a hand bargain with the Portuguese Government in regard to German agents in Portugal.

B Spies Expected.

The existence of three spies destined for this country has been revealed by Most Secret Sources. The first is probably an Austrian employed in a

German steel firm in Lisbon. He will be carrying with him jewellery instead of money. The second is an agent of the Naval Branch of the German Secret Service, and the third is reported to have left Madrid for England. Arrangements have been made to give them a suitable reception.

C <u>Double cross spies</u>.

(1) GARBO

Before his arrival in this country GARBO, an enterprising and ingenious Spaniard operating entirely on his own initiative, double-crossed the Germans and induced them to believe that he was running an espionage network in England while all the time he was inventing his reports in Lisbon. Having gained the confidence of the German Secret Service he offered his services to us and was brought to here in 1942 to continue his work. Since then he has greatly extended his network of imaginary spies and couriers. We have now set him up with a genuine wireless station which has been paid for by the Germans. One of his notional agents, a South African, supposedly went to North Africa with our Expeditionary Force and has since been communicating with the Germans through GARBO using secret ink. Two more of his fictitious spies are sending espionage reports direct to the Germans in secret ink. We know through Most Secret Sources that the enemy believe implicitly in GARBO's 'spy ring' and consider it one of their most important channels of information. His latest and most sensational coup is the arrival of new instructions for wireless procedure and a new and very complicated code. These were contained in sixteen miniature photographs (a specimen is attached) sent to him by the Germans, cleverly concealed in a tube of ointment and notionally brought here by one of his imaginary couriers. The procedure for wireless transmission reveals an entirely new German technique, namely to disguise secret transmissions as ordinary British army type. Through GARBO therefore we have discovered information of great importance to our own interception services. Nor is this all, for it is further probable the new code given to GARBO is used elsewhere by the German Secret Service, and is one which has hitherto proved impossible to break.

(2) JOSEF

Some months ago we succeeded in penetrating the Japanese espionage Service at its Lisbon base through a clever agent of our own of Russian nationality and OGPU training. He has now been instructed by the Japanese Secret Service to report on convoy movements, naval construction

and possible sabotage in the Glasgow docks. JOSEF is now in regular communication with his Japanese spy masters through a seaman courier and the Japanese are proposing to use this courier to send a wireless transmitter and Japanese infernal machines for sabotage.
[XXX]

(2) Recently the Spanish Consul in Cardiff sent to the Spanish Embassy details concerning air-raid damage. These reports have been collected by Spanish Consuls in Great Britain since 1940. There is reason to believe that this information is collected at the request of the German Authorities though the orders to prepare such reports were officially given by the Spanish Ambassador on the orders of the Foreign Office. We are controlling certain of the reports sent in, but in cases where we are not in a position to do this we are keeping a close check on the information which is passed.

E German spies collaborating with the British.
HARLEQUIN
HARLEQUIN, who plied us with invaluable information on the German Secret Service, has become once again an ordinary P/W. Realising that his only asset, his information, had been sucked dry, and that our interest in him was not based on personal affection, his flexible conscience began to give him trouble. He asked to be released from his bargain because it had become evident to him that the Allies were determined to impose crushing terms on a defeated Germany and he did not want to feel that he had played any part in bringing about the oppression of the German people. As the transaction, from our point of view, had been a highly profitable one, we placed no obstacle in the way of HARLEQUIN's proposal. He thus put on his German uniform once again and returned to his former comrades in the cage.

F General Security Measures.
(1) The Chiefs of Staff have now empowered the Inter-Services W/T Security Committee to consider the whole problem of military and civil wireless security. The first meeting has been held and the Committee has reported back to the Chiefs of Staff that the problem is a serious one and must be faced. Ways and means are under discussion by the experts. It will be appreciated that the need for Signals Security is reinforced by the latest developments mentioned at C (1).

(2) The party of technical advisors from this office who were going to the Middle East have at last left the UK. The delay of two months in their departure has not helped the general security position out there. The problem of transporting them there speedily was one of air transport.

G Comintern.

Word of the dissolution of the Communist International first reached the Communist Party leaders in this country through the news agencies. Though completely surprised, the more alert among them were quickly able to accommodate themselves to the new situation, members of the central executive even asserted that they had expected something of the sort, since a message had been sent to the Communist International as long ago as February, 1943, stating the difficulties which the Party is encountering from allegations of foreign control.

At first the Communist Party almost inevitably viewed the dissolution in the light of its own problem of affiliation to the Labour Party, and the Communists felt that the ground had been cut from under the feet of their opponents. Subsequently various Party leaders have speculated on the possibility of forming a Workers' International on broad lines without the strict ideological ties of the Communist International. Such speculations have, however, been frowned upon, and the Party's programme has been strictly limited to the immediate task of affiliation.

This aim is not as innocent as it appears. The Party's record of penetration and fraction work within other organisations is already notable, Comments by the leaders on the suggestion that the Party should disband and seek election to the Labour Party individually show that they believe that the Communist Party has a distinct and corporate role to play within the Labour Party.

In the matter of the prosecution of the war the Communist Party still has a rooted distrust of the Government. Regarding itself as a watchdog for the Soviet Union, it uses its numbers to gather all political, industrial and military intelligence to which they have access in the course of their employment. Considerable information has reached the Communist Party in this way, but there is no evidence that it has been passed out of the country. It appears to have been mainly used to direct and influence the Party's propaganda. In the matter of supplying secret military information, it is to be noted that members of the Communist Party in the Army have permitted their loyalty to Communism to override their allegiance to their King and their duties.

The receivers of such information are well aware of the 'illegal' character
of their activities, as must be the getters as well.

1st June 1943

★ ★ ★

The slightly oblique reference to 'certain Naval and Marine personnel
stranded in South America' deserves some elaboration, for it is at the heart
of Allied concern about the internment of the crew of the *Admiral Graf Spee*
in Argentina. The pocket battleship had been scuttled off Montevideo in
December 1939 and the ship's complement of 1,150 was supposed to have been
interned. Thirty-six were killed in the naval engagement off the River Plate,
but only 850 were repatriated on the troopship *Highland Monarch* in February
1946, among them only six officers, which meant the rest had disappeared.
In fact, as the Allies knew only too well, they had been smuggled back to the
Reich, often as stowaways, to re-join the Kriegsmarine.

The Germans had pulled off something of a coup by arranging for their
men to be landed in Argentina, rather than Uruguay, and they had achieved
this by transferring them covertly from the *Graf Spee* onto another German
ship, the *Tacoma*, a blockaded Hamburg-Amerika line merchantman that had
been moored in the harbour and had accompanied the warship on her final
short voyage out into the estuary. Instead of returning the crew to Montevideo,
as anticipated, the *Tacoma* unexpectedly had transferred them onto smaller
vessels and dispatched them to Buenos Aires. Although all the Kriegsmarine
sailors were required to be detained until the conclusion of hostilities, SIS and
the FBI knew that some of the officers and technicians were slipping away to
Europe with the collusion of the Argentine authorities.

One of the most valuable commodities in any conflict is experienced
personnel, and the internees represented a very valuable, but wasted,
resource for the beleaguered Kriegsmarine. Certainly between thirty
and forty of the crew had been released from internment on parole, and
had vanished, and the evidence suggested that the person masterminding
the operation was Captain Dietrich Niebuhr. Previously the head of
the Abwehr's naval branch, Niebuhr was a highly professional career
intelligence officer who organised an escape route run by his assistant
attachés, Lieutenants Franz Mammen and Johannes Müller. In addition,
Niebuhr had assigned to himself the *Graf Spee*'s only Spanish-speaking
officer, Korvettenkapitän Robert Höpfner, for liaison purposes. Höpfner

had fallen ill during his internment and had been allowed to work in Niebuhr's office in the embassy during his extended convalescence.

Niebuhr's group of subordinates included several who ran their own spy rings, and among them was Rudolf Hepe of the Antonio Delfino Company, which was a subsidiary of the Hamburg-South America Line. Not surprisingly, it was Hepe, working under Niebuhr's instructions, who had supplied the lighter and tugs that had carried the *Graf Spee*'s crew to Argentina even before the Argentine government had agreed to accept them. When they arrived in Buenos Aires the officers and petty officers were accommodated in the Naval Arsenal, with 800 ratings sent to dormitories in the functional, three-storey Immigrants' Hotel nearby.

Mammen and Müller liaised with the internment camps, and passed the evaders on to a local travel agent, Wilhelm von Siedlitz, who arranged for them to be escorted over the Andes and delivered to Friedrich von Schulz-Hausmann, a *reichsdeutschen* who had been the Norddeutscher-Lloyd line's agent in Valparaiso and had been enrolled into the Abwehr during a visit to Hamburg in the summer of 1938. Code-named CASERO, he supervised the travel of about fifty *Graf Spee* crewmen on ships bound for Vladivostock, who completed their long journey home on the Trans-Siberian Express. The groups of *Graf Spee* survivors who slipped away were known, somewhat euphemistically, as the stowaways, and the task of preventing further escapes was considered an intelligence priority in London.

★ ★ ★

Although the detention of Pacheco is well documented, there is little trace of the Vichy agents mentioned, or of the French commando Sibart. Pacheco was detained with his wife, Viviana Diaz, in Trinidad in March 1943 and brought to Camp 020 for interrogation. Pacheco, who had been employed as a dancer at the Piccadilly Hotel before the war, confessed to having been recruited by the Abwehr in Belgium and then sent on a mission to Havana. They were both detained until the end of hostilities and then deported to Cuba.

★ ★ ★

In December 1942 Jean Huysmans appeared in the ISOS traffic as an Abwehr agent recruited in The Hague who had reached Barcelona on a mission to Lisbon where he intended to apply for a visa to travel to England. Two months earlier an ISOS decrypt on a Lisbon channel had shown the Abstellen seeking a cover address for him in Portugal, which had been supplied: Francisco Lopez da Fonseca, rua São Mamede 50 esq 1, Lisbon. Altogether, some forty-six separate messages referring to HALMA or A-1409 provided a very comprehensive picture of Huysmans' activities before he set off for Spain.

When this news reached the Belgians the Sureté in Belgrave Square responded that Huysmans and his wife, Marie, had already applied in Barcelona for a visa to go to the Congo. Although Huysmans did not actually appear in Lisbon until May 1943, ISOS revealed that the 42-year-old university-educated businessman formerly employed by Texaco in Brussels, who was fluent in five languages, was controlled by a Dr Schumann and a series of payments had followed, with a promise of $2,500 and 6,000 escudos when his passage had been purchased.

When Huysmans applied for his visa in Lisbon he was told that he would have to travel to the Congo through England, and soon afterwards he was arrested by the Portuguese police, detained at the rua Augusta Rosa prison, informed that he had over-stayed his residency permit, and bundled onto an aircraft that flew him to Whitchurch, near Bristol.

Huysmans reached Camp 020 on 20 May 1943 where he was considered by the commandant, Colonel Robin Stephens, as 'one of the most fascinating espionage cases of the war'. Initially Huysmans claimed to be the victim of mistaken identity, but when it was suggested he had been blackmailed and his wife was under threat, he began to break. The final incentive was Stephens' shrewd offer to bring his wife to the safety of London, knowing that in fact she was already in Holloway prison. Convinced of the omniscience of the British Secret Service, Huysmans offered a full confession and his complete cooperation, acting as a stool pigeon at Ham for the remainder of the conflict. In his statements Huysmans identified three other Abwehr agents whom he had encountered while being trained in secret writing and encipherment, and gave detailed descriptions of the Abwehr staff.

According to his version of events, Huysmans had been recruited by an Abwehr officer named Schumann in April 1942 after he had been arrested by the Gestapo on a charge of hiding foreign currency. MI5 suspected that 'Schumann' was actually an officer from The Hague previously identified as Schneider, operating from 248 rue Royale in Brussels. Thereafter he had undergone a lengthy course in secret writing and wireless transmission at an office in Ostend but, he claimed, he had participated under duress, following a threat by Schumann to his wife and elderly mother. On this basis, MI5 ruled out Huysmans as a potential double-cross agent. On the other hand, he could not be prosecuted under the Treachery Act as he had not come to England voluntarily. A third alternative was considered by T. A. Robertson, which was to run Huysmans deliberately badly as a double-agent, allowing him to indicate that he was under enemy control. This prearranged signal, by signing himself 'H', had been disclosed by Huysmans, but this option was rejected.

During the six months Huysmans underwent training he met numerous instructors and agents, including an Irishman later identified as Joseph Lenihan. The Abwehr wanted Huysmans to collect intelligence in England, the United States, or Brazil, and prepared him for missions to all those countries, determined that he should not end up in the Congo, and had supplied him with a questionnaire:

(1) ENGLAND.
Economic.
Shipbuilding.
Maritime and fluvial traffic.
Valuation of food and clothing stocks.
Arrivals and sailings of ships and port movements.
Railway traffic.
Female employment in factories.
Reduction of petrol consumption.
Number of agricultural workers.
Coal production.
Conditions of travel in England (for instance, is travel free or restricted?)
What are the reserves of aluminium, copper, paper, etc.
Percentage of ships in repair.

Military.
Location of troops and units.
Strength of the Home Army.
Models of weapons, tanks in use.
Description of new planes, motors and tanks.
Warship and submarine bases, and their strength.
Whether factories and stevedores cease work during air-raid warnings.
Location of munitions depots and new aerodromes.
Strength of USA troops and their armaments arriving in the U.K.
Location of aeroplane factories and submarine shipyards.
Coastal defence, fortifications, guns, troops, aerodromes.
Details of new motors, planes, tanks, munitions, armament.

(2) USA

Degree of mobilisation of Army and instruction of recruits.

Degree of civil mobilisation for war purposes.

Importance of convoys of troops and strength of war material leaving for the front, and their destination.

Food and clothing stocks, and stocks of essential war products.

Quantities of planes, motors, tanks, guns, ammunition, cars, trucks and war materials generally, produced in 1942.

Construction of aircraft carriers and warships, and cargo ships.

Percentage of ships undergoing repair.

Production of synthetic material for war purposes.

Particulars of newly-designed motors or apparatus for war purposes.

Details of the arrivals and destinations of troop-carrying convoys, the amount of armament carried, and the percentage of ships getting through.

(3) BRAZIL and MEXICO

State of mobilisation of the Army and Navy.

To what extent the country has been put on a war footing.

What troop-carrying convoys leave Mexican and Brazilian harbours.

What quantities of food and other goods are being sent to the USA.

What numbers of industrial and agricultural workers are on war-work.

What stocks of raw materials are on hand.

The strength of the Fleet and Air Forces.

What native troops are being sent to the fronts, and what is their armament.

Any information on the production of ships, guns, ammunition, rubber, clothing, etc.

While Huysmans was languishing at Camp 020, his wife was transferred in August 1943 from Holloway to Port Erin on the Isle of Man. Both were released in August 1945 and deported by air from Croydon to Belgium, where they were taken into custody and prosecuted, the military tribunal having been urged to seek a nominal sentence in acknowledgement of Huysmans' alleged assistance to British Intelligence.

★ ★ ★

Joaquin Baticon was a 34-year-old former member of the Blue Division that had fought on the Russian front, and steward on the Ybarra liner *Cabo de Buenos Epseranza* that called into Trinidad on 6 February 1943.

He was described by MI5's Herbert Hart as 'an important German agent likely to be in possession of a mass of information which may have a direct bearing on the war at sea'. Accordingly, he was arrested and on 30 March sent to Gourock on the SS *Maaskerk* via New York, where he was questioned for five days by the FBI.

Upon his arrival at Camp 020, under threat of immediate prosecution and execution, he disclosed a wealth of information that formed the foundation of MI5's understanding of the Axis networks across the western hemisphere, and was the basis of a concerted Allied counter-attack.

In his statement Baticon acknowledged that he had been recruited as a spy by two Germans, the air attaché, Heinz Junge, and his replacement, Peter Wolfmann, in Buenos Aires in March 1942. He also claimed that their principal Spanish contact was Manuel Perez, who exercised control over Spanish seamen travelling to Argentina, and who had the power to place those who were disobedient 'in a concentration camp at will'. Baticon's role was that of a courier, carrying money, documents, micro-photographs and coded letters between Rio de Janeiro, Buenos Aires, Havana, Lisbon, Vigo and Cádiz for two familiar characters, Otto Mesner and Otto Heinrich, both in Bilbao. Although he had no precise knowledge of the content of his deliveries, he possessed an encyclopedic memory of his contacts and their addresses, and incriminated dozens of Axis agents. In his lengthy statements Baticon explained that he had been invalided out of the Blue Division because of a gastric ulcer, and had undergone surgery in Nuremberg before being discharged. He had then sailed in August 1941 on the *Cabo de Bueno Esperanza* to Buenos Aires, where he had received further hospital treatment. After his recruitment by the Abwehr he had sailed on the *Cabo de Hornos* in June 1942 carrying secret documents to Lisbon and Bilbao. In January 1943 he accepted his second mission, to sail from Barcelona to Lisbon on the *Cabo de Buena Esperanza* via Trinidad, with instructions to report to the German embassy in Buenos Aires for a new assignment.

Although Baticon was essentially 'small fry', as Milmo described him, he served to corroborate the accuracy of FBI reports from South America and, of course, ISOS. Furthermore, it was Baticon's testimony about the roles of Manuel Perez, Joaquin Ruiz and José Pujana that led to their arrest soon afterwards. Baticon was kept in custody until August 1945, when he was deported to Gibraltar on HMS *Glasgow*, along with Perez, Ruiz, Urzaiz, Luis Calvo and seven other Spanish detainees.

★ ★ ★

In November 1942 a 48-year-old Mexican, Fernando Lipkau Balleta, was taken off the SS *Marques de Comillas* in Trinidad, based on seven ISOS decrypts that suggested that he was a German spy:

20.8.42. Madrid–B'ona Employment proposal of 17th, Please radio by tomorrow how transfers of money are regulated. HERMANDO. SOMMER.

24.8.42. Madrid–Berlin. To ERUBE. We request permission by FS for estimate of 3,000 USA dollars for journey (out of country) on 28/8 to USA via Mexico of the V-Mann FERNANDO LOPKIU (or LIPKAU) who was placed at disposal of IH by Nevenstelle Barcelona without preliminary report. Employment at Ford or Chrysler works. HERNANDO. KCGP.

21.8.42. B'ona–Madrid. For HERNANDO. Your above message. We are awaiting instructions as whether money can he transferred from South American accounts at your end which are not blocked and are not exposed to suspicion, to V-Mann's American business friend-bank address to follow. Otherwise we should have to purchase money for payment in Mexico here or in Lisbon on the open market. Payable in pesetas or escudos. PORTAL.

21.8.42, B'ona–Madrid. For HERNANDO. ^Ref. both above messages. PASTILO's departure postponed (? on next) steamship, with official permission owing to typhus in the family. Passages remain valid. PORTAL.

22.8.42 Berlin–Madrid. For SOMMER. For HERNANDO. Payment of 3,000 dollars is declined, as we have no evidence here upon which the personality of L and the prospects of success of the undertaking (Rinataz) planned can be judged. KRRF.

3.10.42 B'ona–Madrid. To PORTAL. Proposal for employment V 701 STEP rejected by Berlin; Proposed for employment V-Mann PASTILLA on the other hand approved. HERNANDO SOMOZA.

1.11.42 Lisbon–Madrid via Nauen. To PAGO. Ref proposal for employment of V-Mann PASTILLA. Instructions not possible till a week at the earliest from reason of security. LUDOVICO.

Thus the intercepts appeared to suggest that an Abwehr agent code-named PASTILLA with connections at Ford and Chrysler was being paid to embark on a mission to the United States via Mexico, but had been forced to delay the voyage because of illness. All the details fitted Lipkau, whose daughter had caught typhoid in August 1942, thus postponing the family's departure.

Lipkau had sailed from Vigo on a mission to South America for the Abwehr, destined apparently for an assignment involving him finding work at a factory in the United States. His wife and three children were allowed to continue their journey to Cuba, but meanwhile, when questioned at the St James Internment Camp in Port of Spain, Lipkau identified the matters on which he was to report in secret writing and microphotography to cover addresses in Spain:

1　　To collect and read specialist periodicals, such as the *Army and Navy Journal* for war news.

2　　Shipping intelligence; coverage of vessels. Names of captains, whether armed, convoy posts, whence sailing and destinations.

3　　Number of US Army conscripts, training camps in California, Alaska and Canada, especially those for parachutists, names of officers commanding; officers' insignia, their private lives, potential staff officer, regimental numbers, markings on any army vehicles, etc.

4　　Type, location, calibre and rate of fire of guns.

5　　Location of US munition plants and war activities of different commercial firms.

6　　Location of aircraft factories, origin of components, methods of assembly and caliber of aircraft.

7　　Morale of civilians.

In March 1943 Lipkau, who had been born in Poland, was sent to New York, on the SS *Maaskerk*, accommodated briefly in the Ellis Island hospital, and then transferred to the SS *Ramitata* for Liverpool. When he was interrogated at Camp 020, he made a detailed confession, admitting that he had been expelled from Spain because of a conviction for his black market currency dealing. He had decided to sail for Cuba, but ten days before his planned departure, in August 1942, he had been approached in Barcelona by an acquaintance to spy for the Germans. When shown photographs of German espionage suspects, Lipkau identified one of his contacts as Edmund C. Heine, a former Ford Motor Company executive implicated in the pre-war Duquesne case[1] in New York. Another had played a minor, talent-spotting role in the case of Juan Lecube, a German spy arrested in Trinidad in 1942.[2]

Lipkau was kept in custody, first at Ham, then at the Beltane School in Wimbledon and finally at a Ministry of Health hostel in Retford, Nottinghamshire, until June 1946 when he was deported from London on the SS *Port Huon* to New York.

★ ★ ★

JOSEF was a Russian seaman on the SS *Baron Forbes*, active between August 1942 and December 1944 against the Japanese in Lisbon, and on 13 May 1943 Liddell recorded in his diary:

> Richmond Stopford's agent JOSEF who has just returned from Lisbon, was approached there by the Japanese and asked to act as an agent in this country. They suggested various sabotage schemes to him, one to function in Glasgow in September. He was given a cover address in Lisbon, a seal specially made for him with his monogram on it to seal the letters he would send back by courier, and a promise of a wireless set which would be sent in separate parts by degrees through the courier who would bring his letters.

Among MI5's double-agents, JOSEF is unique because he was actually a fully trained Soviet spy and committed Communist who willingly acted for the Security Service. A case summary drafted in February 1944 set out the background:

> JOSEF is a Russian of whose early history we know very little. He is a little over 30 years old, probably was born in Kiev and lived in Russia until 1919 when he moved to Yugoslavia. At a later date he was trained as an agent by the Russians and since 1934 he has been a seaman for the greater part of that time, with intervals when he was in Spain during the Civil War, in a capacity which is far from clear. He is a communist, fairly well educated, knows a number of languages, and is undoubtedly very clever and astute.
>
> He first came to notice in 1941 when a number of mysterious attempts at sabotage occurred on the Dutch SS *Parklaan*, in which he was then serving. In each case, JOSEF was either the first to discover or report the incident, but in no case was it established who was the perpetrator. JOSEF came to this country at the end of July 1941 and was detained at the Oratory from August 1941 to 28 March 1942. There he became friendly with Matsumoto, the ex-honorary Press Attaché to the Japanese Embassy, about whom and others he supplied reports to the officer-in-charge. Before his release,

Matsumoto asked him to make various contacts on his behalf, and JOSEF was shipped to Lisbon at the end of May 1942. On our instructions, he called at the Japanese Legation, introducing himself as a friend of Matsumoto. On subsequent occasions he was interviewed by a number of Japanese, including the Military and Naval Attachés, who paid him various sums of money and asked him to work for them in this country.

After an unsuccessful attempt in August 1942 to send information to the Japanese by courier, JOSEF returned to Lisbon in February 1943 and re-established contact with the Japanese. He had several interviews with the Assistant Naval and Military Attachés and succeeded in explaining satisfactorily his long absence. They questioned him at length about his activities in England and the information he had been able to obtain, and proposed that he should return and continue to work for them. They also proposed that he should prepare a plan for sabotage in the docks of Liverpool and Glasgow, and offered him £100 in cash.

After JOSEF's return to this country we were able to check his story at various points from other sources, and therefore decided to send him back to Lisbon again with certain information about Glasgow and a plan for sabotaging the Glasgow docks.

As a result of this second visit to Lisbon we learnt particulars of certain persons engaged in espionage on behalf of the Japanese, and details of three addresses in Lisbon used by them for meeting places or for contacts. Further, it appeared that Kiyoi Kisaki was in charge of JOSEF's case. The following was already known to us of Kisaki's previous history: In October 1939 he was staying at the Palace Hotel in Copenhagen, which he left on October 28th, travelling to the Streit Hotel, Hamburg. In January 1940 he was the recipient of a letter from a certain Sekime, c/o Mitsui, New York, enclosing several cheques drawn on Swiss and German accounts with London banks, and mentioning that a certain Moriya (known as a member of the London office of Mitsui) was a subordinate of Kidosaki.

JOSEF was in Lisbon again during April 1943 and had seven meetings with the Japanese. He was interrogated at length, passed over the information he had brought with him and was paid £70. On this visit JOSEF appears to have established himself securely in the confidence of the Japanese. It was arranged that for the future he should work in England collecting information, principally about naval construction, and should send reports by courier. Another of our seamen agents, who had co-operated with JOSEF in the past, was introduced by him to the Japanese, and undertook to carry JOSEF's reports, though not to engage in espionage himself.

JOSEF was given a little seal with the initials 'A.T.' (by which he was known to the Japanese) engraved upon it, with which his reports were to be sealed.

From May to October 1943 JOSEF was resident ashore in this country. At the end of May he sent his first report to Lisbon by courier. As he had only been ashore for about a fortnight, he had not had time to collect a great deal of information, with the result that this report was not of a very high grade. The courier returned with a large sealed envelope which he brought back for JOSEF. This envelope enclosed two similar envelopes and all three bore the official seal of the Japanese Legation in Lisbon. Of the two enclosures one contained the sun of £65 for JOSEF's expenses ashore, while the other contained a letter expressing a certain disappointment in JOSEF's first report and hoping for further information to come. This letter also mentioned that the Japanese were still interested in naval construction and the 'so-called radio electric television' which was explained to the courier as being the latest type of radio location. The letter made no further mention of sabotage. It was signed 'K.K'.

By August 1943 JOSEF had collected a great deal of information for his second report by courier. This related principally to naval construction and, in addition, a certain amount of political and military information. The reply, which reached us at the end of September, this time bore no official seals. It enclosed £150 for JOSEF's expenses, generally commended his last report and contained certain further instructions. Again, no further mention was made of the subject of sabotage. Kidosaki, however, had told the courier that he would be glad to see JOSEF in Lisbon again, as had been provisionally arranged by JOSEF himself last April.

On October 11th JOSEF left again for Lisbon, taking with him a long and detailed report on naval construction collected on the Clyde, on the Tyne and on the Mersey. His report also included a certain amount of political and military information; in addition to his report his courier carried out for him a number of technical shipping magazines, a copy of *Jane's Fighting Ships*, 1942 edition, and a number of aircraft recognition pictures and some Admiralty photographs marked 'Secret – not to be released', which JOSEF had notionally obtained from a friend in the WRNS. JOSEF was also instructed to represent to the Japanese that the method of communication by courier was unsatisfactory and very slow, to ask them for a secret ink for better communication in future and to see how they reacted to the suggestion that he should have a wireless transmitter. He was also to ask for instructions as to how to communicate with them in the event of Portugal declaring war on Japan and their being removed from Lisbon.

JOSEF arrived in Lisbon early in November and stayed there a month, having nine meetings in all with the Japanese. Kidosaki was very pleased to see him, questioned him at length about his voyage and about general conditions and morale in this country. JOSEF handed over his report and the publications he had brought. At his second interview he was interrogated very fully on his report by a Japanese, whom he had not met previously, who has since been identified as Jeikichi Kamikoshimachi. His report was criticised much more severely than on any previous occasion, and he was told to concentrate on information about naval construction, principally of capital ships, convoys, relations between the British and Russian Governments, the coming invasion of the Continent, conditions in this country, radio electric television, and American troops in Britain. He was told that information about the merchant navy was of no interest.

At his next interview he was asked if he would be prepared to work for the Japanese either in Portugal or the United States, both of which suggestions he declined.

On November 26th JOSEF had a long interview with another Japanese, who was clearly a person of higher authority, and he was interrogated from a questionnaire, prepared by someone of greater experience who had examined JOSEF's work in detail. At this meeting, this Japanese professed to be dissatisfied with the accuracy and thoroughness of JOSEF's reporting. At subsequent meetings, Kidosaki, who was still convinced of JOSEF's trustworthiness, told him that his report would have to be examined by still higher authorities, and that until it had been approved, he could only pay him £150. JOSEF told him that he was very annoyed about this treatment, but would wait two or three months till his report had been examined before deciding whether to break with them. In fact, JOSEF's courier left again for Lisbon towards the end of January, bearing a letter from JOSEF in this strain, and a little further information.

JOSEF's requests for secret ink or a radio transmitter had no success, but he was told to get in touch with the Japanese Naval Attaché in Madrid, in the event of war between Japan and Portugal. He was urged to recruit sub-agents to help him in his work, and in particular he was asked if he could get someone employed on the regular trip to North America to bring back American publications; at the same time he was asked to get information from North America on any topics he could.

Miscellaneous Points:

JOSEF has supplied us with eleven addresses in Lisbon, used by the Japanese for meeting places or cover addresses, which were not previously known to us.

JOSEF's own identity documents show him as being stateless and of Russian origin. Because he would not be granted shore leave in Lisbon by the Portuguese International Police on the strength of these documents, it has been necessary to supply him with new ones showing him as a British subject.

It has been agreed with JOSEF that he is working for us on a regular salary, that any sums received from the Japanese are our property and that any bonuses paid to him are purely ex-gratia payments.

The reports which JOSEF has supplied to the Japanese have been largely factual and have not attempted to play any major part in any deception policy. His reports relating to naval construction have however consistently exaggerated our production, particularly of smaller escort vessels.

JOSEF took to the espionage business as a natural, and would eventually disclose details of his past. He was the youngest of three children and his father had been an Imperial Russian Army soldier killed in Romania in 1916. His mother died in Kiev in 1925 and his sister Nina had married the local kommissar. JOSEF's brother, whom he had last seen in 1939, was a high-ranking officer in a tank division stationed in the Soviet Far East. Having graduated from school in 1928 he had enrolled in Kiev's military academy and in 1931 transferred to the Political Military School before undertaking an assignment in Yugoslavia where he was to pose as a White Russian and attend a military academy in Sarajevo. He was then sent on another mission to Louvain University to investigate an anti-Soviet movement sponsored by a Roman Catholic priest.

During his period in Belgium JOSEF reported to an NKVD controller, Victor Pourin, a Comintern activist based at the International Seaman's Club in Antwerp, and to Ivanov, a waiter working at the Imperial Russian Cabaret-Café in Brussels. Later JOSEF was directed by a new controller named Kurtz to join the SS *Hannah* on a voyage to Romania with instructions to report on local conditions and recruit sub-agents. After several voyages he was moved to Rotterdam where he was introduced to a GRU agent, Thelma, who acted as secretary to the local *rezident*, Walter Krivitsky. In 1937, during the Spanish Civil War, he was then switched to sailing between Rotterdam, Barcelona and Valencia. Before the end of that conflict he was moved onto the transatlantic route and at a meeting with Pourin at the City Hotel in Buenos Aires he was ordered to make contact with the German embassy while posing as an anti-Communist White Russian and offer his services as a courier. However, during his second voyage in this capacity the Germans invaded Holland and JOSEF found himself isolated, the Germans having confided that the Nazis planned to attack the Soviet Union. In the absence of Pourin and any local Soviet organisations he could approach, JOSEF went to the British naval attaché, who didn't believe him but was interested to learn more about German plans to sabotage British shipping in Argentina,

JOSEF decided to travel to London to report to the Soviet embassy, and in 1940 joined a ship bound for England, but after a case of suspected sabotage it was diverted to Halifax, where JOSEF was detained by the Canadian authorities. When he finally reached London he was sent to the London Reception Centre at the Oratory School. He was only released, and able to visit the Soviet consulate, on condition that he worked for the LRC as a stool pigeon, a task he undertook willingly.

Once at liberty, JOSEF won over his MI5 case officers, Richmond Stopford in London, Peter Hope in Newcastle, and Jack Hooper in Glasgow, whose confidence was supported by Section V's Graham Greene. He would work from Newcastle and Glasgow, and exploited Matsumoto's mistaken trust by becoming a source for the Japanese naval attaché in Lisbon. In doing so, as his MI5 file reveals, he was code-named RHUBARB by SIS and joined a group of other ship-borne agents, among them SPARK, PEACH, PLATO, IRMA and MADELEINE, who cultivated the enemy whenever they visitied Portugal. However, unlike the others, JOSEF was handled by MI5 in England and was deliberately insulated from local SIS station personnel. His first visit took place in May 1942, with a second in February 1943 when he received instructions to sabotage Glasgow's shipyards. During a third rendezvous, in April 1943, JOSEF held seven meetings with various Japanese intelligence personnel, all of whom he later identified to MI5. In November he had a further nine briefings, all of which served to show that he was highly regarded as a spy.

Later in 1944, following the Italian armistice, SIS learned from the local Italian naval intelligence officer, Commander del Castello, that his Japanese counterparts had acquired an important source in Glasgow, and this turned out to be JOSEF. The same defector also confirmed Kidosaki's true identity as Dr Takeo Saki, the naval attaché's secretary. Actually, JOSEF was an assiduous agent, to the point of being arrested by the Glasgow police in March 1944 after he had been seen making sketches of the Clyde shipyards, but all the information he passed on to the Japanese was cleared for release by Ewen Montagu, the Admiralty's representative on the XX Committee. According to del Castello, who was interviewed by SIS in Lisbon in February 1944, JOSEF's reports 'appeared spasmodically, read most convincingly'.

JOSEF's case came to an end in December 1944, but there would be a curious postscript to it in 1945 when his case officer in Glasgow, Jack Hooper, was identified by Hermann Giskes as a former member of the Passport Control Office staff in The Hague who had sold them SIS secrets before the war. Specifically, he had betrayed SIS's star agent in Germany, Karl Krüger, who had been arrested by the Gestapo. Reportedly, Krüger had committed suicide in prison. When challenged in July 1945 by Herbert Hart and Richmond Stopford, Hooper claimed he had declared his German contacts to SIS. However, when another Abwehr officer, Adolf von Feldmann, was questioned in Germany and confirmed Giskes' version, although there was no evidence, nor suspicion, that Hooper had spied during the war, he was dismissed, but was never charged with any offence. He returned to Holland after the war.[3]

FOURTH REPORT, 2 JULY 1943

The Director-General's fourth report returned to some cases referred to previously, so as to keep the Prime Minister informed of progress on matters with which he was already familiar, and mentioned at the outset an entirely new development, that of the arrest in Trinidad of Oscar Liehr, an Argentine recruited by the Abwehr in Lisbon, trained in wireless and secret writing, and sent on a mission to Buenos Aires. Once again, an enemy spy had been compromised by ISOS and interdicted almost before they had the chance to commence their espionage.

Similarly, access to the Abwehr's communications with Madrid and Lisbon gave advance notice of intended operations, and MI5 was particularly interested in an Austrian, Rudolf Ender. However, there is no record to show that he ever embarked on his mission to England.

The two other major topics were the Spanish consul in Cardiff, the Count of Artaza; and Richard Wurmann, the defector code-named HARLEQUIN, and Gibraltar. Appointed in 1937 to Southampton, the notoriously anti-British Count of Artaza later served as consul in Newcastle and Cardiff, and was often suspected by MI5 as the author of messages, officially protected by the embassy's diplomatic immunity, that were intended for the Abwehr:

FOURTH REPORT
A SPIES ARRESTED.
LIEHR
Oscar Liehr, an Argentine national of German parentage, was arrested at Trinidad on information derived from Most Secret Sources. After interrogation by our representative Liehr confessed that he had been recruited by the German Secret Service in Lisbon as a spy to work in

South America. He described to us in detail the secret inks he was to use to send his reports back to Europe, and has also given us the cover address to which he was to write. This spy is being brought to this country for further interrogation by our officers.

B SPIES EXPECTED

(1) The Austrian spy mentioned in last month's report is still in Lisbon awaiting a passage to this country. He has already received the jewellery which he is bringing with him instead of money. He has also been given the name and address of a British subject in Switzerland as a cover address for his reports. The history and record of this British subject are being investigated, and meanwhile adequate arrangements have been made for the reception of the Austrian when he arrives.

(2) Most Secret Sources show that an agent has been recruited by the German Secret Service in Spain to come to England. He has been given a sum of money in English pounds, secret ink and a cover address. Precise information as to his identity and the date of his departure have still to be obtained.

DOUBLE CROSS SPIES

(1) MUTT

It will be remembered that MUTT recently received money and a wireless set which were dropped by the Germans by parachute. He has just returned from Scotland, where he has been trying to take delivery of sabotage equipment and more money. Unluckily, owing to a combination of misfortunes, the old dropping place and the night arranged were not convenient, and eventually the operation had to be planned for a night when conditions were very bad owing to mist. The Germans dropped the equipment about ten miles away from the spot selected, where it was found by the police the next morning. The sabotage equipment and £100 were contained in a suitcase of British make. The equipment was also British and some of it has been recognised as having been specially made for one particular operation. As the Germans had dropped the suitcase at the wrong place, it was thought inadvisable for MUTT to acknowledge receipt, and he has asked for a repetition of the operation, but the Germans have replied that this would not be possible before the middle of July as the nights are too short. Meanwhile the plan for having an explosion at an electricity undertaking previously referred to as Plan BUNBURY has had to be transferred from Basingstoke to Bury St. Edmunds. Preparations for this are proceeding satisfactorily, and it will take place when the explosives are dropped in the middle of July.

(2) PLAN DREAM

The second part of Plan DREAM has been carried out satisfactorily and £2,373 has been transferred to GARBO by the German Secret Service. To obtain this amount the Germans paid over 225,000 pesetas.

(3) FATHER

It has been found possible to make available the services of this double cross agent to India for deception purposes. He is a member of an Allied Air Force and has been posted to India. He left this country on 29 June 1943. Arrangements have been made for him to be run by the competent Indian authorities. In this connection we sent out to India at the request of DIB an officer from this Department to advise them on the running of double cross spies. This officer will be returning to this country shortly, but we have sent another person who has been fully trained by us to replace him.

(4) ZIGZAG

Most Secret Sources show that the German Secret Service in Madrid is expecting the arrival there of a spy who is likely to be identical with our double cross agent ZIGZAG. Reference has been to a German wireless set with which ZIGZAG is to be equipped, but no indication has been given as to where he is going.

(5) GIBRALTAR

As a result of information received from a double cross agent working in Gibraltar, it has been possible to arrest the following individuals:-

Edouardo Buetto, British.
Luis Lope Cordon Cuenca, Spaniard.
Manuel Serna Botana, Spaniard.

No exact details have been received, but sabotage material has been discovered and it is believed that these people are members of a sabotage organisation of the German Secret Service working against Gibraltar. There is also evidence showing complicity of serving Spanish officers which it may be possible to use as a basis for further protests to the Spanish Government.

D <u>DIPLOMATIC</u>.

Reference was made last month to the reports on air-raid damage which have been supplied by Spanish diplomats and consuls since 1940. There is good reason to believe that this information has been collected at the request of the Germans, who obtain them through their links in the Spanish Foreign Office. The latest report written by the Spanish Consul in Cardiff has come into our hands and has been studied by Home Forces, Home Security and the Air Ministry. All three agree that the information given would be of considerable value to the enemy. We are discussing with the Foreign Office whether the time has not come for a demarche to the Spaniards. We may be able to obtain an account of these activities in a form which could be used by the Foreign Office. Our aim would be, not only to obtain the recall of the extremely anti-British and objectionable Spanish Consul in Cardiff, but also to embarrass the Spanish Embassy here to an extent which might cause them to curtail their reports on subjects of operational importance during the coming critical months.

Previous mention has been made of the arrest of the spy Menezes and his subsequent reprieve at the instance of the Portuguese Government. As a result of evidence obtained through this and other cases which was given to the Portuguese authorities, a number of arrests were made by the Portuguese in Lisbon, and considerable damage was done to some sections of the German Secret Service there. After the first wave of arrests, however, the Germans brought pressure to bear on the Portuguese authorities, who have not only failed to continue their attacks on the Axis organisations, but have actually released some of the more important spies. The Foreign Office has been consulted and is considering whether more energetic protests ought to be made by HM representatives in Portugal. It seems quite clear that the Portuguese authorities have not yet throttled down German Secret Service activities in Lisbon to the extent we were entitled to expect in return for the clemency shown to Menezes at their very special request.

E

It is known from Most Secret Sources that the German Secret Service are most interested in the arrival in Spain from England of Don Antonio Pastor, Professor of Spanish at London University. Pastor has lived here for twenty years and has many interesting contacts in this country. Anticipating before he left for Spain that the Germans would show interest in him we have given considerable information to Pastor which it is hoped he will be indiscreet enough to talk about during his visit.

F COMMUNIST ESPIONAGE

D.F. Springhall, National Organiser of the Communist Party and a member of the Central Committee since 1932, was arrested on June 17th, and has been charged with obtaining information for a purpose prejudicial to the safety or interests of the State. The information in question related to a Most Secret device which is in process of development by the Air Ministry. Olive Mary Sheehan, a Civil Servant employed at the Air Ministry, is charged with communicating this information to Springhall. Springhall is alleged to have told Sheehan that any particulars she could give him would be passed to the Russians, from whom the British Government were withholding information vital to the successful prosecution of the war. This is by no means the first instance known to the Security Service of espionage on the part of the Communist Party, but it is the first case in which we have been able to obtain evidence which can be produced in Court. It is hoped that an exemplary sentence upon Springhall will shock these activities of the Communist Party and of its teachers, particularly those in the Armed Forces who we know to have been guilty of the same kind of offence.

2nd July 1943

★ ★ ★

This report was the first to highlight the challenge represented by the Abwehr to the safety and security of Gibraltar, Britain's vitally important strategic naval and air base at the entrance to the Mediterranean. Of the three enemy saboteurs mentioned in the report, Luis Cordon Cuenca was tried in Gibraltar and executed in January 1944.

A Spaniard born in La Linea in August 1920, Cordon had been arrested in Gibraltar in June 1943 at the fruit shop in Main Street where he worked, and where he stored a cache of explosives and detonators for a group of German-sponsored saboteurs who had been recruited by Spanish army officers. Cordon's intention was to blow up the armaments tunnel in the naval dockyard but his plan was compromised at an early state by Angel Gauceda, a Basque lorry driver living in La Linea, who had been placed under some duress to smuggle a bomb into a munitions store. Gauceda had reported the approach to the Deputy DSO, Philip Kirby Green, a former Metropolitan Police chief inspector, who assigned him the code name NAG, and was full of praise for his conduct:

The wholehearted action on the part of NAG in coming forward as he has done from the very outset, with information about enemy activities against us, is no less praise-worthy than the actions of [XXX] in a recent case and it should be remembered that he did it in admiration for the British and without perhaps the duty which Spanish nationality imposed upon him. NAG did not do it for personal gain, and my total payments to him over four months have been £11, to cover expenses which he actually incurred and which I had some difficulty in persuading him to accept. He has undoubtedly placed himself in considerable danger, both from German reprisals and from the accusation that he was reporting in foreign territory upon matters which were taking place in his own country. If it is possible for some official recognition to be made, say in the form of a testimonial from the British authorities, I feel confident that NAG is really deserving of it.

The actions of [XXX] and [XXX] have been well known to me for some time from secret sources and I have been given reason to suppose that the sabotage of the trawler *Erin* in January 1942 was through their agency. As their activity has now come to our knowledge through the interrogation of a person actually accused of sabotage, this knowledge can without prejudice to any secret sources, be used if necessary for the purpose of any protest which it may be desired to make to the Spanish Government, in respect of the use by Germans of the Spanish nationals.

NAG approached the DSO's office in April 1943 to denounce a pair of saboteurs who planned to bomb the dockyard, and Kirby Green stated that 'as a result of further information received from NAG I caused continuous observation from 4 July to be kept at the frontier with a view to the arrest of José Martin Muñoz if he should enter Gibraltar'.

Muñoz was arrested as he tried to enter Gibraltar on 29 July, almost a month after he had detonated a bomb in the fuel store at Coaling Island. NAG had identified Muñoz as the saboteur, but he supplied much more information that had enabled MI5 to grasp the scale of the German threat:

Both of these men have in fact been actively working for an enemy sabotage organisation which operated from La Linea and which has been engaged in trying to commit sabotage in Gibraltar for over three years. It was this ring which caused the destruction of HMT *Erin* and the explosion of a 'basket of eggs' at Algeciras on 5th April 1942 (intended to explode aboard the water-tanker *Blossom* in Gibraltar Harbour.) Many other attempts were foiled owing to the vigilance of the Security Service here and in 1941, 1942 and 1943 deposits of explosives for use in Gibraltar have been discovered in the Fortress and Dockyard and rendered safe through information received about this gang.

On 10 June 1943 NAG reported that his contact had confided to him that he had recruited MANOLO, who worked in the dockyard, as a saboteur:

> This MANOLO has been identified as Manuel Portalba Carrasco, born 8th January 1920, living at Calle Sagunto 11, La Linea, and employed as a labourer by NAAFI. Recruited by [XXX] as intended saboteur at Coaling Island, was then working NAAFI canteen, HMS *Cormorant*, but later transferred to Trawler Base Canteen as a result of which [XXX] had to find another agent, viz, José Martin Muñoz. Pontalba interrogated 29th July 1941 and has since been excluded from the garrison.

MI5's investigation of Pontalia, completed by Kirby Green in August 1943, noted that:

> During 1942 and 1943 he has been very active as an organiser of sabotage, first under the direction of [XXX] and [XXX]. In the summer of 1942 [XXX] underwent a course under German direction for underwater sabotage to ships. During the past six months he has made many attempts to recruit Spanish workmen as saboteurs. He too is paid a monthly allowance by the Germans. The Spanish police arrested and detained him in San Roque at the beginning of August 1943.

With NAG's assistance the DSO quickly identified Muñoz as the person responsible for the Coaling Island bomb, and he was arrested the moment he tried to cross the frontier. When questioned, Muñoz named his co-conspirators as Carlos Calvo Choas, Fermin Mateos Tapia, Andrés Santos and Paciano Gonzales Perez, who had been promised 40,000 pesetas for the mission.

★ ★ ★

Petrie's report also provided an opportunity for MI5 to explain about GARBO, referred to previously as the recipient of Plan DREAM, an ingenious method of passing him funds in England. The scheme was based on the proposition that Garcia Armas, a fruit merchant trading in London, wanted to transfer money to

Madrid, so GARBO had suggested that the Abwehr pay the nominee in Spain, whereupon the merchant would hand over the identical sum to him in London.

In practice, DREAM worked well, and in May 1943 Garcia Armas deposited £2,375 with Richard Butler for the account of 'Douglas Wills', which was released when 225,000 pesetas were received by his brother in Madrid, and there was a further transaction in March 1944 with a further £3,027 changing hands. Between May 1942 and April 1945 the Germans paid their star agent £31,000, either by delivering it to an SIS cut-out in Lisbon or via DREAM. Under the terms of his contract with MI5, GARBO received £17,554, or slightly more than half the total paid by the Abwehr.

★ ★ ★

MI5's version of the Springhall case was necessarily brief, and there would be plenty more in future reports, but the implications were immensely serious as the information passed to him by Olive Sheehan was a new radar countermeasure code-named WINDOW. As Springhall had been under MI5 and Special Branch scrutiny for years, as a CPGB activist and then commissar of the International Brigade during the Spanish Civil War, his loyalties were considered very dubious. His political extremism dated back to November 1920 when, as Stoker Springhall on HMS *King George V*, he had been dismissed from the Royal Navy as an agitator.

Like her husband Bernard, formerly a Customs & Excise official now serving in the RAF, Sheehan was a CPGB member, and she headed a secret Communist cadre consisting of about a dozen Air Ministry employees. She shared a flat in Prince of Wales Drive, Battersea, with a colleague, Norah Bond, who alerted a friend, Squadron Leader Blackie, to her suspicions. In June 1943 Bond passed him a letter she was supposed to hand to Springhall, and it was found to contain details of WINDOW and a list of six CPGB members in the Air Ministry, together with an assessment of their political reliability. At this point Blackie had contacted MI5 and Sheehan had been arrested the following day, together with Springhall. She promptly confessed, and MI5 made good use of her confession, and of Springhall's diary, as F2(b) described in August 1943:

> Springhall has now been expelled from the Party. It is doubtful whether all the Party leaders were quite so ignorant as they profess to be. The significant fact about Springhall's case is that he was using ordinary Party members to obtain information. When police officers questioned Mrs. Sheehan at the time of her arrest about the secret device, she told them quite seriously

that it was far too secret to communicate to them. At the same time she saw nothing wrong in giving this information to another Party member. This illustrates well the fact that convinced Party members have a divided loyalty which makes it important to keep them away from highly secret information. They regard their loyalty to the Party as over-riding their obligations under the Official Secrets Act. Springhall's diary has given useful information about other contacts.

Among Mrs. Sheehan's possessions were found a number of papers relating to the Air Ministry Group of which she was a member. The average membership of the group was about twelve and it covered the London offices of the Air Ministry. The group used false names for Party purposes and all communications were by hand or over the internal telephone. We found 21 false names and knew at the start only seven of the real names. Others have since been identified and investigations are proceeding. There are similar groups in other Government Departments. From the intimate knowledge which we now have of the machinery of the Air Ministry Group it is clear that these groups can be investigated thoroughly only by the use of agents. The Group never operated openly as such but its members held prominent positions in the branches of such organisations as Anglo-Soviet Committees, the National Council for Civil Liberties and the India League.

Petrie's mention of other instances of CPGB espionage on behalf of the Soviets that had proved impossible to prosecute was a reference to Oliver Green, a printer living above his premises at 293a Edgware Road who had been imprisoned for the crime of counterfeiting petrol coupons. A 36-year-old veteran of the International Brigade who had been wounded in the Spanish Civil War, Green was found by the police in January 1942 to be in possession of classified War Office intelligence bulletins, but he had refused to identify his network of sources. Nevertheless, MI5 surveillance on the CPGB headquarters in King Street revealed that he had sent a message through an intermediary, an ATS girl, to a senior Party functionary, Robbie Robson, who had pretended not to know Green. In reality, according to a report by F2(a)'s David Clarke, dated August 1943:

... he knew that Green was a Soviet agent. Robson also knew of two others. One was a tailor in Stepney named Joe Garber who obtained military information.[1] Garber like Green was connected with the International Brigade. Working for Garber was another, Ted Elly, who has not been identified and had previously been an active member of the Communist Party.

An analysis of Springhall's contacts produced several other suspects, some of whom he had tried to send a warning:

George Rudé
He is a well-known party member in London and a member of the NFS. His telephone number in Springhall's diary. He formerly lived at Flat 4, 6 Gledhoe Gardens, SW. This address appears in the diary and it is probably the flat near Brompton Road which Pollitt said should be closed down after Springhall's arrest. It may have been a meeting-place for service groups.

Richard Kisch
He is a journalist and Party member now employed by Australian Consolidated Press. He has been closely connected with the IBA and was editor for the *Volunteer for Liberty*. In August 1942 he told Springhall that he was bringing him some 'stuff'.

Diana Pym
She is secretary of the North Pancras Branch of the Communist Party, a Borough Councillor and very active in Anglo-Soviet work. Springhall has been in close touch with her on various activities in St Pancras. She told Danny Gibbons that she had not been in touch with Springhall for some months, but Gibbons thought she might have been working for him.

Angela Duckett
She is a solicitor now employed by the *Daily Worker*. She was formerly legal adviser to the NCCL. Springhall is known to have been in touch with her from time to time under the name of Mr Hall and also with Nancy Bell, another member of the NCCL staff.

Ann Pavis
She is a leading member of Unity Theatre and actively interested in the cultural activities of the Communist Party. It was reported at one time that a number of British soldiers visited her house. She has been in touch with Springhall on several occasions. Once he asked her to go to King Street to do some 'plain spying'. She visited Springhall when he was on remand, much to Pollitt's annoyance. Pollitt warned Janet Watson against staying with her.

Mary Wren
She is another leader of Unity Theatre who visited Springhall when on remand. Pollitt made some enquiries about her but was told that she was something of a good-time girl of Springhall's usual type.

Helen Gresson
She is the Scottish organiser of Russia Today. Springhall sent a special message that she should be warned. It is known from the diary that she had put Ray Milne in touch with Springhall.

Harry Berger
He was formerly a clerk at the HQ of the 76th Division and at our instigation was court-martialled for improperly retaining possession of Secret documents. He was reprimanded and later turned up at HQ 2nd Army. He is known to have been in touch with the Forces organisation of the Party and to have supplied Gibbons with secret documents. He once gave Springhall some pay-books. Springhall hastily unloaded them on to Robson. Berger had Geraldine Swingler's telephone number in his diary.

Sidney Dell
He is serving in the Fleet Air Arm and is a friend of Geraldine Swingler. When Springhall was away in Glasgow, Dell brought in some plans of a secret anti-submarine device which he left with Burns but which were intended for Springhall.

Peter Astbury
He is a Captain in the GHQ Liaison Regiment. He admitted to Robson that he had been getting information for Springhall which he thought went to the Soviet embassy through a student. At one time Springhall had put Astbury in direct touch with a 'Red Army fellow'. Robson assumed that this was the Military Attaché.

'Robin'
This appears to be the Christian name of a Civil Servant in the Admiralty. This man may live in Prince of Wales Road, Battersea. He is normally for Party purposes in touch with Beattie Marks. On one occasion he told her that he had changed his job on Springhall's instructions, but Springhall denied all knowledge of him. Robin's contact with the Party does not seem to be very close, as they found great difficulty in sending a warning to him.

<u>Gregory</u>
This man is believed to be a scientist and Springhall asked that he should be warned. It has not been possible to discover his identity.

<u>Norman Henry</u>
Springhall's last message asked that this man should be warned. We have no record of this man.

Springhall sent a message out to say that he had no special organisation of his contacts. This seems natural from the manner in which he was working, since any organisation might have attracted the notice of the Party members responsible for Forces work and the Civil Service Groups. Pollitt was not prepared to believe the denials of those girls whom he interviewed, and he believed that Janet Watson knew far more than she was prepared to admit. It seems likely that Betty Matthews, Freddy Lambert, Val Walker and Geraldine Swingler provided useful contacts and may have acted as couriers. One of the first three probably introduced Astbury to Springhall. The other women referred to may have played a similar role, although there are indications that Ann David was perhaps more deeply in Springhall's confidence. Berger, Dell and Astbury are all known to have worked for Springhall and it must be presumed that the last three names on the list were also working for him. There is also a contact at the Bristol Aeroplane Company, who has not yet been identified.

While Green was at Brixton he was content to be interviewed in November 1942 by two MI5 officers, Hugh Shillito of F2(a) and Geoffrey Wethered, and was reasonably forthcoming:

On the question of the agent who was able to give details of aircraft production, Green told us that this man was not in a factory himself but had access to figures from several factories. As a cross-check on the accuracy of his reports a fitter was recruited in one of the factories who sent in details of production. When these were found to tally with the particulars provided by the more important agent the latter's accuracy was regarded as proved. Further details about this agent were not forthcoming.

On the subject of wireless transmitters Green told us that the job of operator was one which put a great strain upon the nerves. He referred to one particular operator who had previously worked for the organisation in France. This man was married and his wife was much braver than he.

She was taken into the secret, told what her husband was doing and when he got particularly jumpy was even instructed to teach herself morse so that she could take over her husband's job if necessary. He was a wireless technician of great skill and made his own set. He kept the set in the garden inside a post which had been hollowed out. The set was not affected by the damp in any way. The valves were removed before it was concealed in the post. There were four of them stuck into the top of the set. The set was operated by six volt batteries recharged from the main. The reason why it was not operated on power was that if signals had been located by means of RDF in a particular area the electric power could be turned off in that area and if the signals immediately ceased this would form a check on the accuracy of the RDF.

The operator went on the air usually about once a fortnight at a time of night when very few ordinary wireless owners would be listening in. His set was located close to an aerodrome. He began by operating from a semi-detached house. As the house was rather larger than a man of his importance might be expected to occupy an 'uncle and aunt' were provided to share it with him. These were real people, 58 and 61 years of age respectively. All the time there were difficulties with this wireless operator. On one occasion a car drew up outside the house late at night when he was going on the air and he was convinced that it was an RDF van, though in point of fact it contained a courting couple. He began to make difficulties about establishing contact with 'the village' (i.e. Moscow), saying that the set would not work properly. As a result, Green bought a new transmitting set of an American type. He had no idea how it got to this country but had no difficulty in buying it or any other wireless material since he had access to a black market in the neighbourhood of Fetter Lane. Green then broke an invariable rule and went himself to the operator's house and stood by while contact was made with Moscow. After all this trouble had been taken, the operator was in a public bar when he heard a man saying that 'he was doing work for the USSR'. He was so convinced that this would lead to Police enquiries that he insisted on a new house being found and a detached house in a cul-de-sac was found for him. At this period Green's organisation had several transmitting sets so that the same set was not used too often. It was not quite clear whether each set was operated by a different operator though this seems probable. On the occasion when the nervous operator insisted on being found a new house his set was removed and concealed and, meanwhile, another set was used. When he was established in his new house his own set was later moved there. Each transmitter operated on two alternative wavelengths. The set used by the nervous operator was quite small, approximately 12" long, 6" high and 4" wide. Messages were transmitted by means of high speed morse. Unfortunately neither Green nor his interviewers had any knowledge of wireless, but he explained that the morse message which was encoded by the operator was recorded on a piece of perforated paper. The message was then sent out automatically at very high speed and recorded the other end. Certain additional apparatus was necessary for this purpose in addition to the set.

This apparatus was purchased in London after the war [either Spanish Civil War or the Second World War]. It was not brought into the country in the Diplomatic Bag. Green told us that incoming messages were sent in the same way. This appears not to have been an invariable practice because Green said the operators got to know each others touch. He said this particularly applied to the nervous operator who recognised the touch of his Russian colleague in particular over letters in the English alphabet which are not found in the Russian, when he came to these letters the Russian operator would falter slightly. This appears to indicate:

(a) That the Russian was transmitting in English.
(b) That he was not operating in high speed morse, though the experts will no doubt be able to say whether touch can be detected in high speed as well as ordinary morse transmissions.

On the subject of using Party members, Green referred to a particular agent in the Army who was a member and was instructed gradually to sever his connection with the Party. He did this too suddenly, turning over at once to *The New Statesman* and the *Observer*. Since this man was known to a Major who was friendly with the man's Commanding Officer, also a Major, as a Party member it was decided that suspicion might be aroused and he was gradually dropped. There was another good reason for doing this which was that he showed signs of being over zealous.

The method of dropping an agent was to show great concern about his safety and tell him that his welfare was the first consideration and that for the time being it was considered safer for him not to submit any further reports. A man was never told that he was being dropped, but was dropped gradually – 'liquidation was never used'. Green referred to a suggestion made by Krivitsky in his book *I Was Stalin's Agent* that unsatisfactory agents were liquidated by the Fourth Department. He said this was further evidence that Krivitsky was not a genuine Russian Secret Service agent.

On the subject of over zealous agents, Green mentioned with great amusement the case of an agent he had in the mercantile marine. This man had keys made to the Captain's cabin and safe and removed from there all the personal and secret documents he could lay hands on, arriving with his pockets bulging at the rendezvous with Green. Not only did his appearance give him away as a sailor, but he arrived carrying a cage containing a parrot!

On the question of money, Green gave a few further details. He said that he had been supplied with the sum of £500 in £1 notes as an emergency fund. This he had buried and it was still untouched. For ordinary day to day expenses he was supplied with £1 notes by his chief who had a banking account. Though Green himself had a banking account it was always a small one (as we know) and he never used it in connection with the payment of agents. He received the £1 notes and paid them over direct, taking a receipt. He had two receipts on him when arrested by the Police which he had to eat. At one period he discovered that he was being given new notes, straight from the bank, with consecutive serial numbers. He protested against this practice which was stopped. He said that he presumed that the banking account was under the name of 'a trading organisation'. He agreed that a considerable sum of money went through his hands every week, but said that he never made a profit out of his work, on the contrary, he was generally the loser. Very few of the men who worked for him had any idea of making money though he mentioned that the nervous wireless operator was more interested in having the rent of his house paid than in using it for the job which he had agreed to do.

On the subject of aliases Green said that all agents were given these and they were used in all communications with agents, e.g. receipts were signed under the alias. Green also said 'it is, therefore, no use looking for somebody called Dent'. The name Dent appears on the top of the photographic extracts found in Green's possession.

As a safety precaution all agents of Green's organisation would carry out at regular intervals a sort of test rendezvous. The agent would leave his home and, giving every opportunity to possible followers, go to a suitable cafe and have a meal. He would carefully note whether anybody followed him in or out of the café. If the agent suspected then or at any other time that he was under suspicion or being followed his instructions were to do nothing at all. He was to make no attempt to meet his colleague, but would destroy any material of which he was in possession and merely fail to keep his next rendezvous. If he thought it safe, he would go to the stock meeting, or he might think it necessary to avoid one or two stock meetings. He would only go to a rendezvous wearing a 'danger signal' if he discovered at the last moment that he was under suspicion. In order to save time, Green had an arrangement with his chief whereby they would both go to the same cafe where they would have coffee or a meal at different tables without showing signs of recognition. If either wished to see the other he would make some sort of signal, such as scratching his ear. By this means the long process of reaching and leaving a rendezvous could be avoided if it was unnecessary.

Green said that another means of making a rendezvous was for one man to go to the bus terminus. He would then be able to get into the bus when it was empty and there was no danger of being followed. He would then choose a seat downstairs nearest to the door. The person he was to meet would be able to get on at any stop on the bus route and on getting on the bus would go upstairs. He would be the first to get off, followed by the man downstairs who would see him do so. There appear to be inherent difficulties in this method but it seems to be one that Green used if I understood him correctly.

Green explained that it was not always necessary for persons to meet, they could on some occasions leave material to be picked up. On one occasion, when very pressed for time, he went into the Shooting Gallery in Tottenham Court Road with some photographic material in a newspaper. He put down the newspaper and his coat and hat by the side of the gallery and fired a few shots. Meanwhile, his 'friend' had come in and put down his own coat and hat and a newspaper beside Green's. On coming out the friend removed Green's newspaper. On other occasions he used the method described at my first interview with him when he said that he had hidden material in the hole of a tree. He said that perhaps three or four places were chosen either in a park or in open country. The places might be the trunk of a tree, some sandy soil or a suitable bush. These would be alternative hiding places and would be numbered. A poster would be agreed upon in the neighbourhood of the hiding places and on it the person hiding the material would mark one, two or three strokes indicating which hiding place he had chosen to the man who was to pick it.

Green mentioned one instruction which was given to him as a last resort. He never made use of it because it was unnecessary and he regards it as rather a long shot though worth trying. If arrested by the Police in a town with material in his possession drop it on the pavement and make a great scene about picking it up, refusing to do so. This will attract bystanders. With any luck, the Police will pick up the material and force it into the agent's hands. He will then be able to plead at his trial that he has been 'framed' by the Police.

On the point of the number of agents one man can conveniently run, Green said that the most he ever saw in one month was 15, but he stressed the fact that his organisation was very fluid. There was no hard and fast rule that a particular man should only run particular agents.

Green said that he accepted responsibility for the accuracy of the reports which he passed on to his chief. He would speak very severely to an agent whom he thought was exaggerating or reporting on hearsay evidence. The matter of educating agents and keeping their politics up-to-date was regarded as being of the greatest importance. One, a very stupid man, suggested during the period of the Russo-German pact that the information he was passing on might reach the Germans. Green had to jump on him. He reported the matter to his chief who gave him certain 'inside information' with the result that Green jumped still harder at his next meeting.

Green said that he would like to mention one thing. When he was on trial at the Old Bailey on 4 February 1942 a man named Jackson, formerly in the RAF, was sentenced to 18 months for bigamy. After sentence he remarked to Green 'That is all they have got on me except for a few cases of espionage and treason'. Green subsequently cultivated the acquaintance of Jackson in prison and says that he is convinced that Jackson is pro-Nazi and, although Green has no evidence, he says that Jackson was very likely engaged in some sort of espionage work for Germany. Green thinks that the Security Service will have records of Jackson.

Green was rather upset by the manner in which the Police had conducted the search of his house. He did not think it nearly thorough enough, and even when the Detective Inspector had discovered a series of photographs, including photographs of guns, his suspicions remained unaroused. Also in the Dark Room, on an undeveloped film, were details of the organisation. Green watched the searchers while they opened the containers in which this film was contained, thereby rendering it valueless. Another thing which Green said he could not understand was why I had not visited him until he had been in prison for nearly six months. I dealt with these two rather difficult questions to the best of my ability.

I mentioned to Green that it seemed a great risk to photograph a report and then, without developing the photograph, to destroy the original. If the photograph, when developed proved to be a failure the whole report would be lost. He said this was a risk which had to be taken and he invariably took two separate photographs of every report, keeping one himself until the other had safely reached its destination.

After the interview I saw Green for a few moments alone and he said there were one or two things which he would like to mention. Firstly, he would like to make clear his motives for telling me as much as he had done. He wished to help me in the work on which I was engaged (which he believes to be espionage as well as counter-espionage) and he also wished to avoid innocent people, particularly his friends, coming under suspicion. He asked whether I would please omit his name from any report which I might make on the interviews with him as if knowledge of them reached the Russians his motives might be misunderstood. He particularly mentioned this as he had reason to believe that there was 'someone in the War Office'. I asked whether he meant that there was an agent in the War Office proper. He replied 'No, in the Security Side'. I asked what his reasons were for saying this and he said that he had always been told that if he or anybody else in the organisation came under suspicion it would be known at once. He went on to say, without any prompting from me, that it was possible that this story had been told merely to keep up morale, but he thought it unlikely and he thought that in all probability it was a statement of fact.

PS. When speaking of recruiting agents in the Army, Green agreed that the ordinary private soldiery was of little use. He said it was better to try and find someone like a Brigade Secretary. This is an interesting remark because Brigade Secretaries are a new institution. It was not until 21 February 1942 that an Order was promulgated under which the post was created. The Order was in the Press on 25 February 1942. At this time Green was already in Prison where he did not, in theory, have access to the papers, although the Prison Chaplain reads extracts of general interest to the prisoners. I should hardly have thought that this matter was one of general interest and the only other way in which Green could have got to know about it was through advance information acquired from one of his agents before his conviction.

After his release from Brixton at the end of November 1942, having served fifteen months' hard labour for forging petrol coupons, Green was under B6 surveillance and was seen to visit the CPGB headquarters in King Street, Covent Garden, where he discussed his experience, unaware that some of the rooms contained concealed MI5 microphones, and it was by this means that some of the membership of his spy ring had been traced.[2]

During Green's period in prison MI5 attempted to identify his agents, but only felt sure about Private A.M. Elliott, currently posted to the Intelligence

Corps depot at Matlock as a member of No. 4 Field Security Section. A background check revealed that Elliott had served in the International Brigade in Spain with Green, was a CPGB member of long-standing, and had enjoyed access to the intelligence bulletins that had been leaked. The search for an informant inside the Security Service, though pursued by Shillito, simply ran into the sand, although in later years the allegation would be proved correct by the exposure of Anthony Blunt as a Soviet mole. Nor was MI5 able to identify Green's Canadian radio operator, or his source inside the Ministry of Aircraft Production.

Green caused trouble by agitating for trade union representation at his first employers after his release from prison, and was eventually moved by the Ministry of Labour to the Woolwich Arsenal where, he boasted, he was entirely free to wander into areas on the site where classified engineering work was undertaken.

MI5's Michael Serpell eventually closed Green's file, apparently confident that he had not returned to espionage. In a conversation recorded at King Street, Green was heard to tell Robson that he had fooled his inquisitors by pretending, at the time of his arrest, that he had been preparing a stay-behind organisation for the eventuality of a Nazi invasion and occupation as an explanation for all the incriminating material seized by the police from his home when he was arrested. Wisely, Robson had remarked that MI5 probably had not really believed him.

★ ★ ★

There was also more to be said about the case of Dr Antonio Pastor as the true story was not quite as described by Petrie. In fact, as Guy Liddell noted in his diary on 9 June 1943:

> The Abwehr at Vigo are expecting the arrival of an agent from London. This man, code-named PASTOR, will travel via Lisbon. Efforts are being made to identify him.

This information, based on ISOS, assumed that PASTOR was a code name, but as it turned out, this was his surname, and an investigation identified him as a London University academic who was already known to MI5 as he was an informant for Tommy Harris' Spanish section, designated B1(g). A week later, Liddell noted that:

At the weekly meeting Herbert Hart mentioned the case of PASTOR who, from his source, seems to have some contact with the Abwehr. They are at any rate anxious to get into touch with him. From the facts given, Tommy Harris was able to identify this man as a Spanish Professor who had recently left this country and who is in fact a B1(g) agent of a kind. We shall have to consider how we are going to deal with him when he returns.

As well as being somewhat disingenuous in the account offered to the Prime Minister, there was another curious aspect to the case, for PASTOR had already come under suspicion by the Spanish authorities when his name had been passed surreptitiously to a Spanish diplomat in March the previous year. The incident had occurred when a detainee, Luis Calvo, was permitted to attend a supervised meeting at the London Reception Centre with the embassy's second secretary. At the time Calvo had been under arrest at Camp 020 for the past month, having been implicated as an Abwehr agent, but he had been allowed to see Vitturo under controlled conditions, so he had taken the opportunity to slip his visitor a message voicing his suspicions about PASTOR and one other member of the Spanish expatriate community in London. Naturally, this lapse in security was extremely embarrassing for MI5 because their officer, Eric Goodacre, had neither searched Calvo before the meeting, nor spotted the sleight of hand. Indeed, MI5 only learned of what had happened when Calvo finally made a full confession. Thus, far from being frank about PASTOR's role, MI5 had implied to Churchill that he represented a willing, controlled leakage of information to the enemy, when in reality his link to the enemy was unknown to B1(g), and anyway he had been placed in jeopardy by Calvo's denunciation. However, PASTOR evidently survived the experience as he returned safely to his post at London University.

★ ★ ★

Among the references to the double-agents GARBO, MUTT and ZIGZAG was an introduction to FATHER, a Belgian pilot named Pierre Henri Arents, who had reached England from Lisbon in June 1941. In June 1943 he was posted to India to avoid answering some increasingly difficult technical questions submitted by the Abwehr, and supplied with a transmitter code-named DUCK that became operational in August 1944. When FATHER was posted back to Belgium in October 1944 his radio was operated until the end of the war by a police officer in Calcutta, supposedly a disaffected Indian courier based at the Strategic Air Force's headquarters.

★ ★ ★

Oscar Liehr was arrested in Trinidad on 2 June 1943 en route to Buenos Aires, where he was to report on shipping movements, and on that day he confessed to having been recruited by the Abwehr in Lisbon in January when he had been in financial difficulties. He also surrendered his secret writing materials hidden in a pair of neck-ties, and his cover addresses, one in Lisbon and the other in Geneva, as was reported to Kim Philby:

> Oscar Liehr, a passenger for Buenos Aires, Argentina on the SS *Cabo de Esperanza*, was arrested at Trinidad as a German espionage agent. At the time of his arrest, Liehr stated that he was an agricultural machinery mechanic who had been studying in Europe and that he was now returning to Buenos Aires to re-join his father.
>
> Liehr advised that he was born in Buenos Aires on October 10, 1922, of a German father and a Paraguayan mother. He was educated at the Colegio Germania at Buenos Aires until he was fifteen years of age. In 1936, his father arranged with his brother, Ernst Liehr, who was employed by a stained glass window manufacturer in Leipzig, Germany, for Oscar to go to Germany to study as an agricultural machinery mechanic.
>
> Liehr left Buenos Aires on the Polish ship *Kosciusko* in February, 1938, and arrived in Leipzig in March of the same year. He advised that he travelled on this occasion on a German travel docket issued by the German Consulate at Buenos Aires. During his stay in Leipzig, from March, 1938 until November, 1942, Liehr lived with his uncle Ernst at Altenburgerstrasse 82' and with the two sons of his uncle, who are at present serving in the Reichewehr.
>
> In 1938 Liehr took up employment with one Rudolf Sack, a manufacturer of agricultural machinery, where after first being employed as an apprentice, he became a mechanic and was employed by this firm until August, 1942, although Liehr states that he did not work after May 15 1942, due to ill health.
>
> In 1939, Liehr volunteered to the Argentine Consul at Leipzig to be registered for military service in the Argentine. He obtained his present passport in 1941, and also received a mobilization notice from the Wehrmacht during this year. He advises that when he applied to the Argentine Consul he was told that he could not be called for German military service and that the Consul intervened successfully on his behalf. His working permit was obtained for him by the factory and the police granted an Aufenhaltsurlaubnis without difficulty. In May, 1942, he found

that the cold climate did not agree with him and he therefore decided to return to the Argentine to do military service and see his family.

Liehr's father, who is now 61 years of age, has lived for some forty-six years in the Argentine and is a watchmaker in the Calle Lavalle. Liehr states that his father has never been naturalized as an Argentinean but is still a German subject. The father, however, has not returned to Germany since his original immigration to the Argentine.

Liehr states that he started making arrangements at this time to return to the Argentine as a repatriate and was told by the Argentine Consul in Leipzig that the latter had been informed telegraphically by the Argentine Consul in Lisbon that a passage could be arranged on the Argentine ship *Onbu*, which was due to sail from Lisbon in December, 1942.

Accordingly Liehr completed his arrangements to leave and purchased 89 Pounds Sterling and 900 French francs from the Banco Aleman in Leipzig. Upon being questioned as to why he had chosen to buy pounds, he stated that the bank had offered him foreign exchange in either dollars or pounds, but that he had chosen the latter.

Liehr is travelling on an Argentine passport, No. 4/1941, issued at Leipzig on June 9, 1941. The passport also carried a gratis visa issued at Leipzig by the Argentine Consul on November 30, 1942 for a journey to Buenos Aires, Argentina. This passport contained a Spanish transit visa, No. 2672, issued at Berlin on November 10, 1942, and a Portuguese transit visa, 1-Jo. U5Uo, issued at Madrid on December 4, 1942.

This passport shows that Liehr left Germany on November 30, 1942, and he states that he travelled in direct transit via Paris and San Sebastian to Madrid. He had purchased a third-class ticket for this journey prior to leaving Germany. His passport also confirms that he entered Spain on November 30, 1942. Upon his arrival in Madrid, he stayed for a few days in a pension near the Plaza Callao, where he contacted the Argentine Consul and left with him twenty British pounds to pay for his expenses to Lisbon. This Consul also arranged for Liehr's Portuguese visa. Liehr states that he arrived in Lisbon on December 5, 1942, left his suitcase at the Hotel Metropole and went immediately to the Argentine Consulate, which was closed. He tried unsuccessfully to reach the Consul by telephone and then went to the harbour in order to make inquiries on the SS *Onbu*.

He saw one of the officers of this ship who told him that he would have to contact the Captain or the Consul and obtain a Portuguese entry permit and have his passport navicerted by the British Passport Office. He slept on the ship that night but was unsuccessful in finding the Consul the following day, which was Sunday, and as the *Onbu* was sailing that day it was impossible for him to leave as he originally intended. Liehr asked a British official who was visiting the *Onbu* to recommend a pension to him. As a result he went to the Pension Algarbe, where he paid 1,500 escudos per month for his room and board. In January, Liehr moved to a less expensive room in the Rua Escaldenias Marques, Porte de Lima #18.

Liehr further advised that he succeeded in contacting the Argentine Consul the following day, which was Monday, but the latter was not helpful and said that Liehr must wait for another Argentine ship. During the following weeks Liehr called again several times but with negative results, and there seemed to be little hope of his reaching the Argentine at that time. He was rather fearful regarding this matter, inasmuch as his money was dwindling and the Consul would not give him additional money for living expenses. Liehr went on to say that one day toward the end of January he went to the Eden Movie Theater and that while waiting for a ticket he noticed a good-looking Portuguese woman approximately thirty-five years of age looking at the photographs outside the theater. Liehr advised that he offered to purchase this woman's ticket to save her the bother of waiting in line and that she thanked him and gave him the money for two tickets. When he returned with the two tickets he found her talking to a man who spoke Portuguese with a German accent. They had some conversation during which Liehr spoke in German. He told the stranger that he was an Argentinean who had studied in Germany and that he was now returning home. They also spoke on general topics during the interval and when they left the theater the woman left the two men to go shopping. Liehr continued his conversation with the stranger, who suggested another meeting. Liehr pleaded poverty, saying he could get no money from the Consul and was therefore unable to pay his way if they went out together.

The stranger then introduced himself to Liehr as Ernst Schmidt and gave him 200 escudos as a present. Schmidt explained that he was a German engaged in a 'bitter world conflict' and that Liehr might be able to assist him in the Argentine. In return, Schmidt might arrange to assist Liehr financially during his stay in Lisbon. Schmidt told Liehr to come to see him in his house in a few days, bringing his passport and proof of his stay in Germany. Liehr cannot remember Schmidt's address. However, he visited him within a few days, in the early evening, and found that he lived in a small private house with the woman with whom he had seen Schmidt at the theater. This woman does not speak German. Liehr was admitted by a Portuguese servant girl and then had a drink with Schmidt and the woman, whom he presumed was the wife of Schmidt. This woman left the room and Schmidt then asked Liehr about his background.

Liehr is not very precise about this conversation but it seems that Schmidt was interested in where Liehr had lived and worked in Germany, his father's nationality, occupation, and other similar details. Schmidt retained Liehr's passport, the Aufenhaltsurlaubnis stamped on the passport apparently being sufficient proof of Liehr's residence in Germany. They arranged to meet again in a few days.

Liehr's second visit to Schmidt's house also took place in the evening. At this time Schmidt returned Liehr's passport and outlined his proposals, which were that Liehr should proceed to the Argentine and report from there by letter on the following:

(a) Ship movements in the port of Buenos Aires, including details of names of Allied ships arriving and leaving, their tonnage and cargo.
(b) Details of any armament or other factories working on contracts for the USA or England.
(c) Morale and opinion of the Argentine population.

Liehr at present is unable or unwilling to give any more precise details of Schmidt's requirements than the above.

Schmidt also gave Liehr two drop box addresses to which he should direct his correspondence. These actresses are as follows:

1. Helena Fonzeca, Rua Don Franzisco de Almeida #4. Santa Amara de Oeras, Lisbon, Portugal
2. Karl von Presch, Rue de Chene 68, Geneva, Switzerland

Schmidt also told Liehr that his (Liehr's) operating name would be 'Icarus' and that he need not concern himself with any other matters aside from those described above, as other matters were already well covered by other agents. Schmidt emphasized that information was not required concerning purely Argentine matters, in view of the friendly attitude of the Argentine Government.

Following this conversation, Schmidt took Liehr in a snail gray Fiat car with CD plates to a flat in the Rua Padre Antonio Vierira. Liehr states that this house is one house before the last on the left-hand when proceeding towards Quartel de Artilharia #3. Upon their entrance, the door of the flat on the third floor was opened by a young man who treated Schmidt as if

the latter were more important than he. Schmidt introduced Liehr by saying
that he was 'the young man about whom we spoke.' The occupant of this flat
was introduced to Liehr as Stubbs. Liehr advises that he did not see Schmidt
again before leaving Lisbon. Liehr furnished the following descriptions of
Schmidt and Stubbs:

> Name: ERNEST SCHMIDT
> Height: 5'8"
> Hair: Fair, turning gray, closely cut
> Age: Approximately 45
> Build: Medium
> Characteristics: Clean shaven, well dressed
> Languages: Portuguese and German
> Nationality: German
> Peculiarities: Pictures of warships and vessels on the wall of Schmidt's
> sitting room gave Liehr the impression that Schmidt might be a naval
> or merchant marine officer.

> Name: STUBBS
> Height: 5'8"
> Hair: Fair, with a slight wave
> Age: Approximately 27
> Eyes: Blue
> Build: Thin
> Face: Thin and clean shaven
> Peculiarities: Wears ring with a blue stone on the middle finger of his
> left hand. This ring has the initials E, S. engraved on it.
> Address: 63 Rua Almeida, Sousa #1
> Languages: German, Portuguese, Spanish and a little English.
> Nationality: German

Liehr seems to have taken a liking to Stubbs, whom he describes as a
cultivated man, fond of music. Although Liehr states that he never discussed
politics with Stubbs, the latter seems optimistic about the outcome of the
war. Stubbs shares his flat with another German whose name Liehr does not
know, but whom he describes as follows:

Age: Approximately 27
Face: Thick-lipped, clean shaven, wears black horn-rimmed spectacles
Build: Medium
Dress: Well dressed, usually wears sports jacket
Languages: German – does not speak Spanish or Portuguese.

Stubbs and the above-described individual frequently play billiards at the Cafe Llave de Oro in the Plaza Rossio.

Liehr visited Stubbs by prior arrangement about twenty times, from February until he left Lisbon in May. On each occasion Stubbs told him when to come the next time. The interviews took place between 7 and 8 o'clock in the evening and later on, in the morning.

Liehr gained the impression that it was the original intention to train him as a wireless operator, but as there was insufficient time available before his departure, he was only given elementary training by Stubbs, who told him to enter a telegraphy school in Buenos Aires to complete his proficiency. Stubbs told him that when he was fully trained, he would receive a combined transmitter and receiver, together with plans for assembly and operation. Stubbs stated that these articles would be forwarded by an unspecified, indirect route.

On one occasion, Stubbs showed Liehr a combined radio transmitter and receiver contained in a brown leather suitcase about 2'6" x 2'. He was given no technical details concerning it, but believes that it operated between 9,000 and 2,000 kilocycles.

Liehr's course of instruction with Stubbs was the following sequence:

(a)   Tested with morse key and earphones to see if his hearing was suitable
(b)   Morse alphabet
(c)   Cipher code
(d)   Practicing sending and receiving cipher messages with the practice set

About one week after his first meeting with Stubbs, Liehr was introduced by the former to another German named Meier. Stubbs told Liehr that he would instruct him in how to write the letters containing the information. The first meeting took place at Stubbs' flat, but later interviews were held at Meier's flat. Liehr saw Meier about six times in all.

Liehr describes Meier as follows:

Name: Meier
Height: 5' 8"
Age: 26
Hair: Fair
Eyes: Blue, wears spectacles with light-colored frames
Build: Husky and strong
Face: Clean shaven
Nationality: German – typical German type
Address: 35 Rua Manual da Laia, Lisbon

During the course of Meier's instructions as to secret writing, although Meier was informed that Liehr's code name was 'Icarus' Meier advised that for secret writing purposes he would he known as either 'Juan' or 'Carlos'.

Liehr was instructed in two methods of secret writing and was instructed to sign as either 'Juan' or 'Carlos' in the open letter, which was to be in the form of a love letter when writing to the Fonzeca address; and in the form of an acquaintance letter when written in German to 'Lieber Karl' at the Geneva address, supposedly posing as a student. In the secret writing letters, which were to be written in block capitals in German, he was to sign as 'Caru'.

The material to be used in the secret writing letters was found hidden in the two ties found in Liehr's possession. He was informed that in the event he ran short of such material, he was to speak of such material by the code names of 'Juan', 'Carlos', or 'Maria' in the en clair portion of the letters, and that his comments as to the state of health of these persons would indicate whether he was running short.

During the period of his training Liehr was paid 2,500 escudos per month in payments of l,500 escudos, on the fifteenth, and 1,000 escudos on the last day of each month. He was required to sign a receipt under the name of 'Icarus'. These payments were usually made by Stubbs, but on some occasions were made by Meier.

In May 1943 Stubbs gave Liehr a telegraphic code which he was to use in commercial cables sent to his 'cover' addresses announcing his safe arrival, his experience at the Trinidad Control Point, and additional messages concerning his receipt and use of the radio equipment. He was also given a code as to an announcement of his entry into the telegraphy school. Liehr states that in all of these telegrams, the word 'Cesundheit' or 'Gesundheit vater' refers to his safety and 'Stirmung' to the attitude of the German population toward Germany. The six code phrases to be used in open telegrams are as follows:

(1) ANGEKOMMEN – DATUM – GESUNDHEIT MEINE
STUMUNG
(1. Safe arrival) (Experience of Trinidad Control)
(2) POSTEN ARGETRETEH – GESUNDHEIT – STHIIUNG
(Radio equipment received)
(3) BEZAHLUNG – GESUNDHEIT – STINNUNG
(No message received)
(4) URLAUSSBEGINN – GESUNDHEIT – STIMIUNG
(Traffic begins)
(5) URUUB ABGELEHT – GESUNDHEIT – STIMIUNG
(No messages received)
(6) VERLOSUNG VATET NINVERST/JDEN VERLOBUNG
VATER NIGHT NIHVERSTANDEN
(I have entered radio telegraph school)

About May 5, 1943 Liehr again went to the Argentine Consul in
Lisbon to inquire about the possibilities of obtaining passage on an
Argentine ship. Failing to obtain satisfaction, he suggested to Stubbs
that he should sail on the *Cabo de Buena Esperanza*, which he knew
from the newspapers was due in Lisbon shortly. Stubbs told him to find
out the cost of a third-class ticket and he would refer the matter to
his superiors. On inquiry at the Ybarra Company, Liehr was told that
the passage would cost 13,000 escudos but that he first must have his
passport navicerted by the British Control. He obtained the necessary
visas and contacted Stubbs, who gave him the money in 1,000 escudo
notes, telling him that he would be allowed $200 expense money on
the voyage. When Liehr went to Ybarra, he was told that only first-class
passage was available and he accordingly tried to contact Stubbs again
but was unable to do so. He left a note at Stubbs' home and succeeded in
meeting him there on the following day, May 19th, whereupon Stubbs
said he would again consult his superiors as to whether they would pay
the extra 3,000 escudos for a first-class passage.

Liehr offered to pay this amount out of the $200 expense money. Stubbs
told Liehr to wait at the apartment until he returned and then left to consult
his superiors. He was gone approximately two hours and when he returned
he was accompanied by Meier. Liehr received the additional money and was
told to leave the tie he was wearing with Meier. He was further instructed
to report back at midnight.

After some difficulty with the Ybarra Company, which said he was too late, and a telephone call to the British Control, Liehr confirmed his passage and purchased his ticket. When he returned to Stubbs' apartment soon after midnight, he was given two ties and the secret writing material by Meier, and the two cover addresses by Stubbs. One of the ties originally belonged to Stubbs.

Stubbs warned Liehr to memorise the cover addresses and other notes which he had taken, as he would otherwise be arrested at Trinidad.

He also told Liehr that they would give him further instructions concerning contacts in Buenos Aires after he had arrived in the Argentine. He would then introduce himself to these persons as 'Icarus'. Liehr states that he concealed the secret writing materials and papers aboard the vessel a few days before arriving in Trinidad. He denies having been threatened in any way by the Germans with whom he came in contact, nor was he asked to take any oath of service. However, he was told to forget the names of Schmidt, Stubbs, and Meier.

A number of items of personal property were found on the person of Oscar Liehr. Among these was a printed booklet or passenger list for the current voyage of the *Cabo de Buena Esperanza*, on which the following names were marked:

> Juan Pedro Bordelongue
> Martin Ponce de Leon
> Anastacio Monagorre
> Dolores Membrive

At the conclusion of his interrogation by DSO Colonel Henderson, a report was drafted in anticipation of his transfer on 29 August aboard the SS *Empire Settler* to Liverpool, where he landed on 10 October for delivery to Camp 020. In the voyage he was accompanied by three other Spanish detainees, among them Joaquin Ruiz.

FIFTH REPORT, 1 SEPTEMBER 1943

Petrie's report for the period July and August 1943 began with five spies interdicted through ISOS traffic, a demonstration of the source's value. Manuel Perez, destined for Buenos Aires, was taken off a Spanish ship in Trinidad, flown to Panama and then transferred on a warship to Camp 020, arriving at the end of August 1943. Joaquin Ruiz had served as a third officer on the same vessel, having been recruited by the Abwehr in March 1942, and he too was detained at Ham for the rest of the war.

Although the French were anxious to run Georges Feyguine as a double-agent, MI5 was not so sure, and ended up by detaining him on the Isle of Man.

After providing the latest news of MUTT, and introducing TRICYCLE, the report concentrates on Gibraltar and describes an example of sabotage, a recent explosion on Coaling Island, and a coordinated attack by Italian divers on British shipping. The former, caused by the detonation of a magnetic limpet mine attached to a naval fuel tank, was the handiwork of a Spanish dockyard labourer, José Martin Muñoz, who had been identified by the Gibraltar Security Police as a potential suspect. Unaware that he had been compromised, Muñoz was arrested at the border the next time he tried to cross into Gibraltar from La Linea. He readily confessed his role, surrendered a second device hidden in a café, and pleaded guilty when charged. He was hanged in Gibraltar by Albert Pierrepoint in January 1944.

FIFTH REPORT (JULY AND AUGUST)
A. SPIES ARRESTED.
(1) PEREZ GARCIA
This secret Spanish Police agent attached to the Spanish Embassy at Buenos Aires was arrested at Trinidad when homeward bound on the

Spanish SS *Cabo de Hornos* early this month. He was travelling on a Spanish diplomatic passport but his name did not appear on any diplomatic list. Perez, though working on behalf of the German Secret Service in the Argentine, has a background connecting him with the Gestapo. He has been denounced by no less than three confessed German agents whom we have in captivity and was the addressee of a note which was discovered sewn into the flies of one of these gentleman's trousers. There is every reason to believe that we will be able to extract from him a wealth of intelligence concerning German espionage in the Argentine.

(2) RUIZ JOAQUIN

We have known from Most Secret Sources that Joaquin Ruiz, an officer on the Spanish vessel *Cabo de Hornos* plying between Spain and South America, has been working for the German Secret Service chiefly as a courier. Information was recently received that Ruiz was implicated in a plot to smuggle a wireless transmitter across to South America hidden in one of the saloons on the *Cabo de Hornos*. A search was made at Trinidad and the transmitter was found. Ruiz was therefore arrested and will shortly be sent to this country for interrogation.

(3) DILLEBAULE de CHAFFAULT, GABRIEL

In November 1942 Most Secret Sources revealed that a Frenchman, Gabriel Dillebaule de Chaffault, was to be sent on a mission as a spy by the German Secret Service to Montevideo. De Chaffault, a rich aristocrat, has been in German pay since April 1942. He left last week on a Spanish vessel for Uruguay. When the boat called at Gibraltar he was arrested and has since confessed to his connection with the German Secret Service.

(4) FEYGUINE

This one-time fighter pilot in the French Fleet Air Arm came here from Gibraltar in company with a large number of recruits for the French Forces. At our London examination centre he voluntarily confessed that he had been charged with a mission on behalf of the German Secret Service and produced a 'match' with which he had been supplied for the purpose of writing his secret reports. In October last year Feyguine, consumed with a desire to fight Bolshevism, joined the Legion Tricolors and was sent to Paris, where he broadcast an appeal for 200 recruits whom he was to lead against the Russians. The project failed to materialise as Feyguine was rejected upon medical examination, but the proposal was then made to him that he should work for the German Secret Service either in England or in North Africa. He asserts that he accepted this offer as it afforded a means of getting to England and he had changed his outlook upon the war, having been disgusted with the behaviour of Deat and Jacques Doriot and other collaborationists.

(5) JANSSENS

On 29 June 1940 a Belgian named Joseph Janssens arrived in this country en route for the Belgian Congo, where he was to collect military, economic and political information. He was early identified as a spy for the German Secret Service whose previous career in Lisbon and in Belgium was well known to us.

Janssens, who had been in the Germans' service for the past two years was well equipped and well trained for his mission having in his possession secret inks and materials for making them.

B. DOUBLE-CROSS AGENTS.
1) TRICYCLE

TRICYCLE was recruited by the German Secret Service in Yugoslavia before that country was invaded. Since then he has been an active British double-cross agent travelling several times to Lisbon, furthering our deception plans and recruiting for the Germans sub-agents supplied by us.

From August 1941 until October 1942 TRICYCLE was in the United States, where he acted as a wireless agent. He passed through Lisbon on his way to this country, where he managed successfully to remove some doubts that the Germans had had as to his bona fides.

He was sent back by us to Lisbon and it was hoped that through his ingenuity and intelligence he would beguile the Germans into giving their approval to his future plans for luring German agents to this country. It is clear from later developments that these hopes were justified. The Germans believe in TRICYCLE and are providing him with a wireless set to bring back to this country. It is possible that this set may be brought back by TRICYCLE in a faked Yugoslav diplomatic bag which the Germans will fabricate for his.

Among TRICYCLE's successes has been the carrying through of a plan in August 1941 by which he was given in Lisbon $40,000 in exchange for £20,000 to be paid out in London to anyone the Germans chose to nominate. They in fact nominated the double-cross agent TATE, and this put us in the position of controlling their most convenient channel for paying spies in England.

2) MUTT

On the night of the 27th July, the Germans dropped MUTT another consignment of sabotage equipment, a radio set and £1,000 in £1 notes, just
east of the river Ythan in Aberdeenshire. Unfortunately the parachute did
not open. The radio set was smashed and some of the sabotage material, again
of British make, was broken. As this consignment landed only half a mile
from the agreed spot, MUTT has acknowledged receipt of it, reporting the
damage which had occurred.

With this material a faked act of sabotage was committed on 7 August
1943 on a small electricity undertaking at Bury St. Edmunds. A violent
emission occurred in a disused part of the works, and in another part an
unexploded bomb, also part of the equipment dropped to MUTT, was
'planted' and duly found. The local police investigated the case, calling in
experts from this Department, and came to the conclusion that it was the
work of enemy agents. The matter leaked into the Press and the Germans are
highly satisfied with the operation, an account of which they have broadcast
on their Trans-Ocean Service.

C. SABOTAGE.
1) SUCCESSFUL GERMAN SABOTAGE IN GIBRALTAR

On 30 June 1943 there was a serious fire in the petrol stores on Coaling Island,
Gibraltar. The fire was started by a high explosive charge placed against a
large fuel tank. The shape of the hole in the tank caused by the explosion
makes it almost certain that a bomb of British manufacture was used.

The sabotage organisation responsible for this has among its members
a double-cross saboteur run by us. It was thought that if this agent could
commit an act of sabotage he might learn the identity of the Coaling Island
saboteur while collecting his reward. A faked act of sabotage to another
petrol store at Gibraltar was therefore carried out on 7 July 1943. The plan
succeeded and the Coaling Island saboteur was identified as a Spaniard who
normally works in Gibraltar Dockyard. He has since re-entered the fortress,
has been arrested, confessed, and is to be put on trial in the near future.

3) ITALIAN SABOTAGE IN GIBRALTAR BAY

Three Allied ships totaling about 22,000 gross tons were sabotaged on 1 August
1943 in Gibraltar Bay. It was the work of Italians and the Security Service
believes that the saboteurs swam out from the Spanish mainland in light
self-contained diving suits, attached their bombs to the hulls of the three ships,
and returned to Spain. One Italian was captured and is being interrogated.

4) COUNTER-SABOTAGE IN THE MIDDLE EAST

The head of the Sabotage Section of the Security Service has just returned from a six weeks tour of Gibraltar, Middle East, Persia and Iraq, to investigate the problems of sabotage in those areas. His investigations led to the conclusion that the danger of sabotage was greater than was realised locally, and he was able to make a series of recommendations for counter-measures, all of which have been actively taken up by the local military authorities. The most important and the most vulnerable point is the Oil Refinery at Abadan, where proper precautions are now being taken. His visit has been acknowledged by the GOC Iraq and Iran as 'most valuable'.

Another officer of the Security Service has now been sent to Gibraltar to study the sabotage situation there. The German Sabotage organisation in Gibraltar has been largely penetrated by our double-cross agents, but it is hoped to get it even more completely under control.

D. GERMANS WILLING TO COOPERATE WITH THE BRITISH COLOMBINE.

This man is an Obersturmführer of the Waffen SS who, following anti-Nazi activities in Poland, escaped from a Gestapo prison into Sweden and thence, with British aid, to England. His story is significant as an indication of the state of affairs among front line soldiers of the German Army on the Eastern front and he has supplied a great deal of valuable military intelligence to the War Office.

Despite early suspicions of a plant, we are now quite satisfied that this man is genuine in his desire to assist the Allied cause. He belongs to an opposition movement within the German Army, which has its representatives in even the elite formations and which has the general aim of preventing the Nazi extremists from dragging what is left of Germany to its final ruin.

The full and detailed story extracted from this young German soldier provides a valuable guide to the balance of forces inside Germany and, in particular, inside the German Army.

E. COMMUNIST ACTIVITIES.

D. F. Springhall, National Organiser of the Communist Party, whose arrest was mentioned in the previous report, was on July 28th found guilty of offences under the Official Secrets Act and sentenced to seven years' penal servitude. The trial at the Old Bailey was held in camera. Springhall's accomplice, a civil servant in the Air Ministry named Olive Mary Sheehan, who had already received sentence of three months' hard labour at Bow Street Police Court, gave evidence for the prosecution.

The Communist Party has denied any knowledge 'of any activity such as it has been alleged Springhall was engaged in'. Information drawn from Most Secret Sources indicated that the Communist Party leaders did not know of Springhall's espionage activities in any detail, though they did know that he was up to some mischief. The organisation of the underground work of the Party is in the hands of one of the other Party leaders, Robson, and was no part of Springhall's duties.

It is known, again from Most Secret Sources, that Springhall, at the time of his arrest, asked that news of it should be given to the Soviet Embassy. While no proof can be produced, there are strong indications that Springhall was supplying information to the office of the Soviet Military Attaché.

F. VISIT OF PORT SECURITY OFFICER TO THE USA.
At the request of the Chief of the US Office of Naval Intelligence, the Security Service has sent the head of its Port Control Section to America to give a course of instruction with a view to improving US travel and Port security.

1st September 1943.

★ ★ ★

The very first item to be mentioned by Petrie in his report, which was probably not read by Churchill until he returned in mid-September from the QUADRANT conference in Quebec, was that of Manuel Perez. However, he did not go into much detail, even if MI5's Helenus Milmo described it as a 'most important case' and 'the lynch-pin of the extensive German espionage organisation which operates in the Argentine'. Perez, who had been posted to the embassy in Argentina in December 1940, was separated from his wife and son and arrested when the *Cabo de Bueno Esperanza* reached Trinidad on a voyage from Buenos Aires to Spain in July 1943. He had been identified by three Spanish inmates of Camp 020 (among them Joaquin Baticon, the Ybarra courier whom he met in September 1941) as their spymaster, and he was flown to Colon, Panama, on a USAAF aircraft, and then delivered to Greenock from Colon, Panama, aboard the armed merchant cruiser HMCS *Prince Robert* at the end of August.

The incriminating information about Perez had appeared impressive. Apart from Baticon, who said Perez received a large salary from the Germans, there was also some documentary evidence. The Paraguayan consul in Barcelona and Abwehr agent Andrés Blay, arrested in Trinidad, had been found to be carrying a letter of introduction to Perez; the search of another courier revealed Perez's police staff record, which showed his enthusiastic collaboration with the Gestapo in Stuttgart in 1936, and several reports that Perez was supervising a group of Ybarra Line ships' stewards to take secret correspondence to and from Europe. In the absence of anything more specific in ISOS, beyond a reference to Perez's reliability in handling couriers, there was a significant allegation made by the FBI on the basis of information received by a source in Buenos Aires concerning the EFE Spanish news agency. The FBI reported that the German Trans-Ocean News Service wanted to appoint a nominee to run a powerful EFE transmitter located outside Buenos Aires as an alternative communications link in the event that the Argentine government severed relations with Germany.

In his initial interrogation the 46-year-old Perez, who acknowledged being a member of the Dirección General de Seguridad, and a police officer since 1921, claimed that he had served as an aide to the Spanish ambassador in Berlin, Admiral Magaz, from the end of 1938, and then had accompanied him when the envoy was transferred to Buenos Aires.

However, when questioned at Camp 020, a rather different picture of Perez emerged, and although he turned out to be 'a walking encyclopedia of German (and Spanish) activities in Buenos Aires' his interrogators concluded that he 'has never undertaken any major work on behalf of the Axis but he has nevertheless given much valuable assistance on a seemingly small way, to many outstanding personages in the Axis espionage network' and 'his knowledge of German activities in Buenos Aires has been considerable from his earliest days in that city'.

Nevertheless, the Spanish foreign minister pressed Anthony Eden for access to Perez, requests that were denied, partly because of the assurance given to the FBI's representative in London, John Cimperman, that Perez would remain in British custody until the end of the war, but mainly because some of the information against him had come from another Spaniard who was an FBI double-agent in Buenos Aires. Any leak from Camp 020 would have placed this asset in jeopardy but nevertheless the ambassador in London, the Duke of Alba, was offered an interview with Perez, although he declined. Perez was kept in custody until August 1945, when he was transported with eleven other Spanish detainees from Portsmouth to Gibraltar on HMS *Glasgow* and released.

Perez's fellow detainee at Camp 020 was Joaquin Ruiz, and he too had been arrested in Trinidad when, as second officer on the *Cabo de Hornos*, he arrived in Port of Spain, having been compromised in ISOS traffic on the Bilbao–Madrid circuit, which reported his recruitment by the Abwehr in March 1942 as 'Agent 5951'. A quite separate source, described as an SIS agent of unknown reliability, also indicated that when the ship had docked in Cádiz an illicit wireless transmitter had been concealed in August 1943 in the ceiling of the ship's third-class passenger saloon, and Ruiz had an unknown accomplice, probably a passenger. Accordingly, Ruiz was arrested when the radio was found in the hiding place described, but his co-conspirator was never identified. He was interrogated by Eric Goodacre, who deliberately gave the impression that the apparatus, together with a large quantity of cigarettes, had been uncovered during a routine Contraband Control rummage. Examination of the transmitter showed it to be constructed with Telefunken components, but there was a suspicion that it had been hidden on a previous voyage, and had been left on board because of tight security at Buenos Aires. Nevertheless, the ISOS material alone was more than enough to outweigh Ruiz's strenuous denials.

Ruiz, who turned out to be the nephew of Ybarra's general manager, was sent to England on the SS *Empire Settler*, together with his fellow detainees Oscar Leihr, a steward, Miguel Moreno, and another officer, José Pujana, and all three eventually signed confessions.

★ ★ ★

The Italian attack on Allied shipping referred to in the report, which had prompted a visit by Lord Rothschild while embarking on a tour of the Middle East, did not take place on 1 August as claimed, but two days later on the night of 3/4 August when three teams of divers successfully placed limpet mines on the American freighter *Harrison Gray Otis*, the British merchantman *Stanridge* and the Norwegian *Thorshovdi*. Although the British authorities were unaware of it at the time, the enemy divers had been based on the *Olterra*, an interned 5,000-ton Italian oil tanker moored in Algeciras and equipped with underwater hatches that enabled a team of twelve Italian frogmen to conduct underwater sabotage operations in the locality.

In December 1941 two teams of Italian frogmen had attached mines to a pair of moored battleships, HMS *Valiant* and *Queen Elizabeth*, and these had detonated causing extensive damage. Two of the saboteurs were captured, but neither cooperated with their interrogators.[1]

In another operation, in December 1942, divers had swum to the battleship HMS *Nelson* and the carriers *Formidable* and *Furious*. This had resulted in the death of two of the divers and the capture of two others by British patrol boats, but the prisoners insisted they had come from a submarine so the *Olterra*'s role would remain undiscovered until the Italian capitulation in September 1943.

★ ★ ★

The case of COLOMBINE, as described to Churchill, concerned Obersturmführer Hans-Walter Zech-Nenntwich, an SS officer who had defected to the British after his arrival in Sweden. According to Zech-Nenntwich, he was part of an opposition group within Germany that included Eva Braun's brother-in-law, Hermann Fegelein, and accordingly he would be employed as a radio broadcaster on 'black propaganda' programmes transmitted by Tom Sefton Delmer from Woburn Abbey. However, after the war a rather different story emerged.

While Zech-Nenntwich had acknowledged the various Waffen SS units in which he had served, he omitted to mention some of the atrocities he had engaged in, such as the massacre by the 2nd SS Cavalry of 5,000 Jews at Pinsk in the summer of 1941. In his version Zech-Nenntwich had described how he had refused to participate in the arrest and transportation of Jewish children, which had led to his imprisonment by the Gestapo in Warsaw, and to a death sentence. Allegedly he had acquired some false documents while in prison and had escaped to Sweden under the alias Hermann Bottcher. While in Stockholm, when he stayed with Count Folke Bernadotte, he was introduced to the Swedish military intelligence service, and later made contact with the British military attaché, Colonel R. Sutton Pratt, who sponsored his flight to London on 20 October 1943.

In England Zech-Nenntwich had been interrogated by MI5's Brian Melland and by the legendary Klop Ustinov, to whom he admitted having joined the Nazi Party before 1933. He was also questioned in February 1944 by Major Waldemar Caroe about what he knew of the Katyn massacre, and he placed the blame fully on the Soviets. Finally, he was cleared for work with the Political Warfare Executive, but he was not entirely trusted by his colleagues and, using the alias Dr Sven Nansen, was kept separated from most of them. Later in 1944 he was switched to the interrogation of German prisoners of war. In November 1945 he returned to Germany and found a liaison job in Rhine-Westphalia, but in 1950 he was convicted of corruption and imprisoned. He was later thought to be employed as an agent by the US CIA and the Federal German Bundesnachrichtendienst, and attracted adverse publicity when, as the self-styled Baron Zech-Nenntwich, he was divorced from a much younger American heiress. In April 1964 he was convicted of his participation in war crimes committed in Poland during 1941 and sentenced to four years' imprisonment, but four days later escaped from custody in Brunswick and fled to Cairo. He returned voluntarily in August 1964 and received an additional thirty months' imprisonment. Upon his release he lived in Remagen until his death, widely regarded as an untrustworthy adventurer and opportunist.

★ ★ ★

The tantalising reference to the French nobleman Gabriel Dillebaule de Chaffault conceals a remarkable case of German espionage involving a series of interrogation at Camp 020 that continued from 10 September to 4 October 1943, amounting to ten interviews and twenty-six individual statements made by the prisoner.

On 15 August 1943 de Chaffault was arrested aboard the Spanish vessel *Monte Ayala* in Gibraltar on a voyage to Montevideo. He was detained and transferred to Glasgow on the troopship *Cameronia*, which had sailed in a convoy from Egypt. When questioned in Gibraltar de Chaffault admitted only to having taken 4,000 pesetas from the Germans, and to possession of secret writing material and a cover address.

The de Chaffault family was from Veretz, near Tours, and Gabriel's father Jacques had been a diplomat until his dismissal in 1934 by the Laval government when he was chargé d'affaires in Rio de Janeiro. In August 1939 he was called up by the unit in which he had undertaken his military service, the 309th Artillery Regiment, but was evacuated from Dunkirk, taken to Cherbourg and demobilised in August 1940 at Carcassonne, when he returned to his parents' home. In February 1941 he moved to Blida in Algeria, but went back in February 1942 at the request of his father, a German sympathiser, who introduced him to some of his contacts. They invited him to Paris in June 1942 to visit the Sicherheitsdienst headquarters in the Avenue Victor Hugo, where he was recruited as an agent. He had acquiesced to the SD's proposal because he was anyway anxious to travel to Uruguay, where he was engaged to marry a family friend, Yvonne Mola, the daughter of Professor Mola, a physician resident in Montevideo. After several failed attempts, de Chaffault obtained a visa for Uruguay and joined the *Monte Ayala* in Bilbao on 5 August to sail to Gijon, Vigo and Lisbon before reaching Gibraltar on 15 August. Having embarked, de Chaffault hid his money and secret writing material in his cabin, where they remained undiscovered until the ship docked at Montevideo.

Upon arrival at Glasgow de Chaffault was escorted to Camp 020 for interrogation, where he remained until his deportation in June 1945.

★ ★ ★

As for Joseph Janssens, who had been destined for an Abwehr mission to the Congo, he was flown to Poole, questioned at the London Reception Centre, transferred the next day to Camp 020 and repatriated in February 1945, but his case was not quite as clear-cut as Petrie's summary suggested. Born in Antwerp in May 1905, Janssens had come to London as a refugee during the Great War, and had been educated at St Aloysius College in Highgate, but had returned home to work as a shoe salesman in a shop he ran with his brother in the rue Leys.

MI5 first heard of Janssens when an adverse interrogation report from the DSO Trinidad in November 1942, provided by one Robert Lebedoff, identified both brothers as Gestapo informants. Coincidentally, Janssens would later mention Lebedoff, a Belgian Jew with a textile firm in the rue St Hubert, as someone with whom he had traded in currencies, and could vouch for his patriotism.

Then more than a dozen ISOS decrypts referred to an agent code-named JACQUES, and this led to confusion with Frank Steiner, who shared the same Abwehr cryptonym. Both spies were run by the Brussels Abstellen, at the same time, taking much the same route though the Iberian Peninsula, so no wonder the SIS analysts in St Albans, reading the traffic, mixed up the two JACQUES. One message in February 1943 had suggested that JACQUES, a Belgian agent, was probably in Madrid and was planning to embark on a mission to Uruguay. Several other intercepts followed, but they were not associated with Janssens until he was searched in London and found to be carrying a cover address in Madrid, Ezequiel Murietta Llanna, 11 Nuñez de Balboa, already compromised in four other cases, including that of Frank Steiner:

12.12.43   Madrid–Berlin. ERIZO for MARTIN. For GRUBE (Belgium) Ref. 1368 (32 Letters corrupt) entry into Uruguay has requested an influential friend resident there for his acquiescence by wire would like to speed up the matter and requests permission to (rest Corrupt).

15.4.43   Madrid–Berlin. For MARTIN from Belgium (GRUBE) Ref (your message MARTIN) ALFON(S) R no. 25781 of 31st March. In re A 1368 from BELGIUM (Grube).

    1) Prospects of journey to SILO unfavourable. Departure (of) KONGO planned for 5th May. 2) A 1368 asks for sanction for payment of 1500 pesetas for special expenses apart from monthly increase. 3) Consider a

final discussion between A 1568 and Kpt. GARBER of BELGIUM (Grube) to be necessary. Report by W/T requested. KOSP.

7.4.43   Berlin–Madrid. For MARQUES Ref (above message 13/4). GRUBE (Belgium) advises ref your message: I N GRUBE will travel to METRO (Madrid) with money and instructions if operation CONGO really possible on 3/5. Otherwise send A 1568 to GRUBE at once 1500 pesetas sanctioned for special expenses. MARTIN ALFONS.

19.4.43   Madrid–Berlin. To MARTIN for GRUBE (Belgium) Your message of 17/4 (not recd) A I368 will possibly leave the country via WEINBERG (Portugal) at the end of April. We expect a visit from I M (Kan) from GRUBE (Belgium) on 25/4. KOSP.

30/4/43   Madrid–Berlin. For MARTIN to be forwarded to GRUBE (Belgium) A I368 has a chance of leaving on 5th May by means of illegal Belgian organisation via VIGO to LISA (Lisbon). Journey to be continued on 15 May from LISA to BELGIAN CONGO for operation in MATADI or BOMA. Total expenses 30,000 escudos and jewels to value of 2000 Reichsmark already brought to METRO (Madrid). Will report in writing by secret ink to 3 good Spanish cover addresses. Delivery of foreign currency and jewels assured through KOP. There is a prospect of success. Permission (remainder c. 80 letters corrupt).

3.5.43   Berlin–Madrid. For SOUZA for GRUBE (Belgium). representative. Ref. your message of 1/5. employment – 1368 sanctioned, LUDOVICO is receiving from this end instructions to pay out the amount required, MARTIN – ALFONS. BERTA

May 1943   Berlin–Lisbon. For LUDOVICO. Please pay to A 1368 who has been sent to your end by SOMOZA 30,000 escudos. Amount is to be reclaimed through settlement in books at Stelle BELGIUM (Grube). HIOB ZF 74.

4.6.43   Madrid–Berlin. For MARTIN. For GRUBE (Belgium). American citizen MICHED who has arrived here and is a friend of JACQUES reports that both were arrested in Oporto because of unsatisfactory papers and taken to LISA (Lisbon) from where MICHEL was able to escape to Spain, Written report follows.

1.7.43   Lisbon–Berlin. To MARTIN. For ALFONS. Ref ALFONSO 22772 of 20th March 43 and our message 488 of 8th April (not recd.) JACQUES appeared on the evening of the 28th June with WEINBART (Portugal) Secret Policeman at LEVANTINO's house. No announcement of his arrival in LISA (Lisbon) had been received. He had not rung up before (putting in an appearance). It is alleged that JACQUES was flown to GOLFPLATZ (England) on the instructions of the GRUBE (Belgium) KONTO at this end. Later on 28th June, JACQUES asked for Devisen and other material to be deposited in his name at the GRUBE KONTOR at this end. JACQUES believes he will be able after a 4 weeks stay in GOLFPLATZ (England) to continue his journey in the area of operation. KOP fears he may be detained and called up in GOLFPLATZ. Please advise us whether it would be advisable to make a deposit at the GRUBE KONTOR. LUDOVICO leiter I.

12.7.43   Lisbon–Berlin. To MARTIN for ALFONS. Ref. message (not to hand). SOMOZA wishes us to inform him by W/T about contacting JACQUES. Please instruct us concerning depositing. Contents of Msg. referred to are being sent to SOMOZA today. LUDOVICO Leiter I.

15.7.43   Berlin–Lisbon. For LUDOVICO Leiter I. Your message 819 of 1/7 incomprehensible. Message ALFONS 22772 referred to concerns V-Mann JACQUES from KAESEREI (Netherlands) who according to your report left for the zone of operation on 14/4. Your message 488 deals with V-Mann BERNARD from GRUBE (Belgium) who has not yet left the country. The man mentioned in your message 819 is probably identical with V-Mann JACK (A 1368) from GRUBE who was dispatched from METRO (Madrid) and who according to SOMOZA report (message 116) was arrested in Porto. What does BOSNIA mean? Please reply by W/T ALFONS. B no 54180.

18.7.43   Madrid–Berlin. To MARTIN for ALFONS. Please pass same text to LINA (Lisbon) for DIAZ ref LINA (Lisbon) messages 163 and 168 (not recd) It is not advisable to deposit Davison and other documents at the GRUBE (Belgium) office at your end. Do not hand over documents until JACQUES appears at the contact-address at your end only after thorough interrogation, if the continuation of his journey appears credible. The V-Mann has at present no possibility of reporting as he has lost his sticks (staebchen). In the envelope handed over to you there are five stick-heads staebchenkoebfe). It appears unlikely that the V-Mann will make contact at your end. GRUBE (Belgium) is being informed to the same effect. Agreement presumed at this end. KOSB.

Confronted (indirectly) with this evidence, Janssens made a confession, but he could not be prosecuted without the risk of compromising ISOS and Camp 020. MI5 concluded that the case:

… was not of practical importance. In espionage background it tends only to confirm information already in our possession. In contacts it does not lead to further arrests. From an investigation point of view, however, it is of passing interest because a risk was taken and was found justified.

In his interviews, in which he identified various German contacts, he listed 189 Avenue de Belgique as an Abwehr office in Brussels, which matched a building visited by José Pacheco.

Janssen's journey to Lisbon had been interrupted by his arrest on 19 May 1943 in Oporto by the Portuguese police and his incarceration ay Aljube prison in Lisbon, having entered Portugal illegally from Spain the previous night. Ten days later he was moved to Caxias prison, where he remained until the evening of 28 June, when he was driven to the airport and put on a plane for Poole.

★ ★ ★

Although TRICYCLE had been active as a double-agent since his arrival in England in December 1940, Petrie's first reference to him in September 1943 was at a time when he was still on the Continent, shuttling between Madrid and Portugal.

Code-named TRICYCLE by MI5 and SCOUT by SIS, Dusan Popov was the son of a wealthy Dubrovnik merchant who had read law at Freiberg University and had been recruited by his fellow student, Johannes Jebsen, for the Abwehr. His mission was to go to England as a spy, leaving Ivo and their youngest brother, Vlada, in Yugoslavia. Once in London Popov, code-named IVAN, was to make contact with a friend who Popov had claimed would be willing to gather information for the Nazis. In reality, no such person existed outside Popov's fertile imagination.

In mid-December 1940 he turned up at Lisbon and left a prearranged message at the British Passport Control Office for Richmond Stopford, the SIS head of station. Stopford arranged for his flight to Bristol on 20 December where he was met by a suitably briefed MI5 officer, Jock Horsfall, a former racing driver, who escorted him to the Savoy Hotel in London.

When debriefed, Popov revealed that his German contact in Lisbon, 'Ludovico von Karstoff' (actually Albrecht von Auenrode) was attached to the German Legation, and that he had been given the identity of an emergency contact in London, a Czech named Georges Graf. Popov was introduced to 'Bill Matthews', who was to act as his handler and was actually William Luke.

Popov's task of creating an import-export firm was assisted by MI5, which installed him in a prestigious office in Imperial House, Regent Street and a company entitled Tarlair Limited, a name devised by Tommy Robertson. His secretary, Gisela Ashley, was also thoughtfully provided by MI5, as was his manager, Mrs Brander, and although Popov never spotted it, he was kept under constant surveillance and his flat in Park Street was fitted with hidden listening devices.

In January 1941 Popov returned to Lisbon to report on his progress to von Auenrode, and then travelled to Madrid where he was met for further debriefing by Jebsen. In between his meetings with the Germans he kept secret appointments with SIS's Ralph Jarvis, and reported that he had received instructions to develop his operation in London a stage further by recruiting two of his contacts, his attractive Austrian girlfriend, Friedle Gaertner, code-named GELATINE, and a former army officer, Dickie Metcalfe, code-named BALLOON.

As Popov acquired his two sub-agents so MI5 gave him a new, more appropriate cryptonym, TRICYCLE. After his return from Lisbon in February 1941 Popov handed MI5 a questionnaire that he had been instructed to complete that provided a useful insight into the enemy's intelligence requirements and revealed the quality of the information already in its possession. In addition, Popov was requested to complete a detailed study of the defences along a stretch of the English coastline from the Wash in Norfolk to Southampton. He was also specifically asked: 'When are five battleships of *King George V* class ready?' Popov also revealed that the purpose of recruiting GELATINE and BALLOON was so they could continue operations in England, leaving him free to undertake a special mission in America.

This new assignment was discussed by von Auenrode and Popov when they met again in Lisbon at the end of February 1941 as Popov delivered a favourable report on his two new sub-agents and offered a solution to the Abwehr's problem of establishing a permanent, reliable conduit to its agents in England through which they could receive money. Popov's ingenious solution was to suggest Plan MIDAS.

Popov was to go back to Lisbon in March 1941 to make one last interim report before his American assignment and to finalise MIDAS. While the Abwehr was keen to proceed with the plan to finance TATE, it showed less enthusiasm for a map that Popov pretended he had obtained from an acquaintance in the Royal Navy. It supposedly charted the location of minefields along Britain's east coast, but the matter was pursued no further, apparently because the Germans believed the document to be out of date.

The remainder of the visit was spent in preparation of Popov's forthcoming voyage across the Atlantic, which was to be made, theoretically at least, on behalf of the Ministry of Information in London to assess the effect of British propaganda on Yugoslavs in America.

Popov had travelled to Portugal, for the fourth time that year, on 26 June and received a briefing from von Auenrode concerning the tasks he was to undertake while in the United States. In addition he was given a questionnaire that, using microphotography, had been reduced to the size of six full stops concealed on a telegram so as to escape any search Popov would be put through in Bermuda or New York. This development created great interest in London because microphotography was then quite a novelty and this was one of the very first examples of its operational use. As for the questionnaire itself, a large part of it related to naval installations in Hawaii, which, though poorly translated by the FBI, was to take on a greater significance after the Japanese attack on Pearl Harbor four months hence.

Popov arrived in Manhattan on 12 August escorted by SIS's John Pepper and Hamish Mitchell, whom he had met in Bermuda, but while MI5 had been delighted by the double-agent's performance, the FBI was decidedly cool to the prospect of an enemy agent's arrival. Nevertheless, British Security Coordination had arranged for Popov to be interviewed by Lieutenant Chambers from the US Office of Naval Intelligence and G-2's Captain Murray at the Waldorf Hotel on Saturday, 14 August, and according to the official report of the encounter, Popov had information about 'five or six German agents operating in the US'. This news was promptly passed to the FBI on the following Monday morning. The FBI's initial reaction to Popov's arrival appears to have been lukewarm, judging by the twelve-page report written by an FBI Assistant Director, Earl J. Connelley, following a three-hour meeting that was held on Wednesday 18 August, six days after Popov's arrival. The next morning he was introduced to Percy J. Foxworth, the FBI special agent assigned to his case, and it was on this occasion that Popov showed him his personal codebook, and a sample of the crystals the Abwehr had supplied him with to make secret ink. It has been suggested that Hoover did not much care for Popov's behaviour, or his morals. Certainly on one occasion the FBI wrecked an amorous weekend and brought Popov back to New York after he had attempted to take a girlfriend to Florida in September, thereby crossing state lines for an immoral purpose, contrary to the federal statute known as the Mann Act. While Popov was in the US responsibility for supervision of his day-to-day conduct lay with Charles F. Lanman, the special agent reluctantly assigned to his case by the FBI. Popov entrusted Lanman with his code, based on the novel *Night and Day*, and established himself in an apartment at 530 Park Avenue, New York, spending the weekends at a cottage in Locust Valley, Long Island, with his newly acquired girlfriends, Terry Brown and the French movie actress Simone Simon. As agreed with the FBI, he did mail a few reports to Portugal but, by October, he had received no acknowledgement of them, which led MI5 to fear the Abwehr was losing interest in him. The situation was saved by a message from Lisbon ordering Popov to travel to Brazil and report to Albrecht Engels, code-named ALFREDO, at the German firm AEG in Rio.

During his three weeks in Rio Popov held several meetings with ALFREDO and received instructions to establish a radio station in America to communicate with Rio and Lisbon, and to collect information on war production, the composition and destination of transatlantic convoys, and technical developments in the field of anti-submarine warfare. Popov's extended contact with the personable Engels served to compromise him, especially when he topped up IVAN's dwindling funds.

Popov returned by ship to New York triumphant but the FBI remained uncooperative in helping him to collect suitable information for his wireless link, to the point that in March 1942 SIS disclosed that it had learned the Abwehr was having second thoughts about IVAN's loyalty, and there was a belief that he had come under the FBI's control since his arrival in the United States the previous August. This had been revealed in ISOS decrypts that, inexplicably, SIS had refused to share with MI5 until the following May, by which time the situation had deteriorated into a major crisis. Finally SIS revealed an ISOS text from Berlin to Lisbon, dated 21 March, instructing IVAN's handler to test him with a question about his salary. Once again, Popov was running low on funds, had failed to pay several overdue bills, including one on his telephone, and the FBI refused to finance his extravagant partying. He had replied to the query from Lisbon entirely unaware that it had been designed to confirm his bona fides, and was not told that another ISOS intercept from Berlin, dated 5 May, advised that the Abwehr's Luftwaffe branch had concluded IVAN had been 'turned'. In August an exasperated FBI asked SIS to withdraw Popov, and two months later he returned to Portugal, escorted by MI5's Ian Wilson, having been warned by BSC that the he might receive a less than warm welcome. Ignorant of the full circumstances, or that the Abwehr had become very suspicious of him, Popov put on a bravura performance in Lisbon, complaining that German parsimony had handicapped his ability to fulfil his mission, and was rewarded with a new assignment in London and $20,000. Naturally, these events were monitored through ISOS, although

Popov was never indoctrinated into the source used by MI5 to check on his status and integrity. Not all the thirty-six letters he had mailed from the United States had been received at their destination, and there was some dissatisfaction that he had been unable to travel to Hawaii. Popov defended himself vigorously, claiming that shortage of funds had reduced his efficiency, and gradually won the Abwehr over. They rewarded him with $26,000 and 75,000 Escudos, and on 17 October reported to Berlin that Popov's integrity as a German spy was undiminished.

Popov's fourteen months in the western hemisphere served to highlight the different attitudes prevailing in London and Washington DC about the way double-agents should be exploited, but the experience, although damaging for the FBI's increasingly tense relationship with BSC, had proved helpful in solving the problem of authorising the release of information suitable for distribution to double-agents, an obstacle which had hamstrung Popov, was eventually solved in January 1943 by the creation of an Anglo–American coordinating body, known as Joint Security Control.

Popov spent a week in Lisbon placating his German controllers, and then flew back to London with the seeds of yet another ingenious scheme in mind, this time to free some of his brother's friends from Yugoslavia on the pretext that they could be recruited as agents, among them Eugn Sostaric.

Following his success Popov decided to try the same trick again and in mid-July 1943 flew to Portugal but, instead of travelling under his civilian cover of an international commercial lawyer, he went with a diplomatic passport, having been called up for Yugoslav military service, or so he told Jebsen who met him in Lisbon. The idea was to persuade the Abwehr to allow a group of Yugoslav officers who had been interned in Switzerland to escape to Spain. As Popov had anticipated, the Germans had seized on the proposal because it presented them with a useful method of infiltrating agents into the Allied forces. Indeed, the Abwehr had been so taken with the scheme that they had asked Ivo Popov, who had now been enrolled into the organisation with officer rank, to supervise the Yugoslav end of the escape route. This was exactly what Popov had wanted, for it left him with an officially sponsored underground railroad across Europe on which Ivo could send friends with little fear of enemy interference.

TRICYCLE's adventures would continue well into the following year, but by the time Petrie introduced him into the Churchill reports, in September 1943, he was well-established as one of MI5's star performers and the head of its stable of Yugoslav agents, which he was about to expand. The new double-agent mentioned in the report, alongside the familiar characters TRICYCLE and MUTT, was TATE, actually a Dane, Wulf Schmidt, who had parachuted into Cambridgeshire in September 1940 and 'turned' at Camp 020.[3]

Originally from Abenra in the German territory of Schleswig–Holstein, Schmidt had been recruited by the Abwehr in 1939 after his return from working overseas, first as general manager on a cattle ranch in Argentina, and then growing bananas for a fruit company in the Cameroons. Schmidt served in the Danish army, stationed in Copenhagen, and had then volunteered for what he had believed would be a short stay in England. He spoke good English, albeit with a heavy accent, and his task was to carry out a reconnaissance prior to a German invasion. Although he was to parachute solo, he was actually one of several agents to be dropped into England during September 1940. Of the others, Goesta Caroli, a Swede by birth who had made two short visits to the Birmingham area just before the outbreak of hostilities, was known to him as they had been trained in Hamburg together, and they had arranged to meet in England.

Schmidt was flown to England by an ace Luftwaffe pilot, Captain Karl Gartenfeld, and dropped over RAF Oakington, close to the village of Willingham. He spent just a few short hours at liberty for he was challenged by a member of the local Home Guard in Willingham soon after he had completed his breakfast in a cafe. When he was searched Schmidt was found to be carrying £132, $160, a genuine Danish passport in the name of Wulf Schmidt, and a forged British identity card bearing the details of 'Harry Williamson', bearing an address in London that had been suggested to the Abwehr by another of MI5's double-agents, Arthur Owens. Under interrogation Schmidt initially stuck rigidly to his cover story, but when MI5 demonstrated that Caroli had been in custody since his arrival and that he had already made a very full confession, Schmidt cracked. Finally, after a session with MI5's psychiatrist, Dr Harold Dearden, Schmidt agreed to cooperate and accompanied his captors back to Willingham, where he recovered his parachute and radio from their hiding places. At midnight on 16 October he transmitted his call sign, D-F-H, and reported to Hamburg, under the supervision of MI5's wireless expert, Ronnie Reed, that he had found lodgings near Barnet. In reality he had been installed with Tommy Robertson and his wife at Roundbush House, Radlett.

MI5 was persuaded to accept Schmidt as a double-agent by the transparent candor of his initial statement in which he identified a dance band pianist named Pierce as a key member of an existing Abwehr circuit whose name had been given to Schmidt in Hamburg in case of emergencies. In reality the pianist was known to MI5 as RAINBOW and had been operating under Robertson's guidance since February. This item provided MI5 with useful confirmation that Schmidt, now dubbed TATE (because of his resemblance to the music hall comedian Harry Tate), was telling the truth, and that the Abwehr continued to believe RAINBOW was an authentic source.

While claiming to have found work on a farm, Schmidt acquired a notional girlfriend named Mary who often stayed with him at the weekend, and was a cipher clerk based at the Admiralty. In November 1942 she was loaned by the Admiralty to the US Naval Mission and supposedly introduced Schmidt to British and American naval officers who, towards the end of 1942, carelessly left classified documents for him to read.

Schmidt also played a role in the deception campaign to cover the D-Day landings, and was able to report General Dwight D. Eisenhower's arrival in England in January 1944, to take up his appointment as Supreme Allied Commander, even before the news had been officially released. His farm in Radlett was too far from the coast to make any useful observations so Schmidt's employer sent him to spend the summer on a friend's farm near Wye in Kent. From this location he monitored troop movements and he participated in STARKEY, a deception mounted during the summer of 1943 designed to persuade the Germans of an imminent attack in the Pas-de-Calais region, so as to reduce the pressure on the hard-pressed Russian front. As a precaution, a special GPO landline from London was constructed to the notional remote transmitting site in Kent so if the Germans ever decided to use direction-finding equipment to check on the source of Schmidt's transmissions, it would confirm his location in the south-east. In March 1944 Schmidt supported the D-Day cover plan, code-named FORTITUDE NORTH, intended to convey the impression that the forthcoming Allied assault on Europe would take place in Scandinavia, so Schmidt reported that, by chance, he had learned that the British minister in Stockholm, Victor Mallet, had been brought home to London for urgent consultations with the Foreign Office.

After the success of D-Day Schmidt was employed collecting information on the time and location of V-1 explosions. This data was vital for correcting the aim of the weapon and it had been Whitehall's intention to suggest to the enemy that many of the rockets were overflying the capital, or at least impacting north of the centre, so their range would be shortened. On 21 September 1944 Schmidt passed a significant milestone, the transmission of his thousandth signal. His message read: 'On the occasion of this, my 1,000th message I beg to ask you to convey to our Führer my humble greetings and ardent wishes for a speedy victorious termination of the war.' Schmidt maintained contact with Hamburg until the very last days of the war, and was decorated with the Iron Cross.

★ ★ ★

The espionage of Douglas Springhall had been mentioned, in the June 1943 report to the Prime Minister, when he had been arrested, and his would be the only example of a Soviet spy ring. However, the report did not go into any detail beyond passing brief comment on his accomplices, Mrs Olive Sheehan and Mrs Ray Milne. Unexplained was Springhall's significance, for he really represented the very first evidence of the wholesale, deliberate CPGB penetration of Whitehall. MI5's investigation of Springhall began with his diary, which was found to contain a record of his various meetings, among them a rendezvous on 9 April 1943 at the Pop-Inn Café in Leicester Square with Ormond Uren, Milne and Helen Gresson, the Scottish organiser of Russia Today. Springhall's poor tradecraft would reveal the extent of the plot, and in September 1943, two months after Springhall's conviction at the Old Bailey, MI5's Roger Hollis sought the help of Scotland Yard's Special Branch in an effort to identify some of the underground cell membership whose true names had been concealed by the adoption of a 'Party name'. He explained that:

> … a total of twenty-nine individuals who are or have been members of the Air Ministry Group. Of these we know the actual identity of eight, namely:

CONWAY	Miss E.G. GALLEY
HAYNES	Miss Joan MURRELL
JAMES	Miss H.J. DENYER
KELLY	Miss I.M. SCHOLL
LAKE	Miss L. PEPPERELL
LEE	Miss B.M.L HOWARD
LOWE	Miss D.I. PROWSE
PHILLIPS	Mrs. O.K. SHEEHAN

It is possible that the Party name JONES may be a second name for Mss Joan Murrell, who also passes under the party name of Haynes, You will note that ROSKIN is suggested as the Party name of Brian AMBROSE who is said to have joined the Navy in January 1943. The following have not so far been identified:

BLAKE	McKAY	STEVENS
BROWN	MOORE	TRAYNER
CARR	PITT	WELBY
GRANT	SINCLAIR	

MI5's Edward Cussen interviewed Mrs Milne, who had been introduced to Springhall and Uren by Gresson, and she admitted that she had been aware of the further meetings held by Springhall with Uren, but insisted that she was quite unaware that Uren was passing secret information to Springhall. She had, nevertheless, acknowledged that she had drafted an assessment of Uren's political and social background for Springhall:

MI5's B2(b) summarised the case in these terms:

As a result of an enquiry based on notes in Springhall's diary, it was revealed that Springhall had been in contact with a certain Mrs Helen Gresson, a member of the Communist Party and Scottish organiser for the Russia of Today society.

Her husband, Dr Gresson, was a Party number at the University of Edinburgh. Mrs Gresson had suggested to Springhall that it would be a good thing for him to meet a certain friend of hers, Ray Milne, who was engaged in secret work (who was in fact working in a secret Government department). Ray Milne was an adherent of what was known as the Middle Class Group of Communists in Edinburgh and had attended two short courses of Communist training. She was described by Mrs Gresson as being a 'closed member' of the Communist Party. When she was interviewed prior to being employed in a confidential post she stated that she was a Socialist but made no reference to her Communist sympathies.

Ray Milne met Springhall on one occasion in London, and he asked her about her work. On being told that it was secret he asked if she could tell him anything that would be of interest to him, to which she replied that if anything of political interest came her way she would let him know. (Under interrogation she stated that she had in fact no intention of doing this). Ray Milne stated that she had no further interviews with Springhall, but as the result of her contact with Springhall, which she had failed to report to the authorities, and the disclosure of her Communist sympathies, she was dismissed from the Government department in which she was employed.

At the same time Mrs Gresson put Springhall in touch with Ormond Uren, who she also described as being a 'closed member' of the Party. Uren stated that when he attended Edinburgh University as a student he had come in contact with people of Communist views, with which he sympathised, but did not become a member of the Party or take any active part in its work. In 1942, when he joined SOE, he was filled with admiration for the energy and enthusiasm of the Communist Party and openly expressed regret to

Mrs Gresson that he could not do anything active to assist its work. Early in 1943 he had a liaison with a Gertrud Hupenbacker, a German refugee who moved in Communist circles.

Uren stated that he was under the impression that the information which he passed to Springhall would be discussed by the Central Committee of the Communist Party. In his first statement to the authorities Uren merely admitted to passing verbally to Springhall a certain amount of general information, but the next day he made a further statement in which he admitted to supplying this written information.

Springhall was questioned in prison as to what had happened to the document which Uren handed over to him, but refused to disclose anything. In his diary entries were found which clearly referred to meetings which were arranged with Uren.

Springhall, who consistently refused to cooperate with MI5, and declined to give evidence at his trial, served his sentence at Camp Hill on the Isle of Wight, where he attempted to spread political propaganda among the prisoners but, as was noted by the authorities, he never attempted to speak to another convicted Soviet spy, John King.[4] In July 1946 he was transferred to Leyhill open prison in Gloucestershire and during his period there it was alleged that he had attempted to influence a dozen IRA prisoners, and organise the escape of Dr Alan Nunn May, who was promptly transferred to Wakefield prison.[5]

Uren was released from prison in September 1947 and in August 1948 attended the Sorbonne before returning to London in the autumn of 1949.

After his release in March 1948 Springhall lived in London, married an Australian and fellow Communist, Janet Watson, and in February 1950 moved to China. He died in Moscow of throat cancer in September 1963, aged fifty-two.

Apart from Sheehan, Uren and Milne, there were several other CPGB members who came under suspicion as being members of his spy ring, among them Hyman Berger, a long-standing CPGB member who had joined the army in 1940 but who was court-martialled in 1943 for copying classified documents. Another of his contacts was Peter Astbury, an atomic physicist who worked at Manchester University and a CPGB member. Also implicated was a Royal Navy officer, Lieutenant Sydney Dell, who was observed to visit King Street to offer plans of an anti-submarine device. Unresolved was information that Springhall had a source in the Admiralty code-named ROBIN, and another in the Bristol Aircraft Company.

Another loose end, which emerged in 1950, was the precise nature of the role played by Geraldine Peppin, the concert pianist married to an RAF officer, Wing Commander Fisher. She was closely connected both to Springhall and Dell, and was suspected of having acted as a courier between the spy ring and the Soviets, with whom she had strong links via the embassy sponsored by the CPGB's cultural committee. MI5 conducted investigations into all these individuals but there were no further espionage prosecutions. However, in June 1950 Norman Himsworth of B5(b) had some criticisms to add to MI5's official summary of the Springhall case, which had recently been circulated to various Allied security agencies across the globe, but had failed to mention the inconclusive molehunt for a Soviet spy code-named VIPER:

I have just read B2(b)'s very clear and detailed report on the Springhall case. Although we as a Section were not directly involved in the arrest and subsequent conviction of Springhall, we were interested in his activities just prior to his arrest, because of the VIPER case. I was, at first, surprised that no mention was made in the note of Springhall's contact with Geraldine Peppin, of his work with the Party's ARP Co-ordinating Committee, and particularly of his association with Servicemen who used the Peppin's flat when on leave in London. On consulting our own files, however. I found that much of this material, which was obtained by us, was returned to us after it had been read by officers dealing with the VIPER case.

The telephone check on the Peppin's flat at 9b Canonbury Square, Islington, showed quite clearly that Service personnel used the Peppin's flat, and that Springhall had held clandestine meetings with Geraldine Peppin.

For example, on May 12th, 1943, a little over a month before his arrest. Springhall had a telephone conversation with Geraldine Peppin, during which Geraldine said that there was someone who wanted to see him 'very badly'. The conversation continued in a light vein about Mary Peppin's recent marriage to Wing Commander Fisher, and then Geraldine suggested that they should meet on the following Tuesday, May 18th, 'at that funny little place where we met before', Geraldine said that she would be with 'odd people'.

We do know, of course, that the Peppin's flat was used as a reporting centre between the Party's agent VIPER and the Communist Party, and that the two leading characters involved in the case, Wing Commander Fisher (husband of Mary Peppin) and Squadron Leader Norman MacDonald occupied a flat in the same building, either above or below that of the Peppin's.

B2(b)'s note also mentions a contact of Springhall called Sub-Lieutenant Sydney Samuel Dell, who called at King Street with some plans concerning a submarine or anti-submarine devices, is a Naval Officer who was an intimate friend of Geraldine Peppin, and on May 9th, 1943, a man who was presumed to be Emile Burns telephoned Geraldine Peppin and asked her if she had had any news from Dell; she replied that she had not since April, and that he had been at sea and had had an appendicitis. Burns then asked for the man's latest address, which she was able to give him. It is therefore probable that Geraldine Peppin was used either as a recruiting agent for Springhall or that she acted as courier between selected Service personnel and Springhall.

Geraldine Peppin, as a concert pianist, was also closely associated with the Party's cultural work. There is no mention in the note of how Springhall made contact with the Russians, but at that time the cultural leadership of the Party had direct and open contact with the Russian embassy. As Geraldine Peppin was a member of that cultural leadership it would not have been difficult for her to have acted as courier in this respect too.

Clearly Himsworth, who was deputy to MI5's legendary agent-runner Max Knight, felt that the VIPER molehunt had been compromised by Springhall's premature arrest.

SIXTH REPORT

Petrie's sixth report opens with the success stories of Alfredo Manna and Waldemar Janowsky. Manna had operated in Portuguese Mozambique under journalistic cover, but was known to act as a subordinate of the local Italian consul, Umberto Campini. The activities of both men represented a serious threat to Allied shipping along the east coast of Africa so a plot was hatched, with the complicity of the deputy chief of police in Lourenço Marques, Ferreira, to lure Manna to visit Swaziland to see a casino dancer, Anna Levy. Once over the frontier Manna was abducted and then driven into South Africa, where MI5's representative, Major Webster, handed him over to the police for interrogation. Finally, he was transferred to Camp 020, where he was persuaded to make a full statement detailing his past espionage. For his part, Ferreira, an SIS asset managed by Section V's Malcolm Muggeridge, was rewarded with £100 and an MBE.

Janowsky's adventures were rather more profitable, for he was enrolled as a double-agent, code-named WATCHDOG, an Abwehr agent who was landed with a 40-watt radio transmitter near New Carlisle, Quebec, by a U-boat in November 1942. He was run by MI5's Cyril Mills while he was held in custody by the Royal Canadian Mounted Police. A former French Foreign Legionnaire, he had been instructed to carry out a reconnaissance in Canada with a view to assisting six saboteurs who were to land in 1943. He was arrested wearing civilian clothes but under interrogation revealed that he was in fact a lieutenant in the Wehrmacht and had buried a naval uniform upon landing. He also revealed he had been given a code within his code that would indicate to his German controllers if he had fallen under enemy control. If so, he was to insert three 'U's into the fifth group of any message.

Janowsky had three cover addresses and proved entirely cooperative, producing identity documents taken from Canadian prisoners at Dieppe, altered to the name under which he was to live in Canada. He had previously lived in Canada between 1930 and 1933, and had married a Canadian woman still resident in Toronto. He carried $1,000 in US gold pieces, and $5,000 in Canadian notes. He was formerly in the Afrika Korps before being posted to Brussels to recruit agents for the Abwehr. Despite an indiscreet reference to his arrest by a member of the Quebec Parliament, and a report in French language papers in Canada, the WATCHDOG case was judged a success and radio contact was established with the Germans in December, after some delays. However, when it was established that no saboteurs were to be sent to Canada, he was transferred to Camp 020 for the remainder of the war.

★ ★ ★

SIXTH REPORT
A SPIES ARRESTED.
1 ALFREDO MANNA
This man is an Italian subject long resident in Lourenço Marques. In 1941 he was appointed to represent the Stefani Agency there, but this appointment was only a cover for his espionage activities for the Italian and German Consulates. Manna has confessed to controlling four agents who passed to him shipping information for the Italian Consul, Campini, and whom he paid out of funds provided by Campini. He has also admitted to the despatch of two agents to the Union, though neither of these expeditions bore any fruit. Manna has already provided such background of information of his organisation.

Manna fell into our hands with the connivance of a Portuguese police inspector, who arranged for him to be handed across the border to the Swaziland police. The same Portuguese policeman later produced an 'inconclusive' report of his official enquiries into the disappearance of Manna.

2 JANOWSKY
On 9 November 1942 Janowsky, a German national, was landed from a German submarine on the Gaspe Peninsula, Quebec. His mission was the collection of military, naval and economic information in Canada, and his means of communication with Germany were a wireless transmitter and secret writing on letters to cover addresses in neutral countries. His ignorance of local customs and his use of out of date Canadian

currency soon landed him in the hands of the police. Until July 1943 he was used by the Canadians as a double-agent, but when it became clear that no further results were likely from this he was sent to this country for further interrogation.

Janowsky's career before the war included service in the Black Reichswehr, a period in Canada, five years in the Foreign Legion and a short spell in Dachau. In this war he was one of those who infiltrated into Holland dressed in a Dutch uniform shortly before the invasion of that country, and later served in North Africa and in the German espionage organisation in Brussels. He is thus able to provide information on many topics of operational and espionage importance.

B DOUBLE CROSS AGENTS.

I TRICYCLE

TRICYCLE has just returned from three months visit to Lisbon, where he has been in contact with members of the German Secret Service. He gained the impression that they no longer hope to win the war and expect it to be over shortly. He learnt from his spy-master who is also a close personal friend that the latter believes in the existence of the rocket gun for shelling London. The spy-master added that the British raids on Germany had delayed the production of the gun by about two months, but that it should be in action by December and TRICYCLE would be well advised to leave London before then.

The Germans further told TRICYCLE that they are well-informed about the British Order of Battle. Their principal source is wireless interception and, although they are only able to decipher a small percentage of the messages interceded, they have been able by wireless intelligence to establish the positions of 50% of the formations in this country.

The Germans said that they had practically no agents in the USA but that they had ten or twelve in the UK (this corresponds to those under our control). They also told him the story of a major in the German Secret Service in Berlin who had suggested to his superiors that the agents in England were under British control but was sacked for this suggestion within 24 hours.

TRICYCLE brought back with him a large sum of money, a new type of secret ink, new cover addresses and a radio set, which was carried in a bogus Yugoslav diplomatic bag specially forged for him by the Germans.

He is to return to Lisbon soon to continue his original cover plan to which the Germans are now a party, namely to help Yugoslav refugees to come out of Occupied Territory to the UK. The Germans will assist him in this but will slip two of their own agents into the party. These two have in fact been introduced to the Germans by TRICYCLE's brother in Yugoslavia, on the understanding that they will double-cross the Germans.

A difficult situation has, however, arisen over TRICYCLE, since his spy master has recently been in touch with the British Authorities in Madrid and has told them that he is under serious suspicion from the Germans and might have to ask for asylum in the UK. If this takes place, no less than five of our double-agents will be 'blown', including a recent arrival THE WORM (see below).

2 THE WORM

This double-cross agent arrived in the UK at the end of July. He is a Jugoslav and was recruited to work for the Germans by TRICYCLE's brother. He has been handled by the same German Secret Service official who controls the TRICYCLE case. He has been provided with secret ink and is to communicate information of a military nature.

THE WORM makes an extremely good impression and should prove to be a very valuable agent. He has confirmed, among other things, a view which we have held for some time, that there are certain officials in the German Secret Service who would be prepared to sell out to the British because they realise that Germany cannot win the war.

3 FIDO

FIDO is a French Air Force officer who recently arrived from France. He voluntarily confessed that he had been sent over here by the Germans with the specific object of stealing a new aircraft and flying it back. He is now communicating with the Germans in secret ink about Air Force matters.

4 JOSEF

The Japanese have continued to show their interest in the double-agent JOSEF and the information supplied by him, which relates principally to naval construction and has been suitably doctored. They have sent him by his access courier £150 and promised to supply him with secret ink and possibly a wireless transmitter. He is returning to Lisbon to visit them again personally, and make arrangements for another channel of communication to be used if Portugal should declare war on Japan.

5 PLAN DREAM

A further installment of PLAN DREAM has been carried out with the result that £2,600 has been transferred to GARBO by the German Secret Service, to obtain which amount the Germans have paid over 250,000 pesetas.

C Supposed New Sources of German Intelligence from the UK.

Most Secret Sources have recently shown that the German Secret Service believe that they receive information from the UK through three sources of comparatively recent development. These are:

(a)   Portuguese Consulates in the UK
(b)   Swiss Consulates
(c)   a source who is believed by the Germans to report to Stockholm by some means which does not take more than twenty-four hours to transit.

All the reports received by the Germans through these channels have contained information of extremely poor quality and in some cases have been ludicrously mistaken. It is believed that in fact the reports are manufactured at some point before their receipt in Berlin and there is no evidence to show that any communications of this sort are despatched from this country.

D SABOTAGE.

As a result of British protests to the Spanish Government about German and Italian sabotage activities in and around Gibraltar, the Spaniards have arrested a number of German agents in Southern Spain. Some of these are genuinely working for the Germans, others are double-crossing the Germans and working for us, while one, though pretending to be double-crossing the Germans and working for the Security Service, is known really to be still working for the Germans. It is believed that the arrest of these agents is not much more than a gesture and the conditions of their indiscretion are such that the German Secret Service in Madrid is communicating with some of the agents who are in prison, while others are regularly reporting to us at Gibraltar. Friedrich Baumann, the German sabotage expert in Madrid, writes in secret ink to one German agent in prison, the letters being taken by a trusted courier. This courier is in fact working for us and a recent letter from Baumann was flown to England where the secret ink message was temporarily developed by special processes, photographed and allowed to sink back into this paper and become invisible, (see attached photostat). The letter was flown back to Gibraltar and has been delivered to the German

Agent in the Spanish prison. It is evident that imprisonment does not prevent this German agent from having the necessary chemicals to develop his master's secret writing.

These mass arrests have interfered with our double-cross organisation in so far as we now have no one to 'commit' sabotage for the Germans. This lack however is also felt by the Germans, who have instructed one of our agents to recruit some more saboteurs. They are only going to commit imaginary sabotage for the Germans, though it may be necessary to commit faked sabotage for them.

The German Secret Service officer who escaped from Germany is now being used for secret broadcasts in German. He speaks as a German officer without giving his real name. There has recently been a very satisfactory round up of a German spy agency in Persia.

E <u>Germans willing to collaborate with the British</u>.
It is now proposed to use the German officer who was mentioned in Report No. 5 to speak in the secret broadcasts in German to Germany. He will operate as a German officer, but without giving his real name. He may also have other uses in the future.

F <u>SABOTAGE and SUBVERSIVE ACTIVITIES in PERSIA and IRAQ</u>.
In recent months the Germans have increased their efforts to establish agents in the Middle East, and more particularly in Persia and Iraq. Seeing their chance of invading the area becoming more and more remote, the Germans seem now to be turning their attention to sabotaging our lines of communication and supply. They also aim, by incitement of local tribes to open revolt, to tie down Allied troops in the area.

In June a party of four – three Germans and an Iraqi – were dropped by parachute in the Mosul area of Iraq and, after a few days at large, were arrested. This party was primarily concerned with encouraging Kurdish insurrection but, after establishing itself, it was to signal Berlin by wireless for a further party who were to land with sabotage equipment. The original party is now supplying us with a considerable amount of new and useful information on German sabotage methods and training.

It has been known for some considerable time that German agents were at large in Persia. Left behind when Russia and ourselves invaded Persia in

1941 they have remained in hiding, helped by high-ranking Persian officials and by officers and by tribal chieftains of Axis sentiment.

Most prominent among these agents was Franz Mayr whom we captured in August. His aim was to influence Persian polities, and so thwart British policy and assist the expected German attack through the Caucasus by subversive activity.

Until March this year Mayr had been occasionally in touch with the German Embassy in Ankara by courier – a Teheran merchant who engaged in smuggling activities across the Turko-Persian frontier. Mayr's primary need was for money and for an operator to work his wireless set – one of five handed over to him by the Japanese Legation when they left plain code messages in the form of greetings programmes broadcast from Germany which told him that help was on its way. This came at the end of March when a party of six German agents were dropped by parachute south of Teheran. They contacted Mayr and, until they were all arrested in August, they were in wireless communication with Germany. Although they were prepared for sabotage Mayr dissuaded them, as he considered his political activities would be endangered.

A later party of German agents is known to have been dropped in Persia by parachute in July, and there is reason to believe that others may have followed. For the moment these further expeditions are still at large.

★ ★ ★

This sixth report is quite unusual in the whole series because part of an earlier draft has been left in the original MI5 file, and a comparison between the two makes interesting reading, and shows that in the editing process a few items were omitted from the final version. The original draft reads:

Several more spies have been arrested during the period under report. These include an Italian who had been working for the Italian and German consulates at Lourenço Marques; a German who was landed from a German submarine near Quebec; a French artillery officer whom we removed at Gibraltar from a vessel sailing from Bilbao to Montevideo; a Portuguese who was caught at Capetown en voyage for Lourenço Marques; an Icelander who arrived in a rubber boat in Iceland and succeeded in convincing the

American authorities of his bona fides, but who after he had been received in London broke down under interrogation; and a Belgian who came here under the pretence of wishing to enlist in the Belgian forces, but has been proved to be working with the German Secret Service.

TRICYCLE, the Yugoslav double-cross agent who has been working for us for two and a half years, has recently spent three months in Lisbon where he had some interesting contacts with the chief German spy-master in that town.

The spy-master firmly believes in the existence of the rocket gun, the production of which has he says, been delayed for about two months by British raids. It should be in action by December.

The spy master also gave TRICYCLE the impression that he was aware that TRICYCLE was double-crossing him, and was anxious himself to come over to our side. He said that he saw no hope of a German victory and that if he could get a British passport which would enable him to live in peace after the war, he might be prepared to consider any reasonable offer. While this spy master has in his possession an enormous amount of knowledge which would be very valuable, his defection at the present time would compromise a great many of the agents who are working under him, and in whom the Germans hitherto have had confidence, such as TRICYCLE himself and several others. TRICYCLE returned from Portugal with a further large sum of German money.

The German Secret Service believe at the present time that they were receiving information from the Portuguese and Swiss Consulates in the United Kingdom, and also from a source which is supposed to report to Stockholm from Great Britain. The information which they receive from these various sources is of extraordinarily poor quality, and we believe the reports are, in fact, manufactured by some neutral country and largely fabricated.

This short draft is curious because although the second version expanded and identified the Italian spy from Lourenço Marques as Manfredo Manna, and the German spy in Canada as Waldemar Janowsky, references to four recently captured, unnamed enemy agents, the French artillery officer detained in Gibraltar, the Portuguese at Cape Town, the Icelander and the Belgian were removed entirely. While it is true that the Icelandic case of the spy named Fridrikson would be reinstated in the very next report (Chapter 7), the other three were never mentioned again. Nor was the intriguing source reporting to Stockholm, which almost certainly was a reference to the then very current JOSEPHINE investigation in which Anthony Blunt had played a major role. The source was discovered to be the Swedish naval attaché, Count Johan G. Oxenstierna, who was quietly removed from his post at the Foreign Office's request and replaced by the King's grandson, Prince Bertil. For whatever reason, this passage was removed from the report's final version, and the JOSEPHINE investigation was not mentioned again.

★ ★ ★

Petrie's account of the Franz Mayr case is the first of the MI5 reports to deal with the Middle East, where Security Intelligence Middle East (SIME) operated as the organisation's regional surrogate. Mayr himself was a Sicherheitsdienst officer who had worked separately from his Abwehr counterpart, Berthold Schultze-Holtus, operating under vice consular cover in Tabriz. Wireless traffic from both men was monitored, and Mayr only narrowly escaped a trap in November 1942 when he was betrayed by an associate. However, some of his documents were recovered, and these compromised much of his network, leading to the arrest of 150 suspects, including General Fazlallah Zahedi, the senior Persian officer in Isfahan, and forty of his subordinates. Meanwhile, ISOS intercepts showed that three SD agents accompanied by a Farsi interpreter had been dropped in support of Schultze-Holtus at the end of July.

Mayr's arrest, at gunpoint in August 1943 by the Defence Security Officer Joe Spencer, was a major breakthrough for SIME and won Spencer, a pre-war petroleum engineer, the DSO. He and his deputy, Alan Roger, were then preoccupied with the analysis of the captured material, which resulted in the construction of a vast registry of enemy agents and their contacts, amounting to 13,700 individual files and 30,000 index cards.[1]

According to MI5, Mayr was a 'master of subterfuge' with a 'strange personality' who, aged 25, had fought in Poland with the 1st Prussian Armoured Division before working in Moscow for a German economic mission between December 1939 and February 1940. Upon his return to Berlin he had joined the SD, and in October that year travelled to Pavlevi with Ramon Gamotha, under Nouvelle Iran Express Company cover. Much of his activities became known following the discovery of his diary in Isfahan in November 1942 and he was forced into hiding. Nevertheless, at the end of March 1943 he was joined by six more agents who landed by parachute at Siyah Kuh on a mission code-named FRANZ, consisting of Karl Korel, a Persian interpreter who would succumb to illness soon afterwards, and radio operators Georg Grille, Hans Holzapel, Werner Rockstroh, Hans Graepe and Otto Schwerdt.

The first of the FRANZ team to be captured was Rockstroh, caught with his transmitter in a house in Tehran where Spencer soon afterwards also detained a dentist, Dr Qudsi. He turned out to be the uncle of Lily Sanjari, a 19-year-old who had been Gamotha's secretary, and was still Mayr's mistress. When the dentist's home was raided Holzapel and his radio set were seized, and on 26 August Sanjari led Spencer to Grille's hideout, where his transmitter was also recovered. Finally, Mayr too was betrayed, and he was taken into custody. Spencer then exploited the situation further by using Mayr's name to lure two more saboteurs, members of the ANTON mission, Günther Blume and Ernst Kondgen, into an ambush.

In October Mayr was flown to Cairo for further interrogation, and while in captivity was the subject of an exchange offer from the Germans, who evidently regarded him highly. The approach was rejected by the British authorities, and Mayr escaped from custody on 26 August 1946 with a fellow German PoW, Rudolf Nussbaumer. When Nussbaumer was recaptured he claimed that as a fugitive Mayr had been protected by high-ranking Egyptian army officers.

Mayr then turned up in Switzerland, carrying a forged British passport with French visas, and was arrested on 9 December in Zurich, only to be deported on 3 February 1947 into French hands to Letestetten, near Schaffhausen. He escaped from Malsbach on 5 March and was thought either to have travelled into the American zone or returned to Egypt. He later adopted the alias Peter Studermayer and became active in the Middle East, selling weapons in Syria, Lebanon and Egypt. In March 1952 he was alleged to be in contact with General Gehlen's Bundesnachrichtedienst.

★ ★ ★

In April 1943 an Italian pianist, Alfredo Manna, was identified by SIS's Stopford Adams as Umberto Campini's principal agent in Lourenço Marques, and it was decided, because of the threat he and his wife Berta posed through their reporting of Allied shipping on a radio channel to the Japanese Imperial Navy, that he should be brought to England for interrogation. As well as ISOS evidence, there was testimony from three of Campini's other agents who had fallen into British hands. One was a Greek merchant marine officer, Homer Serafimides, who had been lured aboard a Greek vessel, the *Leonidas*, and taken to Durban. Also arrested was a pair of Portuguese, José Muno Im Oliveira and José Lourenço Manira, who both confirmed Manna's status and admitted they had gathered shipping information from the docks for him. In addition, there was concern about German U-boats operating in the Mozambique Channel, and a wireless on the interned Italian tanker SS *Gerusalemme*.

The task of his abduction fell to SOE's Nero Grieve and the local SIS officer, Malcolm Muggeridge, and his MI5 counterpart in South Africa, Michael Ryde. Their plan involved the beautiful Anna Levy, a 22-year-old South African dancer at the Casino Costa whom Manna had been attempting to seduce, but on 2 May she had agreed to a rendezvous at 9 p.m. behind the Variatas Theatre and to accompany him to a café on the road to Maranchas, some 12 miles from Lourenço Marques. On the way the couple were stopped by another car that had supposedly broken down that contained the local police chief, Abel Figuera (who was on Muggeridge's payroll), and Levy's most recent lover, Harry Maigger. When Manna stopped his Oldsmobile he was seized by the two men and driven across the border in Swaziland, where he was delivered to the police commissioner, Major Percy, and interrogated, using a questionnaire sent from London. Soon afterwards, without the knowledge of any South African officials, Manna was escorted to Durban, where he was hospitalised with appendicitis, but was then transported to England from Cape Town on 4 August aboard HMS *Revenge*. Manna finally reached London on 11 September and, in the mistaken belief that he had been attacked by Levy's lover, who had dumped him in Swaziland, proceeded to make a lengthy confession. Almost immediately Manna acknowledged having been recruited by Campini in late 1941, and of having acted as his intermediary in dealing with agents. He identified many of them and later Manna would admit that he also worked as an agent for the German vice consul, Dr Leopold Werz, under cover of the Trans-Ocean News Agency, and had tried unsuccessfully to infiltrate two spies into South Africa. One, named Gonsales, had undertaken a mission in February 1942, but had not been heard of after the receipt of four letters, which were incomprehensible. The other agent failed when he was turned away at the border. He also confirmed the existence of a clandestine wireless operated in Lourenço Marques by Eduardo Quintinho.

★ ★ ★

The double-agents mentioned in the report were TRICYCLE, whose exploits would appear frequently, and JOSEF, the Russian seaman, but two, FIDO and THE WORM were entirely new. THE WORM was Stefan Zeiss, a 27-year-old Czech from Belgrade who had been recruited by Ivo Popov. He would eventually be employed by the Ministry of Economic Warfare in London. FIDO was a French pilot, Roger Grosjean, who arrived in England in

July 1943 from Lisbon and when he underwent screening at the Royal Victoria Patriotic School he confessed that he had been recruited as an Abwehr spy and instructed to steal a plane, preferably a Mosquito, and fly it to Nazi-occupied territory. He was enrolled as a double-agent by MI5 but actually worked for the Bureau Central de Renseignements et d'Action at its headquarters in Duke Street, St James's, before being transferred in July 1944 to Algiers for a posting to a squadron at Meknes in Morocco, adopting the alias Francois Perrin. His contact with the Abwehr ceased in February 1944 when a last attempt to obtain further instructions from the Germans failed. In April 1954 Grosjean completed a manuscript, *The Sun is in Leo*, in which he described his adventures, but it was not published before his death in Corsica in June 1975.[2]

★ ★ ★

The problem of TRICYCLE's spymaster seeking to defect, as mentioned briefly by Petrie, was a dilemma that threatened the entire double-cross system. The Abwehr officer in question was Popov's old friend Johnnie Jebsen, who had been assigned to Madrid and therefore was in possession of information about his organisation's agents supposedly operating in England, including GARBO. If he defected, his German colleagues would assume that he would compromise all the agents he knew of, and take the appropriate countermeasures, which did not suit MI5. The solution was to persuade Jebsen to remain in place, giving him no hint that all his sources were actually already under British control. It was a dangerous strategy, but much of the double-cross system hinged on Lisbon and Madrid, and the priority was to retain the deception channels that had been so carefully developed. Thus a policy of procrastination was adopted, until the Gestapo intervened to settle the issue finally.

★ ★ ★

Friedrich Baumann, described as the Abwehr II sabotage expert in Madrid, was a very familiar figure to MI5, which had monitored his activities through ISOS since October 1940 and knew his real name to be Friedrich Blaum. This intercept material was the skeleton upon which other sources would add flesh for SIS's analysts, and in August 1945 he was taken insto custody in Bremen by the US Counterintelligence Corps.

Although he was unaware of it, Baumann had been a target for SIS, which had skilfully placed a 22-year-old Czech girl, code-named ECCLESIASTIC in his path in Lisbon. She had been deployed successfully against one of his Abwehr colleagues, Franz Koschnik, and that operation had proved very successful. However, ECCLESIASTIC's substantial feminine charms, directed by the redoubtable Klop Ustinov, evidently had not achieved quite the same results against Baumann.

When first questioned Blaum, aged 34, was cooperative and explained that before the war he had been employed by Nord-Deutsche Lloyd shipping line, and for five years had been in Cristóbal, Panama. He had been drafted into the Brandenburg Regiment in February 1940, and posted to Madrid in March as deputy to Hans Kreuger in the KO's Abwehr II branch. He remained in Spain until February 1945, when he was expelled and flown to Italy on a new assignment. Part of his very extensive knowledge was attributed to the fact that his brother, Rudolf Blaum, had headed the Abwehr II branch in Portugal.

Blaum's interrogation covered the activities of Abwehr II in several regions, and revealed his connections with ZIGZAG, known to the Abwehr by the code name FRITZCHEN:

1. North Africa

Possibilities for sabotage in North Africa appeared after the Allied invasion of November 1942. In January 1943 Hummel went to Spanish Morocco and contacted Krueger, who had recruited two Arabs for sabotage work in Algeria. Hummel instructed the new agents in the use of British materials he had brought from Spain, and accompanied them to the border, which they crossed illegally. One of the men was caught by the French. The other returned with claims of having blown up railway tracks in several places. Further details are not known to Blaum, since Kreuger's Tangier office was directly responsible to Berlin and not under KO Spanien.

2. Central Africa

Berlin sought to send agents to Spanish Guinea for the purpose of using that colony as a base for operations in Guinea and Central Africa, with the ultimate aim of sabotaging the extensive British communication lines in the Near East. Berlin did not realise, however, that these Spanish possessions were not accessible from other parts of North and Central Africa.

Two volunteers were found for the mission. One was the brother of Gregorio Moreno Bravo, well known for his Abwehr work in Barcelona. Both men were trained in sabotage work. Carrying sabotage materials disguised as food parcels, a secret code and invisible ink, and other equipment, the two agents began their expedition in summer 1941. The first man returned in 1942, and Moreno Bravo in late 1943. Neither could report success. The information they had – transmitted by mail, the only available means of communication – had been worthless.

Despite Blaum's suggestion in 1942 that both agents be recalled because of the high cost of maintaining them and of the technical impossibility of setting up a radio station in Guinea, Berlin, which prided itself on having men in key locations all over the world, had refused to do so.

3. Mexico

In 1940 Rakowski left for Mexico via Russia and Japan to make contacts in the US regarding the Irish affairs section of Abwehr II. Late the same year KO Spanien was ordered to dispatch an agent to Mexico to meet Rakowski. Thereupon Ernesto Pena was sent to Cuba with his wife for the ostensible purpose of visiting friends and relatives. Obtaining a Mexican visa in Havana, Pena went to Mexico City and delivered money and instructions in invisible ink to Rakowski. Ordered to return with a detailed report from Rakowski, Pena was delayed until summer 1941, when he arrived in Bilbao aboard a steamship of the Ybarra line.

Another opportunity to contact Mexico arose with the arrival in Spain of Carlos Cuesta. A Mexican citizen, Blaum met Cuesta through Dr Dietrich of the press section of the German Embassy in Madrid. Cuesta claimed to be leader of a chauvinistic and pro-German group of Mexican students. This was confirmed by Dietrich, who had known Cuesta in Mexico for many years. Abwehr II decided to utilize Cuesta's group, establishing a W/T net in Mexico as a first step toward initiating Abwehr operations in that country. It was also decided that some sympathizer should come to Spain from Mexico with a report on conditions there, especially the possibility of II and even I work. This person had to be able to return to Mexico after reporting to Spain. Cuesta claimed that were he to return he was certain to be arrested by the Mexican police. A fanatical anti-Semite, Cuesta received a scholarship to the Frankfurt Institute for Race Research in 1943. Nothing was ever heard of him after his return to Spain in 1944.

Finally chosen to make the trip was Carmen Fonseca, a Mexican citizen who had inherited money in her homeland but lacked the foreign exchange necessary for a trip to Mexico. Miss Fonseca was to contact Cuesta's organisation by using the password 'Juan Diaz', and was to deliver a secret code with invisible ink for future correspondence with Spain, as well as a schedule for the operation of the planned W/T station. Miss Fonseca was then to break off connections with the Cuesta group, after sending coded cables to Spain announcing the success of her mission. Only one such cable arrived in Spain, and no further news was ever received from the Fonseca woman, in spite of repeated efforts by the IJ (monitoring) department of KO Spanien to contact her.

4. South America

Following urgent orders from Berlin to begin operations in South America, the following project was started by II KO Spanien in early 1943:

Bernardo Carrasco (or Cassascal), who was being repatriated to Argentina by the Spanish Falange in recognition of his service during the Civil War, was engaged by Referat II to work his way into Brazil and Uruguay and investigate sabotage possibilities in those countries. In Brazil inflammable cargoes were to be sabotaged before being loaded onto Allied vessels. Carrasco was to recruit agents, using Buenos Aires as a base. He was instructed in the preparation of home-made incendiaries and given several British fuses. His reports were to be written with invisible ink. Leaving Bilbao on a Spanish ship in January 1943, Carrasco passed the British control at Trinidad and arrived at Buenos Aires safely. No more was ever heard of him.

5. England

FRITZCHEN, a fabulous figure in Abwehr II operations, related the following account of his activities in England to Blaum: He was serving a prison term on the isle of Jersey when the German Army landed there in 1940. Imprisoned after his conviction for a minor theft, FRITZCHEN was also suspected by the British police of heading a criminal gang. His original plan had been to go to South America, but until German forces arrived he had reason to expect a prison sentence of ten to twenty years.

Offering his services to the Abwehr, FRITZCHEN was released on orders of Ast Paris, trained in sabotage and operation of W/T sets, and in 1942 parachuted into England. He was to blast the huge transformers of the Mosquito aircraft plant near London, for which he was to receive 100,000 DM. FRITZCHEN, claiming complete success, reported by W/T communication that he had personally witnessed the explosion and that confirmation of his success had been obtained from other sources. Leaving England for Lisbon, FRITZCHEN carried papers provided by friends which identified him as a member of the crew. A secret agency (not Abwehr II) in Lisbon gave him a German passport, enabling him to cross into Spain. Paris was his ultimate destination. Although his subsequent whereabouts are unknown to Blaum, it was rumoured that he was to return to England on an Abwehr I assignment.

FRITZCHEN also offered to sabotage the boat aboard which he had travelled from England to Lisbon. Blaum doubts the truth of some of FRITZCHEN's claims, and suspects he may have been a British Counter-Intelligence agent.

6. Wales

In 1940 Berlin ordered an agent sent to Wales to contact Williams, of the Welsh National Party. In autumn 1940 Miguel Poernavieja left Spain in the role of a representative of the Instituto de Estudios Politicos, a cover arranged for by Angel Alcazar de Velasco, Kuhlenthal's chief agent. Poernavieja was therefore to work for both Abwehr I and II.

Poernavieja's assignment for Referat I primarily concerned air attacks on England (details unknown). For Referat II he was to deliver money and pass on suggestions for J-work (insurgierungsversuche) to Williams. Upon his return he was to report on the Welsh National Party. Poernavieja's assignment was in line with the German programme of propaganda for a Welsh independence movement.

Poernavieja returned to Spain early in 1941 after a quarrel with Alcazar de Velasco, who had followed Poernavieja into England as a press agent with the Spanish Embassy. The reason for Poernavieja's expulsion from England is not known. Blaum considers it possible that Williams was a British Counter-Intelligence agent. Nothing more was heard from Berlin regarding the Welsh National Party.

7. Eire

From 1940 to 1942 the Abwehr attempted to establish contact with anti-British elements in Eire and to set up an espionage net there. In 1942 all Abwehr functions in this field were assumed by the German Foreign Office.

In May 1940 Blaum was instructed to contact Frank Ryan, an Irish citizen.[3] Ryan had commanded an Irish volunteer brigade with the Loyalist forces in the Spanish Civil War until his capture and imprisonment. Abwehr II in Berlin became interested in Ryan, who had formerly been a leader in the Irish Republican Army. With the aid of Jaime Michels de Champourcin, Ryan's lawyer, Blaum was able to see Ryan at the prison, and he persuaded Ryan to go to Germany if he were released. Blaum agreed to Ryan's stipulation that he go to Germany as a free man, and not as a paid German agent.

His release was obtained through Admiral Canaris, who saw high Spanish authorities while visiting Spain in Summer 1940. The Spanish officials insisted, however, that Ryan's release be disguised as a prison break.

Taken by car to Hendaye, Ryan was there turned over to a representative of II Berlin. Ryan was well treated during his stay in Germany, according to information received by Blaum. Eventually he was taken over by the Foreign Office, which planned to parachute him into Eire. However, Veesemeyer, then in charge of Irish affairs at the Foreign Office, reported that Ryan's physical condition was deteriorating rapidly, and that the parachute project would have to be abandoned. Ryan was instead placed on a German submarine in a Spanish port, with the cooperation of Kerney, Eire minister in Madrid. Ryan died en route to Eire. Veesemeyer then considered parachuting Clissmann, long a university lecturer in Eire, into the country. Blaum knows no further details.

In summer 1940 Berlin ordered that a man be found to travel to Eire and establish contact with certain Irish Republican Army officials. Through Champourcin Blaum met Mary Mains, an Irish citizen known to be an Anglophobe and Irish Republican Army sympathizer. She agreed to go to Eire, not as a paid agent, but as an Irish nationalist. Departing from Lisbon in September 1940 aboard a Japanese vessel, Miss Mains went directly to Dublin, where she was to give a message and money to a Jim O'Donovan and receive a message for Abwehr II from him. Since the messages were written in invisible ink which could be made legible only in Berlin, Blaum is not acquainted with any details. He believes it was intended to drop a W/T operator with wireless equipment into Eire, with time of arrival and landing place to be arranged through Miss Mains. She was also to check the whereabouts of Leutnant Goetz, of Abwehr II, who had landed in Eire in spring 1940 but had failed to establish a W/T connection.[4]

One particular area of interest for MI5 was Blaum's knowledge of sabotage operations in Gibraltar, Spanish ports, and the extent of the Spanish government's collusion with these activities:

The order to proceed with German sabotage of Allied shipping was received from Berlin in 1940. By 1942 the sabotage program was well under way, and it had reached its high point in 1943 when an explosion in a Spanish harbour led to a cease-action order from Berlin.

The first actions, in 1940 and 1941, were directed by Heinrich Schomlier, who was later killed in Russia. In Seville and Huelva, two five-kilo explosive charges were to be camouflaged as chunks of iron ore and smuggled aboard Allied freighters. The fact that the explosions never materialized was attributed to two possible reasons: either the Spanish sub-agents did not place the charges in the loads of ore, or the German time fuses broke when the ore was loaded into the hatches. Later Schomlier attempted to have home-made mines, each holding about 15 kilos of explosives in an iron container with chain and shackle, fastened near the keel of allied ships by Spanish divers, once at Seville, twice at Melilla, and once at Huelva.

At the time, however, there had been no technical research to establish how and where the bombs could be most effectively attached, and the pull exerted by the moving ship had not been correctly estimated. Thus the early attempts were merely the work of enthusiastic amateurs, and showed doubtful results.

One Spanish agent insisted that, outfitted in a Draeger diving suit, he had dived more than 12 metres to attach a charge to the bottom of the British freighter *Greenwood*. It was later learned that diving with the Draeger hood required extensive training as well as courage, and it was therefore considered doubtful whether the mine, if fastened, ever exploded. It was definitely established that the *Greenwood* had gone down off Melilla at the exact time predicted by the agent, in December 1944, and Major Rudolph immediately reported the success of the mission to Berlin. The Navy later announced that without doubt the *Greenwood* had been sunk by a submarine's torpedo.

Other mine-laying undertakings were reported to Berlin by the II chief during 1941, but the 'sabotaged' ships reappeared repeatedly with no signs of damage. These false claims of success finally led to the recall of Rudolph and his specialist assistant, Schommer. This ended the first phase of German sabotage activities against Allied shipping.

The experience gained from the failures of 1941, together with the efforts of Hummel, who had taken charge of Referat II in early 1942, were the main factors leading to the decision to intensify the sabotage program. A new type of mine, intended to be fastened to a ship's 'Schlingerleiste', was designed in Berlin according to instructions prepared by Hummel. The mine was constructed in three separate parts, thus facilitating its handling and transportation. The air contained in the empty head of the mine kept it afloat. The middle part held 15 kilos of explosives, and the rear part consisted of a fuse, set for distance rather than time, which could be adjusted to a maximum distance of 80 miles. The fuse was simply a small wheel, kept revolving by the current produced by the motion of the ship. Several pincers were welded onto the mine so that it could be easily fastened to the 'Schlingerleiste'. If it was discovered that the mine could be used successfully only if diving and fastening of the device were repeatedly practiced by the agents who were to execute the operation.

The German freighter *Lipari*, anchored in Cartagena bay, was selected by Hummel as the location for a sabotage diving school. At first only Hummel was able to swim and dive with the Draeger outfit, since II-T in Berlin had failed to provide the necessary aids, such as artificial flippers to be fastened to the swimmer's feet and adequate weights to counteract the updraft of the Draeger mask. In summer 1942 Hummel and Waber, assisted by Memmel and Alejandro Mejias, made numerous attempts to fasten the mine to Allied ships docked at Seville. At that port it was possible to guide a rowboat underneath the piers and thus to approach to within a few feet of the target without being detected. Hummel would dive silently while Waber held a thin guide and emergency rope.

Many of the first attempts failed because of the diver's physical exhaustion and the danger of discovery of the mission. Finally a mine was attached to a freighter, the *Imber* (Blaum is not certain of the name). The freighter later turned up in Gibraltar as scheduled.

In September another graduate of the *Lipari* school, Francisco Lopez of Melilla, succeeded in attaching a mine to a British vessel. Not only did the mine fail to explode, but the I-M observation post in Algeciras reported that a British diver had been observed removing the mine from the 'Schlingerleiste'. Thereupon all training at Cartagena ceased, and it was decided that the sabotage of ships from the outside would be abandoned.

It was then attempted to smuggle explosives aboard British ships at Seville. In late 1942 two successes were reported. In both instances, orange crates loaded on barges awaiting transfer to Allied freighters had been partly filled with explosives fitted with time fuses. The operations were performed at night from rowboats. In both cases, 15–30 kilos of explosives were packed into each of several orange crates. One ship, the *Ravonspoint*, was blown up at Gibraltar, while the other, *The City of* ... had to put in at Lisbon because of the heavy damage it sustained.

A similar project was started in late 1943. Explosive charges had to be planted in crates farther upstream, along the banks of the Guadalquivir river, instead of Seville harbour, since the British anti-sabotage organisation was maintaining a close watch over the orange barges in the harbour. Three crates were filled with sabotage materials of British origin and loaded onto one or possibly two vessels. The results of this operation were never discovered by the Germans, although they made extensive efforts to learn of the fate of the two vessels.

At Valencia sabotage along similar lines was committed. Onion and orange crates were filled with charges at night along the road leading to the harbour where the cargo ships were docked. A serious blunder was made when German fuses were used in several bombs instead of the usual British fuses, of which there was a temporary shortage, 'The sabotaged orange ships' were widely publicized by the Allies, who in this case had definite proof of German complicity. Further evidence of German origin came to light when several crates exploded aboard a British cargo ship in Valencia harbour, following an unexpected postponement of the ship's sailing date. (Once the charges were placed inside the crates it was impossible to regulate the time fuses.)

No further sabotage of this sort was attempted in Spanish ports. Numerous investigations by Blaum and his associates showed conditions everywhere to be adverse. Very few Spaniards were implicated in the sabotage of orange ships, Hummel and Blaum having both planned and executed this project.

Two final attempts to sabotage Allied ships were made in Seville and Huelva respectively. Bombs camouflaged as chunks of coal were thrown in the coal bins of two freighters. Neither attempt was successful.

Sabotage of Italian Ships in Spanish Harbours after Italy's Surrender
Shortly after Italy's surrender it became known in Berlin that Spain, under Allied pressure, was to deliver to the Allies Italian ships which had remained in Spanish harbours. KO Spanien was thereupon ordered to prevent these ships from sailing to Allied ports. As a result the following sabotage missions were undertaken:

The *Fulgor*, a tanker in Cádiz harbour: Screw and rudder damaged by an explosive charge of 15 kilos fastened to the ship's 'Schlingerleiste' by ANTE.

Gaeta, freighter, Huelva: Same method as above. Charge, 30 kilos. Results: Screw and rudder damaged.

Tanker (name unknown), Cartagena. An unsuccessful attempt was made by Leutnant Kampen, who planned to use the same method as that used on the Fulgor. As Kampen and his assistant, Richter, rowed from the *Lipari* to the tanker, the fuse ignited prematurely. Kampen was instantly killed, and Richter and one of the *Lipari* officers were injured.

A second attempt was carried out with the help of Giuseppe Faber, an Italian Fascist officer residing in Madrid. Faber persuaded two members of the tanker's crew to assist him. Originally it was intended to destroy the screwshaft inside the ship and some bearings. Some of the charges did not go off, however, and only minor damage was inflicted.

Cesena, freighter, Barcelona: Blaum directed this mission, assisted by the second engineer of the Cesena. Blaum suggested the shaft be destroyed, but the engineer, whose cabin was located nearby, feared his life would be imperiled in the attempt. Without Blaum's knowledge, the bomb was placed in another section of the ship, and little damage was caused by the explosion.

At Vigo an attempt to sabotage an Italian ship failed. Sasso, a friend of Faber's, claimed to have fastened two British magnetic mines to the ship's hull. Sasso was probably not well acquainted with the handling of these mines.

At Las Palmas and Tenerife the crews of two Italian ships, acting on their own initiative or at the urging of the German consulates, opened a number of valves and destroyed several engine parts in each ship. The II agent at Las Palmas, José Segura, claimed to have smuggled a 15 kilo charge aboard one of the vessels. Neither attempt was successful.

Sabotage of Allied Ocean Cables

In summer 1942, Referat II attempted to cut British cables leading from Vigo to Gibraltar and Lisbon, and in 1943 an attempt to cut the Bilbao–Great Britain cable was undertaken. Both actions were ordered by Berlin despite the fact that the cables were officially out of use. To cut the cables, a three-pronged anchor was dragged along the bottom of the ocean about a mile offshore, in the general vicinity of the cables. When the anchor hooked a cable, it was raised, thus exerting maximum tension and causing a break. The participants in these missions – the II staff plus Juan José Dominguez at Vigo and José Luis Echazarra at Bilbao – claimed success.

Use of Torpedoes for Sabotage

In 1943 a small torpedo was to be fired from a ship outside Huelva harbour. The torpedo, constructed for shipment in sections, had an S-charge weighing about 50 kilos. After being fired in the desired direction the torpedo could be guided automatically. The torpedo was never used, however, because permission was not received from Berlin. A supply of these torpedoes brought to Huelva in 1943 was returned to Germany in early 1944, when S-operations in Spain were discontinued.

This MI5 interrogation report contained no analysis, but the reference to the Welsh Nationalist contact named Williams must have given B1(a) some cause for satisfaction, for he was actually the double-agent Gwylym Williams, code-named G.W., who had been part of a larger Welsh network supposedly based in Swansea. Evidently Blaum's justified suspicions about Williams had not been shared with any of his Abwehr colleagues.

Blaum also had some interesting observations about the Abwehr's efforts to attack Allied shipping in Gibraltar, a subject often mentioned in Petrie's reports:

Following Italy's entry into the war and the collapse of France and its possessions, Gibraltar, because of its unique geographical position, its military strength, and its political status, became an important objective of German Intelligence Service activities in the Iberian peninsula. This report will summarize chronologically the activities of Referat II KO Spanien in Gibraltar.

The first permission to operate in Gibraltar was received in late autumn. Later, orders were received to study possibilities for sabotage work and to begin recruiting agents.

1941
The first shipment of explosive and incendiary charges was smuggled into the fortress at the beginning of the year. It was intended to attack various targets, eg, fuel dumps and grounded aircraft, in a simultaneous action. The first attempt failed because the timing mechanisms furnished by Berlin proved to be 24-day clocks, whereas it had been assumed that they were 24-hour devices, although one agent reported some success. Referat I notified Major Rudolf that most of the sabotage materials had been discovered by the British, who had neutralized them. Positive results were reported to Berlin, however, since at the time it was general Abwehr policy to shield its inexperience with exaggerated claims of success.

In June a bathing hut was rented at Puente Majorca and a 25 kilo mine was concealed there. An agent was to row to the vicinity of one of the cargo vessels anchored off Puente Majorca and lay the mine. British Secret Service agents foiled the attempt, however, when they discovered the mine in the bathing hut.

The chief agent for these missions and a subsequent one was Juan José Dominguez, of Seville, another agent, Emilio Plazas, was hired in late 1941. He was unsuccessful in his first mission placing a charge inside an artillery shell, he forgot the necessary explosives.

1942
The first sabotage attempt was made by Dominguez, who in late December 1941 or early January 1942 concealed a five kilo British plastic charge with corrosion igniter in a case of eggs aboard a transport in

Algeciras. The case was discovered by Spanish customs officials and was exploded on the pier. Dominguez was later arrested and sentenced to death because of an alleged attempt on the life of Spanish War Minister Varela in summer 1942.

A project resulting in the destruction of two airplanes on the ground was undertaken by Alfonso Olmo, a sub-agent of Plazas, in January 1942. Olmo later proved to be completely unreliable, and his claims could never be verified.

Two of Plazas's subordinates, Ramon Correa and Manolo Tapli, succeeded in a mission undertaken in February 1942. A British adhesive mine with corrosion igniter was placed inside a water-bomb aboard a patrol boat. The boat was sunk and a nearby vessel damaged by the explosion.

1943

In late 1942 Berlin had authorized large-scale sabotage activities against Gibraltar. At the same time Hummel had taken over Referat II. These changes brought new ideas and impetus to an organisation lacking in imagination and enthusiasm.

In January a small tanker was set afire by means of a thermite incendiary charge smuggled aboard by Ramon Galves. Since the time and place of the action were known in advance, the success of the mission was definitely ascertained. Another mission executed by Galves proved equally successful. Galves affixed a small British adhesive mine to a water-bomb aboard a submarine chaser, which was later seen sinking off Gibraltar.

An ammunition dump next to an anti-aircraft position was blown up in early 1943 by means of a small British plastic charge with corrosion igniter inserted into an anti-aircraft shell. As in previous actions, advance notice of this mission had been given. The principal agent was Carlos Calvo.

In June three Spanish agents used a British plastic charge with corrosion igniter to set afire two fuel dumps. The agents were Angel Sarasol and Pariano Gonzales, and another Spanish agent employed by Calvo. The latter was later captured by the British. Hummel had been notified of this mission in advance, and its success was unquestioned.

Also in summer 1943 Hummel met an Italian naval officer who had been directing Italian sabotage against Gibraltar, independently. The Italian, (name unknown), was consul at Algeciras and closely connected with the GAMMA swimming school, which trained men in long-distance swiping and deep-sea diving as prerequisites for sabotaging Allied shipping, by fastening sabotage charges to the vessel's 'Schlingerleiste'. Although close cooperation between the Axis countries was precluded by Italy's surrender, GAMMA swimmer sabotage methods were followed by Referat II in subsequent actions, especially against Allied shipping.

A mission of considerable importance was undertaken in late summer 1943 by a group of Spanish officers headed by Narciso. They intended to blow up the main ammunition dump of Gibraltar proper by inserting a large charge in a stored shell or water-bomb. The mission was never executed, however, since a number of participants gave information on the project to the British, Later, complete details of the undertaking were secured by the British through the trial of Luis Cuenco and others. Blaum claims none of the Spaniards involved, including Perales, had been paid Abwehr agents. Its participation in the action was limited to technical advice, supply of British S-charges, and financial aid, according to Blaum.

Blaum's information was added to other material supplied by Colonel Paul Fuchs, an Abwehr officer who had been based in Biarritz, and from a former KO Spanien agent, Hermann Amende, to create a very accurate order-of-battle for the Abwehr's wartime organisation across the Iberian peninsula:

During the war, Spain was the scene of numerous acts of sabotage committed by Germans and agents of the Germans against Allied shipping and military installations. In addition, the Iberian peninsula was used as a base from which agents with a wide variety of missions were sent to many parts of the globe.

This report is a study of the organisation responsible for all these activities.

History and Organisation of Referat II KO Spanien
Abwehr II's first representative in Spain, sent there in early 1940, was Sonderfuehrer Krueger. Kreuger was instructed to set up an office in Madrid and to study conditions in general as well as possibilities for II operations in Spain. At the time, headquarters in Berlin had not yet devised a plan for carrying out its insurrection and minority program (J-work) in Spain. No sabotage activities were planned, principally because 'S' and 'J' were still separate departments of Abwehr II, and both Kreuger and Blaum, who went to Spain in March 1940, were sent there on orders of the J-section.

Upon his arrival in Madrid, Blaum reported to Freg/Kptn Lenz, CO of KO Spanien. Blaum was told that his first mission was to make contacts of possible future value. Permission for Blaum to remain in Spain was obtained by the German Embassy, where he was registered as an employee. Later the entire staff of Referat II was incorporated into the Embassy as a section of KO Spanien. Thus Lenz became Blaum's and Kreuger's superior. Although matters of II interest were settled directly with Abwehr II in Berlin, Lenz still influenced II operations, since all general policies had to be approved by him.

In 1941 Kreuger was transferred to Tangier, where he was put in charge of a small, independent KO organisation. Major Rudolf was appointed new head of II in Spain. The failure of most of the projects initiated under Rudolf was largely due to his inexperience and lack of initiative.

The appointment of Friedrich Hummel, a well-known swimmer, to succeed Rudolf in 1943 paved the way for the most successful period of II KO Spanien's history. Missions were completed against Gibraltar, Allied orange freighters, and, after Italy's surrender, Italian vessels in Spanish harbours. A 'cease action' order was received from Berlin in March 1944, however, and Hummel was recalled for a more important assignment as head of Leitstelle II Jest, FA.

The new chief of Referat II, Hptm Naumann zu Koenigsbrueck, was handcuffed by the order prohibiting S-operations in Spain. He had only begun work on an R-organisation (Rueckzugs Organisation – withdrawal plan) when he was ordered to return to Germany. In February 1945 Blaum was also recalled, and Referat II's remaining activities were entrusted to Werner Schulz, an inexperienced man from Berlin.

The following is a list of all personnel assigned to KO Spanien from 1940 through March 1945:

1940 – Chief: Hans Krueger, Sonderfuehrer (Z)
        Wolfgang Blaum, Pionier alias Friedrich Baumann. Franz Zimmerman, V-Mann
1941 – Chief: Rudolf, Hptm alias Rudolph Wolfgang Blaum
        Gefr Joseph Waber
        Gefr Heinrich Schommer, Uffz (killed in Russia)
        Frl Charlotte Hilgert, secretary
        Franz Zummermanm, employee
1942 – Chief: Friedrich Hummel, O/Lt
        Wolfgang Blaum
        Gefr Hans Richter, employee alias Ritter
        Joseph Faber, Gefr

Franz Zimmmermann, employee (died 1942)
Victor Ante, Gefr alias Hoffmann
Frl Guntrud Heise, secretary
Frl Lilo Niemann, secretary alias Nehrkorn

1943 – Mar 44 Chief: Friedrich Hummel
HptmWolfgang Blaum
Gefr Hans Richter
Pvt Joseph Waber
O/Gefr Victor Ante
Gefr Fritz Rossbund
Gefr Alfred Strickner
Uffz Frl Lore Daumer
Secretary Frl Charlotte Kriesch
Secretary Karl Kampen, Lt (temp) (killed Nov 43)

Mar 44 – Dec 44 Chief: Guenther Neumann zu Koenigsbrueck
Wolfgang Blaum, Uffz, Sonderfuehrer (Z)
Joseph Waber
Uffz Fritz Rossbund
Gefr Frl Guntrud Heise, secretary

Cooperation with Spanish Agencies

At no time did Referat II cooperate with the Spanish General Staff or any official Spanish agencies, according to Blaum. Such contact was restricted to Referats I and III. It was never officially admitted that II was active in Spain, and therefore Referat II was not permitted official outside assistance. Referat II was, of course, very unpopular in Spain, and the KO chief was repeatedly advised by the Spanish General Staff to cease all S-operations. Blaum emphasizes that Spain does not have an equivalent to the German Abwehr II.

Orders from Berlin

No specific orders concerning the nature of sabotage work were ever given by Berlin headquarters, which merely issued statements of general policy. Changes in policy were frequently necessitated by political or military reverses, the exact nature of which were unknown to the lower echelons. One rule, however, was always emphasized: all sabotage against Allied shipping was to be timed so that the explosion would occur outside Spanish territorial waters, that Spanish neutrality would never be openly violated, and that no proof of German origin would be found at the scene of the sabotage. (Proof of German complicity in the explosion of an orange ship at Valencia brought a succession of reprimands from the Foreign Office, the High Command, and Spanish authorities, directed against Abwehr II in Berlin and passed down to Hummel in Madrid.)

Only one exception was allowed to this regulation. At the last minute, permission was granted to sabotage Italian ships in Spanish harbours, but again, it was emphasized that no clue of German complicity be found, and that, should the Spanish Government make an official protest, blame be placed on the Italian crews.

A last and definite order from Berlin was received in early 1944, prohibiting all S-operations in Spain and ordering the destruction or removal of all remaining S-materials.

Origin of Sabotage Materials

Whenever possible, II KO Spanien used British sabotage equipment. The reason for this was twofold: (a) British material was far superior to, as well as more reliable and safer to handle than, the German equivalent; (b) its use also prevented detection of German origin in case an action was prematurely discovered. This equipment, sent from Berlin under diplomatic privileges, had been captured in France, either after the British withdrawal of 1940 or from underground forces, to whom great quantities had been parachuted by the Allies.

Efficiency of Abwehr II

Personnel of Abwehr II was generally ill-suited for its job, according to Blaum and Amende. In most cases the KOs were headed by old reserve officers, intent on keeping their position and rank but lacking intelligence training and knowledge of the country to which they were assigned. Strict adherence to the rigid military hierarchy prevented abler, more experienced subordinates from making their voices heard in the operations of the KOs. As a result, plans were always vague, specific operations had little chance of success, and throughout the war the slogan in Berlin remained, 'Something must be done, no matter what.' Abwehr II was characterized by a marked tendency to claim tremendous successes and to report constant activity, even when nothing was going on.

II KO Spanien at Work
The activities of Abwehr II in Spain fall into three separate phases:
First phase, 1940–1941: No large-scale sabotage.
Second Phase, 1942–43: Several unsuccessful missions against Gibraltar and Allied shipping. Important activity in connection with J-work, with Spain used as an intermediary.
Third Phase: 1944 to the end of war: Activity in many fields, especially against Gibraltar and Allied shipping.

All S-activities prohibited by Berlin, Drafting of plans for R-activities (Rueckzugsorganasation). II staff reduced at beginning of 1945.

R-Organisation
In late 1942 KO Spanien began to fear an Allied invasion of Spain. This attitude, based in part on persistent reports from Berlin pointing to the probability of Allied landings in Spain, prevailed throughout 1943. Shortly after the Allied invasion of North Africa orders were received to build up an R-organisation in the Iberian peninsula. Referat II's part in the project consisted of burying small quantities of S-materials in south and south-east Spain, where the invasion was anticipated. To avoid possible indiscretions, only the German staff was allowed to participate in the burying parties.

The plan was to send agents across the front lines or to parachute them in the vicinity of hidden dumps. Thus future Abwehr missions, once arrived behind enemy lines, would be assured of adequate supplies. Approximately 30 small crates were buried at a depth of about 30 cm, at locations calculated to be both easily accessible and close to future sabotage targets. These crates were corrosion-proof and contained five to ten charges of different types and sizes, such as incendiaries, demolitions, and camouflaged coal, all of British origin. Instructions for use were attached to each charge.

The location of the dumps was described in great detail by means of a series of charts and photographs, of which three sets were made. One set was kept at II headquarters in Berlin, one sent to Ast Paris, and one to the Iberia Abw Trupp, a unit set up at the same time as the E-organisation for employment in the event of an Allied invasion of the peninsula. None of the charts or photographs remained in Spain. The three existing sets were destroyed before the end of the war. The copy in Paris disappeared in 1944, coincident with the rumoured desertion of a member of the II staff of Ast Paris.

Organisational Chart of the KO Spain

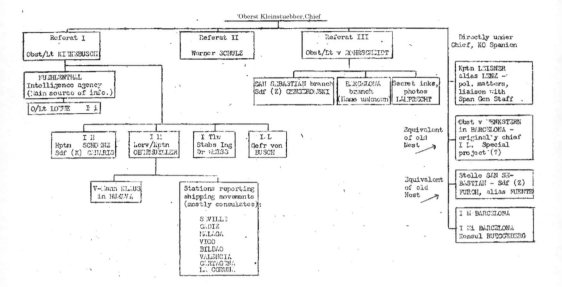

Also in line with the R-organization, Referat II began in late 1943 to train ten to 15 Spaniards in the handling of S-materials. These men were to be left behind enemy lines. However, when all 3 operations in Spain were discontinued on orders from Berlin in early 1944, this plan had to be abandoned. Of the participants in this sabotage course, Blaum remembers Francisco Borjabad, the recruiting agent, and Ricardo Zusait and Emilio Diaz, both students. Since the training had to be suspended in its early stages, the Spanish agents never received any sabotage materials.

KO Spanien envisioned another possibility for R-work in the support of a clandestine right-wing Falange group led by Perales, one of the earliest Falangists and a sincere idealist. Extreme political activities were of little interest to Abwehr II, which, despite its new designation, Mil Amt D, had remained a purely military organisation. It was suggested to Berlin, however, that as a demonstration of goodwill 20,000 pesetas be allotted to Perales' organisation for its propaganda programme.

Perales and his followers were in opposition to Franco's foreign policy, which in their opinion had become increasingly favourable to the Allies. Perales was also a fanatic Catholic, a rabid opponent of Communism, and a thorough Germanophile.

Perales' group consisted of old Falangists who had supposedly remained honest and not joined in the frequent attempts by Falange leaders to enrich themselves. They considered themselves the 'Falange autentica', as opposed to the regular Falange organisation founded by Primo de Riviera,

Perales, known as a very secretive person, never divulged more than vague information regarding the composition of his organisation. Moreover, it was felt by KO Spanien that his tremendous enthusiasm caused him to exaggerate the importance of his group. He claimed that such military leaders as Generals Yague and Munez Grande supported his movement, and that even Serrano Suner was sympathetic to his cause. It was considered doubtful, however, whether these important figures would openly ally themselves with Franco's enemies.

Despite suspicions of wishful thinking on the part of Perales, Referat II agreed that he could be of value in R-operations in the event that Franco should break diplomatic relations with Germany, or that Spain should be invaded by the Allies. In July 1944 a plan for making use of Perales was submitted to Berlin. Since approval was not immediately forthcoming and Perales needed time to round up and brief his collaborators, little progress was made in 1944. The project was still in its preliminary stages when Blaum left Spain in February 1945.

The first step of the plan was to set up a W/T net which would assure permanent contact with Perales after a break between Germany and Spain. This net would have been the basis for future II work. The remainder of the plan, including S-training, could not be carried out because the blanket order prohibiting all S-activities was still in effect.

Three W/T stations were to be established, at Madrid, Barcelona and Seville. The procurement of personnel and appropriate sites for the stations was entrusted to Fernando Alzag, head of the anti-communist department of the Falange Information Services. It had also been decided to turn over to Perales a set of the documents revealing the location of the S-deposits mentioned above. Since the documents were not available in Spain, a set was requested from Berlin. They were to be given to Perales just before the contemplated diplomatic rupture or invasion. In February 1945 this had not been done.

Cooperation with Other Sections of KO Spanien
Only a minimum of news and opinions were exchanged between Referat II and the other sub-sections. Information of I and III interest which was gathered along with II material was merely passed on to the interested sections. There were, however, some exceptions to this policy:

In Seville, Captain Antonio Ojed, and Patricio Drexel, neither of whom were connected with II, were used in sabotage activities. Ojeda, a member of the Spanish Intelligence Service, volunteered information on maritime traffic to and from Gibraltar. Most of his reports came through Referat I. Drexel, a German resident of Seville, contributed reports on the internal political situation, police records, etc, some of which were used by III.

Referat II obtained an especially valuable item of information for I-TLw through Drexel. A Spanish Air Force colonel supplied a complete description of a US four-engined bomber which had made an emergency landing in Southern Spain. Various technical manuals were included in the report. At the time (summer 1943), the Abwehr was looking for such material, and was anxious to obtain data on radar equipment, which was supplied in this report.

Some III-F functions were taken over by the II office after all S-operations had been forbidden by Berlin. Perfecto Brioso, a Falange Information Services agent, had contacted Baldwin, of the US Embassy. Brioso, who had been engaged by the Spanish III-F service, had offered his services to the II office without the knowledge of III-F. Thus Blaum was able to learn what questions Baldwin had asked Brioso and what cover answers Brioso had been furnished by his own intelligence service. In one case, when Baldwin screened a number of Germans with Brioso's aid, Brioso's cover answers were supplied by the II office. Brioso's activities came to an end when Spain decided to discontinue III-F connections with the US Embassy and Brioso refused to carry on without the shield of his own organisation.

Enrique Zabal, a Spanish friend of a member of the II staff, claimed to have established III-F contacts with the British Embassy through certain left-wing and anarchist circles, who in turn claimed to know Varel, a Spaniard in the service of the British. KO Spanien had always been extremely interested in the results of Allied measures to gain support from the Spanish leftist parties. Zabal, however, was arrested by the Spanish police and admitted having worked as a III-F agent for the Germans.

Another III man, Fernandez-Fernandez, was engaged by Referat II. A Spanish police agent in Seville, Fernandez-Fernandez worked in a III-F capacity with the British Consulate, supplying British Intelligence with lists of arrivals and departures of aliens. He had also been asked to investigate suspect German agents. Necessary answers were, of course, supplied by the II office.

In December 1945 Blaum was released from CIC custody and transferred to a PoW camp at Ziegenheim.

SEVENTH REPORT, I NOVEMBER 1943

The arrival in Scotland of Nicolay Hansen at the end of September 1943 was, in counter-espionage terms, an important event, as Petrie made clear. Additionally, it was evident from the outset that Hansen, an uneducated labourer from the Norwegian island of Spitzbergen, could not be prosecuted because of the circumstances of his arrest when he had immediately volunteered that he had been equipped with two transmitters, a British one, constructed by SOE, that he had been instructed to surrender, but the second, a German apparatus, he was to conceal. Instead of obeying his German controller, he had given up both. This act appeared to demonstrate his true loyalty, but under interrogation in his own language at Camp 020 two problems emerged. Firstly, ISOS had betrayed the fact that he had been issued with two cover addresses in Sweden, but when challenged on this point he had initially denied the accusation. Secondly, he only admitted the existence of a false tooth in his mouth, in which secret writing material had been concealed, after he had been given the opportunity to acknowledge it. Once again, he had lied to his well-briefed interrogators.

Having given himself up to the police soon after he landed, Hansen was questioned in Fraserburgh by the RSLO, Peter Perfect, and had made a lengthy statement in which he described how he had been recruited by the Abwehr while serving a 20-month prison sentence for theft from a German naval depot at Harstad. He had agreed to undergo espionage training in exchange for an immediate release from jail, and this had commenced in May 1943 in anticipation of a mission to Spitzbergen. However, his destination was switched to Scotland and after his first flight on 17 September was cancelled because of bad weather, he completed his journey three nights later. The German plan called for him to find a job in Glasgow, perhaps as a miner, and then begin transmitting military information on his second, undeclared wireless set. After nine months he was to travel to Portugal or Spain and identify himself as HEINI to a German diplomat for passage to Oslo.

When questioned, Hansen appeared cooperative, and identified the Germans he had encountered, and a dozen other trainees. However, doubts about his integrity led to a debate about the possibility of a prosecution, and eventually Liddell and the DPP concluded that no case could be brought without the risk of compromising Camp 020 as witnesses would have to be called to give evidence of Hansen's lies. Accordingly, Hansen was detained for the remainder of the war.[1]

SEVENTH REPORT
A SPIES ARRESTED.
Our special interrogation camp has been particularly busy during the last month as no less than ten new spies have arrived there; eight of them have been arrested at various points overseas.

For the first time since December 1942, when double-cross agent ZIGZAG arrived in this country, a German spy called Nikolay Hansen was dropped by parachute in the neighbourhood of Fraserburgh on the night of 30th September. The choice of that neighbourhood for the dropping of Hansen is interesting. In the past parachute spies coming to this country are best dropped in the Midlands and East Anglia, but it is possible that the success, as they see it, of the dropping of sabotage equipment and wireless sets to MUTT and JEFF has led the German Secret Service to believe that Scotland is the safest venue for such clandestine operations. Hansen, a Norwegian miner by profession, at once gave himself up and revealed that he had been supplied by the enemy with two wireless transmitters. He had been instructed to bury one of these, and to give himself up with the other. The Germans imagined that the credulous British security Authorities would believe his story, release him and allow him to find himself a job in this country, when he was to pick up his second transmitter and start operating. It was subsequently found that this story was not quite complete, as under interrogation by our officers, Hansen revealed that he had been supplied with a cover address in Stockholm to which he was to write in secret ink, this ink being concealed in crystal form in a rubber container beneath a tooth stopping. We are satisfied that the reason Hansen concealed this last piece of intelligence was fear, as he had been threatened with dire penalties to himself and his family if he should ever reveal the Stockholm cover address which might compromise the Germans with the Swedish Government.

Hansen's training was cut short as after the capitulation of Italy, the German Secret Service were anxious to send a spy to this country as soon as possible. Hansen has stated that other agents are in training in Scandinavia for missions so it is possible that we may have some more aerial visitors.

Another spy, also from Scandinavia, arrived in Iceland in September. He told the American military authorities there that he was a genuine refugee who had made his way from Norway in a fishing boat. He managed to persuade them that this story was genuine, but we regarded it as unconvincing, and induced the Americans to send him to the UK for further interrogation. As expected, this man, Fridrikson, confessed that he had been landed from a German submarine, equipped with a wireless transmitter which he had buried, and $9,000. One of his tasks was to finance another agent who is operating under Allied control in Iceland, and with whom Fridrikson was to be put in touch after he had made wireless contact with his masters. He is being sent back to Iceland to carry out his mission under control.

Recently the Security Service has adopted a policy of harassing and arresting, whenever possible, Spanish seamen known to be working for the enemy. Pursuing this policy we arrested at Trinidad two Spanish officers of the Ybarra line whose ships ply between Spain and South America. After interrogation here both made written confessions of espionage on behalf of the Germans. There is ample evidence that this harassing policy is achieving notable success and is seriously impeding, not just the German espionage, but also the brisk German contraband traffic between the Argentine and Spain.

In connection with espionage in South America, we arrested recently an Argentinian, an agent of the German Secret Service station in Berlin who was en route thither. He has now arrived in this country and is under interrogation.

A spy of the Italian Secret Service named Bonzo has been arrested in Gibraltar. He also had a mission in the Argentine, having been sent to Buenos Aires from Europe in June 1942. He was arrested on his return to Europe with his family, the first purely Italian spy to be handled at our international centre.

B SPIES EXPECTED.

Another spy also connected with the Argentine will shortly be arrested and sent here for interrogation. This man, Osnar Alberto Hellmuth, has been sent on a special mission to Berlin as the personal emissary of President Ramirez to the Germans. On arrival, he was to be introduced at once to Himmler and also to the Führer. It is believed that one of the objects of his mission is the negotiation for the sale of German arms to the Argentine, and that it also covers the general arrangements for the safeguarding of German interests in the Argentine if relations with Germany are broken off. Hellmuth enjoys the confidence of an inner ring of the Argentine Government which includes, as well as the President, Admiral Sueyrro (Minister of Marine) and Colonel Gilbert (Minister of Interior). Hellmuth has been given as cover the ad hoc appointment of Argentine Consul at Barcelona, but the real object of his journey is being kept a secret from the rest of the Argentine Government and from the Argentine Ambassador in Berlin. He has recently been arrested in Trinidad on his way to Europe, and arrangements have been made for his rapid transfer to the UK, partly by air, and partly in one of HM ships.

As regards espionage directed against this country, there has recently been intense activity in the Lisbon branch of the German Secret Service which is concerned with Air Force matters. It is known that they are attempting to send spies to this country in the guise of Allied Air Force volunteers. The object of this type of espionage venture is for the spy to become a pilot in an operational unit, and, when flying an aircraft of the latest model, to land in German-occupied territory. This type of espionage is not new to us, and there have been several previous examples, such as FATHER and FIDO, to whom reference has been made in previous reports. One such spy, a Belgian named Bertrand, is now on his way to this country. Two other Belgians, agents of the German Secret Service, are also intended for the UK and we shall not obstruct their journey, but arrest them on arrival.

C DOUBLE CROSS AGENTS.

As mentioned in the last summary, a difficult situation had arisen. TRICYCLE's spy-master has been in touch in Madrid with the British Authorities and said that he was under serious suspicion with the Germans and might have to ask for asylum in the UK. During the last month this situation has improved, as it has been possible to persuade TRICYCLE's spy-master to retain his position in the German Secret Service. It also means that the suspicions have been somewhat allayed, and that his position is not as bad as we thought it was. His main rival in the German Secret Service had expressed doubts about the bona fides of TRICYCLE, but his criticism had been unsuccessful and he had been sent to the Eastern front. The spy-master has also been providing useful information on various subjects of great interest and importance, including changes in the higher ranks of the German Secret Service, and details regarding the activities of its Head, Admiral Canaris, during his recent visit to Spain.

It is hoped that within a short time TRICYCLE will pay a further visit to Lisbon, accompanied by an officer from this department, when it is hoped that through contact with his spy-master he will obtain more useful information.

Through the medium of double cross agent GARBO, we have recently been able to continue our policy of harassing and impeding the German Secret Service. We have already completed an operation which will force their branch in Lisbon to find new cover addresses, a task which is becoming increasingly hard for them. It was arranged that a batch of GARBO's letters should be 'intercepted' by the British censorship and enquiries then made in Lisbon about the persons to whom these secret ink letters were addressed, which showed the Germans that these addresses, twelve in number, were blown. The Germans have sent a special officer from Madrid to Lisbon to conduct an investigation and have told GARBO to lie low for the next six weeks or two months, by which time they hope that the storm will have blown over.

D SABOTAGE.

Allied shipping at anchor in Gibraltar Bay has suffered a number of successful attacks by Italian divers carrying explosive charges. 52,459 gross tons of shipping have been seriously damaged. Although the Security Service has long suspected that these attacks were based on the Spanish mainland, we could not exclude the possibility that the attacks originated from Italian submarines. After the armistice with Italy, the Chief Engineer of an Italian tanker, interned since the outbreak of war with Spain in Algeciras harbour, gave information to the British Vice-Consul at Algeciras which made it clear that since the end of 1942 all the sabotage attacks had been based on this tanker, which had been specially modified to become a sabotage depot ship. Underwater hatches had been constructed so that Italians in light diving-suits could leave the tanker below the water and proceed with human torpedoes and other types of sabotage equipment into Gibraltar Bay, attaching them to the hulls of our ships. The Italian personnel came overland across Italy, and hid in the tanker until the time of the attack. The sabotage equipment was also brought across Spain and housed in the tanker. Despite this, even after the armistice, the Italian Authorities persisted in their denials that the sabotage was shore-based.

The Italian tanker is now at Gibraltar and is being minutely examined. Statements are being taken from the Italians concerned with the attacks. The complicity of the Spanish Government, or at any rate Spanish officials in the neighbourhood of Gibraltar, will it is hoped be proved, and will provide more formidable material for protests to Spain than any we have previously used.

The interrogation of the Tanker's engineer has provided interesting information. He has told us that the German Sabotage Service in Spain attempted to procure him to continue his sabotage activities against the Allies on behalf of the Germans, after the armistice with Italy, and also asked him to provide details of the Gibraltar water supply, presumably with a view to sabotaging it. Adequate precautions have been taken long since to deal with this type of plan.

An officer of the Security Service is on his way to Gibraltar to conduct an expert examination of the tanker and its equipment.

E COMMUNIST ACTIVITIES.

Further investigation of the activities and associations of D.F. Springhall, the late National Organiser of the Communist Party who in July was sentenced to seven years' penal servitude for offences under the Official Secrets Act, has disclosed other contacts in other Government departments. A girl clerk, employed in highly secret work in MI6, was seen by Springhall in April this year, and was asked for details of the work she was doing. She claims to have refused to supply them and we believe this claim to be true, but it was nevertheless thought prudent to remove her from her work in view of her membership of the Communist Party and has admitted loyalty to it.

Another contact of Springhall was Captain O.L. Uren, a young officer employed in the Balkan Section of SOE. Uren volunteered to help the Communist Party and was put in touch with Springhall. After a number of introductory meetings, Springhall asked for a written statement of the make-up and functions of SOE and Uren supplied him with a detailed and accurate account. This revealed the identity of the then Head of SOE, the location of Headquarters, organisation, policy and methods of work of SOE with the Allied Governments. The association of Uren and Springhall was only brought to an end by the arrest of Springhall. Uren appeared before a court martial on October 21st. The findings of the court have just been announced and Uren has been sentenced to seven years' imprisonment.

This Department has not been entirely immune from Springhall's attentions, for he is believed to have been in touch with a late member of our canteen staff. Enquiries are proceeding. He was also receiving information, some of it of a highly secret character, from officers in the Navy and the Army. A number of cases are under investigation.

While Springhall was perhaps acting without the Party's authority in these matters, the Security Service has good cause to know that the more official underground organisation of the Party continues to have a measure of success in obtaining information about the policy of the Government, forthcoming operations and the development of new and secret weapons and devices. Two new anti-submarine devices were betrayed to the Communist Party, one by an officer and another by a civilian engaged on instructional work. Two radio devices for use in paratroop operations were disclosed by a technician engaged in their manufacture. In those cases no prosecution has been possible, both because the evidence, though clear, was not legally admissible and because the source of the information would have been imperiled. Many similar cases of leakage to the Communist Party are known to us.

A common feature of all cases of this nature, which, by their growing numbers and seriousness, are viewed very gravely by the Security Service, is that the offender sets loyalty to Communism (and thence to Russia) above every consideration of duty, honour and allegiance to his own King and country. The study of these cases goes far to support the conclusion that every Communist has a 'soft side' in this respect and is better not employed in any capacity which gives him access to confidential or secret material. It is interesting that the above growing conviction of the Security Service should have been confirmed by a comment made by Captain Uren in his own defence during his trial, its gist being that, although he knew it was in no way necessary for Springhall to have it, he disclosed to him vitally important information in order to demonstrate that he had complete faith in Springhall and to persuade Springhall to trust him in return as a sincere believer in Communism. If this creed, which has now found open avowal, is general among members of the Communist Party, the possible reactions on national security can scarcely fail to be serious.

1 November 1943

★ ★ ★

The arrest of Andrés Bonzo was fully justified in being mentioned by Petrie to the Prime Minister as it was one of the most remarkable, if undocumented, cases of wartime espionage of the entire conflict, and originated with Kim Philby in September 1943. At that time Bonzo, carrying an Argentine passport, was aboard the Spanish ship *Monte Albertini* retuning to Spain from Buenos Aires. He had travelled to South America on the *Cabo de Buena Esperanze* in

June 1942 from Genoa, accompanied by his wife Maria and son Dario, and by José Trotti, a wireless operator. Bonzo described himself as a correspondent for *La Stampa*, but was actually an agent of the Italian intelligence service. However, according to an SIS source, Angelo Pozzi, in Buenos Aires, Bonzo was a senior figure in a local spy ring headed by Ricardo Prati, the assistant military attaché at the Italian embassy. Pozzi had approached the SIS station with this information, apparently in an attempt to penetrate any British organisation, and had been regarded with suspicion and scepticism, but nevertheless his information seemed to link Bonzo, employed as a lawyer by the Roman Catholic church, to an agent code-named FRANCISCO who appeared with some frequency in the intercepted Italian wireless traffic.

When his ship docked at Gibraltar on 12 September Bonzo was arrested, and upon his arrival at Camp 020 he promptly supplied a lengthy and detailed statement describing his recruitment in Rome by the Italian foreign intelligence service, the Servicio Informazione Extere (SIE), his assignment in Argentina, and the SIE's network of personnel across South America. In his account of the SIE's operations and personnel, Bonzo described how his organisation was dependent upon funds provided by the Italian naval attaché, Eugenio Torriani who, unfortunately, had been killed in a car accident, thereby cutting him off from any financial support. A bitter row had then ensued, and Bonzo had decided to return to Rome to obtain further instructions from his superior, Colonel de Renzi, at headquarters in the Palazzo Baracchini.

Born in Argentina in April 1896, Bonzo had been taken by his parents to Italy, where he had qualified as a lawyer and, during the First World War, had served with the 252nd Infantry regiment on Monte Grappa in the Italian Alps.

In his confession Bonzo, who had been a reservist officer with the rank of captain with the 37th Infantry Regiment until he was called up in December 1940, identified his entire network, its agents, their methods, communications and cover addresses, and cooperated fully with his interrogators, developing a very comprehensive picture of the SIE, including its premises and staff. He also named members of his network in Chile and Uruguay so, by any standard, Bonzo's material represented a major intelligence coup, although MI5 observed that 'this story of Italian adventure in espionage is one of appalling muddle, personal rivalry and sordid intrigue'.

The unforeseen complication in the Bonzo interrogation occurred in March 1944 when it was reported by SIS the Servicio Informazione Militare (SIM) representative in Buenos Aires, Major Prati, had boasted that he had recently seen a copy of the interrogation of Bonzo conducted in Gibraltar. This allegation, if true, amounted to a significant breach of security, especially as one detail, mentioning a 'red-headed Jewess' employed in Bonzo's office, appeared to be authentic. Prati had claimed to have seen a photostat document, and although Bonzo had not been questioned in Gibraltar, the description sounded like one of two interim case reports issued by Camp 020, dated 1 and 16 November 1943. These had been shared with Joseph Lynch, an FBI liaison officer in Washington, who had distributed copies to the FBI representatives in Buenos Aires, Montevideo and Rio de Janeiro. Evidently one of these three copies had reached Prati, and once the FBI special agent in Argentina, Ken Crosby, had been eliminated, suspicion fell on Carl Spaeth in Uruguay, who had unwittingly passed a copy to a representative from the Argentine police.[2] Soon afterwards, there was further evidence of a leak when details of Osmar Hellmuth's case reached Argentina, and an FBI investigation in October 1943 concluded that the documents probably had been removed, copied and replaced from an unaccompanied State Department bag that had been sent to Buenos Aires. However, MI5 was not quite so confident, and Cyril Mills informed Liddell that:

> … strictly between ourselves this may be the Bureau's official explanation of an occurrence which is highly embarrassing to them but I am not altogether satisfied that if it is the real one although I do not suggest that the FBI know what the real one is.

The matter remained unresolved, and by August 1944, with the political position transformed in Italy, SIS pressed MI5 to release Bonzo on the grounds that 'there seems no good reason to keep Bonzo in captivity and every reason why he should be released'. Even Colonel Stephens, Camp 020's fierce commandant, conceded that Bonzo had been fully cooperative and had assisted in breaking another Italian, Philippe Manfredi de Blasis. Accordingly, on 12 December 1944 Bonzo was escorted to Liverpool where he was placed aboard a ship bound for Italy and deported, to continue his work as an intelligence officer, this time for SIM.

★ ★ ★

The detention of Osmar Hellmuth, an ostensibly innocuous insurance broker, was one of the great unsung intelligence coups of the entire conflict, and would have a profound impact in Argentina. He was arrested in Trinidad on the *Cabo de Hornos* on 29 October 1943, flown to Bermuda and the taken by HMS *Ajax* to Plymouth.

Hellmuth was born in Buenos Aires to a German father and later became friendly with another member of the Argentine Yacht Club, Hans Harnisch, who had boasted of his Nazi connections, and in particular his friendship with SS Obergruppenführer Walter Schellenberg. Allegedly he had fulfilled the role of an intermediary, negotiating between President Castillo and Berlin, but after the military coup of April 1943, which had brought Pedro Ramirez to power, Harnisch had lost his influence. He complained to Hellmuth, who happened to know Ramirez because they had once shared a long rail journey together when the future president had been a mere commander of a cavalry brigade. Furthermore, Hellmuth was on particularly good terms with the president's secretary, Colonel Enrique Gonzalez. Seeing an opportunity to exploit Harnisch's contacts in Germany, Hellmuth asked him to intervene in the protracted talks that had been taking place over the fate of the *Buenos Aires*. This *cause célèbre* was a tanker bought from its Greek owners that required a safe conduct pass from the Germans before it could make the voyage through the Baltic from Gothenburg to Argentina. Harnisch not only offered his support to have the *Buenos Aires* put to sea, but suggested that he could also assist in the Ramirez government's desire to buy German weapons.

In September 1943 Hellmuth was appointed an auxiliary consul and given travel papers, ostensibly to fulfil an appointment at the Argentine consulate-general in Barcelona, but actually to negotiate with the SD, and embarked on the *Cabo de Hornos* for Bilbao early the following month with instructions, not from Harnisch, but from Hauptsturmführer Johannes Becker and Colonel Juan Perón, then an assistant to the Minister of War, General Edelmiro Farrell. Under the scheme agreed, Hellmuth would be contacted in Bilbao once he had checked in to the Carlton Hotel, and then he would be flown to Berlin to meet General Schellenberg, and possibly even Reichsmarshal Heinrich Himmler. He would be accompanied by Colonel Alberto Vélez, the new Argentine military attaché to Spain and Portugal, who would handle the weapons procurement negotiations once the *Buenos Aires* had been released. The complicating factor in all this preparatory work was the mutual distrust between the regular diplomats at the German embassy in Buenos Aires and Becker as the SD's representative. Similarly, there was considerable rivalry between the various factions in the Ramirez government, all of which had different ideas about what should be negotiated in Berlin, and who should go there, but Hellmuth had been promised by his friend Gonzalez, and Ramirez's foreign minister, Colonel Alberto Gilbert, that if his mission was successful he would become one of the president's inner circle, or at least one of those who would be enriched.

Although Hellmuth during his interrogation was given the impression that his detention had been opportunistic, it was in fact the culmination of a carefully prepared plan to capture a man who was suspected of being despatched to Berlin by either Ramirez, or people close to him, so an unofficial line of communication could be kept open in the event that his government was forced to sever diplomatic relations. Hellmuth's arrest, of course, was the most flagrant abuse of his diplomatic immunity, but the excuse to detain him was a single letter, erroneously omitted from the diplomatic bag, from Harnisch addressed to a certain Dr Holm that served to introduce Hellmuth and listed various 'precision measuring instruments' which would be subject of future, profitable business. This reasonably innocuous letter was the pretext for Hellmuth's arrest on the grounds that he was engaged in contraband, which was timed to take place shortly before his ship was due to sail. An attempt by another Argentine diplomat to send a telegram to Buenos Aires to report the arrest was also stymied by ensuring that Imperial Censorship did not clear the text for a further five days. By the time other Argentine diplomats had been alerted to find Hellmuth he had, for all intents and purposes, simply disappeared.

In reality an infuriated Hellmuth was told that he had been let down twice, once by Colonel Gonzalez, who had failed to include the incriminating letter in the supposedly sacrosanct diplomatic bag, and also by the German embassy, which, his interrogators hinted, had tipped the British off to the true nature of his mission. Outraged by what he believed was gross treachery, Hellmuth made the most comprehensive confession, naming Becker as the SD Chief in Argentina, and describing in considerable detail everything that had occurred before his departure. To assist the preparation of his statement he was given a typewriter, but MI5 also examined a pad on which Hellmuth made a first draft of everything he intended to include in his confession, plus a few additional items he decided to omit. The result was that MI5 could undertake a comparison of both versions, which assisted in his interrogation. When Hellmuth finally realised he had been tricked, and the implications of his admissions, he refused all further cooperation and remained a recalcitrant prisoner at Camp 020 for the next two years.

Hellmuth's very comprehensive confession provided the Foreign Office, which had been pressed by the indignant Argentine ambassador, Miguel Carcano, for an explanation for the arrest of what he called 'a career Argentine diplomat' with a splendid opportunity to exploit what might otherwise have been a very embarrassing diplomatic incident. In fact the Foreign Office would not admit that Hellmuth was a prisoner until 25 November 1943, and a fortnight later Carcano was summoned by Anthony Eden to be told that Hellmuth had admitted to being a 'secret representative of a subversive German organisation in Argentina' and that:

> ... before the departure of Hellmuth, the British government was informed by a prominent member of the German colony in Buenos Aires that Hellmuth would soon travel to Germany via Spain in representation of a branch of the German espionage service in Buenos Aires.

Technically this assertion was perfectly true, as the original tip to Hellmuth's mission had originated from an ISOS sub-set code-named IZAK in October 1943, but the inference was that the British were referring to a willing source, and Colonel Gonzalez and Colonel Gilbert immediately jumped to the conclusion that the traitor had been Ludwig Freude, the owner of a construction business and one of the richest Germans in Argentina. Both men knew that Freude had used his influence, at the request of the German chargé, Erich von Meynen, to scrap Hellmuth's mission, and wrongly concluded that their opponents had stooped to alerting the British, never suspecting that their own communications had been severely compromised.

The consequences of this extraordinary episode were to be far-reaching. With the trump card of Hellmuth's confession, Carcano proposed a face-saving exercise in which Hellmuth would be released so the Argentine government could revoke his diplomatic status and he then could be re-arrested. The British, on the other hand, had a counter-proposal: unless the Argentine government denounced Hellmuth publicly and severed relations with Berlin, a detailed statement on the whole affair would be released. Whatever the nature of the confidential discussions that followed, President Ramirez removed Hellmuth's diplomatic status on 21 January 1944 and the next day cut its diplomatic links with the Nazis. Almost simultaneously, Colonel Gonzalez ordered the chief of the federal police, Colonel Emilio Ramirez, to crack down on any known German spies. None of this was enough to save Pedro Ramirez, who was deposed by General Edelmiro Farrell on 23 February, nor indeed to prevent Admiral Canaris being removed as chief of the Abwehr. The Hellmuth debacle was to be one contributor in a series of coincidental intelligence disasters that undermined the Abwehr's status and led to the Abwehr's absorption into the Reich Security Agency, the RHSA. One additional factor had been the embarrassment caused to the Spanish AEM, headed by Canaris' friend General Arsenio Martinez de Campos, which demanded that much of the Abwehr's structure in Spain be dismantled, and that it cease using German diplomatic and consular posts as cover. Dismayed, Canaris had flown to Biarritz to retrieve the situation, confident that the Abwehr had enjoyed the closest relations with its Spanish counterpart since the Civil War, but had returned to Berlin humiliated and empty-handed, leaving his KO in Spain severely depleted.

★ ★ ★

The complications over the BEETLE case were rather more challenging, as Guy Liddell's version infers in his diary entry for 30 September 1943:

> Blanshard Stamp and I went over to see General Crockatt about the Icelandic subject Petur Tomsen who arrived a short time ago in Iceland ostensibly from Bodo. His story was obviously a poor one and when reported to Harold Blyth the SIS man he communicated with his headquarters. We also expressed doubts and said we thought it was desirable that the man should be sent here. The Americans, however, took a different view. They believed in Tomsen and very reluctantly agreed to us having him sent to this country, provided he were treated as a guest and remunerated for the information that he had provided. There appears to have been some undertaking of this sort between the American general in command and the British admiral who was responsible for bringing him to the country. When we got him to the London Reception Centre and heard this story Baxter was quite convinced he was a spy. Taxed with this he collapsed and has now made a full confession. He was, in fact, dropped by submarine from Bergen. He had a wireless set, $5,000 and a code and instructions, all of which he had buried in Iceland. He has pinpointed the place where they are hidden. We broke this news to General Crockatt, who called in Colonel Calvert and also Colonel Stevens, who recently arrived from Iceland and was conversant with the case of COBWEB. It seems that Tomsen was to communicate with his masters by wireless and would then be informed how to dispose of the money. He would be given the name of a contact, which it almost certain would be COBWEB. We impressed upon Crockatt and Calvert that, by virtue of the large fund of information carefully indexed here, we had a very definite advantage over any intelligence people in Iceland. We thought therefore that some arrangement by which characters of this sort were put on a plane at once and sent here for examination would be profitable to all concerned, particularly since the time factor might on occasion be important. In this particular case for example it would be for consideration whether Thomsen should be turned round. Crockatt and Calvert were more than co-operative and said that they would be delighted to fall in with

any recommendations that we liked to make. I made it clear that the disposal of the body was really a matter between G-2 and SIS since they operated in Iceland and we did not. We would let them have a full report on the case at the earliest possible moment.

BEETLE would be run in Reykjavik by Harold Blyth of SIS's Section V, which meant that three Abwehr agents were under local SIS supervision: Ib Riis, code-named COBWEB, who had been landed near Langanes by the U-252^3 in April the previous year, and a seaman code-named LAND SPIDER. The fact that BEETLE had duped the Americans upon his arrival meant that potentially he could have jeopardised the other two cases, but fortunately the episode ended happily, with the Americans learning an important lesson about the handling of plausible enemy spies. The only remaining curiosity in Petrie's report is his identification of Tomsen as Jens 'Fridriksen', which was his alias.

Although Tomsen initially had claimed to have landed from a Norwegian fishing boat, he had in fact been delivered to the coast near Glettinganes by the U-279,[4] having embarked at Kiel on 2 September. Nevertheless his American captors believed his story, which disintegrated upon his arrival at Camp 020 where his interrogators had been expecting the arrival of an ISOS character code-named ILSE. Tomsen signed a confession within two hours of encountering Colonel Stephens in which he explained that his cooperation had been coerced under the threat of imprisonment for his black market activities in occupied Norway. He also claimed that the Germans had seduced his wife and threatened his mother, who was living in Iceland. After six weeks in custody, Tomsen was returned to Iceland to begin his role as BEETLE.

★ ★ ★

FATHER was Pierre Henri Arend, who reached England from Lisbon in June 1941. In June 1943 he was posted to India to avoid answering some increasingly difficult technical questions submitted by the Abwehr, and supplied with a transmitter code-named DUCK, which became operational in August 1944. When FATHER was posted back to Belgium in October 1944 his radio was operated until the end of the war by a police officer in Calcutta, supposedly a disaffected Indian courier based at the Strategic Air Force's headquarters.

EIGHTH REPORT, 1 DECEMBER 1943

The eighth report, delivered to Churchill in the first week of December 1943, introduced a British traitor, Oswald Job, who would be the first Briton of the war to be hanged in a London prison. It also dealt with two other interesting categories, those of MI5's double-agents, DRAGONFLY, TREASURE and SNIPER, and the enemy defector, Hans Ruser.

EIGHTH REPORT
A. <u>SPIES ARRESTED</u>.
The special interrogation camp staff continues to be extremely busy as in the past month eight new spies have arrived there, three of them being arrested overseas.

One of the most interesting of these spies is Oscar John Job, a British subject of German parents, and a resident for many years in France. Job escaped from France, where he had been in internment, but the story which he told in Lisbon regarding his escape aroused our suspicions and we gave instructions that he was to be interrogated carefully on his arrival in the UK. During the course of the examination, it was noticed that he was carrying certain pieces of jewellery which corresponded closely to the description of jewellery which the Germans had intended to send by courier to our double-cross agent DRAGONFLY, who has been working under control for the last two and a half years. Job was allowed to proceed normally to London and his suspicions were not aroused. He was kept under close observation for twenty days, in the hope that he would disclose his hand and deliver the jewellery to DRAGONFLY. He made no attempt to do this, and as it was certain that he was DRAGONFLY's courier, he was arrested.

Under interrogation Job admitted, not only to having the mission to deliver jewellery from the Germans to an address in London, but also that he was a spy as well. He had secret ink concealed in the hollow handle of an old razor and in the hollow shank of a key, and was to receive instructions broadcast in code over the ordinary German radio network. He himself was to write letters in secret ink to ten internees at St. Denis Internment Camp, purporting to come from people in this country whom the Germans knew to be writing regularly to these internees. Job has not told the full truth, as he stated that his instructions were to obtain information regarding bomb damage and political feeling in this country, while we know from Most Secret Sources that he was in fact a spy sent by the Section of the German Secret Service based on Bordeaux dealing with technical Air Force matters. Job is an unpleasant character and a crook as well as a spy. He clearly had no intention of passing the jewellery to DRAGONFLY, but was going to keep it and sell it himself. It has been decided that Job should be prosecuted under the Treachery Act and the DRAGONFLY case should be closed down.

Hans Ruser, a German who has been connected with the German Intelligence Service from at least 1937, has also arrived in this country. Since the outbreak of war he has been working for the German Secret Service in the Iberian Peninsula, mainly recruiting agents. He fell into disfavour on the suspicion of double-crossing in 1942 but managed however to satisfy his German masters though remaining under a cloud. A short time ago, he was reported again to be in grave danger from the Gestapo, and in view of the serious damage which he could have done to the British Intelligence Service by revealing information under Gestapo interrogation, he was induced to flee from Spain and was detained on arrival here.

Mention was made in the last report of Hellmuth, who was being sent from the Argentine on a special mission to Berlin as a personal emissary of President Ramirez to the Germans. He has arrived in this country and confessed. The full nature of his mission has not yet been revealed by him, but it included the procuring of technicians, arms and precision instruments from Germany which were to be transported in an Argentine tanker now in Gothenburg. He has also given us the name of the Head of the Argentine branch of the section of the German Secret Service dealing mainly with political intelligence.

B. DOUBLE CROSS AGENTS.

Two new double-agents have arrived in this country in the last month. The first arrival was TREASURE, a French citizen of Russian origin. She has lived most of her life in Paris, where she occupied herself with journalism, and at one time gained considerable reputation as an artist. As a journalist she travelled all over Europe, and at the outbreak of war found herself in Syria city while undertaking a bicycle trip from Paris to Saigon.

Through a fellow journalist, a German whom she had known before the war, TREASURE obtained her first introduction, after the fall of France, to the German Secret Service. It was a long time before TREASURE was able to persuade her German masters to send her to this country as they planned various other missions for her in different parts of the world, all of which, for one reason or another, broke down. She has had extensive training in wireless transmission and reception and in secret ink writing. She did not bring a wireless set with her, but was assured that arrangements had been made for one to be sent. Her mission is primarily to collect information on air matters.

The other double-agent is SNIPER, who is also concerned with air affairs, as he was recruited to come here by the Head of that section of the German Secret Service dealing with technical Air Force matters. SNIPER is a Belgian, educated in London and Brussels, who joined the Belgian Air Force just after the end of the last war. He left the Air Force in 1926 and from then till 1940 he was a mining engineer in the Belgian Congo. On his return to Belgium he re-joined the Air Force and was under training when the Germans invaded. SNIPER's escape from Belgium through France was facilitated by the Germans, but after crossing the Franco–Spanish frontier, he freely reported the true facts to the Belgian Authorities. His instructions from his German masters were that on his arrival here he was to buy a wireless receiver on which he would receive his instructions from Brussels. He was told that he would be sent a transmitter in due course, either by parachute, or delivered to him by another German spy in this country. In the meanwhile he was to communicate in secret ink to cover addresses in Switzerland, Spain and Portugal. Apart from being given a certain amount of money for his immediate needs, SNIPER was promised very large rewards for technical information on anti-submarine devices, night-fighter devices etc. One of the most interesting points regarding SNIPER'S instructions was that he had been told to contact two other German spies who were already in this country.

One of them, Leon Jude, had already been arrested, and the other one, Jean Creteur, is one of those who were sent to our special interrogation camp this month. He has not yet admitted to being a spy, or that he was sent here as one. Like SNIPER, both Jude and Creteur were Belgian Air Force officers.

C. SABOTAGE.

Since the capitulation of Italy the German sabotage service in Spain and Spanish territories has been engaged in frantic endeavours to sabotage Italian merchant ships in Spanish ports and prevent them from falling into British hands. So far these efforts have only proved partially successful. The first scheme was to bribe the crews to flood the ships by opening the sea-cocks, but this idea was abandoned. The Germans, therefore, had to fall back on sabotage, using as their instruments either members of their crews who were faithful to Mussolini or independent saboteurs.

Apart from a number of ships in the Canary Islands, there were three Italian ships in Spanish ports, at Cádiz, Huelva and Cartagena respectively. The German Sabotage Service attached a bomb to the ship in Cádiz which exploded and damaged the hull and propeller shaft, but the ship was refloated, partially repaired and will, it is hoped, be towed to Gibraltar.

The ship at Huelva was partially flooded by the crew, who opened the sea-cocks. The Germans later tried to damage this ship in the same way as the one at Cádiz, but the attempt failed owing to the boatman who was involved becoming frightened. The Germans were forced to leave the task of sabotaging this ship to the Captain and First Officer if and when they were ordered to sail.

The Germans' attempt to sabotage the ship in Cartagena ended rather unfortunately for them, as the bomb which was being taken by boat from the German sabotage depot ship, SS *Lipari* in the same port, exploded prematurely and killed a member of the sabotage service. This premature explosion was probably due to the Germans using British time fuses and mistaking the meaning of the colours on them, a mistake which may lead to a bomb exploding in ten minutes instead of ten hours.

An attempt to sabotage the British SS *Greathope* at Huelva was foiled by our underwater counter sabotage squad which had recently been instituted. This squad is composed of trained divers, and one of them discovered an object wired to the ship's rudder. As there was a very strong tide running at the Bay, the help of a Spanish diver was enlisted to remove the object. After removal it fell to the bottom of the harbour and was lost.

D. GENERAL SECURITY MEASURES.

Evidence from the field has recently suggested a leakage to the Germans in France, possibly originating from this country, as to the real names of agents employed by the French in France. It has been stated by a Free French agent who is still operating in France that the Gestapo have a list of all the French agents sent to France in September. The antecedents of all the personnel who might have had access to this information in either the French or British organisations concerned are being investigated, it is also proposed to censor fully all documents carried by departing agents, and also to search them thoroughly before they leave, both for their own protection and that of the organisations to which they belong. Neither step has been taken to date, and it is hoped that the British and French organisations will agree to the application of this very necessary security procedure.

1st December 1943

★ ★ ★

TREASURE would make an appearance in three of the Prime Minister's reports, and was not just an adventuress, but one with some potentially sinister connections. For example, her uncle had been General Yevgenni Miller, the White Russian leader who had been abducted in Paris in September 1937 by the NKVD. The crime was never solved but Miller had left a written record of his rendezvous with his intelligence chief, Nikolai Skoblin, thereby implicating him and his wife, the singer Nadezhda Plevitskaya, who was imprisoned while her husband escaped abroad. Miller's daughter, Lily Sergueiev's cousin, was (Dame) Elizabeth Hill, then a lecturer in Russian at Cambridge University, who acted as her referee when she applied in June 1943 for a British visa.

Another example of Sergueiev's unconventional life was her approach to journalism, in which she was the centre of attention. In 1933 she walked from Paris to Berlin, arriving in October, and then continued her tour a month later, returning to France via Denmark. Over the next six years she embarked on numerous similar journeys, often writing about her experiences in books and articles, gaining a reputation too as a painter. When she was in Belgrade, to report on the Yugoslav king's funeral, she had obtained an interview with Hermann Göring, a scoop that was rewarded with employment by the French newspaper *Le Jour*. This was followed in March 1935 by a longer visit to Berlin, sponsored by the official press bureau and *Le Petit Journal*, and two tours, one to Norway and the other to Bad Ems.

TREASURE had been in Aleppo when war broke out, and had abandoned her travel plans to train as a Red Cross nurse in Beirut. Upon her return to France she sought out a German acquaintance, Felix Dressel, who turned out to be an Abwehr recruiter, and it was his introduction that launched her espionage career, which became known to MI5 through ISOS in July 1943 when an Abwehr report of her arrival in Madrid was intercepted. Sergueiev's link to Dressel, she later explained, had been driven by her suspicion that he had been implicated in Miller's assassination.

When SIS and MI5 debated the merits of accepting Sergueiev's offer to act as a double-agent, there was an adverse report on her from Virginia Hall, an American SOE agent who had known her in pre-war Paris and suspected she might be a Nazi sympathiser. She was also known to Anthony Blunt, who declared that she had been 'slightly left-wing'. However, by October the decision had been taken to enroll Sergueiev as TREASURE, and she was flown from Gibraltar to Whitchurch via Rabat on 5 November 1943.

Long before TREASURE arrived in England she had earned a lengthy MI5 file, based on ISOS, dating back to September 1942:

1   Sergueiev's name first appeared on MOST SECRET SOURCES on 24 September 1942 in a message from Paris to Lisbon. This message requested Lisbon to despatch immediately a telegram to Nathalie Sergueiev chez Cholay, Finances Exterieurs, Charlton, Vichy France, purporting to come from her Aunt Louise, asking her to come immediately because her aunt Marie Therese was very ill. The message ended by saying that the telegram was only to serve as a basis for the issue of a French passport and exit permit.

2   Nothing further was seen until 11 June 1943 when Paris asked Lisbon to supply an address and telephone number where TRAMP could make contact.

3   15 June 1943. Lisbon replied giving the name Morgener of Rua Joaquim Antonio de Aguiar, Telephone 52030. They advised caution in telephoning and visits after dark. Also, they requested advice of TRAMP's arrival in good time.

4   29 June 1943. Paris asked Madrid whether Vaufrau TRAMP had reported to Miret under the name of Canuto and given special information. Also, saying that if any letters arrived with Miret for Octave Bernhard signed Solange they were to be sent as soon as possible to Paris for Kliemann.

5   Nothing more was seen on these sources until 3 March 1944 when Lisbon informed Paris that Madame Solange had arrived from London and reported under the password CANUTO. They wanted to know what assignments she had and what arrangements were to be made for looking after her. They ended by saying that their relevant documents had been destroyed.

6   4 March 1944. Lisbon informed Paris that Solange was going back to London in a week and wanted to see Kliemann in Lisbon without fail.

7   5 March 1944. Paris replied saying that contact by Madame Solange was quite unexpected but was, nevertheless, an excellent piece of luck. Paris went on to say that she had repeatedly sent reports by letter which were of great value and that she was a first-class Paris link. Great caution in meeting her was advocated. Paris stated that the object of her making contact was to meet Kliemann and to take over a W/T set. Paris also said that if she wanted money she was to have an advance up to 5,000 escudos.

8   6 March 1944. Lisbon informed Paris that Madame Solange declined any meetings before Kliemann arrived for security reasons.

9   9 March 1944. Paris informed Lisbon that Kliemann would be arriving on the 12th or 13th, and that a few days' discussion would be necessary.

10   11 March 1944. Paris informed Lisbon and Berlin that Kliemann had not made any arrangements with Wireless Control about the English traffic that was about to be established with V. Frau TRAMP.

11   14 March 1944. Lisbon informed Paris that Solange had to leave in a few days, and asked where Kliemann was.

12   15 March 1944. Bordeaux informed Lisbon that Kliemann had been delayed because of Portuguese visa difficulties. If Solange's departure could not be delayed Lisbon were told to inform her that all her communications via the SABINA address had arrived safely with excellent results. That communications to her would be continued by radio from 25 March 1944 and she was to continue to use the SABINA address. Also, Solange was to leave behind precise instructions as to where the suitcase and radio were to be deposited. These instructions were only in case Kliemann did not arrive in time.

13   16 March 1944. Paris to Lisbon asking that facilities be given to Major Kliemann who was arriving in Lisbon. Also asking Lisbon to fix a traffic plan with TRAMP because there were no instructions in Paris. This message ended by saying that one of the six megacycle crystals was only a reserve.

14   17 March 1944. Madrid to Lisbon said that Kliemann was arriving on 17th and would visit the Consulate during the morning and requested that contact be arranged with Solange.

15   18 March 1944. Lisbon to Berlin requesting instructions from the Finance Department regarding 10,000 Escudos for Solange.

16   20 March 1944. Lisbon to Madrid stating that the sum of £1,200 was intended for Solange.

17   23 March 1944. Berlin to Lisbon, that £1,200 in notes of the smallest denominations were being remitted for payment for TRAMP, the book entry to be debited to Paris I Luft.

18   3 April 1944. Lisbon to Bordeaux, for Paris, asking confirmation of the
arrival of V-TRAMP's W/T instructions.

19   11 April 1944. Paris informed Lisbon via Berlin, that the TRAMP
instructions had arrived.

20   2 June 1944. On the Wiesbaden–Paris circuit, TRAMP's message No. 5
was relayed verbatim.

21   Since 26 April 1944 nearly all the references to Sergueiev in MOST
SECRET SOURCES have been verbatim re-transmissions of her outgoing
messages and incoming messages, except for a few exceptions.

22   16 May 1944. Paris to Lisbon, via Madrid, stating that W/T traffic with
V-TRAMP was functioning flawlessly.

23   25 May 1944. Paris asked Wiesbaden to send at once TRAMP's
transmitting and receiving times along with the appropriate frequencies
according to the last arrangement.

24   7 June 1944.   Paris asked Wiesbaden to signal when TRAMP last
gave traffic and whether she had been heard since, even if badly.

TREASURE turned out to be a temperamental case to handle, and exasperated her MI5 case officer, Mary Sherer, but she proved to be an exceptionally
valuable asset as her instructions and questionnaire, supplied by Emil Kliemann,
indicated a close interest in the Cromwell tanks as well as preparations for
the anticipated invasion of Europe. As well as illustrating what the enemy
knew already, the questionnaire had the additional benefit of revealing areas
of weakness:

All British, Canadian and American army motor vehicles which belong to
a division, either Army Corps or army bear insignia on the front and rear.
These insignia are divisional signs, unit signs and occasionally a painted flag
(e.g. red-black-red). The divisional sign is most important of all. It is
represented by coats-of-arms, geometrical figures, letters, flowers, leaves,
trees, animals, etc. The size is about 20 by 20 cm. Exact description is
absolutely necessary when reproducing them.

The unit signs appear on a rectangular metal plate (measurement 24 by
21 cm) with backgrounds of various colours and a white inscription (letters,
figures). If the metal bears on the upper edge or the lower edge the white
stripe 50 mm broad, this is to be mentioned in the report.

The signs painted on the sides of the motor vehicles and on the turrets of
armoured cars are not to be given in the report.

When observing signs on vehicles particular care must be taken that only the recognition of the same signs on a large number of vehicles justifies the conclusion that a formation (Verband) is involved.

Occasionally soldiers wear on the left or on both upper sleeves the sign of their division on a cloth square (e.g. Canadian troops wear coloured rectangles and geometrical figures in various colours on the upper arm).

Commando, Royal Marine and similar units wear these designations on both sleeves and sometimes a number. Pay attention to, and report on, both of these.

In armoured units, where possible, give the type of tank.

If numbers can be discovered (i.e. divisional numbers, number of brigades, numbers of artillery regiments) in the case of the infantry battalions care must be taken that the traditional name of the regiment is reported along with the number of the stated battalion.

1) Report technical details on the new English tank which is alleged to be in production. Series A27 (M).

2) Information about 'Caiaouflet' apparatus for exploding mines which has been adopted by the English; construction, weight, packing, appearance and method of working, explosives formula for blowing cavities (Minenkammersprengungen) and possibly service instructions.

3) Reports on new English 'Cromwell' type of tank.

4) Numbers (Nummern) of troop transports which come to or from England, giving destinations, etc.

5) Which American forces are in England? Division, regiment, etc.

6) Where is the staff of the 5th American Army Corps?) Area Oxford – Swindon – Reading). Which infantry divisions belong to it? Signs on motor vehicles.

7) What view is taken in authoritative English circles of landing preparations?

8) Where are the barracks placed in coastal areas, exact locations?

9) Information on the presence of landing craft or vessels suitable for landing purposes particularly on the south coast of England, but also in other coastal areas.

(Locations, number and possibly concentration) Are some of these vessels dismantled, and if so, where are the dismantled vessels?

10) Information about the stoppage of leave of British and American troops should be reported urgently, giving place and time.

11) How many and which British Divisions have been organised since commencement of the war?

12) How many and which British Armoured Divisions have been organised since commencement of the war?

13) How many and which English County Divisions still exist?

14) What is the organisation and armament of these English County Divisions?

15) Which English County Divisions have since been made into ordinary divisions? Give numbers they now have been allotted.

16) How many and which Independent Brigade Groups are in existence?

17) Have Brigades with numbers over '200' any particular role? If so what is their task?

18) Are there British Tank Battalions with numbers nine to thirty-seven? If so state Armoured Divisions? or Army Tank Brigades (as the case may be) in which Divisions are they?

19) Have the British Royal Horse Artillery with numbers six to ten and over twelve? In which Divisions are they?

20) Are there British Field Artillery Regiments with numbers thirty-four to fifty and over one hundred and sixty-five? In which Divisions are they?

21) How many and which Field Artillery Regiments were formed into Anti Tank Regiments?

22) What is the difference between the Coast Artillery Regiments and the Defence Regiments? Name the task of the Defence Regiment.

23) What is the role of the seventieth battalion of regiments?

24) How many Infantry and Armoured Divisions and Army Tank Battalions are at present in Canada? Give their numbers and/or names.

25) Give number and types of tanks produced monthly in Britain.

26) Give number and types of tanks produced monthly in Canada.

27) Give number and types of Armd. Cars produced monthly in Britain.

28) Give number and types of Armd. Cars produced monthly in Canada.

29) Give number and types of landing craft produced monthly in Britain.

30) Name shipyards where these craft are produced.

31) Name factories where tanks and cars produced in Britain.

32) Name factories where tanks and cars produced in Canada.

33) Are the Commandos organised and armed uniformly? If not, give details of each.

34) Give details of strength and composition and armament of Commandos.

35) Give official numbers of Free French and Norwegian Commandos.

36) Organisation, strength and armament of all Royal Marine Commandos. Give basis of information.

37) What is organisation of staff of Chief of Combined Ops?

38) Name parachute units now in Britain.

39) Give location of paratroop HQ.

40) How many machines are used in their organisation for transport purposes?

41) Give regimental or brigade numbers used on baggage for troops going overseas and destinations.

42) What units of the USA army are now in Gt. Britain and what units are in Northern Ireland?

43) Give shipping numbers of troop transports leaving or arriving with destinations, etc.

Sergueiev remained in contact with the Abwehr until December 1944, when she returned to Paris and was assigned a job as an interpreter to a US Army officer, Major John Collings, whom she married in 1946. She moved with her husband to Detroit, died of kidney failure in 1951 and her memoirs, *Secret Service Rendered*, were published posthumously in 1968.[1] Perhaps the most remarkable aspect of her entire history is that years later MI5 would conclude that most probably Sergueiev had been a long-term Soviet agent.

★ ★ ★

SNIPER was a Belgian pilot, Hans Bertrand, who reached England in November 1943 and was allowed to join a Belgian squadron of the RAF. When he was posted back to Belgium in December 1944 he sent a letter in secret ink to his controller in Lisbon, and at the end of March he received confirmation that money for him had been buried near Aachen, but it was never recovered and the German surrender happened before the case could be pursued any further. Nevertheless, part of his value had been to incriminate two other Belgian pilots, Leon Jude and Jean Creteur, about whom he had been instructed by his Abwehr handler, Werner Unversagt, to make enquiries. Interestingly, Bertrand, who had been betrayed by ISOS even before be reached England, developed into a double-agent.

In the case of Jean Creteur, MI5 was badly mistaken, and had mixed up Jean Creteur, who had been flying with the RAF's 609 Squadron since May 1942. It was his brother Georges who was the espionage suspect, and Jean was freed from Camp 020.

Leon Jude was a Belgian pilot who before the war had worked for Sabena, flying between Leopoldville and Brussels, but in March 1942 he was denounced by FATHER, another Belgian pilot, as having been associated with an Abwehr figure, Dr Hacke. At the time Jude was at Malvern, awaiting a posting to an RAF squadron, so his appointment was delayed while MI5 investigated him. At first, in April 1942, the Belgian Sureté interrogated him, but when inconsistencies appeared in his story, he was arrested and interrogated at Camp 020.

Jude had arrived in England in March 1942 from Halifax, Nova Scotia, having travelled from Bilbao to Cuba on the *Marques de Comillas* in August 1941 under Abwehr sponsorship. In Havana he had reported to the Belgian legation and had been ordered to re-enlist in Canada, even though, aged 35, he was considered too old for operational duties. Released from the Tiscornia refugee camp, he flew via Haiti and Maracaibo to Caracas where, on 30 October he embarked on the SS *Santa Rosa* for New York, finally reaching the Belgian Army headquarters at Juliette, Quebec, on 22 November. By the time he arrived in England, in March 1942, he had never been asked about the circumstances of his escape from enemy-occupied Belgium, and had never been vetted.

When questioned, Jude eventually acknowledged his recruitment by the Abwehr and conceded that his failure to declare this relationship at the first opportunity had prejudiced his case. Although MI5's Eric Goodacre elicited the truth, the challenge was to cross-examine Jude without him realising that his colleague FATHER was an active double-agent. Particularly irksome was information possessed about the enemy, such as three cover addresses that he had failed to disclose:

Gottfried Richter, Rua Linda 188, São Paulo
Georges Lotina Rheima, 55 East 35th Street, New York
Karl Lotz, 149/150 20th Avenue, Whitestone, Long Island, New York

He had also failed to denounce FATHER, whom he knew had been approached by his Abwehr recruiter, the ubiquitous Dr Hacke. In the circumstances, it was felt that the safest course was to intern Jude for the duration of hostilities, but on July 1945 he was still in custody because FATHER was still active in the Far East, and consideration was given to handing him over to the Belgian Auditeur Militaire. Finally in August 1945, he was served with a Deportation Order and flown from Croydon to Brussels, where he was detained by the Sureté d'Etat.

★ ★ ★

Code-named JUNIOR, Hans Ruser was an Abwehr officer based in Lisbon. His father, Commodore Ruser, had been the master of the transatlantic liner SS *Imperator*, and Hans had been brought up in the United States. In February 1941 he had suggested to CELERY that he might be interested in defecting to the British. A year later he approached the SIS station in Lisbon with a view to defecting. He had been rebuffed, on MI5's advice, for fear of jeopardising Dusan Popov, who had been known to him because of his meetings with Albrecht von Auenrode. To MI5's relief, JUNIOR had pursued the matter no further, but in January 1943 he had been transferred to the German embassy in Madrid, where he had made another pitch to SIS. On this occasion he had been accepted, but on the condition he remained in place. JUNIOR had agreed these terms and fortunately this arrangement had worked well, although it presented a definite risk for Popov because JUNIOR had been able to deduce that Popov must have been operating as a double-agent. The unexpected complexity arose when, later in the year, JUNIOR had been consulted by Johnann Jebsen when the latter visited Madrid and had been put in touch with Colonel Walter Wren, then the new SIS station commander.

On 20 December 1943 Guy Liddell recorded in his diary that he had read a long report about Ruser over the weekend:

> It is extremely interesting since it was through Dr Kurt Johannsen of Hamburg that he first came into contact with the Abwehr. Before the war a number of journalists in this country, including Kurt Singer and Karl Abshagen, used to send reports to Johannsen on political and economic matters, marked 'Confidential and not for publication'. Ostensibly, Johannsen was dealing solely with the advertising of German import and export business. He was, however, financed by the Ministry of Propaganda and did a considerable amount of work for the German Ministry of Economic Warfare. Later Ruser worked in the Fremdenienst, a propaganda service which was set up for bear-leading visitors from this country and the United States to Germany. Ruser obtained this job through his shipping connections. His father had been employed by Norddeutscher Lloyd, had been captain of the *Leviathan*, and was interned in the United States. Ruser and his mother were at liberty and Ruser himself received most of his education in the United States. He eventually drifted to Spain and it was there that he became definitely connected with the Abwehr. There is no doubt that the Germans were giving assistance to General Franco in the very early stages of the revolution. The Ruser report shows how the KriegsOrganisation Spain and KO Portugal were gradually built up, through professional Abwehr officers

making use of local business people. Ruser complains quite moderately that he never actually wished to leave Spain and that it was only on the insistence of Thompson that he did so. Definite promises were made to him that he would be given his liberty in this country. He thinks that he should still be of great use to us to Spain and Portugal owing to the number of contacts that he has there outside the Abwehr, and he is quite prepared to go back if we provide him with some sort of papers which will prevent him from being picked up by a junior member of the Spanish police and expelled from the country. The usual practice of the Gestapo in dealing with a recalcitrant German is to arrange that his passport should not be renewed. Immediately it expires the Spanish police arrest the man and push him over the frontier in conjunction with the Gestapo. Ruser thinks, however, that the tide in Spain is beginning to turn in our favour, and that certainly the junior Spanish officers would not now be prepared to act in this way.

★ ★ ★

Oswald Job would be mentioned several times (see Chapters 10 and 18) and was relevant only because of his connection with DRAGONFLY. A Briton resident in Paris before the war, Job was interned during the Nazi occupation but released to act as a spy for the Abwehr in London. Betrayed by ISOS, Job was arrested in November 1943 in possession of a diamond-studded tie-pin that he had been instructed to hand over to DRAGONFLY. MI5's interrogation of Job proved sensitive because of the need to protect DRAGONFLY, who could also compromise FATHER and another valued double-agent. Having stuck to his cover story, and lied to his interrogators, Job was hanged at Pentonville in March 1944.

NINTH REPORT, 1 JANUARY 1944

MI5's ninth report covered six double-agents, of whom GARBO, MUTT and JEFF were familiar figures; it introduced a Catalan, LIPSTICK, and the Yugoslav FREAK as recent additions. Once again, MI5's role across the Empire was emphasised by references to the enemy spies Ernesto Hoppe, Diego Beltrán-Leiro and José Olivera arrested in Gibraltar, and to Basil Batos, an Abwehr agent recently detained in Kenya. The only other spy to be included, Guy Wijckaert, was a more conventional espionage suspect, having arrived in England as a refugee from occupied France.

NINTH REPORT

A <u>SPIES ARRESTED</u>

The three most interesting spies captured this month, and under examination at our special interrogation centre, are of Argentine or Spanish nationality.

The Argentinian is one Ernesto Hoppe, who though of Argentinian nationality is of German birth, and who was arrested on his way from Germany to the Argentine. He was known to have been given a mission by the German Secret Service, but for a considerable time after his capture, he strenuously denied all connection with the Germans. While he was undergoing treatment at the hospital, he managed to escape for a short period, and the somewhat unexpected result of his speedy re-capture was that he then confessed. It appears that the Germans had been preparing a scheme to take certain material to the Argentine by submarine and to land it at a lonely point on the coast south of Buenos Aires. Hoppe had not seen this material, but from conversations with his spymaster he understood it to be of three kinds. The first consisted of securities and cash which was being sent abroad by high Nazi officials to be invested in real estate in the Argentine.

The second was a wireless transmitter and other technical equipment, and the third important documents. The scheme put forward in the first instance was for Hoppe and a wireless operator to travel as passengers in the U-boat, but Hoppe refused to do this on account of his wife's health. As modified, the plan was that he should travel in advance by passenger boat and make the arrangements for the reception of the material and its disposal. The provisional date for the arrival of the U-boat was mid-February, but as the Germans know of Hoppe's capture it is thought that the plan will be dropped or substantially altered.[1]

The other two interesting arrests are those of two Spaniards, José Olivera and Diego Beltrán-Leiro, who were two wireless operators on Spanish ships plying between Spain and the Americas. These two men had been acting as couriers for the Germans for a considerable period. Olivera was reported to be carrying platinum as well as mail, but the platinum turned out to be lead discs of no value. The mail was a package of documents consisting for the most part of economic reports, but it also included certain material in code. The capture of Beltrán-Leiro produced even more interesting results. In addition to similar economic and political reports, he had two documents of particular value. One contains the names and particulars in cypher of a large number of German agents in the Argentine. The other was a private letter from the Head of Himmler's Secret Service in Buenos Aires to his opposite number in Madrid. In this letter the writer expresses his views freely on his relations with German Embassy officials in Buenos Aires and other personalities. It also appears from this letter that Beltrán-Leiro was regarded as the second best courier in the service of the Germans. It is hoped that an opportunity will shortly arise to capture the best man. A photograph is attached of some of the documents showing a page of the private letter, an example of the technical information, a graph showing wireless frequencies for secret communication with the Argentine, and the first page of the coded list of agencies, which code we can now read.

Another arrival at our special interrogation camp is Basil Batos, a Greek journalist, who has been known for a considerable tine as the Head of the organisation for collecting shipping reports for the German Consulate in Lourenço Marques. Batos was expelled from Portuguese East Africa and detained by us in Kenya, and has now been brought to this country, where he is under interrogation.

A young Belgian, aged 20, called Guy Wijckaert, has arrived here; he had been recruited by the German Secret Service, and trained to perform sabotage in this country. He was passed through France in the company of genuine escapers on a route which the Germans have penetrated, and was assisted by a German agent posing as an Allied helper. On arrival in Spain Wijckaert gave certain information to the authorities and his case is now being investigated with a view to extracting the fullest intelligence information from him, and to determine whether his story that he accepted the German proposals in order to escape to this country is likely to be true.

B DOUBLE-CROSS AGENTS

Our double-agent, LIPSTICK, returned to this country in the beginning of December, after a short visit to the Peninsula.

He brought with him a long questionnaire from his Secret Service masters containing nine micro-photographs in duplicate, which were in the form of spots gummed on to both ends of a silk spotted tie. This questionnaire dealt chiefly with technical matters relating to Radar and various forms of rocket propulsion. His trip appears to have been successful and he has built himself up in the eyes of the Germans. He also provided a certain amount of useful counter-espionage material.

An interesting exchange of messages dealing with CROSSBOW activities has been going on during the past month between GARBO and his German masters. GARBO has been instructed to make arrangements to move out of London. There is no indication, however, in the messages that they require him to take action immediately. This is borne out by the fact that, when GARBO suggested that he should remove his transmitter now so that it should not be destroyed, the Germans replied that they attached more importance to continuous contact with him for the present. In saying this they pointed out that in the next few months events of great importance would occur. It is probable from the context that this refers to the invasion of the Continent by the Allies.

A new agent, FREAK, has arrived in this country. He was a naval officer in Yugoslavia, and was brought over here under the instigation of double-agent TRICYCLE, and will, among other things, perform the duty of TRICYCLE's wireless operator in the United Kingdom. He came to this country from Yugoslavia, through the Peninsula, the journey being arranged by the German Secret Service. The cover story which he was supposed to tell us on arrival was a good one, and would have been difficult to break him. His main mission, it appears, was to contact Englishmen in high places and to impress upon them very strongly the view that Germany is open to approaches from this country with a view to stemming the flow of Communism across the Continent of Europe, and for this purpose they required the assistance of the British. He was not, of course, to make it appear that he was acting on behalf of the Germans, but was to report by wireless and secret writing the progress he was making in his task of influencing people in high places with this doctrine, to give the names of people who he found to be receptive of these ideas. The core of his instructions was that Germany was not to be forced to capitulate, but should be granted terms by this country to enable her to maintain a barrier in Eastern Europe against the Communist peril. It was emphasised that Germany was willing, in order to obtain these terms, to get rid of Hitler, to introduce a Democratic form of Government acceptable to the British and Americans, to withdraw from all Occupied Territory, and to accept Allied conditions about frontiers – provided Germany herself was not seriously touched. Apart from this mission, he was to obtain details about troop movements and concentrations and details about factory production. He was also required to try and find out details through his naval contacts about ship-building activities, convoy routes, and to attempt to obtain details of the Allied U-boat location apparatus. The officer who gave him these instructions was candid enough to explain that the object in asking for details about what ships arrived is in part out of a concern and what ships were sunk was because they were unable to rely on unconfirmed reports of U-boat Commanders.

Arrangements were made by the Germans to drop another consignment of sabotage equipment in Scotland to MUTT and JEFF. Owing to unsatisfactory weather conditions, the Germans postponed the operation.

1st January 1944

★ ★ ★

Of all the German agents accommodated at Camp 020, the 52-year-old Argentine Ernesto Hoppe may have been the most extraordinary, entrusted with one of the most remarkable espionage assignments ever.

Hoppe was betrayed by ISOS in September 1943 and SIS requested his arrest when he applied to the British consulate in Bilbao for a visa for him and his pregnant wife Ella to travel to Buenos Aires via Trinidad, so when his ship, the SS *Monte Albertia*, docked at Gibraltar, he was detained. According to six ISOS texts, Hoppe was code-named HEROLD and was on an unknown mission to his adopted country, where SIS had received other reports about his role as a senior figure in the local SS. According to the US Office of Naval Intelligence, Hoppe, who described himself as the proprietor of a thriving driving school business in Buenos Aires, had been recruited by the Abwehr in 1936 and had been a full-time agent ever since, travelling pre-war to Austria and Czechoslovakia, and in Holland just before the German invasion.

After a fortnight of interrogation on Gibraltar, Hoppe was flown by the RAF to Lyneham via Portreath on 28 October and escorted to Camp 020. In his initial statement Hoppe confirmed that he had been born in Brandenburg, near Berlin, and had emigrated to Argentina in 1908 when he was 16, but denied any connection with Nazi espionage. However, after a month at Latchmere House he changed his story and made a detailed confession. His conversion had been prompted by his brief escape, while staying at a hospital in Woolwich, for medical treatment. He was at liberty for just two and a half hours, when he was able to post several letters, one of which was addressed to the Argentine ambassador in London. When it became apparent that the embassy would not assist Hoppe, he underwent a change of heart and described how he had been recruited by a Luftwaffe officer, Colonel Rosenstretter, and instructed to prepare a landing place at a remote site on the Argentine coast for a U-boat to land contraband.

Hoppe's account of Colonel Rosenstretter's plan to use a U-boat for the transport of certain cases to the Argentine, and the part Hoppe was expected to take in its execution, is as follows:

It was intended to ship various cases to the Argentine by U-boat and land them secretly on the coast during the Carnival period (Shrove Monday and Tuesday, 21st/22nd February 1944). This time was chosen because there would be much traffic on the coast roads during this festival and transport connected with the landing would be less likely to arouse suspicion.

The cases were already lying at the Censor's Office in Bordeaux. They would be marked 'A', 'B' and 'C'. Those marked 'A' were to be handed over to a bank (probably the Banco Aleman, Buenos Aires.) Those marked 'B' would also bear the word 'Vorsicht' ('With Care') and were to be delivered to the Villa Balestero, some 8 kilometres outside Buenos Aires, owned by the Brothers Schmidt. Those marked 'C' were to be delivered to Herr Baumgarten, at an address in the Florida District of Buenos Aires. The number of cases was not specified, but Hoppe thinks there would probably be about forty. The contents of the cases marked 'C', Rosenstretter said, were politically the most dangerous and would be of corresponding value to the British. Hoppe assumes that important Party documents were referred to whereas the other cases might contain bonds, gold, jewellery and foreign exchange. In addition, there would be a wireless transmitter in a suitcase and a microphotographic apparatus. These were to be handled especially carefully.

The U-Boat was to land its cargo at a point off the Argentine coast, possibly off El Rancho, some 180 kilometres south-west of Buenos Aires. At the point of landing the cases would be loaded on to a three ton lorry, the wireless and photographic apparatus being transported in a private car. Hoppe would travel in advance by boat. His job would be to give advice and assistance in the arrangements for the transport of the cargo from the beach. This would need to be done by a man well acquainted with the coast, able to provide labour and mechanised transport discreetly, after a previous study of the sea depths and the state of tides and moon at the place and time of landing.

On arrival in the Argentine, Hoppe would be contacted by a man, presumably the individual to whom he was to deliver the package entrusted to him by Rosenstretter. This man would use a password 'vengo para tomar leccion, dene la hora' (I have come for a lesson, give me the time) and, although in charge of the operation at that end, would have to keep in the background. It was essential, therefore, that Hoppe should be well versed in their needs, in case he had to work on his own.

From the fact that Rosenstreter several times hinted that a Herr Imhof of the German embassy in Buenos Aires was a man whom Hoppe could always trust, Hoppe presumed that Filip Imhof would be the man in question. From various remarks let fall, Hoppe knew the wireless operator at the German embassy and that he signed his wireless messages PATIO. The suitcase containing the wireless transmitter, which Hoppe was to handle with care and deliver either to Baumgarten or to the brothers Schmidt, would be for Imhof to collect.

As a safeguard against the discovery of Hoppe's identity, the cover name HEROLD would be used by the Germans in all their communications concerning him to the Argentine.

The U-boat would take two passengers. Since Hoppe had turned down the proposal to travel in it, some other unspecified agent was to take his place.

The man who was to have been Hoppe's companion on board, and who was to go in any case, was one of Germany's most expert W/T operators. Hoppe understood that this man had also received training in microphotography and the making of full-stops, and that the microphotographic apparatus to be part of the U-boat's cargo was for his use.

Hoppe cannot recall this man's name, if he ever heard it, although he was told many facts about him. Apparently he was of an adventurous type who had already returned to Germany from a mission in one of the South American republics, where 'he had blown up a radio mast'. He had fought in the Spanish War with the Condor Air Legion.

From his South American mission he was supposed to have returned to Germany via Japan and Russia and held then a good position at the German Foreign Ministry in Berlin. Part of Hoppe's job was to procure identity papers and a safe lodging for this man on arrival. This, Hoppe said, would have been a comparatively easy matter, for – at a price – anyone could obtain false identity papers in the provincial towns in the Argentine. At the time Hoppe left Germany, this agent was still in Berlin, Hoppe says he was told nothing about the second passenger and it may have been that this man had not been decided on at the time of Hoppe's departure. Further duties expected of Hoppe concerned the reward to the U-boat crew. He was to prepare some fifty attaché cases for the fifty members of the crew – first packing them with tea, coffee and cigarettes – to the value of 50 Pesos each. He was to advance the money, Pesos 2,500, and present a bill for this, plus his other outlay, and would receive, he presumes through the German Embassy, the full amount plus a substantial 'present' for himself. A further inducement was held out to him at this time by Rosenstreter when discussing plans. It was intimated to him that there would be large purchases of land undertaken in the Argentine, that Hoppe's services would be needed, whereby he would earn large sums in commission.

Hoppe was naturally never told the exact value of the U-boat's cargo which he was to handle, but he thinks it could not have been less than 10,000,000 Marks. While discussing this subject, Hoppe volunteered the information that there were no jewels or jewellery left today in Germany or any of the occupied countries of Europe. Rosenstreter's suggestion that Hoppe should go to Bordeaux and stay there, at the Germans' expense, until it was time for him to go on to Bilbao, was refused by Hoppe.

Hoppe makes it clear that the plan to send a U-boat was still in its infancy when he left Germany and he can only presume that if it materialises the boat will carry the two unnamed agents mentioned above.

Possibility: At El Rancho there is no village but merely a restaurant and a cluster of out-buildings, built in Indian style. It lies about half a mile from the coastal road and between the restaurant and the sea proper. For a distance of some 600 yards, there is swampy land with grass and bushes, dangerous to traverse save on the footpaths.

For what it is worth, Hoppe's opinion is that a landing at El Rancho would not be possible because the transport of forty cases would be extremely difficult across the marshy ground adjoining the shore.

Plenty of other places would be more suitable, Hoppe says, and there are numerous estates belonging to Germans and pro-Axis Argentines scattered along the coast. The owner of El Rancho, Emil Fuchs, an Austrian born in the Argentine, is known to Hoppe, who recalls excursions to this picnic resort in 1935, 1937 and 1938. He describes Fuchs as a dark, Spanish-looking type, active as a smuggler and owner of small boats which met ships lying off-shore.

It came out in conversation with Rosenstreter that an earlier U-boat trip had been made, but the date of this voyage was not mentioned. On this occasion a wireless transmitter had been put ashore at El Rancho; it had fallen into the water in transit and had subsequently not functioned well. The set to be taken on Hoppe's U-boat was intended to replace this damaged apparatus. This first U-boat had used a landing point approximately opposite El Rancho and, in view of its rather doubtful suitability, a final decision on the second U-boat's objective was to depend on Hoppe's information, after he had personally investigated and made soundings along the coast. That information would probably be sent by wireless to Germany.

The foregoing outline of Rosenstreter's U-boat scheme covers the information obtained from Hoppe and mention should here be made of the reasons Rosenstreter gave for choosing him for an important part in it. According to Hoppe, Rosenstreter told him that his information from Buenos Aires on Hoppe was that he was a lukewarm Nazi, but a sound and independent man of business. When it was pointed out to Hoppe that this was scarcely sufficient reason for the Germans to trust him with such an important and secret mission, Hoppe said that his importance in the scheme was being over-estimated; he was merely to be the intermediary and his particular job was actually little more than that of a better-class chauffeur.

Rosenstreter picked on Hoppe firstly because, being financially independent, he was unlikely to keep asking for money and would be more free to work for them in the Argentine than if he were a man with a business to look after. Lastly, Hoppe was a motor expert and knew the roads and coastline of the Argentine well. Hoppe thinks Rosenstreter heard possibly from Rienhard Schroeder about his (Hoppe's) knowledge of the coastline, but this is a guess only on Hoppe's part. Hoppe states emphatically that he was never taught to communicate in secret writing, nor did he know or receive instruction in wireless transmission. He says he knows nothing about microphotography beyond what he has read or seen in shops. He points out always that the time that elapsed between his first meeting with Rosenstreter and his departure from Germany was much too short to have enabled him to receive any useful knowledge on these subjects. His mission, had he carried it out, he says, would not have involved any correspondence with Germany and he admits to no cover addresses.

During his examination here, Hoppe has repeatedly stated that from the time of his first contact with Rosenstreter he had no intention of carrying out the latter's plan. To support this declaration he mentions the hiding of the sealed tin given him by Rosenstreter. Hoppe concealed a packet, handed to him in Bilbao by an emissary of Rosenstreter, in a junk room on board the *Monte Albertia*. When asked what then his intentions were, Hoppe said that he would have betrayed the whole matter to the Argentine government, after he had obtained information as to the time and place of arrival of the U-boat. This would presumably have meant that Hoppe would have perforce, in order to get that information, carried out Rosenstreter's instructions up to a certain point at least. On the one hand, Hoppe was to benefit considerably if he performed the job expected of him by the Germans, namely by a monetary reward and subsequent commissions on the purchase of land for his Nazi employers. On the other hand, by betraying contraband to the Argentine government to the tune of 10,000,000 Marks, he would be entitled by Argentine law to 10% of that sum.

Hoppe remained in custody until October 1945 when he was repatriated, together with Oscar Liehr, on the SS *Deseado*, which sailed from Liverpool for Buenos Aires.

★ ★ ★

José Olivera del Rio was a highly motivated ship's telegraphist whose Spanish vessel, the SS *Habana*, en route from Buenos Aires to Teneriffe, was stopped at sea in October 1943 by a Dutch patrol vessel, the *Johann Mauritius*, operating from Curaçao. The initial identification of Olivera had come in late 1941 from a double-agent in Buenos Aires, Jesus Aguilar, and it was only when it sounded as though the courier was likely to be carrying codebooks, secret correspondence and a quantity of some mysterious metal to Spain that the decision was taken to intercept him. On 7 November Olivera was flown from Gibraltar to Lyneham and transferred to Camp 020 for questioning.

Under interrogation, and after some initial resistance, Olivera made a very full statement and described how he had been recruited by the Abwehr after he had served as a radio operator attached to a squadron of Junkers bombers, part of the Condor Legion, during the Spanish Civil War. There he had worked with Otto Hinrischen, who was later to stay in Bilbao on behalf of the Abwehr. Hinrischen had suggested he collect information on Allied shipping and act as a courier, and they had used another contact, Carlos Imaz, as an intermediary. Unfortunately, at the time of his arrest, no codebooks had been recovered, and it was not until his final confession at Camp 020 that his hiding place was revealed. He had concealed a bag of material behind the reflector of his ship's starboard running lights, and when this was retrieved the contents proved to be of exceptional value.

When asked about Diego Beltrán-Leiro, whom he never realised had also been detained at Camp 020, Olivera acknowledged that he too was in the pay of the Germans, but refused to say anything more about anyone else. This, nevertheless, was further evidence that was used to good effect against Beltrán-Leiro. Olivera also admitted that he had been on the payroll of the Italian Servizio Internazionale Militare (SIM) which had recruited him in August 1942 during a visit to Seville while he was working aboard the *Motimar*, and given the code name RODOLFO. He was invited by the local Italian consul to collect information during his imminent voyage to Baltimore, and to obtain a copy of Lloyds' *Register of Shipping*.

When his ship returned in October from Baltimore and Philadelphia, Olivera had submitted a report to Hinrischen in Bilbao, and then the following month gave the same material to his Italian contact in Seville. His last voyage on the *Motimar* was in December to Philadephia, returning to Cádiz in January. He signed off the *Motimar* in February 1943, and joined the *Habana* as second officer in May in Bilbao, bound for New Orleans. His ship returned to Barcelona in July, and then sailed for Buenos Aires in August.

As for Jesus Aguilar, the double-agent who had given the tip about Olivera, he was a cabin steward on the *Cabo de Buena Esperanza*, and had proved useful in alerting the DSO in Trinidad to passengers whom he had been paid by the Abwehr to keep an eye on. He and the ship's pastry chef, Bernardino Solana, were low-level agents who were typical of those working for the Germans on the route between Argentina and Europe. Some were employed to carry messages and compile shipping reports, especially in enemy ports, while others, like Aguilar, fulfilled the role of minder, keeping an eye on important passengers. It had been Aguilar, supported by ISOS intercepts, who had alerted MI5 to the mission of Andrés Blay, Paraguay's consul-general in Barcelona. Blay had developed a good trade in selling his country's passports and visas to desperate refugees, but had also acquired some financial problems. Before they embarked at Bilbao, Aguilar knew Blay was working for the Abwehr, so when the *Cabo de Buena Esperanza* reached Trinidad in September 1942 he was detained. Although nothing incriminating was found in his cabin, when Blay himself was searched, despite his protests of his diplomatic status, a small packet was found stitched behind his fly-buttons. Inside was a letter of introduction addressed to the Spanish consul-general in Buenos Aires, seeking him to supply Blay with courier facilities, and signed by Joaquin Baticón, another Ybarra Line steward and Abwehr agent already known to MI5. Blay was promptly shipped to England for interrogation at Camp 020 where the questions, based on ISOS material, proved rather more difficult to evade, and he made a confession, naming his Abwehr contact as Horst Müller of the German consulate-general in Barcelona.

The real significance of Blay's statement was the light it shed on the activities of the Spanish intelligence service, which was known to be extremely active in Buenos Aires, although little was known about another organisation believed to be Franco's personal intelligence service, which concentrated on political issues.

Baticón himself was arrested in Trinidad in February 1943 and his statement, combined with Blay's confession and ISOS information, led to the arrest of three more Ybarra stewards between June and August 1943 and, most significantly, to the capture of a valued prize, Manuel Perez, the Spanish police attaché in Buenos Aires.

★ ★ ★

On 6 December 1943 Diego Beltrán-Leiro, a wireless operator on the SS *Monte Monjuich*, sailing from Buenos Aires, was arrested when his ship was stopped at the Strairs of Gibraltar by the anti-submarine trawler HMS *Lady Hogarth* and escorted into the dockyard. A fortnight later Beltrán-Leiro was flown to Whitchurch for interrogation at Camp 020. According to Herbert Hart's analysis of the ISOS traffic, Beltrán-Leiro had been recruited by the Abwehr two years earlier, and when his vessel was rummaged some incriminating documents and mircodots, some of them dealing with secret radio-location apparatus, were recovered from a ventilator. His SD controller, Hauptsturmführer Johannes Becker, considered Beltrán his 'best and most trustworthy man', apart from a courier code-named BRAVO. Four rolls of photographic film, amounting to eighty-eight frames, were also retrieved from inside the ship's wireless transmitter, to which only Beltrán-Leiro had access. When his cache of papers was studied in London it revealed details, including code names and cover addresses, of some forty hitherto unknown German spies in South America. There were also photographs of various Germans, including Becker and another character, Hans Harnisch, and a lengthy report on the Hellmuth affair, blaming various members of the embassy staff for the fiasco.

Quite apart from the ISOS evidence, MI5 had acquired a statement from Olivero incriminating Beltrán-Leiro, which served to settle the matter of his seizure on the high seas by the Admiralty upon his return to Europe. When questioned the 23-year-old Beltrán-Leiro, code-named GORRA and usually based in Vigo, immediately offered a confession. Formerly a radio operator in the Spanish navy, Beltrán-Leiro admitted having been recruited by the Germans in November 1941 and had successfully completed six missions. For this he had received 1,000 pesetas from an intermediary, Carlos Fuentes, later identified as an alias adopted by a known Abwehr officer, Fritz Furch. SIS would eventually identify BRAVO as Cuevas Mins, a seaman serving on the SS *Rita Garcia*.

Beltrán-Leiro was kept in custody until August 1945, when he was escorted to Portsmouth to embark on HMS *Glasgow* for his release in Gibraltar.

★ ★ ★

In August 1943 Basil Batos, a Greek Communist and journalist, was expelled from Portuguese East Africa, having been identified in ISOS traffic as an Axis spy engaged in the collecting of shipping information for the Italian consul Umberto Campini, which was delivered to a bookshop, Cardoso & Cardoso, in the rua Salazar. ISOS revealed that since July 1942 Batos had receved £15 a month for his material, supplied under the code name LEO. He had also been seen associating with a German, Alois Muellner, although ISOS suggested a link with Otto Werz or the German consul, Paul Tromke. The SIS representative in Lourenço Marques, Malcolm Muggeridge,[2] tipped off the local police about Batos's alleged communism, and this resulted in his expulsion, ostensibly to Turkey via Egypt. Accordingly, when Batos reached Mombasa by the Imperial Airways flying-boat *Castor* he was arrested by the Kenyan police and questioned at Nairobi prison.

Aged 52, Batos was married to an Englishwoman, Mary O'Neill, had lived in New York, and had a 23-year-old son, Richard, in the US Navy. He reached Glasgow on the P&O liner *Rampura* in December and was escorted to Camp 020, where he was interrogated. However, when questioned Batos denied any involvement with espionage and, in the absence of a confession, was kept in custody until July 1945, when he was served with a deportation order and flown to Athens.

★ ★ ★

At the time Petrie presented a brief account of Guy Wijckaert's arrival in England he had only been in British custody at Camp 020 for a few days, and Churchill was never given the full story.

When Wijckaert turned up at the Belgian consulate in Barcelona he admitted that he had been recruited by the Germans, but insisted that he had pretended to collaborate as a means to escape from the occupation. Certainly his role as a spy had been compromised already, but when he was questioned he made significant omissions relating to his intended Abwehr assignment, to undertake sabotage in England, Canada or Africa, and was untruthful about the payments he had received. After a period of interrogation he reluctantly revealed three cover addresses and admitted to the large sums he had been paid. He also conceded that after he had visited the Barcelona consulate he had mailed a letter to an intermediary to inform the Germans that he had begun his journey to England. In his defence Wijckaert claimed that he had adopted this course to ensure continued payments to his father in Belgium, but his lack of candour meant he would remain in detention for the next two years.

★ ★ ★

LIPSTICK was Josef Terradellas, a Catalan separatist who was sent by the Abwehr to England in November 1942. He declared his mission and his secret writing instructions to the SIS station in Madrid before his departure, and was managed until December 1944 by MI5, although his political activism became increasingly embarrassing to his handlers.

★ ★ ★

FREAK was Marquis Frano de Bona, an aristocrat from Dubrovnik and an old family friend of the Popovs. De Bona had undergone an Abwehr training course in the use of secret ink and Morse, and had also been provided with a radio transmitter that he handed over when he was welcomed to Madrid by Dusan Popov. The Marquis eventually reached London via Gibraltar in December 1943, where he was assigned the cryptonym FREAK by MI5, and began using his wireless to signal his German controllers as soon as Popov returned from Lisbon the following month. Holding the rank of commander in the Yugoslav navy, de Bona joined the King's entourage, and maintained radio contact under MI5's supervision with the Abwehr in Paris, and then Hamburg, until May 1944, acting as Popov's wireless operator. On 24 February 1944 Liddell recorded in his diary:

FREAK has got through satisfactorily. The fact that the enemy put two stations on to the job of receiving his traffic confirms that they regard it as of the greatest importance.

After the war de Bona moved to Trieste, and he died in 1991.

TENTH REPORT, I FEBRUARY 1944

In this report, covering three months of MI5 activity, Petrie makes oblique references to Oswald Job, earlier identified in Chapter 8 by name, who was mentioned as having been sentenced to hang at his trial on 24 January 1944, and the two Gibraltar saboteurs, Luis Cordon-Cuenca and José Muñoz. The case of Hellmuth, previously mentioned in the Seventh Report, was touched on, and GARBO, introduced in Chapter 3, was trumpeted as a double-agent of growing significance.[1] Thus, at this critical juncture of the war, MI5's first report after an accumulated period of silence contained very little of substance and only the most fleeting of references to TRICYCLE's triumphant return to London in September 1943.

NOVEMBER, DECEMBER AND JANUARY

During the last three months five new spies have been arrested, one of whom has recently been condemned to death. Three new special agents have been brought to this country and two Spanish saboteurs have been executed in Gibraltar. The Germans have made five attempts at sabotage, most of them unsuccessful.

Of the spies who have recently been arrested, two are of particular importance. The first is of interest on the grounds that he is a British subject, although of German origin. He was detected in a somewhat unusual way owing to the fact that he was carrying jewellery for which we had been on the look-out as the Germans had promised to send it to one of our special agents in this country. This man, who turned out also to have a spy mission of his own, has now been prosecuted under the Treachery Act and condemned to death.[2]

The second spy, Hellmuth, whose arrest has been mentioned in the Press, is of interest from the political point of view. He was arrested while carrying out a mission to Europe for General Ramirez and other extreme Fascist elements in the Argentine Government in collusion with Himmler's special Secret Service. He had been promised an interview with Himmler, and if possible with Hitler, in order to carry out certain clandestine political and economic negotiations of which the German Embassy in Buenos Aires was unaware. The statements obtained from him by the Security Service have led to noteworthy political developments.

Considerable political significance also attaches to recent German sabotage attempts in Spain. The main object of the German Sabotage Service recently has been the sabotaging of Italian merchant ships in Spanish ports with some measure of success. An attempt on a British ship was, however, frustrated by the preventive measures of the Security Service. The Germans have, as has been reported in the Press, also attempted sabotage on cargoes of oranges to this country. Four of the bombs which had been placed in the oranges exploded on board ship, and the fifth was finally located in a case of onions in Kettering. This bomb, which was still active and of a formidable character, was dismantled by a member of the Security Service. In view of the attempt by the Spanish Government to deny that the Germans were responsible for this sabotage it is of interest to note that the intact specimen secured at Kettering is clearly of German origin. Two German saboteurs have, moreover, recently been executed at Gibraltar, and it is known that one of them was acting for serving Spanish officers who themselves were working for the Germans. A strong memorandum has been prepared by SIS and the Security Service, and it is understood that this is being presented to the Spanish Government, which is being pressed to expel from Spain the German saboteurs known to us by name. We have lately obtained from a recently arrived Italian spy information about the organisation which Himmler has prepared to operate sabotage and espionage behind the Allied lines in Italy.[3]

Our special agents have also been active. Several new ones have arrived, some with instructions to obtain technical information, and one with a political mission. This was a Yugoslav naval officer whose object was to explore the possibility of gaining sympathy for Germany in British circles on an anti-Communist basis.[4]

Two of our long-standing special agents have recently returned to this country after a visit to the Peninsula with large sums of money, detailed and instructive questionnaires, new contacts, and reputations apparently greatly enhanced in the eyes of the Germans.[5]

GARBO has been probing German intentions over CROSSBOW. He has been instructed to make arrangements to move out of London, but the Germans do not appear to think that much action will be necessary immediately.

Some light has been thrown on morale in the Nazi party by the confession of another character who recently fell into our hands. He was engaged in arranging to transport to the Argentine by submarine securities and cash to be invested in real estate for certain high Nazi officials.

1st February 1944

★ ★ ★

The reference to a German sabotage device defused in Kettering was one of the more remarkable episodes of the war, and created great controversy within the Security Service. Guy Liddell provded the details on 2 February 1944:

Victor Rothschild rang up to say that he had just dismantled a bomb found in a case of onions at Kettering. This bomb consisted of a number of blocks of TNT, and two German time clocks enclosed in plastic. Owing to some mechanical defect, the clocks had stopped, but on getting a bump in course of transit from the docks one of them had re-started and would have gone off in seven days. Meanwhile, Peter Hope has been ringing up from Newcastle. He says that the Chief Constable is slightly annoyed that he was never told about the explosions in the orange ships *Stanhope* and *Haywood*. He is worried about some 3,000 cases which are still on the quay and also about the remaining 7,000 cases which have been distributed throughout the UK down to retailers. He was thinking of communicating with Home Office in order that all these cases could be traced and ripped open. I told him to calm the Chief Constable down since we had reason to think that there would be no further explosions (ISOS had disclosed that there were five bombs. Three went off on the *Stanhope* and one on the *Haywood*. The discovery of the fifth, therefore, account for them all). I told Hope that he could also tell the Chief Constable that the chances of anymore bombs going off now was remote owing to the time factor, and that in any case the public had been warned in the press and would doubtless report any suspicious circumstances to the police.

The details of this incident became known quite widely, mainly because a transcript of Rothschild's commentary, dictated remotely over a field telephone to his secretary Tess Mayer (whom he later married) mysteriously circulated and resulted in the recommendation by the Chief Constable of Northamptonshire for a decoration. This caused controversy and adverse comment within the Security Service, where by convention individual acts go without public recognition, but Churchill had intervened and approved the award of the George Medal, which was gazetted on 4 April 1944 'for dangerous work in hazardous circumstances'.[6]

According to Kenneth Rose's discredited 2003 biography *Elusive Rothschild*,[7] the decoration was personally recommended by Churchill, who had been so impressed by the account of his bravery given in Petrie's report that he had asked his military aide, General Ismay, to make further enquiries, which had elicited the name of the gallant officer, but this version is quite at odds with the recollection of MI5's staff at the time.

What makes this particular report so unusual is that it is studiously vague, and only refers to cases of espionage that had been covered by earlier reports, such as Hellmuth, who is described as though for the first time. Similarly, the Italian SD spy was Manfredo de Blasis, although his case would not be described until the following year (Chapter 23).

11

NINTH REPORT, 7 MARCH 1944*

In his report, dated 7 March 1944, Petrie concentrated on Belgian spies, but described a strange twist to TRICYCLE's adventures, as previously mentioned in Chapters 5, 6 and 7, which had referred to him as a Yugoslav who had spent a long period in the United States.

A. SPIES.

1. Eleven German agents have been taken into custody during the past month. Of these six were Belgians. The two most interesting specimens were a Belgian, Pierre Neukermans, an agent of the Abwehr (German Military Intelligence) and a Dutchman Aben, an agent of the SD (Himmler's organisation). Both were spies of long standing. The former had first served the Germans during the winter of 1939 as a casual informant in the matter of Belgian troop movements. More recently he had formed part of the network of agents along the Belgian coast designed by the Germans to operate in the event of an Allied landing. The latter, Aben, had been an agent of the SD and the German Security Police since April 1942.

2. Neukermans arrived in this country as an escaper on 17 July 1943. He had travelled from Belgium through France and the Peninsula with two compatriots, Omer Sevenans and Roger Louant. There was nothing abnormal in their story and after the customary interrogation the three were released. Some while afterwards a captured spy under interrogation mentioned these three men as among those whose escape from Belgium had been forwarded by one Louis de Bray, an organiser of spurious escape

---

*   There are two ninth reports!

routes on the Germans' behalf, with whom we had long been familiar. An examination of the files show that Neukermans, Sevenans and Louant had in fact been assisted on the first stage of their journey by a certain LUIS whom we were now able to identify with Louis de Bray. The three were, therefore, detained and under further interrogation Neukermans confessed to being a German agent.

3. Neukermans further admitted that since his arrival in England he had written nine letters in secret ink to cover addresses in the Peninsula. These had contained accurate information about the disposition of Belgian forces in this country and other less accurate information about convoy movements and public morale which Neukermans had either invented or derived from the press. So far as we can ascertain the sum of all this information cannot have been of great value to the enemy.

4. This episode shows that it is possible for a spy who has evaded capture on his arrival to follow his trade at least for some months without detection. This immunity depends to a great extent on the spy's willingness to avoid risks and not to seek information beyond what comes naturally under his daily notice. If by routine security measures he can be denied access to those parts of the country where vital information about forthcoming operations is to be had, his activities will be an irritant rather than a menace.

5. The Dutchman Franciscus Aben was the Master of a vessel plying between Sweden and Delfzijl in Holland. He was employed as a courier by certain Dutch resistance organisations in which both SIS and SOE were interested. He was also engaged in smuggling Allied agents and other persons in and out of Holland. After he had been occupied in this manner for some while Aben was denounced by members of an Allied organisation in Sweden. At the same time he had the misfortune to entangle himself in a love affair of which murder appeared the most probable outcome. For these reasons he was invited to withdraw to England.

6. Aben arrived here on board his own vessel. When this boat was rummaged at the port two things were discovered: a paper showing Aben to be employed by the German Security Police and a code characteristic of the SD. When Aben was confronted with these documents he confessed to being a German agent and to having been employed to penetrate and inform against the Dutch resistance organisation whose courier he had been. We anticipate

that his further interrogation will provide valuable information about the combating of resistance groups in Holland and the extent to which they are known to, or have been penetrated by, the Germans.

Job, the German spy of British nationality mentioned in our last report, has been sentenced to death at the Old Bailey. He appealed, but the appeal was dismissed.

B. SABOTAGE.

1. We are informed from most secret sources that the sabotage department of the Abwehr has recently been collecting British and American uniforms on the Italian front. A number of these have been sent to Abwehr Stations in France. It is reasonable to assume that they are intended for use in the event of an Allied landing.

The possibility also exists that the Abwehr may anticipate this event by attempting to introduce into the UK agents disguised as British or American soldiers. Any such agents will, of necessity, be landed by parachute or by boat and will be subject to many of the same disabilities as previous clandestine arrivals of this kind.

2. The representations recently made to the Spanish Government and the Press campaign which followed the discovery of bombs in crates of oranges and onions reaching this country from Spain have had their effect. The officer in charge of the Abwehr sabotage department has now issued an order forbidding any further sabotage in Spain particularly if it is directed against Allied shipping. The Abwehr station in Madrid is, therefore, withdrawing the sabotage equipment of the various out-stations in Spain and returning it to Germany. Two sabotage organisations will, however, remain. First a German controlled network of Spanish agents who are to operate in the event of an Allied invasion or a withdrawal of the German organisation proper. Secondly an independent organisation composed entirely of certain Falangists who are fiercely anti-British and anxious to impede or overturn General Franco's present policy of reconciliation. This organisation will devote its attention to Gibraltar.

It has already been penetrated by agents in our employ and will continue to receive our careful attention.

C. SPECIAL AGENTS.

1. TRICYCLE, a special agent already described in earlier reports, has returned to Lisbon to report to his German employers. He was provided with a quantity of tendentious information of apparent importance and we

are informed that his first interview with his spymasters passed off in a most satisfactory manner. A slight complication has, however, been introduced into his affairs by the fact that his principal spy master is himself now acting as a British agent. This individual's zeal and ability in a new role has verged upon the embarrassing. He has begun to provide us with information about the networks of agents maintained by the Germans in this country. Of these it appears that the principal one is the GARBO organisation of which it is clearly undesirable that he should make us too fully aware. We are engaged at the moment in the delicate operation of diverting this valuable agent's attention elsewhere. There is good promise of success.

2. We hope that two further special agents will presently be provided with wireless transmitters. The agent TREASURE has recently left for Lisbon where we anticipate that she will be given a transmitter to bring back to this country. The agent BRUTUS is at the moment discussing by wireless with the Abwehr station in Paris the dropping of a fresh set and a new code by parachute.

D. SECURITY MEASURES.
1. A member of a firm of Cartographers engaged in drawing maps for use in impending operations saw fit to draw upon his knowledge of these matters during a discussion of the Second Front in a London hotel. He has since been taken sternly to task and measures are in hand to ensure that he will not know whether or not his deductions were correct.

2. A letter bearing the impress BIGOT from COHQ to an address in Cambridge came into the hands of the 'Return letter section' of the GPO as it had been wrongly addressed. Investigation has shown that the matters with which the letter dealt have not been compromised by this event and steps have been taken to ensure that it will not be repeated.

3. An engineer, who divulging to an Army officer in a hotel information about PLUTO that he had acquired in the course of his duties, has been prosecuted and been fined £60 with 16 guineas costs.

4. A Trades Union despatched to various addresses in the UK/Eire copies of the minutes of a committee meeting at which measures had been discussed for consolidating the production of Phoenix and particulars given of this device. The single copy of this document which was addressed to Eire was

intercepted in censorship. Arrangements have now been taken, devised by the Home Secretary and executed by an officer of MI5 to recover all the copies discreetly, and have now been carried into effect.

7th March 1944

★ ★ ★

A Belgian pilot, Pierre Neukermans, was sent to England as a refugee to spy for the Abwehr. He had served as an Belgian army officer and claimed to have engineered his own escape to London, arriving in July 1943. Cleared and allowed to re-enlist with the Belgian forces, he had peddled a plausible story of his escape from Belgium to Spain, but in December 1943 SIS learned from a source in Lisbon that the group in which Neukermans had moved across France had contained a spy. SIS traced the other two members of Neukermans' party and concluded that he was the spy. MI5 interviewed him, having traced ISOS references to a source who had written eleven messages in secret writing, and he confessed that he had worked for the Abwehr since 1939. On 4 February 1944 Guy Liddell recorded in his diary that Neukermans:

> … had a good cover story and was extremely skilful under cross-examination. He was later denounced by Wyckaert and brought back. He has since confessed not only that he got his secret ink through the London Reception Centre and communicated with the Germans but that he had other means of communication if all others broken down, i.e. transmitting from an aircraft in flight. Neukermans is a Belgian and a trained pilot.

Under interrogation Neukermans revealed how he had succeeded in taking secret ink undetected through MI5's screening, and had reported his safe arrival to the Germans in two letters that had been passed by censorship, even though the cover addresses had been on the suspect index. At his trial Neukermans pleaded insanity, but was convicted and executed at Pentonville in June 1944.

★ ★ ★

For two years before his arrival in England Franciscus Aben worked as an SD penetration agent for the organisation's chief in The Hague, Hauptsturmführer Walter W. Müller, infiltrating SIS, SOE and Dutch networks that in July 1943 he betrayed, sending their membership into German captivity and, in many cases, death. One of his victims was Gevers Deynoot, a former police chief in The Hague who was also a leader of the 'WIM' resistance movement, and another was Dr Oosterhuis of Haaren. Both men had been accidentally compromised by the Dutch Consul in Stockholm, de Jong, who had taken up Aben's offer to act as a courier in March 1943 when he had produced what appeared to be good references to confirm his loyalty. On that occasion Aben claimed to be in contact with a Baron van Asch, an American living in The Hague, and supposedly a significant figure in the resistance. Aben also declared his willingness to exfiltrate individual escapees at a rate of 5,000 kroner each. A further detainee was a contact in Delfzijl named Zwaantje, who disappeared into a German prison.

Aben, a former Dutch Nazi Party member and Holland–America Line officer, had been identified as a Gestapo agent in September 1943 when the SIS station in Stockholm was informed that he was intending to sail to Westervik with a stowaway, Anton van der Waals, who was also a notorious German spy known to have used the aliases de Wilde and Baron van Lynden. Allegedly their 'escape' across the Baltic had been sponsored by the Germans. After their arrival van der Waals asserted that he was the organiser of a large resistance movement, and demanded to be put in touch with British Intelligence in London.

As the owner of a 194-ton Groningen coaster, the SS *Excelsior*, plying between Delfzijl and Sweden, he was given the task of collecting political intelligence, especially relating to the Dutch resistance, and arranged through the deliberate sabotage of his ship to spend some months developing local contacts. He then acted as a courier, passing messages to and from the Netherlands, which he shared with the SD, leading to the arrest of the leadership and the infiltration of other SD *agent provocateurs*. The result was the wholesale destruction of two circuits, although Aben himself talked his way out of complicity. However, one of those who denounced him to SIS demanded that he be removed to England without allowing him to make a return voyage to Holland, making a very credible threat to murder him if he remained in Sweden.

Suspicion had been aroused when Aben tried to expand his activities by investing in Nettogvist, a ship's chandlery business, and introduced as a new personality, he was invited to England in the pretext of receiving the thanks of the government in exile. In his absence his ship was searched and a highly incriminating letter was discovered, signed by a German officer named Mueller, who confirmed that Aben was 'a member of the Dienstelle'. The document, intended as a pass to ensure the cooperation of any German naval authorities, had been found among the possessions of Aben's second mate, Gerhardus van der Moolen.

Upon his arrival at RAF Leuchars on 30 January 1944 he was arrested and interrogated at Camp 020, where he was confronted with evidence that his employee, van der Moolen, had been recruited by the SD on his recommendation. As soon as he saw Mueller's *laisser-passez* he confessed and admitted that he had been recruited by Müller in April 1942 to work for the Sipo, and in March 1943 had been taken to Berlin to meet an SD Amt VI officer, Seidler, and his assistant, Werner Hoose. As well as acting as an informer, compromising all those he smuggled to Sweden and more besides, he attended a radio course at Scheveningen and had been instructed to send a warning about any impending invasion over a high-powered transmitter installed for the purpose on his ship. As Aben revealed the scale of his treachery, MI5 circulated SIS and SOE with the grim news on 27 April 1944:

WIM and ZWANTJE Organisations appear badly blown.
A certain Cohen of the WIM Organisation was arrested in Brussels. He was broken under interrogation and blew ZWANTJE I. Rossien and Dykstra have been arrested and have been broken in interrogation in turn. Consul Lindberg of Stockholm appointed Dr Osterhuis as ZWANTJE II. This second organisation has now been blown by the wife of Osterhuis to Schreider of the Gestapo in The Hague.

The SD officer credited with handling Aben was Joseph Schreider, a Bavarian policeman and former border guard who seized the opportunity to have his subordinate, Hauptsturmführer Müller, create a German-sponsored replacement resistance group named Paulani.

Although Aben confessed to collaboration with the Germans, he could not be charged under the Treachery Act. Accordingly, he remained in MI5's custody until the end of the war, when he was deported to the Netherlands to face trial.

★ ★ ★

More would be learned about Louis de Bray when Werner Unversagt, a leading member of the Brussels Abwehr, was arrested in Bad Ems in May 1945 and interrogated at Camp 020. He recalled that de Bray had peddled a plan, intended to make him some money, which he claimed could deliver German agents to England through an escape route managed by the local resistance for evading Allied airmen. Unversagt had tested the route by deploying Pierre Neukermans, but a few days later Neukermans had reported that the whole scheme was bogus, thus earning de Bray a certain reputation with both the British and their German adversaries.[1]

12

CHURCHILL INTERVENES

In his report dated 7 March 1944 Petrie referred to a breach of security concerning the PHOENIX component of the artificial harbours code-named MULBERRY that were under construction in anticipation of D-Day. The invasion plan, in the absence of a convenient port available for capture in Normandy, involved towing two entire prefabricated unloading and disembarkation docks across the Channel from their construction site in Weymouth.

> 4. A Trades Union despatched to various addresses in the UK/Eire copies of the minutes of a committee meeting at which measures had been discussed for consolidating the production of Phoenix and particulars given of this device. The single copy of this document which was addressed to Eire was intercepted in censorship. Arrangements have now been taken, devised by the Home Secretary and executed by an officer of MI5 to recover all the copies discreetly, and have now been carried into effect.

Churchill was dismayed by the news and demanded more information, which Petrie supplied to his private secretary, Tom Bromley, on 20 March:

> The answer to the Prime Minister's query in Para D4 of the attached report is as follows.
> The Trades Union official responsible for the issue of the minutes was interviewed in the presence of the chief official of the Union. The former, who is an official of many years standing, was in a state of great distress. He explained that his motive in raising the matter at the Committee Meeting had been to ensure that the work of PHOENIX should proceed as

smoothly as possible from the labour standpoint. He made no attempt to excuse his error in allowing the minutes to go out with his remarks reported in detail. He undertook that he would never be guilty of such an error of judgement again.

With the cooperation of the Trades Union officials concerned, the whole of the 265 copies of the minutes have been recovered and will be destroyed. The Union concerned has made arrangements to ensure an efficient check on all their correspondence in future, and Sir Walter Citrine is, at the request of the Home Secretary, drawing the attention of all Trades Unions to the need for the very greatest care being exercised in their correspondence.[1]

In these circumstances the taking of criminal proceedings against either the Union or the responsible official is considered inexpedient.

The return of this report in due course is requested.

Arguably the most secret aspect of the Allies' D-Day plan was the actual location of the invasion, and the Germans had naturally anticipated that any viable large-scale landing would require huge logistical support to handle the transport, food and ammunition necessary for such a major undertaking. The merest hint that a scheme had been devised to make the capture of port facilities redundant would betray a central plank of the entire project, and this was Churchill's fear, and the reason for his fury at the hapless trade union official who, through sheer carelessness, had jeopardised the greatest military operation of the era. The Prime Minister was rightly concerned that, having been sent to a neutral country, other copies might fall into enemy hands, and even the most unimaginative intelligence analyst would recognise its significance and draw the appropriate conclusions.

13

3 APRIL 1944

In the month before D-Day MI5 was preoccupied by SHAEF's strategic deception campaign, designed to mislead the enemy about the imminent Allied invasion, and by the fear that uncontrolled spies might be infiltrated into the country on missions to verify intelligence reports from existing sources. Tension was high, as the invasion season approached, yet the Prime Minister's report seems almost mundane, dealing with two Frenchmen, Henri Chambard and Jean Fraval, two unnamed Belgians, and a Norwegian, Knut Brodersen. In terms of double-agents, only TREASURE, TATE and GARBO are mentioned, with no indication of the crucial role they were playing in the strategic deception operation code-named FORTITUDE, arguably the greatest military gamble of all time.

MARCH 1944

A. SPIES

1. Since the last report was made, four more enemy agents, two Belgians and two Frenchman, have been arrested. Of these, the Frenchmen are of the greater interest. One, Henri Gravet Chambard, is of particular importance as he was recruited on behalf of the Japanese. He arrived in the Argentine from Spain in May of last year. At that time it was known from Most Secret Sources that he had a mission to perform for the Japanese on the Pacific coast of the United States. While in Buenos Aires, Chambard was kept under observation by the FBI and is known to have been in touch with Japanese agents. He was arrested at Trinidad in November last while on his way back to Spain. The exact nature of Chambard's projected mission has not yet been discovered. It is known, however, that he had been recruited

by, and was working for, Angel Alcazar de Velasco, a man well-known to us. This person was in London in 1944 as the Spanish Press Attaché, a post for which his previous experience as a bull-fighter indifferently qualified him. He was at that time engaged in organising a network of spies on behalf of the Germans. Subsequently, he worked for both the Germans and the Japanese simultaneously. He has now severed his connection with the Germans and peddles his wares, which are mostly of a dubious quality, only to the Japanese.

2. The other Frenchman, Fraval, is an air-pilot by profession and the latest in the series of agents sent to this country by the German Secret Service with instructions to join the Airforce and fly back to Occupied Territory an aircraft of the latest type.

3. It is known from Most Secret Sources that a certain Norwegian is at present in Madrid, awaiting an opportunity to come to this country as a spy. He has already been supplied with money by the German Secret Service and, after his arrival here, a cover-address will be communicated to him by wireless. It is almost certain that the man in question is one Knut Brodersen, who has applied in Madrid for permission to travel to the UK. His journey here will be facilitated and suitable arrangements have been made for his reception.

B. <u>SPECIAL AGENTS</u>

The agent TREASURE has returned to this country after a visit to Lisbon for the purpose of meeting Dr. Emil Kliemann, her spymaster. She has received a new questionnaire from which it appears that the Germans urgently require exact information about the whereabouts of General Eisenhower's headquarters; and that they are interested in the specifications of a new and apparently non-existent type of aircraft which has neither a propeller nor is Jet-propelled. The instructions issued earlier to the agent TATE, to go to Cambridge to obtain information about the points at which British and American aircraft assemble before taking part in raids on Germany have now been cancelled in favour of instructions to report (by reference to the nearest cross-roads) the position of anti-aircraft batteries in Greater London. The agent GARBO's financial position has been further improved by another transaction under the terms of Plan DREAM, by which he has received £2,775 in exchange for a quarter of a million pesetas, paid by the German Secret Service to his nominees in Madrid.

C. SABOTAGE

1. The activities of the group of Falangist saboteurs, referred to in the last report, continue. Our representative in Gibraltar has informed us that sufficient information about their doings to form the basis of a protest to the Spanish Government may soon be available. We have advised that such a protest would be unavailing unless supported by specific and factual evidence. We have therefore proposed that the question of a protest should be deferred until after one of these saboteurs has been caught red-handed.

2. On the Italian front the Germans are showing greater skill in the targets which they select for sabotage. The quality of the agents whom they employ remains poor. A fair number have now been captured, all of whom were Italians with little stomach for their work. The equipment which they employ is, however, excellent being of British manufacture. It appears that the Germans now employ exclusively equipment captured from British secret organisations. This includes such ingenious devices as explosive dogs and rats stuffed with plastic explosive.

3. Information has been received from Most Secret Sources that a detachment of Himmler's Secret Service in Russia has applied to headquarters for thirty bottles of poisoned brandy, thirty packets of poisoned cigarettes, an equal number of pairs of rubber gloves and a supply of dog poison. These accessories are presumably either for the use of agents behind the Russian lines or for employment against Russian partisans. They are an index of the methods employed by Himmler's organisation.

3rd April 1944

★ ★ ★

The mention of Emil Kliemann as a key figure in the TREASURE double-agent case shows that MI5 considered him a significant adversary, and his capture at the home of his French mistress, Yvonne Delidaise, in Bougival on 16 August 1944 proved to be a major intelligence breakthrough. Arrested by the FFI, who were suspicious of Yvonne's brother Richard. He had been extracted from his prison cell by OSS personnel, who had handed him over to an SCI. His name cropped up in numerous espionage cases and he was a highly energetic professional, travelling frequently between Paris, Madrid and Lisbon to manage his very considerable stable of agents. Some of Kliemann's career was already known, either supplied by the double-agents TREASURE, DRAGONFLY, WEASEL and BASKET, or by the defector HARLEQUIN, or by the wretched Oswald Job. All, to varying degrees, were acquainted with Kliemann, and his interrogators were also assisted by lengthy statements from his mistress and her mother.

Under an interrogation conducted by CSDIC and not at Camp 020, he volunteered that he was an Austrian, and never a Nazi, and had decided to cooperate fully with the Allies in the hope of building a better Austria. At the time of his capture he was finding excuses not to return to Wiesbaden where, ISOS had revealed, the Gestapo wished to question him about the 20 July plot to assassinate Adolf Hitler. He was kept a prisoner until his release in the British zone in Germany in December 1945.

Originally a businessman in Vienna working for a wholesale grain merchant Kliemann, who was still married to his second wife, had been called up by the Luftwaffe in 1939 and posted to Wiesbaden as an intelligence officer, attached to the Abwehr's Eins Luft branch. In June 1940 he was transferred to Paris, where he remained for the rest of the war, although his role changed from the analysis of captured French documents to the recruitment and management of agents. According to his large MI5 dossier, he was also a violinist who collected old porcelain, and suffered from a coronary illness.

On 23 September 1944 Kliemann was flown from Paris to Heston, treated as a prisoner-of-war and accommodated by MI-19 at Trent Park, Cockfosters, where he described his work for the Abwehr, unaware of his paper trail in ISOS and the British control over four of his agents. His star source, of course, was the temperamental Russian journalist Lily Sergueiev, code-named TREASURE by MI5 and TRAMP by the Abwehr, but his first encounter with the recruitment and management of individual agents was with DRAGONFLY's German sister, Lilian Rindermann, in Frankfurt in February 1940.

DRAGONFLY was Hans George, born in London of German parentage, who travelled in April 1940 to meet his sister in The Hague, and accepted a message and a supply of secret ink from her in order to ensure his family's safety, but immediately upon his return to England declared the approach to MI5. In November 1940 he went to Lisbon under business cover, as a wine importer, to meet Kliemann, who claimed to represent the German Chamber of Commerce, and receive his instructions. Having been briefed, and been given a wireless transmitter disguised as a gramophone, DRAGONFLY went back to England in the expectation that he would be paid through a commercial licensing scheme in which he would be funded by an intermediary company in Switzerland for the manufacturing rights to a cosmetic product, Trixale, This arrangement involved Kliemann's nominee, Colonel Bertil Martenson, formerly the Finnish military attaché in Paris, who had moved to Lisbon. DRAGONFLY's wireless link became operational at the end of March 1941 but in April 1942 Kliemann confided to HARLEQUIN that he suspected his agent had been compromised, although he did not submit a formal report. Paris maintained the radio connection until the end January 1944 up to twice a week, but DRAGONFLY usually demanded money. In an effort to send jewellery to DRAGONFLY, Oswald Job had been employed to act as a courier, but he was quickly identified, arrested in November 1943, tried, and hanged in March 1944. DRAGONFLY's controlling station was moved to Wiesbaden in January 1944, but finally abandoned in July.

Kliemann first met TREASURE through an introduction in Paris made by his mistress, Yvonne, in a café in June 1941, although he did not recruit her until October 1941. She completed her training in June 1942 but visa problems delayed her mission, and Kliemann saw her again in October 1942 at 2 Villa Boileau, 16 rue Molitor, but could not acquire the necessary travel permits until June 1943, when he gave her the address of a contact in Lisbon, an Abwehr officer named Morgener.

On 17 September 1943 Kliemann met TREASURE in Madrid, accompanied by a colleague, von Buch, and she received a final briefing at a villa on the Ciudad Ordinal. Unaware that she had already contacted Kenneth Benton at the SIS station at the British embassy on 17 July, Kliemann sent her on her mission, and remained in contact using secret writing to cover addresses in Sweden and Spain until her return to Lisbon in March 1944. Over a period of a week they had frequent meetings, in a flat at 9 rue San Pedro, and during a day trip to Sintra, before she returned to England on 23 March 1944. Even during his interrogation, Kliemann never realised that TREASURE had worked against him from the outset, and his interrogators gave him no clue to the wealth of their knowledge so as to avoid compromising either her or ISOS.

Kliemann's relationship with the Irishman Joseph Lenihan, code-named BASKET, was rather fleeting. His assignment in July 1941 had been to escort him to the Château Buc, where he was paid £500 and prepared for a flight the following day from Brest to Ireland. In February 1935 BASKET had been convicted of smuggling for the IRA, and had been serving a prison sentence in Jersey when the Channel Islands had been occupied. After an unsuccessful escape attempt he had been recruited by the Abwehr and taken to Paris for a parachute mission to County Meath, where he was to transmit daily weather reports. He landed on 18 July but five days later travelled north from Dublin to surrender to the Royal Ulster Constabulary and thereafter was sent to Camp 020. He was eventually released with a promise of good behaviour as he could not be run as a double-agent, the RAF banning any suggestion of transmitting accurate weather reports to the enemy.

BASKET's role as an MI5 double-agent would remain secret for many years, and his Security Service file has never been declassified because of Whitehall's sensitivity about the Lenihans, a family prominent in Athlone, because his nephew Brian Lenihan was a prominent Fianna Fáil politician who became Eire's deputy Prime Minister, foreign minister and minister of justice.

THE WEASEL was a Belgian ship's physician, Dr Hilaire Westerlinck, who had been working aboard the liner *Thysville,* and was not much more successful in his intended mission to the Congo. He arrived in Paris in July 1941 but did not reach Lisbon until 15 August 1941, and landed in England with his wife in May 1942. Not only had Westerlinck's assignment been compromised by ISOS, but his pro-Nazi sympathies had been reported by two other Belgians, Jack Verlinden and Albert de Jaeger, both later employed at Camp 020 as stool pigeons. His role as a double-agent terminated in December the same year, probably because he alerted the Germans that he was mailing his secret writing messages under British control.

Although Kliemann filled in many of the gaps in MI5's knowledge of the four double-agents, his real value was in his account of the Abwehr's stay-behind organisation in France, which he estimated consisted of twenty-five transmitters, most of which were captured British sets following the bombing of the Abwehr's depot in Berlin. He recalled the code names and the locations of many agents, among them OMI in Caen; BERNARD in Nantes, where he owned a theatrical agency; PRIMO, a 24-year-old garage mechanic; SECUNDO, a 26-year-old electrician named Roger Fournier employed at the Laleu aerodrome near La Pallice; a factory draughtsman, Francois Kretz, code-named JUX, in Bordeaux; BANJO, a half-caste garage mechanic named Megele from Guadaloupe, based in Rayan; Tisserand, code-named FLUTE, a worker in an electrical plant in Perpignan; Marcel Guillouard, code-named CELLO, in Toulon; ALTO in Marseilles; FIDELO in Cannes; Harduin, a former airman and taxi driver code-named PERCY, in Nice; and CALAIS in Saint-Girons. There were others established in Saint-Malo, Arles and Montpellier, with a separate Abwehr Eins Marine IM network in the ports Le Havre, Cherbourg, Brest, Lorient and maybe Quimper. Because Kliemann could remember several true identities and other details, all these agents would be tracked down by SCI units.

★ ★ ★

Henri Chambard was arrested in Trinidad in November 1943. Aged 37, and travelling on a French passport issued at the consulate in Barcelona in January 1943, he was married to an Argentine, Maria Dou, and had lived in Spain since the age of 8. Between 1934 and 1927 he served in the Spanish Fleet Air Arm as an aviator. He emigrated to Argentina in 1928, but returned to Spain in 1931.

According to ISOS, he had been recruited by Angel Alcazar de Velasco in April to act as a spy for the Japanese and undertake a mission to Guatemala, Mexico and California, where he was to establish a network equipped with wireless transmitters. While in Madrid his principal contact was Alcazar de Velaso's secretary and assistant, Dr Celestino Moliner. Having accepted this assignment, and a promise of $5,000, he had boarded the *Cabo de Hornos* in Bilbao and sailed to Argentina. When he reached Buenos Aires on 11 May 1943 he was placed under intensive surveillance by the FBI and seen to meet a Japanese diplomat, Shozo Murai. However, within a month he was trying to return to Spain and, after many visa delays, he embarked on the *Cabo de Buena Esperanzia,* on 13 November bound for Spain, having spent most of his money and abandoned his mission.

Chambard was arrested when he called in at Trinidad on 6 December and interrogated, but claimed that he had not been in contact with the Japanese until after his arrival in Buenos Aires in May, and that admission was only made after he was confronted with surveillance evidence from the FBI. He was sent to England in February 1944 aboard the Dutch freighter SS *Maaskerk*, arriving on 11 March, when he was escorted to Camp 020. When questioned by MI5 Chambard made a detailed confession and he would remain in custody until June 1945 when he was flown from Croydon to Le Bourget with Gabriel De Chaffault and delivered to Inspector Latruberce of the Direction de la Surveillance du Territoire. In September 1948 he was sentenced by a French military tribunal to fifteen years' hard labour.

Velasco, the man who recruited Chambard, was a very familiar figure to MI5, and for a long period was the most active authentic German spy in London, although he was surrounded by MI5 informants and most of his sources were actually double-agents. He was appointed to the post in January 1941 and succeeded Miguel Piernavieja del Pozo, code-named POGO by MI5, and thoroughly compromised by an MI5 double-agent, G.W., who supposedly ran a network of Nazi-sympathising Welsh Nationalists.[1] This bogus organisation, created by MI5, had established a link between the Abwehr and the Spanish embassy, and had incriminated POGO and a Spanish journalist, Luis Calvo. However, during the few weeks Velasco was in England, before his departure at the end of February 1941, when he was under intense technical and physical surveillance, he was not spotted engaging in espionage, although more would be heard of him from both German and Japanese sources.

★ ★ ★

Lieutenant Knut Brodersen of the Norwegian army had been recruited by the Abwehr in Norway after his arrest for dealing in black market cognac and sent to Spain with a cover story of an escapee from the Todt Organisation in southern France.

Born in 1904 and educated in Oslo, Brodersen had completed his military service with the 3rd Infantry Regiment and then travelled to France to learn the wine trade. He then worked for the Croft port business in Portugal until August 1926, when he travelled to Rio de Janeiro to join the Calorie Oil Company. By August 1931 he was back in Norway, as a tennis coach, and had several different jobs until he was recalled by the army in April 1940. His unit surrendered to German troops five days later, and in September 1941 he was employed as a bookkeeper by the Luftwaffe. Two years later, in November 1943, he was posted to Bayonne in France, and on New Year's Eve he crossed the Spanish border, reaching Madrid on 12 January, where he approached the Norwegian legation.

By this time the Norwegians had developed reservations about Brodersen and alerted SIS, which matched him to FRANK in the ISOS traffic. Since November 1943 thirteen messages about 'V-Mann FRANK of Stelle Norway' had been decrypted. He remained in Spain until March while his case was considered, when he was sent to Gibraltar by SIS, the decision having been reached by Helenus Milmo that he 'would be a valuable acquisition to our intelligence sources at Camp 020, more particularly in view of his connection with Bayonne where he must have been in a position to know about the large number of German agents who have been decanted into Spain by this method'. Three days later, he travelled on the SS *Norefjord* to Leith, and on 8 May he signed a confession at Camp 020, disclosing his cover addresses, in Oviedo, Spain, and Bergen, Norway, to which he was to communicate in secret writing. His instructions were to be concealed in numbers spoken over conventional radio broadcasts, concealed in prearranged transmissions three times a week. Eventually, he was supposed to acquire his own transmitter and establish a direct radio link.

Compromised by ISOS references to 'V-mann FRANK' long before his arrival, Brodersen had actually been recruited as a spy in Bergen in September 1943, and thereafter had been escorted by a German intelligence officer to St-Jean-de-Luze and seen safely over the frontier into Spain. His intention was to establish himself in England where his younger sister Cero was married to a London stockbroker, Billy Bennett.

His secret writing material was found concealed in a tooth and under a toe, and because Brodersen had not taken the opportunity when questioned in Leith to reveal his espionage mission, the decision was taken in June to charge him under the Treachery Act. He was remanded at Bow Street Magistrates' Court to Brixton prison and sent for trial at the Old Bailey, but in preparation for the hearing Brodersen's solicitor demanded that Captain Torgersen, the Norwegian master of the SS *Norefjord*, should be called as a witness, together with the four unnamed MI5 interrogators who had questioned the prisoner at Camp 020. Both requests caused the greatest anxiety because Torgersen was by then in Baltimore, and Petrie would not allow any of his staff to be subjected to cross-examination about Camp 020. The central problem lay in the threat made by Major Samson when he first met Brodersen on 8 May, the morning after his delivery to Ham:

This is the British Secret Service prison, to which all German spies are sent for investigation. The British Secret Service has a great deal of information obtained from Germany and from countries occupied by Germany. That information is obtained from various sources. One is people like yourself who have been sent over here and have come to this place – they all come here. The other is from our own agents in Germany and in German-occupied countries, many of them are Germans themselves, who are always willing to receive money to betray their own cause. That is why so many people come here. We do not bring people here without good reason and on mere suspicion; when they come here it is a very serious matter. It is a matter of life and death. We have had hundreds of people here, and many of them have been executed. I have here a few obituary notices about people who have come through here: 'Spy hanged', 'German agent executed'; 'Dutch refugee, Nazi spy executed'; 'German spy executed in London', 'Traitor's end', and so on, many of them. You must understand we are at war, and we have no compunction with anyone who tries to hinder our effort. Anyone who does that is liquidated pitilessly. On the other hand, we do not execute people out of simple inhumanity. Our object here, our main objective, is to obtain information which may help us in the war.

Now you are in as dangerous a position as any man might be and I make no promise to you, but what I do say is that you can help yourself by helping us. Have you anything to say?

The prosecuting authorities considered that this explicit threat rendered his subsequent confession inadmissable and, combined with the reluctance to discuss Camp 020 in a courtroom, resulted in the withdrawal of the charge. In order to prevent Brodersen's solicitor, a Mr Head from Ludlow & Co., from realising that it had been his demand for witnesses that had led to the collapse of the case, the court was informed that the Norwegian captain was unavailable:

> Colonel Hinchley Cooke explained that the DG had instructed him to say that a witness from Camp 020 could not be made available either for the prosecution or for the defence, and that in the circumstances, the case must be withdrawn. Colonel Hinchley-Cooke suggested that the withdrawal could be accomplished fairly easily without in any way putting Mr. Head wise to the fact that the real difficulty lay in calling evidence from Camp 020; the whole burden of the withdrawal could be placed upon the captain of the Norwegian vessel from whom a statement would be taken at the earliest opportunity.

The Attorney-General, Sir Donald Somervell, somewhat reluctantly gave his consent to entering a *nolle prosequi*, which effectively dropped the case, leaving MI5 to apply for Brodersen's detention in Dartmoor so as to prevent him returning to 020, as was explained to the Home Office:

> At Camp 020 Brodersen made a confession which he subsequently repeated under caution. In this he admitted to a Quisling background and to the fact that he was recruited by the German Secret Service in Bergen in September of last year. He was subsequently despatched to this country via the Peninsula with instructions to communicate information in secret writing to cover addresses in Spain and Norway respectively. An abundance of secret writing material was found concealed on his person and amongst his belongings. He was also instructed to procure a radio receiving set with which he was to pick up broadcasts sent to him in code from Norway. A watch has been kept on these broadcasts which show that the German Intelligence Service are still attempting to contact him. We have independent evidence from a most reliable but delicate source confirming Brodersen's confession.

Brodersen's defence to the charge under the Treachery Act was disclosed for the first time at the close of the case for the prosecution at the Police

Court. He then contended that it had been his intention all along to tell the British Secret Service everything about his recruitment and mission. This defence was ingenious and there was a considerable amount of material to substantiate it. It is, in fact, quite possible that had the prosecution continued the Jury would have been left with a sufficient element of doubt to justify them in returning a verdict of not guilty. There is however little doubt in our minds that if this man had not gone to Camp 020 where it at once became apparent to him that he was known to be a spy he would have said nothing and probably endeavoured to carry out his espionage assignments. In this connection it is significant that the story which he told to the Security Officer at the port of his arrival after having been warned in express terms that this was the time when he should tell everything that he knew, was precisely the cover story which his German master had instructed him to tell ...

The next question which arises is the place of detention to which Brodersen should be sent. In the ordinary way we would strongly recommend that he should be returned to Camp 020, but since he has been in touch with a solicitor, namely the gentleman who was appointed to look after his interests under the Poor Persons Rules, we feel that it would be taking an undue risk to send him back there. Were he to ask to be allowed to communicate with this solicitor he would probably have to be allowed to do so and although I do not think that any great harm would be likely to occur in this particular case, were such a communication permitted it would undoubtedly come to the knowledge of other internees and probably involve us in a spate of correspondence and possible litigation. In the light of these considerations we feel that Brodersen should be sent to Dartmoor assuming that accommodation is available for him in the special wing of the prison.

Thus Brodersen became the only German spy ever to have a prosecution withdrawn. Suitably impressed, he subsequently pressed a claim for compensation for the loss of his possessions, which had been tested to destruction in a search for secret writing material, plenty of which was found. He never knew the full weight of the case against him, or of the ISOS intercepts that had heralded his arrival in Spain. His only utility to MI5 was the assistance he gave to the cryptanalyst Denys Page in solving an Abwehr triple transposition code used over a broadcast station for Norwegian seamen. He had been directed to listen to the transmissions on Oslo Radio for his instructions, but the messages had defeated the Radio Intelligence Section, requiring him to seek further guidance through a letter to one of his cover addresses. This was duly accomplished, although the only message addressed to him, sent by his Abwehr handler HENRY, consisted of complaints about the lack of contact.

The extent to which Brodersen was prepared to cooperate with MI5 was always open to doubt, and Robertson's B1(a) section rejected him as a potential double-agent. There was also concern about Brodersen's insistence that he had been required to report on Allied invasion plans by his secret writing channel, as this method of communication could entail a delay of up to six weeks. This obvious inconsistency suggested he was not entirely candid. As Colonel Stephens pointed out on 26 May 1944:

> What has exercised all of us is Brodersen's insistence that he had to report invasion movements by secret ink. This story, due regard being had to the inefficiency of the German Secret Service, is not necessarily false, but it does give rise to the possibility that Brodersen might have been instructed by radio to report to some other contact in this country with a W/T set of his own. Some colour is lent to this theory by the fact that code messages of the type indicated by Brodersen are being received at the present time and that they may be intended for some other agent.

In September 1944 he was interviewed by Norwegian Security Service officers, who recommended his continuing internment, and his case was referred to Colonel Roscher Lund, head of the Norwegian Security Service. Brodersen was later transferred to the Isle of Man and, upon his return to Norway with fifteen other detainees in June 1945, was sentenced to fifteen years' imprisonment in May 1947.

Soon after the German surrender several Abwehr officers who had worked in Bergen were questioned by the Norwegian authorities and a Leutnant Franger was identified as Brodersen's Eins Heer recruiter and handler, whom he had known only as HENRY. According to SIS, Franger had previously served at the Abstelle in Algeciras between February 1942 and January 1943 under the alias Henry Bender.

★ ★ ★

Aged 27, Sergeant Jean Fraval was a French Air Force pilot from Brittany who had qualified as a pilot in 1936 and had been posted to 38 Squadron at Metz. After his demobilisation, by which time he had accumulated 800 hours

of flying experience, he had moved to Paris where, in July 1943, he had
been recruited by Werner Unversagt, an Abwehr officer whom he knew only
as WERNER, who gave him a refugee cover story and a mission to steal
an aircraft in England, preferably a Typhoon, Thunderbolt or Spitfire. His
instruction in secret writing and espionage was conducted by Unversagt at
the Abwehr office on the third floor of 29 rue Royale in Brussels between
August and November. That address was familiar to SIS analysts as it had been
described by another pilot, Georges Feyguine. During this training he lived
with Unversagt, who had previously been mentioned by José Pacheco and
Waldemar Janowsky, at 54 rue Dautzenberg, an address already compromised
by the Belgian spy Pierre Neukermans, and was supplied with several cover
addresses in Barcelona, Brussels, Brabant and Geneva.

Upon his arrival at the British consulate in Barcelona in February 1943 he
was interviewed by an SIS officer, to whom he confessed that he had been
recruited as a German agent. Initially he had tried to peddle a completely
false cover story about his escape from France over the Pyrenees that, under
cross-examination, he admitted was untrue. Nevertheless, he continued to
Lisbon on 29 February under SIS's sponsorship and was accommodated by
the Belgian legation at a pension in Santa Amara, and four days later was flown
to Bristol on an Imperial Airways flight.

Once landed in England he was escorted to Camp 020, where he remained
for the rest of war, and was then delivered to the French authorities in
May 1945 by air. At the conclusion of his interrogation, MI5 reported that:

On presenting himself to the British Consulate in Barcelona, Fraval carried
out the orders of his German masters, and tried to make the authorities
believe that he was a genuine refugee.

Fraval's own story of his interview with the Consul differs entirely from
the report made by the Consulate, but although it is not clear how much
pressure was brought to bear on him before the truth was extracted, Fraval's
account cannot be accepted. The extract from the Consul's report reads
as follows – 'The story was obviously false and under cross-questioning
he admitted that he had been recruited by the Germans for their services
in England.'

It can safely be assumed that Fraval never intended to fulfil his mission
for the Germans. On the other hand, his claim that he was resolved to make
a complete disclosure to the British authorities is totally inadmissible. It
is most probable that, true to form, he intended to take the middle way,
committing himself as little as possible to either party, while trying to retain

an advantage to himself. Thus, while it may be in a measure true that he intended to deceive his German masters, in that he was not prepared to carry out the work entrusted to him, to give full information to the British would have meant for him the forfeiting of the advantage he had gained, namely, the monthly payment to his wife. It would therefore seem that Fraval took a chance with the cover story as outlined to him by the Germans, but, on seeing that it was being received with scepticism, gave up the attempt and made a deposition as described in the Barcelona report.

In his favour, however, it must be stated that when he found himself forced to tell the truth, Fraval made no attempt to go back to his German masters and tell them this, or suggest that it would probably be wiser to send him back again to France, as he was obviously a suspect case. He decided rather to tell them that his story had been believed implicitly, and to continue his journey to this country.

Fraval is a very weak character and thoroughly unreliable. He certainly does not inspire sufficient confidence to allow him to join the Fighting French Air Force especially in view of the instructions he received from WERNER that he was to try to fly back to France the latest type of Allied aircraft.

Although intelligent and willing to give all the information possible, he is definitely not a man to be trusted, especially in view of coining operations. It is strongly recommended, therefore, that he be detained.

MI5's submission was accepted and Fraval spent the remainder of the war on the Isle of Man. This episode brought to an end what might have looked like a very specific tactic adopted by the Abwehr involving French and Belgian airmen who had been recruited to masquerade as refugees and for some, having joined the Allied air forces, to steal an aircraft and fly it to Axis territory. This strategy was the common denominator in the cases put before Churchill, such as FATHER, FIDO, SNIPER, Feyguine, Creteur, Jude and Neukermans.

More light was shed on this in July 1945 when Werner Unversagt was detained and interrogated about his role in the HAMLET case (Chapter 2). He had been named by a captured colleague, Julius Hagemann, and several Trupp 121 stay-behind agents, identified as a *sonderführer* or *oberleutnant*, although he never wore a uniform. Actually, he had been born in November 1908 and attached to Eins Heer from Wiesbaden. In the opinion of Waldemar Janowsky, who had known him in Brussels, he controlled about 150 agents and was extremely hard working.

Before the war Unversagt had been a professional dancer and had performed across Europe with his wife, Ula, visiting Paris, Brussels and Spain.

According to one report, his mother had run a health sanatorium near Cologne, and he had given an exhibition in St Moritz as a dance champion. By April 1945 he was thought to be in hiding in Amsterdam or Rotterdam, very conscious that the Allies were searching for him. He was caught on 25 May in Bad Ems by the US Counter-Intelligence Corps acting on a tip from Julius Hagemann, who had revealed his mother's address, the Villa Balzer in Bad Ems, and his ownership of the Hotel Metropole in Wiesbaden. In fact, Unversagt had turned himself in to American troops when they occupied the town at the end of March, but had been told to go home and await instructions.

What made Unversagt of such great interest to MI5 was the number of reports from captured agents suggesting that in June 1940 he had been based in Boulogne to supervise the despatch of several spies across the Channel, some of whom had claimed that Unversagt himself intended to be parachuted into England in September 1940. He was also thought to have visited London in August 1939 to contact an existing spy ring. The opportunity to question such an active adversary raised the prospect of clearing up quite a few unresolved investigations that dated back to before the war, including that of the Duchesse de Château-Thierry, a woman suspected of having engaged in German espionage.[2] Although Unversagt volunteered to be dropped into England, he was instead posted to an Abwehr training centre at 48 rue Joseph II in Brussels. However, during the 'invasion summer' of 1940 Unversagt was known to have helped prepare several agents, among them Sjoerd Pons and Charles van den Kieboom, who landed in Kent, and Francois de Deeker, who rowed ashore in Scotland. All three had made comprehensive confessions, and had identified WERNER as their Abwehr contact.

On 5 June 1945 Unversagt was flown from Wiesbaden to RAF Harrington and escorted to the London Cage in Kensington Palace Gardens so he could be transferred to Camp 020, where he underwent a lengthy interrogation. The resulting reports proved fascinating, and revealed several cases of espionage about which MI5 had minimal previous knowledge, such as the escaped PoW Gunner William Hewson, code-named WILLI:

> … who had served at Dunkirk, Greece and captured in Crete serving with an Anti-Aircraft unit. It is not known why he was picked for training or from what camp he originated. He was sent to Brussels with instructions to be trained for a mission in England forthwith (September 1942). He spent two months living with Unversagt and was trained in S/W by a woman instructor of Eins Gruppe. For his cover story of 'escaped PoW' he was sent to a Black Forest camp where he remained about four weeks before

an 'escape' was arranged and he was helped to the Swiss border. Unversagt personally received a few post cards and a letter or two during the next few months. None, it is claimed, contained anything except greetings and thanks for having been assisted out of Germany. Nothing of intelligence interest was ever received; what happened to WILLI eventually is not known. One of his cover addresses was a Stalag,

In fact, Hewson had reported his escape, and his recruitment by the Abwehr, as soon as he had reached the British consulate in Basel. Another very similar case involved Conrad Bach, a 25-year-old RASC soldier code-named SEBASTIAN:

British POW RASC, captured at Dunkirk. Of dual English Swiss nationality; spoke good German. Was from a prison camp on the Prussian border where he had been an interpreter. Was willing to be sent on and was sent to Brussels for training. He was to give information on any military matters and trained in S/W, methods cannot be recalled. He remained in Brussels for about two months and was then taken to the Swiss border towards the end of the summer of 1941. He had an uncle who was a schoolmaster near Frouenfeld, Switzerland, and it was anticipated that with this contact his journey to England would be facilitated. Cover story was that of POW escaping. After this man crossed the border he was never heard of again although it was rumoured that he was employed at his uncle's school.

In Bach's case his reported version was slightly contradicted by Unversagt, so he was re-interviewed by MI5 to clear up the apparent discrepancies.

Unversagt's lengthy statements to his interrogators showed that he had been a very active Abwehr recruiter based in Brussels until August 1944, when he had fallen ill with jaundice and had returned home to Bad Ems. In his absence the Brussels Abstellen had collapsed in September 1944 and been withdrawn to Wiesbaden where, from November 1944, he was assigned the task of preparing a stay-behind organisation composed of refugees from Belgium and Luxembourg. However, not a single recruitment was achieved before the entire organisation had been disbanded in February, following the destruction of the Abwehr office in Wiesbaden in an Allied air raid in February 1945. Thereafter, Unversagt claimed he had simply stayed at home, running his family's hotel.

Inversagt's value was his intimate knowledge of so much espionage that had been investigated by MI5, and his willingness to complete a comprehensive organisational chart of the Abwehr in France and Belgium. He also proved willing to provide his perspective on some important cases, such as Joseph Van Hove:

Joseph Jan Van Hove, a Belgian national, was executed in England on 12th July, 1944. It has been possible to check his German Secret Service activities with his spy master Werner Unversagt, and the impression gained is that Van Hove was elaborating on his entire story, hence the following observations:

In 1941 Mayer, an agent of the Abwehr once attached to Oberst Recke of Tangiers – introduced Unversagt to Vanhove (who was working on an airfield in Lille). When the latter paid a visit to Brussels, the question of a mission to North Africa was discussed and Vanhove was willing to accept it. He was informed he would be contacted again later. He left the airfield, went to Calais and was contacted there for the second time. This briefly dismisses a long story given by Vanhove which contains something of the truth; the reference he made to receiving letters from Unversagt is incorrect, although it is possible he received a note from Mayer inviting him to Brussels. Unversagt states that he did not give a post box number or instructions to write Poste Restante at any time.

In July 1942 Unversagt was paying some anti-invasion network agents when he heard of the whereabouts of Vanhove and called on him. (He was living with Rombaut connected with the ROBERT Stelle and although Unversagt did not know those agents, he presumes they worked for Group III IM). Unversagt agrees he may have given the impression that he found Vanhove through his parents – this, however, is not true; he denies having given the man 600 francs.

As Vanhove had been employed on ships, it was decided that he would best be employed as a steward and it was decided to place him on a Swiss ship running from Italy to the USA. Vanhove was contacted in Antwerp, informed of the mission, and asked if he could find a companion for the task (two refugees making a better cover story than a man alone). Vanhove introduced Romyn who was given the alias Robinson.

According to Vanhove, the second clause of his contract mentioned that he would obey all orders, even to being dropped over England by parachute. Unversagt maintains that no such clause was ever given to an agent.

Vanhove's last mission was to be via Sweden against the UK or USA. It is not correct, according to Unversagt, that he was to try and infiltrate the British Intelligence Service and later drop over the continent by parachute; Unversagt also denies the threat of reprisals and denunciation.

It is correct that Vanhove was taken to Antwerp for instruction on a naval mission; he was handed over to an officer of Eins Heer whom Unversagt cannot recall or identify.

In Stettin, Vanhove mentioned that he saw Unversagt with another person. This is correct, the other person being an Oberleutnant of the Ast in that town, and it is believed covered IH and IM matters. Unversagt met him twice whilst arranging the departure of Vanhove for Sweden; his name cannot be recalled.

With regard to letters, several, but not all, of the letters sent from Sweden to Brussels, were received (it is known that others went astray.) Vanhove stated that he was not expected to write every day, but once or twice per week: this Unversagt also states is incorrect, since every effort was made to impress the agents that quality and not quantity was desired.

Although Vanhove arrived in England, was tried and executed, his masters in Brussels never knew what happened after they received no further letters from Sweden.

Vanhove was not the only Abwehr agent managed by Unversagt who ended up in one of Petrie's reports to Churchill, and on the scaffold at Pentonville, for a month before him another of Unversagt's spies had suffered the same fate:

Pierre Richard Charles Neukermans was the fifteenth spy to be executed in Britain during the war. The Liquidation Report on Neukermans was used when interrogating Unversagt, with the result that hitherto unknown facts have come to light and complete the picture of Neukermans.

Neukermans, during the last days of his interrogations, admitted he had been an agent in 1939; Unversagt confirms this and is inclined to think that he may have been employed even before the outbreak of war. At that time Rumpe was in Brussels and the history of how he recruited Neukermans is not known. In 1940 Brinkhaus took over and inherited Neukermans. The man was found to be very pro-German, a loyal and zealous worker. His information and results had already proved him trustworthy.

Unversagt first met Neukermans in the summer of 1941 and was charged with the administration side of the case. It is confirmed that there was no mission until the spring of 1942 when order was received to build up a network of W/T agents on the Belgian coast and Neukermans was sent to Westende; according to Neukermans, he had been sent for training only. Of the W/T training in Brussels Unversagt knows little since agents were handed over to Ii and the OTTO and Baron George von Widera are thought to be cover names used by the NCOs who instructed. It may be recalled that Neukermans stated that he did not wish to leave Belgium when it was proposed that he should go on a mission to Turkey, Britain or a neutral country. Unversagt states, however, that Neukermans was continually pressing to be allowed to go on a mission, preferably to England. (Turkey could not have been mentioned as it was Abwehr OST territory.) He adds that Neukermans was continually probing for information in Brussels and regularly handed in information on resistance movements, other Abwehr departments and rumours. It was reported by Neukermans that we encouraged him to visit bars where members of the underground movement were to be found, bars where Unversagt already had agents; to this Unversagt stated that he was probably asked to obtain any information of a direct espionage nature (not counter-espionage which was the prerogative of Abt III). Of agents working in cafes Unversagt knows nothing.

As a result of pressure from Berlin demanding results from England, it was decided to prepare Neukermans for a mission. He was trained in secret writing by I.g. whose instructor, Berger, was known to Neukermans as Bicker or Beckmann. (Berger did not invent the match head for S/W as claimed).

Through von Bassewitz, Major Brinkhaus (alias Ackermann alias Bergman) was introduced to Louis de Bray and arrangements made to assist Neukermans. After two attempts failed, Neukermans returned to Brussels for other instructions and it was learned that de Bray had admitted his story was a fraud in order to obtain money. In April 1943, arrangements were made to send Neukermans to Britain via Iberia. Neukermans was given his mission, but Unversagt points out that Neukermans, exaggerating as usual, has added 'Targets for British Bombers, U-Boat Detectors and Plans of Towns'. The idea of stealing a British plane is another example of the imagination. Eins Heer were not interested in these activities at that time.

In relating his story of the voyage from Brussels to Perpignan, Neukermans mentions that he was accompanied by Brinkhaus, whereas it was in fact Unversagt. It is correct, however, that they were joined at Toulouse by PEDRO, but Unversagt is positive that no mention was made of a Dutch agent whom PEDRO was arranging to send to England. In the first place such a case cannot be recalled, and secondly it is most unlikely that such a statement, even if it were true, would be made in the presence of another agent under such conditions.

Of the letters sent by Neukermans from England to the enemy, about twelve were received. The value of the information cannot be ascertained by

Unversagt who was not as yet, in charge of assessing the value of information received in agents' reports.

The report of the execution of Neukermans on 23rd June 1944 was heard by Unversagt over the wireless and came as a great blow. Arrangements were made for Neukermans' wife to stay with Unversagt's wife for a short while, and to receive some 50,000 francs as compensation from Berlin (though it is claimed she was at no time aware that her husband was an agent). As Unversagt lost touch with her shortly afterwards, he cannot say whether she received all the money.

Other points which can now be cleared up in the Neukermans case are as follows:-

Rue Dauzenburg, 54: This was Unversagt's home, not that of Brinkhaus.

Place du Grand Sablon: Address of Mayer, one of Brinkhaus's agents.

Place de Barricades: Where it was thought the Abwehr had an office, was one of the roads used to approach the rue Royale offices and used to confuse agents.

Le Lion Belge, Chausee de Wavre: Artist known as 'Le Marocain' is identified with Mayer. The name 'Le Marocain' is not known to Unversagt.

Place Collignon: Doctor of Medicine described as an agent was, in fact, Unversagt's doctor, Dr. Laurent, to whom Neukermans was asked to call at a period when Unversagt was under treatment in order to obtain some medicine.

ALBERTI: Unversagt has never heard this cover name which was thought by Neukermans to apply to Brinkhaus.

CHARRON: Believed to be the cover name of Wagner.

St Moritz Badge: Neukermans stated that he had seen Unversagt wearing a badge with 'St. Moritz' written on it, states that he has been to St. Moritz but has never worn such a badge.

Neukermans reported seeing a coloured agent undergoing W/T training. Unversagt has no knowledge of such a person.

Unversagt is unable to recall the information which was received from Neukermans. It was the duty of Leutnant Kohler to collate and examine all information received. Neukermans wrote in secret ink from England regarding troop movements from Belfast to Liverpool and later Africa (without details). Badges observed. Belgian soldiers in No. 10 Commando in Corsica. Belgian war materiel in a camp near Rochdale. Number of French soldiers in England. Communist movements. Building of a factory in Wales with a drawing of a munitions factory. Belgian troops moving to camps on the south coast of England and shipping movements to the

Congo. The name of a double-agent was mentioned (no details can be recalled) and the copies of German documents from the Belgian Military Administration Department which had been transferred to Britain. These documents referred to the food problem in Belgium. There were also two messages for Eins Luft containing plans and full descriptions of three German airfields in Belgium and France and some details, which cannot be recalled, regarding the 8th US Air Force in Britain. Berlin's comment on this information averaged from bad to satisfactory. One of the Eins Luft messages was reported to be good and useful.

Unversagt also had some recollections of Waldemar Janowsky, the spy captured in Canada:

Unversagt first met Janowsky in Brussels during the spring of 1942, shortly after this man had arrived from the Brandenburg Regiment. It is understood that he had previously been in Africa in the Waffenstillstandkommission. Their contact was slight, but Unversagt accompanied Janowsky on two or three occasions to the coast during the building up of the coastal network which was later taken over by Janowsky.

Janowsky was under the direct orders of Leiter I, Major Kramer, and was not attached to Referat Eins Heer.

In about September Unversagt again saw Janowsky when he handed back the coastal network organisation and on which occasion Unversagt learned of Janowsky's proposed mission to Canada. At a later date Unversagt learned from various secretaries in Leiter 1 that Janowsky had been in W/T contact from Canada and that the messages had suddenly stopped. Unversagt admires Janowsky's record and learned that as a result of the Canadian mission Janowsky was promoted to the rank of officer.

In the case of Jean Fraval, the pilot who arrived at Camp 020 in March 1944, having travelled via Barcelona, Unversagt had much to say:

Unversagt confirms that report, with the exception of containing exaggerations and incorrect deductions by Fraval, is correct. Unversagt formed a good impression of Fraval at the first meeting with de Granville in July 1943, and as the man lived in Brittany, it was decided to let him return home and find out the prospects of travelling to England by sea.

In the meantime arrangements would be made to train him. The sea route proved impractical, and Fraval went to Brussels. Fraval's statement that he made a similar enquiry at Paimpol is incorrect. He stayed at a pension, 15 rue aux Laines, where the two agents Desgranges and Aubert had previously stayed. The Abwehr held the room in the name of Dr Lang. According to Unversagt, Fraval did not leave this address because it was too expensive for him, and further, Fraval did not pay the rent as he suggests. He left and stayed with Unversagt because it was more suitable for observation and discipline. (Fraval and Tocabens[3] were becoming a little careless at the time.)

Although Fraval has stated that he received his S/W training mostly from Unversagt, the latter is doubtful of this though he adds that he probably gave some instruction. I.g. were responsible for the training. In addition to confirming the account of a letter containing secret ink being passed from Paris to Brussels to show Fraval it would pass the censorship, Eins Heer carried this out as a test to see whether the German censorship worked; it did not in this case.

For communication with England Fraval said he would send his British address to the Germans who would then communicate with him. Unversagt, however, doubts the authenticity of this statement but cannot certify it as incorrect. Again Fraval mentioned that it was proposed he should fly a plane back to the enemy and that Unversagt told him which aircraft were of the greatest interest. Unversagt observes that Eins Luft may have suggested stealing an aircraft, but that he himself certainly did not mention types of aircraft, this being outside the province of Eins Heer.

Fraval mentioned that Unversagt was interested in obtaining a Swiss passport which the former mentioned accidentally he had been trying to buy. Unversagt denies that there is any truth in this and adds that passports and any other papers were obtainable with ease through Berlin. It was Group III's task to obtain passports.

In his statements Fraval was confused over the crossing of the Franco/Spanish frontier in four cars. Unversagt explained that one new car was for a Spaniard on the frontier and therefore only three of the four cars continued into Spain; this necessitated a change of seating accommodation. There are no other observations on the report and it remains to identify various vague persons described by Fraval.

Similarly, with Feyguine, Unversagt had some observations that were helpful for MI5's reassessment of the case:

Not until the alias Riquier was mentioned did Unversagt recognise Feyguine as an agent who had twice been in Brussels. The name Feyguine is unknown to him and he could not recall this individual from the photograph shown to him.

It was in about February 1943, whilst in Paris, that Unversagt was introduced to a French agent who it was suggested could be sent to England. Unversagt suggested that he be sent to Brussels where a meeting first took place at the Rotisserie Ardennaise in the Boulevard Adolphe Max. Subsequently this agent paid another visit to Brussels, but it cannot be recalled why he was not taken on for training by Ast Belgium. At this time Unversagt was paying frequent visits to Germany in connection with his brother's illness.

As regards Unversagt's pre-war activities, he provided a detailed account of his movements, and this suggested his only visit to England had been five months in 1931 when he stayed with the Hewlett family at the Palace Hotel in Brixton as an exchange student while their daughter was at Bad Ems. Soon afterwards he had contracted tuberculosis, and when he was called up for military service in September 1939 he was posted as an interpreter to Stalag XIIA, a PoW camp in Limburg, In February 1940 he was transferred to Colonel Walter Sensburg's Abstelle in Wiesbaden, but actually spent several months at a tuberculosis sanatorium in Davos. When he was declared medically fit he was sent to an Abwehr training school at Le Touquet where two agents, José Waldberg and Karl Meier, were undergoing training for missions to England. Both would be captured, examined at Camp 020, and hanged.[4]

Unversagt was released from Camp 020 in October 1945 and returned to the American zone of occupation in Germany.

14

5 MAY 1944

As well as mentioning the now familiar figures of TRICYCLE and DREADNOUGHT, the thirteenth of Petrie's reports described the interdiction of three enemy spies, Joseph Vanhove, Alejandro Urzaiz and José Polo, the recent trial of Pierre Neukermans, whose case had been described in Chapter 11, and the subversive activities of a group of local Communist revolutionaries.

At the time of drafting, José Polo was still held in custody in Gibraltar, awaiting a flight to England, and it was only when he was interrogated at Camp 020, a week or so after the report had been delivered to the Prime Minister, that SIS realised that their man in Barcelona had been duped by a very plausible liar. Far from offering interesting information about the Abwehr, Polo proved to be an accomplished fraudster who had sold his services to both the British and the Germans, and had played each off against the other, to the point that SIS had invited him to spend a fortnight in Gibraltar, meeting someone who was promised to be a senior intelligence officer. Worse, SIS had obligingly passed Polo down a clandestine escape route through an SOE safe house in Seville, where he had joined an MI9 felucca for the voyage to Gibraltar.

When it was finally acknowledged that Polo was nothing more than a fabricator, SIS was left with quite a dilemma, because by then he had acquired some sensitive information about SOE, MI9 and Camp 020. In those circumstances he could hardly be allowed to return to Spain so, to ensure his silence, he was detained until four months after the end of hostilities in Europe, by which time his information could do no harm.

APRIL 1944

A. SPIES.

1) Three more enemy agents of interest have been placed under detention, two Spaniards and one Belgian. The latter-named, Joseph Jan Van Hove, arrived in Sweden early last year, ostensibly as a deserter from the crew of a German merchant ship. He said that he wished to come to England in order to join the Belgian Forces. Owing to various difficulties of transport he was not brought to this country until recently. On his first examination he persisted in his original story, but has now confessed that he was sent to England as a spy. He had been provided with instruments for secret writing disguised as matches, one of which was found on him, and during his time in Sweden had in fact written some fifteen letters to his spy-master. He awaits prosecution.

2) The first of the two Spaniards, Alejandro Urzaiz Guzman, was detained at Trinidad, He was then returning to Spain from a journey in Cuba, Mexico and the United States as a representative of a Spanish bank. Urzaiz is known to us from Most Secret Sources as an enemy agent. While he was at Cuba the German Secret Service paid considerable sums of money to him, partly for himself and partly for the use of their local representative. So far, however, Urzaiz, who is now under interrogation in this country, has maintained a stubborn silence. He admits that he received the sums referred to, but protests that the transaction was not in any way connected with the Germans, and that any mysterious circumstances surrounding it are attributable to his desire to avoid Spanish currency restrictions. It is evident, however, that the Germans attach importance to Urzaiz as, since his arrest, a protest has been received from the Spanish Government at the instigation of General Jordana, who has in fact been moved to intervene in the matter by another of the Spanish Government who, there is reason to believe, is acting on behalf of the Germans.

3) The second Spaniard, an individual named José Polo, was arrested in Gibraltar. It is not clear whether he had at that time a mission from the Germans to spy in Gibraltar, but it is known that he had previously worked for the Secret Service in France, Germany and Spain. He will be transferred to this country, as it is anticipated that he may have information of interest to say about his employers.

4) It appears from Most Secret sources that Juan Brandes, one of the representatives of the German Secret Service in Lisbon, claims to have

despatched an agent to England on the 15th April and expects to be in a position to send another at some date after the 29th. Particulars are available about these two agents which should enable us to identify them if indeed they exist, but previous enquiries which we have had occasion to make into the workings of Brandes' organisation suggest that they are more likely to be products of his imagination. Our information is that Brandes himself, a disagreeable young man of 23, is far from loyal to his employers, and has been maintaining himself in Lisbon as a Secret Service agent for some years as a means, among other things, of avoiding military service.

5) Neukermans, the Belgian spy mentioned in previous reports, was sentenced to death at the Old Bailey on Monday, 1st May. It will be recalled that after passing through the London Reception Centre, Neukermans was at large for some six months in this country before he was recognised by someone who had known him on the continent and was exposed in his true colours.

There has been the possibility of other persons like Neukermans slipping through the net that has led the Security Service uniformly to resist the pressure sometimes brought to bear on them to shorten the period of detention at the LRC of aliens arriving in this country, which could only result in lowering of the standard of thoroughness required for the proper scrutiny of these persons.

B. SPECIAL AGENTS.

The agent TRICYCLE has now returned from visiting his masters in Lisbon. He has once more succeeded in convincing them of his complete reliability and has extracted from them a large sum in dollars as an advance against his future services. So far as the Germans knew, his reason for visiting Lisbon was that he is acting as the organiser of an escape route on behalf of the Yugoslav Government. This undertaking has now the cordial support of the German Secret Service, who hope to use it as a means of reinforcing their network in England. In practice, however, the effect will be the opposite, since the escapers are selected in London and sent from Yugoslavia by TRICYCLE's brother, DREADNOUGHT. The latter, who visited TRICYCLE while he was in Lisbon, and brought with him a number of personal messages from General Mihailovitch to King Peter, has now become one of the Abwehr's most important agents in Yugoslavia. He has been advanced to the rank of Sonder-führer or Lieutenant-Colonel. He has since returned to Yugoslavia to continue his work of sabotaging the local manifestations of Goering's Four Year Plan. Apart from his work for German Military Intelligence, TRICYCLE has now also established a connection in Himmler's organisation to whom he has delivered a political report, and from whom he has received an interesting questionnaire. They appear to have the highest opinion of him and are taking steps to ensure that his work for them remains unknown to other German masters.

C. SABOTAGE.

1. The Security Service has been investigating a case of sabotage on HMS *Aylmer*, when sand was placed in the gearing of the mainshaft of the turbo-blower. One culprit was identified as Stoker Petty-Officer P.E.L. Land. He pleaded in extenuation of his offence that he had domestic troubles, and therefore wished to delay the sailing of the ship. He was dismissed from the service and sentenced to two years' imprisonment.

2. Three more saboteurs belonging to Himmler's organisation have been arrested in Italy. They had been instructed to destroy one target of the ordinary type, and in addition to assassinate Generals Alexander and Mark Clark.

C. TROTSKYITE.

Correspondence between Roy Tearse, an industrial organiser of the Revolutionary Communist Party, and Heaton Lee, a Tyneside organiser, was intercepted and showed that they were naively interesting themselves in the strike of ship-yard apprentices. Papers were submitted to the Director of Public Prosecutions, who instructed that searches be made of the premises of the Party and certain of its leaders in London, Newcastle, Glasgow and Nottingham. On evidence revealed in the searches, warrants were issued for the arrest of Roy Tearse, Jock Haston, the national organiser of the Party, and Heaton Lee and his assistant Anne Keen. All these persons are new in custody and have been charged with conspiracy to incite or instigate a strike contrary to the provisions of the Trade Unions and Trade Disputes Act of 1927.

E. LEAKAGES.

Despite the efforts which have been made in so many ways to prevent leakage of information occurring through careless talk and the like, cases continue to be reported, of which the following are examples:-

A woman employed as a book-folder in the Confidential Section of HM Stationery Office disclosed to fellow-workers at a Civil Defence

First Aid Post, where she did part-time duty, information regarding a confidential publication with which she had been dealing. She was prosecuted and sentence to three months' imprisonment with hard labour.

A fireman telephonist wrote a letter to a friend disclosing information which he had received in the course of his duties recording air raid damage. He was prosecuted and fined £50.

A doctor at Portsmouth saw fit to draw a sketch of certain devices which were being prepared in connection with future operations. He was prosecuted and fined in all £75.10.00.

A workman employed in connection with the preparation of devices for use in future operations wrote a letter describing their nature and purpose. He was prosecuted and fined £25.

5th May 1944

★ ★ ★

The Spanish case referred to, Alejandro Guzman Urzaiz, originated in January 1944 with the FBI when the routine inspection of the transatlantic mail showed a payment made to him in Cuba from a compromised source, a 24-year-old model, Valentina Kurz, in Spain and Portugal. This led the FBI's liaison officer in London, Arthur Thurston, to alert MI5's Herbert Hart, and to a request that the 45-year-old Urzaiz, a Siemens employee, be detained when he sailed from New Orleans to Spain in February on the Spanish SS *Magallanes*. When the ship docked at Trinidad in February there would be an opportunity to seize Urzaiz, who had been identified from decrypts as a Nazi spy, although the FBI's surveillance of him in the United States and Cuba had not produced any evidence. However, ISOS had incriminated him when he left Bilbao at the end of August 1943 bound for Havana on the *Marques de Comillas*, apparently representing the Banco Exterior de España but without a diplomatic passport. In several of the decrypts he was referred to by the code name VIENTO. After Urzaiz's arrest his wife, Matilde, was allowed to continue her journey.

When questioned by the FBI in Trinidad Urzaiz insisted that his trip to Cuba had been an opportunity to visit his wife's relatives in Mexico and conduct some banking business. When challenged about the transfer of large sums from Spain and Portugal, he claimed that the money, amounting to $21,000, was a black market currency transaction. Further than that, he admitted nothing apart from acknowledging that he had spotted surveillance and lodged a complaint about it to the Mexican intelligence service, which happened to be headed by a friend of his wife's family.

Coincidentally, Fernando Kobbe was sailing on the same vessel, but he was protected by his consular status. However, when word reached Madrid of Urzaiz's arrest, either through Kobbe or a report in the *Daily Express*, the Spanish foreign minister, Francisco Jordana, immediately protested, through the British embassy in Madrid and the Spanish ambassador in London. Meanwhile, Urzaiz was flown to Bermuda and placed on the frigate HMS *Torrington* for the voyage, via a brief stop at St John's, Newfoundland, to Belfast, where he landed in 20 April 1944 for transfer to Brixton prison and then Camp 020.

Under interrogation Urzaiz conceded only that he had broken Spanish currency regulations, and refused to name the source of the money he received in Cuba, which ISOS confirmed was the Abwehr. In conclusion, Camp 020 could 'not prove Urzaiz guilty of any intent or action on behalf of the enemy and against the interest of the Allies although it is implicit in his refusal to identify material contacts and satisfactorily explain his financial arrangements'. Nevertheless, his detention was continued and the stalemate was perpetuated with MI5 unwilling to divulge the nature of the evidence against him. 'Either the FBI and the British authorities were bluffing, in which case Urzaiz saw no reason to confess, or we had evidence which we were unwilling to produce. The latter is correct, for the security of Source is worth more than an admission from Urzaiz.'

Given that it is likely that the clumsy surveillance warned off Urzaiz from incriminating himself, and there was really no evidence that he had accomplished more than making contact with the Abwehr in Madrid, it is remarkable that Petrie singled him out for the Prime Minister's attention. So far as could be ascertained, Urzaiz had not completed any espionage assignment, and although some of his currency was unaccounted for, it seemed unlikely that he had been able to hand on very much cash to any alleged Abwehr representative in Cuba. In July 1944 Kim Philby, as head of SIS's Iberian counter-intelligence branch, was consulted on what statement should be made to the Spanish government, and the decision was taken to say the bare minimum. Accordingly, Urzaiz remained in custody until August 1945, when he was escorted by a pair of Special Branch detectives to Portsmouth, placed aboard HMS *Glasgow* and released in Gibraltar.

★ ★ ★

Identified in ISOS as the head of the Berlin Ast in Lisbon, Juan Brandes appeared initially to be an exceptionally able and dangerous adversary, managing agents in many theatres, including one in Egypt in July 1942, although this information only emerged from the cryptanalysts in December of that year. Other reports on Brandes were supplied by Section V's Martin Lloyd, who handled a double-agent code-named VIPER, actually the concierge at the Hotel Aviz, and had been assigned the task of penetrating the Lisbon Abwehr. To assist in the cause MI5's Richmond Stopford and Section V's John de Salis were posted to Portugal and offered another asset, code-named CHLOE, to be introduced by VIPER to Brandes. By way of background, ARTIST mentioned that Brandes was partly Jewish and had been posted to Lisbon personally by Admiral Canaris to keep him out of danger. TRICYCLE confirmed this, and opined that Brandes was anti-Nazi and very pro-British. He was also strongly suspected of having fabricated his network of Swiss sub-agents, which meant that his sole source was VIPER, whose principal function was to photocopy the passports of his hotel's guests.

Brandes claimed to have an agent in England, another in the United States, and two in South America, with whom he maintained contact through Swiss diplomats. However, there was growing belief in London that Brandes was a fraud, emulating notorious fabricator Paul Fidrmuc, code-named OSTRO.

1. Hans Brandes is an agent or representative of Ast Berlin and of HKW who has made Lisbon the centre of his operations. He controls or claims to control a fairly extensive network of agents. A number of them appear to be Jewish, or at least to be based on Switzerland. The particulars available about them on secret sources suggest that they are, at least ostensibly, of a higher grade than most Abwehr agents. The principal ones of whom we have knowledge are:

> INSTERBURG, tentatively identified by SIS as Paul Rene Keller of a Swiss transport firm in Lisbon.
> AESCULAP who was said to have been in Cairo in July, 1942, and subsequently to have left for de Gaulle's headquarters at Fort Lamy. He was later reported in Portuguese Guinea and last heard of in Freetown in January 1943.
> BUNSEN probably a Swiss, who was in New York in October when he returned to Switzerland via London.

In December of the same year he was said to be about to return to England. More recent evidence shows that he has now returned to Switzerland after having apparently been in London.

The IRA Man. Nothing is known of this man except that he is an Irishman member of the IRA, who was intended in November 1942 for Estonia, which may, in that context, have been a cover name for England.
PETTERMANN Another agent, possibly connected in some way with AESCULAP, who was intended for this country in January 1941. We know nothing of him except that according to Brandes was full of good prospects.
BARINKI d'ARNOUX @ DANNEMANN. A Frenchman who was in Vichy in March 1943, awaiting a visa for the USA where he was to take up the position of secretary to the representative of the Swiss Mercantile Marine in New York.

2. No actual reports from any of Brandes' agents have so far appeared on secret sources. There is not the same positive evidence, therefore, as there is with Fidrmuc, that the organisation which he claims to run is fictitious. There are, nevertheless, reasonable grounds for supposing that this may in fact be the case. The following facts may be cited:

3. Endeavours to identity BUNSEN and AESCALAP were attended by wholly negative results, though in each case the facts available should have been sufficient to produce, if not an identification, at least a short list of possible candidates;

4. Similar attempts to identify DANNEMANN failed completely, even though we were informed of his real name. According to the FBI, no application was made in Vichy at the material time for a U.S. visa by anyone named d'Arnoux, nor did any alternative candidates suggest themselves;

5. According to both TRICYCLE and ARTIST, Brandes is not only anti-Nazi but positively pro-British and has, according to his own statement, been a party to at least one deliberate fraud on the Abwehr.

6. These facts afford at least some reason for supposing that Brandes might accept a proposition along similar lines to that suggested above in connection with Fidrmuc. The method of approach would be broadly the same with, however, these qualifications. There is no evidence that Brandes is an adventurer of the same type as Fidrmuc. His motives, to judge from what he said to TRICYCLE, are not so much to make money as to keep himself in safety in Lisbon. It appears probable that his outlook is, broadly

speaking, similar to that of JUNIOR. It would not, therefore, be appropriate to put the matter as bluntly to him as to Fidrmuc. On the other hand, two powerful arguments can be advanced in his case which would not be applicable to Fidrmuc. In the first place Brandes is fit and of military age. He is, in fact, only 24. He is also half Jewish. It is certain, therefore, that if he fails to maintain his position and still more if any fraudulent practice of his were exposed, that he would find himself very rapidly on the Eastern front. If he were offered a straight choice between comparative security under our control and the Pripet marshes, it is not to be supposed that he would hesitate very long. It is true that we should find even greater difficulty in exposing Fidrmuc. There is, however, no reason why Brandes should realise this. However, though it would be difficult to expose him, it would be comparatively easy to dislodge him from Portugal, since he is engaged in various black-market and smuggling activities on behalf of Sonderstab HWK. Unlike Fidrmuc, Brandes would regard the threat of being expelled from the Peninsula as a very real one. Secondly, there is Brandes' political outlook to be considered. If the reports of TRICYCLE and ARTIST are to be trusted, he would have a positive motive in accepting our proposition as a means towards defeating the Nazis and bringing the war to an end.

7. In the event of Brandes rejecting the proposition, the same arguments apply as were noted above in connection with Fidrmuc. The only difference is that the possibility of Brandes' network actually existing is higher and must be reckoned with. It does not necessarily follow, however, if Brandes' political attitude has been correctly reported, that this would cause him, as it would almost certainly cause Fidrmuc, to reject our proposition. If he did so, and if he informed the Abwehr of what had occurred, no greater danger to secret sources would be involved than in the case of Fidrmuc. The Abwehr's suspicions would naturally tend to fall. It is true that some suspicion might also attach to ARTIST and TRICYCLE. This could be mitigated, if not wholly removed, by a careful planning of what was actually said to Brandes in the first place. If it were made plain to him that we knew not only of the agents whom he claims to have in England, but also of the agent whom he claimed previously to have in North Africa, it would be difficult for the Abwehr subsequently to lay the blame for the leakage on either ARTIST or TRICYCLE. They are not (I understand) aware of any of the details of Brandes' organisation except in so far as ARTIST has been concerned with Brandes' Swiss connections. It might well be possible at the same time to leave Brandes under the impression that the ultimate source

of much of our information was Erich Geweyer, on official of Ast Berlin, who is now one of Cramer's assistants in Lisbon. This man, though new a member of Gruppe III KO Portugal and not associated with Brandes' work, is connected with him through VIPER and through Werner Deussen who acts as an intermediary between Brandes and VIPER. As a late member of Ast Berlin, it is reasonable to suppose that Geweyer is, or could be, familiar with the nature of Brandes' work. He was before the war a receptionist at the Savoy Hotel in London. Although we are not, in fact, in contact with him, it is reasonable and probable that we should be.

At one point, early in January 1944, consideration was given to the idea that Klop Ustinov should travel to Lisbon and approach Brandes, but in the end the proposal was dropped, partly because of the growing complexity of the situation with ARTIST and TRICYCLE speculating on the extent to which Brandes was simply inventing his network's reports from English newspapers. The ramifications, as D-Day approached, became apparent when in April 1944 Popov's MI5 case officer Ian Wilson circulated an assessment that compared TRICYCLE's standing to GARBO:

In discussion with Kuebarth, Hansen, Bohlen, Weiss and Kammler about the valuation of the various England connections by 'Fremde Heere' in Berlin, Brandes has learned the following:

The only connections working really well are the Red–Spanish Group and the IVAN group. The correspondence with a number of other agents, amongst which are presumably also Sostaric, CAIS, IVAN II etc, has even before the cancellation of the postal traffic not been very productive. In Brandes' opinion there are no other wireless connections. He said, however, that possibly only connections carried on from the Iberian Peninsular were discussed with him, and that perhaps there are other connections from Sweden or from Switzerland. However, he thinks that the latter is very unlikely, as in the long discussion with him a comparison would surely have been drawn between the performances of these people as against IVAN and the Spaniards.

It can therefore be said that, as I reported previously, from the Iberian Peninsular, and probably from anywhere, only these two really good connections exist, after OSTRO has dropped out. The valuation of these connections has, however, altered considerably lately as IVAN is now considered to be by far the best connection, and the Spaniards as regards quality of their reports are following a long way behind. Lately there has been the strong suspicion as regards the Spaniards that they are being controlled by the British. IVAN, about whom similar doubts existed until the last report, is still not considered to be 100% safe, but the confidence in him has grown very much and it is thought very probably that he is genuine. Brandes told me to advise IVAN for the time being only to give reports which he has checked himself and not to rely on stories. If he would give a few more reports, which later are proved to be correct, there would no longer be the slightest doubt in his genuineness, and if he wanted to become a little lazy later on he could do so and also once in a while report rumours or indulge, in his fancies. Brandes told me these things with the intention to help my friend and thus me. It can therefore be assumed that his remarks reflect Berlin's opinion fairly accurately. If therefore IVAN would bring two to three bits of really good information, it can be counted upon with certainty that any doubt in his genuineness will be removed.

As regards the Spaniards, however it will mean considerably greater efforts to regain the full confidence of the 'Abt. Fremde Heere', although, of course their reports are still being given attention.

The above valuation is in contrast to my former reports (sources: Karnap, Wiegand, etc.) There can, however, be no doubt that Brandes' report is reliable and that the valuation in Berlin has changed completely since my last reports. The KO Spain nevertheless still maintain that their people are doubtless genuine and IVAN, to say the least, is suspicious, and that this too is Berlin's opinion. This point of view of the KO Spain is, however, probably based on jealousy.

In a further report dealing with KO Spain, containing information obtained by ARTIST from Franzbach, ARTIST writes as follows: 'The Red-Spanish group which is working in England for the KO Spain and which according to Kuhlenthal is now 17 men strong, will shortly also open a wireless station in America. The payment for this group for the next nine months.

'Mention has made with £7,500, for which 750,000 pesetas were paid in the way reported previously. If I remember rightly, the amount of this payment was at variance with the details given me by the same source previously. As I assume that in London there is exact knowledge of this group I have made no further enquiries, but can do so if required.'

With access to ISOS, but unable to share the intelligence derived with either ARTIST or TRICYCLE, MI5 and SIS found themselves powerless as Brandes manoeuvred in Lisbon and Abwehr III's counter-espionage experts in Berlin came to distrust both men. Although Brandes seemed sympathetic to the Allies, he submitted adverse reports on ARTIST, apparently motivated by a desire to shorten the war and prevent him, as he saw it, from helping the Nazis. He also seems to have been concerned about his own status when he was unable to comply with a directive to send his agents to France for training. His inability to produce them on demand heightened suspicions, not just in London but apparently shared in Berlin, that they were imaginary. ARTIST was warned in general terms by SIS not to trust Brandes, but the need to protect the ISOS source prevented his case officer from spelling out the precise nature of the danger he was in, and in April 1944 Jebsen was abducted in Lisbon, leading to recriminations between the SIS station commander in Lisbon and MI5 in London. The loss of such a well-placed agent was hugely disappointing for SIS, and after the war efforts were made to learn his fate. The interrogation of various prisoners suggested that Jebsen had been lured to the Abwehr office in the rua Buenos Aires where he had been overpowered, drugged, and driven in a box across Spain to the French border. There the Gestapo had taken him into custody and placed him in a concentration camp, never to be seen again. One of those captured was Wilhelm Kuebart, who was questioned at Camp 020 in August 1945 and provided his version of events.

Kuebart, described to Dusko Popov by Johnny Jebsen as 'the most intelligent man in the Abwehr', had been detained by the Americans in Michelau in April 1945 and transferred on 24 May to Camp 020. There he made a lengthy statement in which he described having encountered the Abwehr for the first time in September 1941 when he was transferred to Fremde Heere Ost at Mauerwald as a staff officer to work on intelligence from Turkey, Persia and Iraq.

In August 1943 Kuebart had been sent to Brussels to look into a request to send RM50,000 to an Abwehr agent, Dr Johann Koessler, who had established himself with his wife in Lisbon. Kuebart had expressed doubts about Koessler's loyalty to his senior officer, Georg Hansen, who ordered Koessler to be dropped. He was also briefed on a network in England headed by IVAN and managed from the KO Madrid by Johannes Jebsen, whom he said he 'instinctively distrusted'. In mid-September 1943 Kuebart had visited Lisbon, and later the same month he accompanied Admiral Canaris to Madrid for talks with Spanish ministers. They then travelled to Lisbon, where he was briefed on three agents: IVAN, a woman in England code-named IWI 'who appeared to be of little use' and a Portuguese, MARINO, who reported on shipping movements in Lisbon. He also met an Abwehr agent, von Wolff, who introduced him to a journalist, Paul Fidrmuc, who had been to England and the United States. Fidrmuc's role was to produce information on:

a)   Aircraft production in England and the USA (this was considered reliable information by the I Luft since it was greatly appreciated by the evaluation section of the Luftwaffefuehrungsstab). This at that time was Fidrmuc's main activity.

b)   Allied convoys, shipping movements and tonnage. (Although this was sent to IM Kuebart does not know whether it was regarded as reliable).

c)   Reports on troop identification, divisional signs and/or numbers in England. (Those were judged inaccurate by IH on checking with Fremde Heere).

Channels of Fidrmuc's Information. Kuebart claims that he was unaware of the precise channels through which Fidrmuc derived his information. When it was put to him that he, as Fidrmuc's chief, should surely know this, he replied that he purposely did not burden himself with such details as he, in his capacity as head of Abwehr IH, had little time for complete knowledge of these.

Kuebart's opinion of Fidrmuc. Kuebart was not prepared to say whether he considered Fidrmuc's work good or bad. In some ways, such as the IH information from England, it was unreliable but in others it more than balanced the information sent to IH. In the whole he was inclined to feel that the balance stood in Fidrmuc's favour.

Naturally, Kuebart's MI5 interrogators gave him no clue that all these individuals were well known to the Allied counter-intelligence authorities, but his recollections threw new light on Jebsen's abduction and the 20 July plot to assassinate Hitler. According to Kuebart, Jebsen was suspected of preparing to desert, and had been embezzling money from the SD, so therefore he 'deserved everything he got', although he was uncertain about his ultimate fate. He was informed in May that Jebsen has been summoned by Alois Schreiber to the Lisbon KO with one of his friends, an I Wi agent named Molderhauer, where they were overpowered, placed in a trunk and driven to Biarritz. They were kept in military detection in Wunsdorf for ten days and then, on orders from General Keitel, handed over to the SD.

Kuebart also described how in March 1944 Georg Hansen had begun to confide details of the plan to overthrow the regime. This knowledge led to his arrest by the Gestapo, but he would be acquitted on charges of his complicity in October for lack of evidence. Nevertheless, he was dismissed from the Wehrmacht in November and eventually found a job on a farm near Michelau owned by Klaus von Stauffenburg's cousin. It was here that he encountered

US troops and made himself known to the occupation forces. He was detained on 27 April at Bamberg and then Wiesbaden before being flown to England on 24 May for interrogation at Camp 020.

After the war Brandes remained in Portugal but he was repatriated in March 1946 and was detained briefly in December 1946 by the US 7th Amy Counter-Intelligence Corps in Berlin. He gave them a very limited account of his activities in Lisbon, confirming only that he had operated there as a representative of his mother's machine-tool manufacturing firm, Fritz Werner AG, selling armaments to the Portuguese government. Although he acknowledged a friendship with Dr Alois Schreiber of the Lisbon Abwehr, he denied ever having worked for the organisation. Accordingly, the CIC released him, causing great consternation in London where the FBI's Win Scott was aghast. Nevertheless, Brandes received a clearance and went back into the arms dealing business, apparently with the support of the West German Bundesnachrichtendiest. He died in April 1971 in Schaftlarn, Bavaria.

★ ★ ★

Born in Valencia in December 1919, José Polo was interned at the end of the Spanish Civil War and then released. In July 1941 he volunteered to join the Blue Division to fight in Russia but was returned to face a court martial for insubordination in May 1942, although he never stood trial. In November 1942 he accepted a job offer in Germany and was employed until May 1943 as a pay clerk at a factory in Kiel assembling U-boats.

While on leave in San Sebastian in July 1943 Polo approached both the German and British consulates to offer his services as a spy. To the Germans he declared that he had already been recruited by the British, who had instructed him to penetrate the German organisation, and to the British he claimed to be willing to collect information while travelling through Germany. He also said that his uncle owned a fruit business in Covent Garden.

In March 1944 Polo went through the same routine in Barcelona, offering his services to the British and German consulates and being paid by both, but on this occasion a German named Hampler suggested a mission to Gibraltar, requiring him to surrender upon arrival and pretend to be a double-agent. However, a Section V officer, Captain Matthews, spotted that one part of this scheme had appeared in an ISOS intercept on the Paris-Madrid circuit, which referred to him as 'a swindler and has apparently invented the whole affair'. Polo's activities in Spain attracted the attention of Kim Philby, who alerted MI5's Herbert Hart to him:

Apart from contacting our Barcelona representative Aparicio also approached the Vice-Consul at San Sebastian with an offer of service. He stated that he had information about sabotage operations based on Algeciras. At the same time as Aparicio presented himself at the San Sebastian Consulate, the following report was received from an independent source:-

José Aparicio Polo, a Spaniard who lives in Hotel Arana in San Sebastian where he has an account, was a member of the Blue Division, but he was demoted for some unknown reason. The head of the German organisation took a great interest in this man because, some time ago apparently he, Gensorowski, was approached by subject, who offered to work for him. Subject told him at the same time that he was in contact with an Englishman living in Valencia, named Sheldon, and said that this was in order to obtain information about Russia and the situation concerning the Blue Division. Gensorowski gave subject some money on various occasions, although he apparently produced information of very little importance. Gensorowski suspected that subject was connected with the Allied I.S. and that he should be watched; he went so far as to send someone to the Hotel Arena to watch subject, but so far nothing has been discovered.

In view of this, it was thought that Aparicio was working as an '*agent provocateur*' for the Germans and nothing than mild encouragement was given him. This, I think, confirms our view that Aparicio will prove an interesting character.

Accordingly, when Polo was smuggled into Gibraltar by boat from Seville on 9 April 1944 by SIS he remained under Section V's sponsorship until, after ten days of embarrassment and debate, he was taken into custody and flown to Whitchurch for transfer to Camp 020 for interrogation.

When questioned Polo was able to give a limited amount of information about the factories he had visited in Germany, but initially obfuscated about his attempts to engage in espionage, causing one of his MI5 interrogators to describe him as 'a trickster who duped the German and British intelligence services in turn' and 'an inveterate liar'. In his summary of the case in June 1943, Buster Milmo concluded:

After a thorough interrogation at Camp 020 it became clear that during the year prior to his arrest and transportation to this country José Polo was trying to obtain a livelihood both from the British and German Intelligence services. He lied to both though it is only fair to say that certain information given to the British authorities in Barcelona may have been both true and of value – we have no information as to whether it was true or not.

Aparicia Polo maintains that all the information he gave to the Germans was either untrue or common knowledge whilst information given to the British was true but sometimes exaggerated unimportant details with the view to enhancement of his apparent value as an agent. He claims that his favouritism of the British was due to his having heard that the British Intelligence Service paid better than the Germans, and also because he came to the conclusion that the bad state of affairs in Spain at that time was due to Fascism. The latter reason appears to be an afterthought and is not convincing. In fact, he has lied so much to the Germans, and also whilst under interrogation, that it is reasonable to suppose that during his contact with the British authorities in Spain he lied as much as he thought he could without being found out. Moreover, we only have his word that the information he gave to the Germans was either untrue or obvious.

There is little doubt that through completely false representation Aparicio Polo wormed his way into the confidence of MI6 in Barcelona and induced them to evacuate him from Spain to this country through secret channels. Having found himself, on his arrival in this country, under close detention, he lied volubly about the missions entrusted to him by the German Intelligence Service and proved without a doubt that no confidence whatsoever can be placed in him.

Thus, because Polo had learned about SIS's clandestine route to Gibraltar from Seville, stayed overnight at an SOE safe house in Seville, seen MI5 techniques, and experienced Camp 020, he remained in detention, although by August 1944 it had been discovered that he was suffering from epilepsy, and was transferred to the Royal Marsden Hospital for specialist treatment. He was deported to Madrid by air in September 1945, and this might have been the last to be heard of him. However, in October 1949 the French Direction de la Surveillance du Territoire contacted SIS and asked for any background information held on Polo, who was then representing himself in Paris as a Spanish intelligence officer offering information about the Soviets. In his version of events, passed to MI5's Ronnie Reed by SIS, Polo claimed that he had:

> … fought with the Republican Army during the Civil War, and also with the Blue Division in Russia, where he was wounded. During his convalescence in Austria he met Major Kammler of the Abwehr (or SD), through whom

he was repatriated to Spain where he was planted on Sheldon of SIS at Barcelona. Polo was sent to England via Gibraltar and on arrival in the UK admitted to being a German agent.

★ ★ ★

A 27-year-old Belgian waiter, Joseph Vanhove landed at RAF Leuchars in February 1944 having been flown in from Stockholm, where he had been living since jumping ship in April 1943. Under interrogation at the Royal Victoria Patriotic School he broke down and admitted having been recruited by the Abwehr in Antwerp for a mission to find out about Allied preparations for the invasion, and when he was questioned at Camp 020 in April he confessed and acknowledged links to several other Belgian spies recruited by the Germans. He was tried in May 1944 and hanged at Pentonville on 12 July 1944.

★ ★ ★

The issue of wartime industrial unrest and labour stoppages was always of concern to the Cabinet, especially as the Minister of Labour, Ernest Bevin, had founded the Transport and General Workers' Union in 1922 and had been general-secretary for eighteen years before he joined the coalition government in 1940. The introduction of conscription into the mines was deeply unpopular and on 28 March 1944 a shipyard apprentice and former Young Communist League member organised a strike which spread across the industrial north of England to the Clyde. Such an interference with production had the gravest strategic implications and MI5 identified three veteran Communists, Jack Haston, Roy Tearse, Keaton Lee, as having influenced the ringleader, Bill Davey. They were arrested on 8 April, along with Lee's girlfriend Anne Keen, and prosecuted under the terms of the 1927 Act. As we shall see, the case would go awry.

15

3 JUNE 1944

In the month before the D-Day assault in Normandy, when the true Allied objectives for the invasion were the top priority, MI5's monthly report disclosed a veritable German espionage offensive through Iceland, a territory under Anglo-American military control, but with only a small SIS office in the capital, Reykjavik.

MAY 1944
A. SPIES.
The most interesting development this month has been the sudden influx of a comparatively large number of spies into Iceland.

As far is known, the enemy had sent only three espionage expeditions to Iceland till April of this year. All three of these were enterprises of the German Military Intelligence Service, two of the agents concerned have since been operating under control, while the third committed suicide. In the latter half of April no less than seven new agents arrived in Iceland; these were grouped into three parties, two of which were controlled by Military Intelligence, and one by Himmler's Secret Service. These agents had between them six wireless transmitters.

They were instructed to send weather reports, and at least two of the spies were equipped with instruments to assist them. They also had orders to send information on the presence of ski troops, landing craft for invasion, and on the number of ships in the fjords, and to keep a special watch on six named harbours.

Two of the parties comprising four spies in all were captured within a very short time of their arrival, but the third party was at large for over a week, during which time its members endeavoured to make contact with the enemy by wireless.

During the course of the war there has been no comparable activity by the German Secret Service since the autumn of 1940, when similar tactics were employed for the despatch to this country of invasion spies. However the questionnaires given to these Icelandic agents present a marked contrast to those given to spies sent here at the time when the enemy were preparing themselves to invade. These new cases strongly suggest that the enemy anticipates an offensive operation of some magnitude to be launched from Iceland at some not far distant date, and the fact that both Military Intelligence and Himmler's Secret Service have despatched expeditions thither suggest that this expectation is not confined to the Intelligence Service, but may well be occupying the mind of the German Supreme Command itself.

As mentioned in a previous report, Most Secret Sources disclosed that a spy was on route from Norway to this country through the Peninsula. This character was identified as one Knut Brodersen, and on his arrival here he was at once arrested. He has confessed that he had a mission on behalf of the German Secret Service to supply them with information regarding invasion details here. This information was to be sent in secret writing to a cover address in Spain, and Brodersen was to receive further instructions by means of broadcasts in code sent over the German controlled Norwegian radio. Particulars of this code have been given by Brodersen and attempts are now being made to decypher messages broadcast over this service which appear to be intended for him. His secret ink was concealed in one of the straps of his plus-fours and in a pocket knife. More material for secret writing had been hidden underneath his big toe nail and in his tooth, but the former came out when he had a bath, and the tooth broke off while he was eating.

A Pole, Wladyslaw Wilman, arrived recently in Gibraltar, where he volunteered the story of his adventures, including his recruitment by the German Secret Service.

In the course of Wilman's career, both before and after he was recruited into the German Secret Service, he has been imprisoned by various powers no less than six times, and of course once again now in detention in this country. On his arrival here he produced a handkerchief from which he developed secret writing and microphotographs. The latter contained a diagram of a powerful wireless transmitter which he was to build when he reached this country or Canada, and also gave details of codes, call signs, cover addresses etc. The mission given him by the German Secret Service was to transmit technical details of new aircraft, which he was to obtain by getting work in an aircraft factory.

Joseph Jan Vanhove, the Belgian spy mentioned in the previous report, was sentenced to death at the Old Bailey on Wednesday, 24th May.

B. SPECIAL AGENTS.

1) News has been received regarding special agent ZIGZAG, an Englishman, who was dropped by parachute in December 1942, and subsequently was returned to the Germans via Lisbon after having caused a notional explosion in the de Havilland Mosquito factory. It is now known that ZIGZAG is established as the chief instructor to the German Secret Service in sabotage at Oslo, where he is living prosperously, dressed in a pepper and salt suit and with a private yacht. It is hoped that in the fullness of time he will contrive to work his way back and tell us all he has learnt in the course of his present employment.

2) There has been an unfortunate development in the case of TRICYCLE, the true purport and consequences of which have not yet been determined. It was learnt from Most Secret Sources that ARTIST, his spymaster, was at the beginning of May, lured with great secrecy into France and from there despatched to Berlin. The reasons for this action are for the moment obscure, but it is certain that the TRICYCLE case is passing through a most critical phase and must be handled with the greatest care in view of OVERLORD.

A denunciation of FREAK, who was brought over here under TRICYCLE's auspices, was received from Mihailovic circles. (It is from Most Secret Sources that this denunciation was intercepted by the Germans.) This denunciation has provided an excuse for closing down the FREAK transmitter, at least temporarily.

3) The special agent TATE, on the 24th May, 1944, transmitted his 1,000th message, in which he took the opportunity of referring to this fact and expressing his loyal devotion to the Führer. A cordial reply has been received, and it is hoped that this will be followed up by the further advancement of TATE in the Order of the Iron Cross, of which he already holds the First and Second Class.

4) The Government Code and Cypher School have reported that the messages of TREASURE and BRUTUS are being so consistently relayed

verbatim on the German Intelligence W/T network that, with the assistance of this 'crib', there has been a very considerable saving of time and manpower in decyphering Most Secret Sources. Thus, special agents have, at a critical period, acquired a value which it is scarcely possible to overestimate.

C. SABOTAGE.

The special agent, GARBO, has been asked to give the exact locations, including street numbers, of the Service Headquarters concerned with the Second Front. This, coupled with the mission to assassinate Generals Alexander and Clark in Italy, and the known interest of Himmler's Secret Service in terrorism, makes it possible that parachute attacks against key persons may be attempted during coming operations. But this type of warfare is not beyond the Germans as confirmed by the recent parachute glider attack on Marshal Tito's Headquarters.[1]

D. LEAKAGE OF INFORMATION.

Among the cases which have come to notice, are the following:-

1) A man who was formerly employed by a firm concerned with the manufacture of a special type of tank to be used in forthcoming operations, gave details about its purpose and performance to a casual acquaintance in a public house. He was prosecuted and sentenced to three months' imprisonment. There is no doubt that this man had been making use of his knowledge in order to attract attention to himself for some time before his apprehension.

2) An American Naval Officer, at a dinner party, gave, in the course of general conversation, very detailed information as to the probable date of future operations and the forces to be engaged in them. A report was made by a general officer who was present and also by a retired officer of the Royal Air Force. Steps have been taken to warn all those present as to the need for complete discretion. The American officer is being dealt with by the American naval authorities.

3) A ship's fireman wrote a letter in which he explained that the ship on which he was serving was to be used as a block ship in the course of forthcoming operations. The letter revealed the port where the ship was then lying, together with other ships designated for similar use. The offender was prosecuted and was sentenced to thirty days' imprisonment.

4) A case at present under investigation concerns a Dutch ship's officer in an hotel at Port Talbot who stated that his ship would be off the French coast within the next two weeks, that she was loaded with petrol and ammunition, had sufficient men on board to carry out unloading. He added that all the ships in Port Talbot were similarly loaded and were ready to sail to twenty-four hours' notice.

5) A woman living in a southern county wrote to relations in Lancashire giving the precise whereabouts of the house which General Montgomery will be using as his Headquarters. Proceedings are being taken against her.

3rd June 1944.

★ ★ ★

Disappointingly, Petrie offered few details of the enemy's espionage offensive in Iceland, which, as he pointed out, was on an unprecedented scale. Altogether seven spies had landed, and all had been captured within a week, but who were they? In the days and weeks before the much-anticipated Allied invasion of Europe, the German High Command was preoccupied with clues to the likely landing areas, and FORTITUDE NORTH had been designed to draw attention to a planned amphibious assault on Norway. The need for accurate information about the build-up of troops near embarkation ports in Iceland and Scotland was the only rational explanation for the sudden interest shown by the Abwehr in Iceland, and this suggested that the Germans had taken the bait.

Hitherto, as reported accurately by Petrie, there had been just three earlier Abwehr missions to Iceland, and of them COBWEB and BEETLE had become double-agents, maintaining contact with the enemy from Reykjavik under SIS's supervision. Chronologically, the first had been a Norwegian, Olav Saetrang, who landed in Iceland in August with a group of genuine refugees off a boat from northern Norway, but he committed suicide before he could be questioned. According to ISOS, he may have been a spy code-named SVERRA, intending to travel to England, and the episode was recorded by Liddell:

There has been an interesting ISOS case. It became apparent that three Norwegians, Sverre [sic], Stefansen and Elverstadt [sic],[2] were preparing for some expedition. The message said Iraq but it was difficult to see why three Norwegians should be going to that country. Hugh Trevor Roper discovered that the 'Q' was probably a misprint for 'X' and that the 'R' was probably a misprint for a 'D'. This left IDA in inverted commas since X is used for this purpose. IDA is the speller in German Morse code for I. This leaves I in inverted commas and from the context it seemed likely to be Iceland. A telegram to Iceland has produced a reply that a boat called the *Hornfjell* recently arrived with eight crew and passengers, three of them being Saetrang, Stefansen, and Elverstad so they are all being sent over here for examination. This case is a clear indication of Trevor Roper's value.

Two weeks later, on 17 September, Liddell learned of Saetrang's suicide from Camp 020's commandant, and took the appropriate measures to keep the matter secret, and informed Lord Swinton:

Colonel Stephens rang me up early this morning to say that Saetrang, one of the Norwegians who arrived on the *Hornfjell*, had committed suicide, by hanging himself from a water pipe with his scarf. He had stripped himself to the waist and gagged himself by stuffing a handkerchief down his throat. He had only been interrogated for three minutes on his arrival on the previous day. He had been told that he had information which connected him with the German secret service and that he had better consider the advisability of making a written statement. He had been seen by the guard at 4am and must have committed suicide sometime between four and six o'clock.

On arrival at the office I got hold of Edward Hinchley-Cooke and Edward Cussen in order that we could make arrangements for a coroner's inquest with the least possible publicity. They have made arrangements to do this effectively, through a tame coroner in the north of London.

Lord Swinton was in the office in the morning and I explained the facts to him. From the intelligence point of view it is a pity that Saetrang had done himself in. We think he is identical with a man called Sverra and that he could have told us a good deal.

The next spy, Ib Riis, landed from *U-252* in April 1942, and he had been enrolled as COBWEB.[3] Born in Hallerup, Denmark, to Icelandic parents, he had trained as a ship's radio operator and served on the *George Stage*. In July 1939 he joined a hunting expedition to Greenland on the *Gustav Holm*, and in October 1941 was back in Denmark to be recruited by the Abwehr in Copenhagen. He attended a course in Hamburg in February 1942, and set off on the *U-252* for Iceland.

Having surrendered on his arrival to British personnel, he was escorted to Reykjavik on 22 April, and soon afterwards took his captors back to a site near the beach where he had hidden his transmitter. When questioned, he described Jens Palsson as another agent destined for a similar mission. Always anxious to cooperate, Riis maintained his radio channel with the Abwehr until the end of the war, supervised first by MI5's Ronnie Reed and then later by SIS's Harold Blyth.

Riis was followed by Sigurjon Jonsson, the 53-year-old captain of the *Arctic*, a three-masted trawler with a crew of fifteen, and his 26-year-old radio operator, Jens Palsson. Both had been recruited by the Abwehr during a visit to Vigo lasting two months in December 1941, when they had been entrusted with codes, a transmitter and instructions on the collection of military and meteorological data. As they would later reveal, they had been threatened with a torpedo attack on their ship unless they cooperated, so they had transmitted the requested information on eight successive days. Both men were arrested on 14 April 1942 after Jonsson had taken the apparatus ashore in anticipation of a voyage to England, and the episode was reported to Dick White in London:

Major Ferguson rang up to say that the M/V *Arctic* was being held by the Navy in Iceland. Meanwhile Wise had managed to extract confessions from the Captain and the Wireless Operator and as a result of his investigations four persons are now under arrest in Reykjavik. These are:

Sigurjon Jonsson – Captain of the *Arctic*

Jens Palsson – W/T operator of the *Arctic*

Marel Magnusson and Hallgrimur Dagland, residents of Iceland

The story as understood so far is as follows:

The *Arctic* started its Abwehr career at Vigo and is probably one of those ships run by the Schuchmann organisation. Its principal function is Naval reconnaissance and the *Arctic* is fitted with a short wave transmitter by which it can signal ships sighted on sea lanes or evidence of convoy movements. These signals are I understand picked up by Schuchmann's organisation at Le Havre and there has recently been information from Secret Sources as having had 100% reception of such signals as were sent by the *Arctic* on its voyage from Vigo to Reykjavik.

The *Arctic* carried to Reykjavik a cargo of oranges. It was not, however, intercepted by the Navy until it reached the Westman Islands on the continuation of its voyage from Reykjavik. It went to the Westman Islands ostensibly to collect a cargo of fish for transport to the UK.

It is not clear how the further details of the story have been extracted, presumably by interrogation either by the Navy or Wise – and I gather that the Captain and the Wireless Operator together with the 14 members of the crew have been taken back to Reykjavik. Anyway the important facts emerging from their story are:

(a) That on their first arrival at Reykjavik they had managed to smuggle a wireless set on shore and deliver it to a resident in Iceland named Magnusson. This is the man referred to above who is now under arrest.

(b) That they were also able to smuggle a code book on shore and to pass it to a resident in Iceland named Dalberg. This is the man referred to above who is also under arrest.

After discussion with Ferguson, and subsequently with Keith Liversidge, the following plan of action was agreed:

(1)   That we should request Wise to send Jonsson and Palsson to England as soon as possible for further interrogation.

(2)   That the two Iceland residents, whose cases must obviously be of considerable local interest, should be dealt with by Wise until such time as he could report that he had obtained sufficient information on their mission for his purpose, when they should be sent on here.

(3)   That careful examination should be given to the possibility of using the *Arctic* and its wireless transmitter as a XX station with all the possibilities thus offered of strategic deception in the war at sea.

(4)   That in view of (3) we should request Iceland to send us as urgently as possible complete technical specifications of the wireless sets in use by these enemy agents.

The opportunity to exploit the *Arctic*'s established relationship with the Abwehr evidently appealed to MI5, which prepared an ambition deception scheme, code-named SPIDER:

The capture of two German W/T stations, one in Iceland and the other on board a trawler of 477 gross tonnage, the SS *Arctic*, which was taken in the Westmann Islands and is at present en route under guard to Reykjavik, offers good opportunities for strategic deception in the war at sea. The known facts under which we could operate those two German stations are as follows:

(a) Complete knowledge of W/T procedure in the case of the SS *Arctic* station;

(b) Probable knowledge of the procedure of the Iceland (o\c) mainland station.

(c) It is known that the *Arctic* left Vigo on 10 February 1942, and arrived at Reykjavik on 24 February 1942. It left Reykjavik in ballast on 10 April 1942 for the Westmann Island with a load of fish for the UK, its personnel having smuggled the Iceland W/T ashore in a sea bag on 9 April 1942.

The German intentions with regard to the *Arctic* were that the trawler should report her departure from Reykjavik and course outward bound. If the behaviour of the *Arctic* on its voyage Vigo–Reykjavik may be taken as a model, one is to report weather conditions and shipping movements observed during the voyage. This is corroborated by the confession of the skipper and W/T operator.

2. It is suggested that if this station is worked under our control and corroborated by working the Iceland station as well, it should be possible to mislead the enemy to a major extent. This would involve sailing the SS *Arctic* under guard with a British operator to monitor the transformation to be carried out by the *Arctic's* present operator. It is essential in view of the fact that the set has already worked that the original operator should operate the set himself. He has confessed and therefore will probably cooperate.

3. It is suggested that the plan for strategic deception should be conceived on a short-term basis with definite naval objectives. It has been suggested that the object should be the luring of the German major units from Trondheim during the passage to Russia of one of the convoys, by the giving of a false position of the Home Fleet. The plan so far put forward is that the *Arctic* should leave Reykjavik on a date to be fixed and on a given day sight the Home Fleet en route towards Reykjavik (This should probably not be done until the Home Fleet has left Scapa in view of the danger of a PRU check of the message). After an appropriate interval according to the position in which the *Arctic* makes the signal, the Iceland station should report the arrival of the Home Fleet, specifying a similar number and type of units. A message should also be provided for the Iceland station so that if an enemy reconnaissance comes over Iceland after that, he can announce that the Home Fleet left a few hours before on a westerly course.

4. To create the proper mis-en-scene the vital signals regarding movements of the Home Fleet we must envisage a period of some fourteen days during which that Iceland station must establish contact with the German control and supply, in accordance with German instructions, daily weather reports and some information (which may be checked by PRU) about Iceland and military forces and ships in port. It should be appreciated that it may take anything up to a fortnight or three weeks to establish a satisfactory two-way contact on the part of the Iceland station, and until this has been done the *Arctic* will probably have to remain in port.

5. If it is impossible to sail the *Arctic* in the manner set out above, a similar but weaker deception might be worked with the Iceland set only.

6. In order satisfactorily to plan the details of this operation it will be necessary for SIS to send an intelligence officer experienced in this work and a wireless operator at once by air to Iceland there to get into touch with Major Wise, who is at present conducting investigations into the enemy agents concerned, and with other necessary authorities.

7. If this plan is approved in principle, authority is requested for the following:
(a) Air passage for the officer and wireless operator mentioned above;
(b) The sending from the time contact is established of regular and accurate weather reports.
(c) The sending of the reports mentioned in paragraph 4 above, which will have to be accurate insofar they can be checked by PRU. If the agent is to see the arrival of the Home Fleet, he must be in a position to see the arrival of the other ships.
(d) A decision at the appropriate moment and before the *Arctic* would have to sail of the time and position in which the Home Fleet is to be sighted and what units are to be reported.
(e) Provision to be made by ACIC for assistance in operating this plan, which may involve the loan of a wireless operator to the shore station once or twice a day, and the provision of personnel to control the *Arctic*'s voyage to England; this will include the provision of a wireless operator to ensure that the *Arctic*'s own operator does not double-cross us.

The proposal of SPIDER was welcomed at MI5, where on 22 April John Marriott, then secretary of the XX Committee, assigned Richmond Stopford to the case and liaised with Ewen Montagu at the Admiralty to bring the four

Arctic suspects to Glasgow for further interrogation, and send an MI5 radio operator, Ronnie Reed, to Iceland. However, four days later, Marriott had learned about COBWEB, and hastened to alert Stopford:

> We last night received a cable from Iceland informing us that a certain Ib Riis Icelandic national landed in north-east Iceland from a German submarine on 5 April 1942. He is at present under arrest and has stated that he brought with him a wireless transmitter, code books and secret ink, all of which he buried. He was originally recruited in Copenhagen by Kapitan-Leutant Otto Kiesel alias Knudsen and another German named Edward Franz. Both men are known and are either members of the Abwehrstelle in Copenhagen or Hamburg. Riis had stated that he was originally to go to Greenland, that this was changed to Iceland via Portugal, but that finally he went to Iceland direct. He was given a course in Hamburg in wireless, codes, inks, etc. and left Heligoland on 29 March 1942 in *U-252*. Wise has sent a party to collect the set and code books from their hiding place and he has been cabled to keep the body and belongings in Iceland until your arrival. No further details are yet available at this end but Riis may prove to be a valuable reinforcement for you.

The prospect of mounting a sophisticated deception scheme in Iceland certainly appealed to the Admiralty, and on 26 April the Commander-in-Chief Home Fleet issued a secret directive, introducing an operation code-named BALDERDASH:

> It has been decided by the Admiralty that use shall be made of the two wireless sets captured with the trawler *Arctic* in an attempt to deceive the enemy.
>
> 2. The general idea is to work the set which was landed in Iceland in such a way as to cause the Germans to believe that it is being operated by one of their agents. It will probably take some time to establish satisfactory communication with Germany and to establish confidence: it is hoped to effect this by the time PQ16 sails. The build up must include truthful reports of the arrivals of convoys at Reykjavik and a few bogus reports of convoy's sailings so as to mask the actual movement of PQ16.
>
> 3. If this initial success is achieved it is intended that the *Arctic* should be sailed for Fleetwood about two days after PQ16 sails. One or two days after the *Arctic* leaves Reykjavik she should transmit a report – in accordance with the instructions arranged by the Germans – that she has sighted the main

surface forces of the Home Fleet steaming on a course for Hvalfiord. This
report should, if possible, be transmitted near sunset in order to make D/F
difficult and prohibit confirmation by German air reconnaissance.

4. The agent, using the W/T set in Iceland, should report the arrival of
the Fleet at Hvalfiord on the day on which PQ16 passes Jan Mayen Island.
Subsequently, whether the absence of the Fleet from Hvalfiord is discovered
by enemy air reconnaissance or whether the actual position of the fleet is
revealed at sea by some form of sighting report, it is at present intended to
continue with the ruse in order to confuse the enemy.

5. Mr. J.R. Stopford and Mr. R.T. Reed, officers from MI5, will bring this
letter to you. Under your direction they will control and advise on the
conduct of this ruse.

6. They will transmit a number of messages to the Germans containing
information which must be accurate if it is subject to possible air
reconnaissance confirmation. Other information which is not subject to
easy confirmation need not be accurate, though it must, of course, be
credible. Weather reports must form a part of these transmissions and they
must be accurate.

7. Should this ruse not be discovered by the Germans during the period of
passage of PQ16 it is intended to consider its possible re-employment on a
subsequent occasion.

8. It is requested that you will assist the officers with the preparation of the
messages which they will send with the object of building up a convincing
picture in the enemy's mind before PQ16 sails, and without presenting him
with dangerous information. The intermittent assistance of one or more
W/T operators will be required.

9. The enemy W/T operator who belonged to the *Arctic* is being sent back
to Iceland as it is necessary for him to perform the actual transmissions from
the *Arctic* as in paragraph 3. He will be under the charge of one of the officers
from MI5 during this part of the programme. Transmissions from the *Arctic*
will include sightings of shipping and weather reports both before and after
the sighting of the Fleet referred to in paragraph 3.

10. It is desired that this ruse should be disclosed only to the absolute minimum of personnel; under your command.

11. In order to preserve secrecy it is desired that the MI5 officers should send their signals through you prefixed 'For DNI personal'.

12. The codeword for this operation is BALDERDASH.

Thus the Admiralty's scheme was to provide protection for a large convoy of thirty-five ships, destined for Murmansk and Archangel, and scheduled to sail on 21 May, which was assembling in Iceland, by pretending that the Home Fleet was operating in the same area. PQ16 was particularly vulnerable because of the lack of darkness at night during the summer months, and the poor protection from enemy aircraft. However, when Stopford reached Reykjavik he was disturbed to learn that before their departure for Scotland Major Wise had subjected his four prisoners to 'violent third degree methods', prompting a diplomatic incident and a formal court of enquiry to investigate the abuse. This, of course, was extraordinarily embarrassing and threatened to expose the Allied double-agent operations. Accordingly, Stopford had to persuade the local British military commander, a brigadier, to keep the matter quiet and he agreed upon the withdrawal of Wise and his staff. The British consul-general, Howard Smith, also reported to the Foreign Office that 'highly irregular methods were used in interrogating the crew', which were likely to create gossip, and a summary of the known events was compiled by Milmo as Captain Seddon was arrested in anticipation of a court martial:

> Following upon the receipt of information from most secret sources Major Wise was notified by MI6 by cable dated 13 April 1942 that the auxiliary schooner *Arctic* then sailing from Reykjavik to the Westmann Islands was working on behalf of the German Secret Service, and Major Wise was instructed to submit the vessel and her crew to a thorough examination. By a further cable from MI6 dated 16 April 1942 Major Wise was informed that the captain and wireless operator of the *Arctic* were considered very suspect and was asked to cross-examine the entire crew.
>
> By cable dated 18 April 1942 addressed to MI6 Major Wise reported that the captain of the *Arctic*, Jonsson and the wireless operator Palsson had confessed that they had been enlisted as agents by the German Secret Service in Vigo and had been supplied with a wireless transmitter and a code book with which to transmit weather reports and details as to

shipping and convoys observed during their return voyage from Vigo to Iceland. Particulars of call signs and other technical information obtained were also given. Major Wise further reported that two Icelandic residents were implicated namely Magnusson and Dalberg, both of whom had been arrested. In Magnusson's house there was found the wireless transmitter, in Dalberg's house the code book. It was stated that the rest of the crew of the *Arctic* were being brought to Reykjavik for further examination.

3. On the 19 April 1942 MI6 cabled to Wise their congratulations on the success of his interrogations.

4. A full written report on the interrogations to date was sent to MI6 by Wise on the 19 April 1942. This report shows that the initial interrogations achieved no success, and that it was not until Jonsson's fourth interrogation that the truth was extracted from him. It is evident that up to this point the interrogating staff had performed an excellent job of work within a very limited time in a case where it was of the utmost urgency to obtain information with the minimum of delay both in the interests of the security of convoys proceeding through Icelandic waters, and for the purposes of LAND SPIDER. Captain Seddon, Major Wise's subordinate officer, obtained detailed and what is believed to be substantially accurate information on the following essential points:
    (i) Who were the principals in the conspiracy?
    (ii) What were the instructions which they had received from the Germans?
    (iii) What communications had been sent already?
    (iv) Where was the wireless transmitter?
    (v) Where was the code?
    (vi) Particulars of call signs, frequencies and other technical information essential for the purposes of PLAN SPIDER.
In the limited time available it was not possible to come to any conclusion as to the extent to which the remaining members of the crew of the *Arctic* were implicated, but Major Wise intimated that his investigations were proceeding.

    Meanwhile Plan SPIDER was being evolved and on 21 April 1942 MI6 (Major Cowgill) have his assent, subject to what might be construed as a mild protest, to the plan and to MI5 handling the case.

6. On the 7 May 1942 a cable was received through M16 from Mr Stopford in Iceland informing us that unorthodox methods had apparently been

used by Major Wise's staff in conducting the interrogation of the crew of the *Arctic*, and that a Court of Enquiry had been called. It appeared that American Military Police had assisted and that Third Degree methods and violence had been employed. A further cable from Stopford stated that as a result of the finding of the Court of Enquiry, Captain Seddon had been arrested and that the British Military Commander had stated that the evidence warranted the arrest and Court Martial of Wise.

7. On the 9 May 1942 the Foreign Office sent us for our observations a copy of a cable from the British Minister at Reykjavik dated 7 May 1942 in which it was stated that irregular methods had been used in the course of the interrogation. A copy of our reply to the Foreign Office appears at 7IA on the file. No other particulars of the allegations made against Major Wise's staff were notified to us.

8. On the evening of the 11 May 1942 Major Rupert Speir discovered through an acquaintance in the JAG's office that the papers relating to contemplated charges against Captain Seddon and Major Wise had already passed through that department and had been returned to AG3 at the War Office for a decision as to whether Court Martial proceedings should be launched. Major Speir communicated with AG3 (Colonel Barnwell) from whom he learned that the War Office file containing the report of the Court of Enquiry in Iceland had been referred to MI6 for their views as to whether there was any objection to the Court Martial taking place, and that MI6 had replied in the negative. Despite the fact that the case of the *Arctic* was being handled by MI5 with the knowledge and consent of MI6 and that the interrogations in Iceland were being carried out on our behalf and in our interests, not only was this reply given by MI6 without reference of any sort to this department but we were kept completely in the dark in respect of the whole affair.

9. On the instructions of ADB1 in company with Major Speir I saw Colonel Barnwell at the War Office at mid-day yesterday (12 May 1942). A separate note of this interview is set out at serial 73A on the file. Colonel Barnwell was surprised that MI5 should not have seen the papers and undertook that we should receive the findings of the Court of Enquiry the moment they were returned to the War Office by MI6.

10. At approximately 5:30 p.m. on the 12 May 1942 we received for the first time a copy of the proceedings of the Court of Enquiry which had been held in Iceland on the 5 May 1942, and from which it appeared that the incident referred to took place on the 23 April 1942 during the interrogation of three members of the crew of the *Arctic* – the first mate, the second mate and the cook. The report is attached. The findings of the Court appear on the final page. Briefly they were that the prisoners had received superficial injuries, not of a serious character, as a result of blows struck with the open hands and fists of two American Policemen, the blows having been struck in order to induce them to part with information; the action was taken with the concurrence of Captain Seddon who had acted on the instructions of Major Wise. From reading the evidence the following facts appear:

(i) The methods complained of were only adopted when all other methods had failed.

(ii) In each case they were not resorted to until the prisoner had deliberately withheld information and had either avoided or refused to answer questions.

(iii) It appears that the men had made admissions which implicated them in the espionage conspiracy and were regarded by Captain Seddon and Major Wise as falling within the category of spies.

(iv) The men had resisted and free fights had ensued with the American Police.

(v) The two American Military Police who had struck the blows were 'specialists in this kind of work'.

This potentially disastrous turn of events required some deft manoeuvring behind the scenes, and persuasive arguments were deployed to prevent the War Office from taking the matter further. Petrie intervened personally to write to the War Office:

It is not my purpose to suggest that the conduct which formed the subject of enquiry by the Court should be condoned or regarded as undeserving of official notice. There were, however, certain extenuating circumstances, among them that the interrogators did not act in a fit of temper or from any feeling of personal resentment, but because they believed that the information in possession of the prisoners was so valuable that in obtaining it the end would justify the means.

Their view as to the extreme importance of the information was correct, though their ideas on methods may have been misguided. There has been no loss of temper or deliberate cruelty, but rather an excess of zeal, which even if reprehensible, has redounded greatly to the advantage of our war effort.

In all the circumstances it is clear that most valuable information has been obtained, albeit through unorthodox methods. The officers concerned are Army officers and I feel that it is not within my province to do more than describe the facts which underlie the history of the incidents so that you may be assisted in reaching your decision as to what disciplinary steps should be taken.

Petrie prevailed, and H.J.D. Seddon was released from custody with a very stiff warning from the Deputy Director of Military Intelligence, with Wise escaping all punishment. The two American military policemen, Sergeant Lyons and Warrant Office Wooldridge, were removed from Iceland and posted elsewhere. Meanwhile, there were complications with Palsson, now code-named LAND SPIDER, who suffered from a crippling stammer that made conversation, and verbal interrogation, next to impossible. Exchanges with his interrogator, Major Samson, were conducted in writing, and he agreed to be flown back to Iceland so he could perform his role in Plan SPIDER and, when that project was replaced by Plan E.S., be returned to Camp 020. He would later suggest a plan to plant another Icelandic ship, the *Katla*, with a reliable wireless operator, Adolf Dundunderson, on the Germans in Vigo, but the proposal was vetoed by Tommy Robertson, who remarked that 'we don't want to have another *Arctic* on our hands, still less to create one'.

No sooner had MI5 extricated itself from one crisis, than it was plunged into another. On 28 May, under naval supervision, the remainder of the *Arctic*'s crew sailed the ship to Gourock and internment, but one of them, Arne Magnusson, the 40-year-old second engineer, committed suicide during the voyage. When the vessel docked on 30 May the local police informed the Icelandic vice consul of the death, and he began to take an interest in Magnusson, the rest of the crew, and the *Arctic*'s precise status. These awkward enquiries sent the SCO at Gourock, Major Brown, scrambling to plug the potential leak, and to avoid any public statement the procurator fiscal was persuaded to grant a death certificate without the usual formalities.

The Icelandic crewmen were finally questioned at Camp 020, the full truth emerged, and Jonsson explained how he had been introduced by the Danish vice consul, Alvarez Tome, to the German captain of one of the tankers moored at Vigo, and had been coerced into assisting the Abwehr.

The crewmen were interrogated at Camp 020, but on 13 July 1943 Jonsson, who suffered from tuberculosis and kidney stones, died in St Clement's

Hospital, in east London, from bowel cancer. The rest of the crew sailed back to Iceland, where they arrived on 19 September 1942, but Palsson was interned until the end of the war. Magnusson and Dalberg were repatriated in August 1942, and the latter, who had been studying law at Reykjavik University, was paid £100 in compensation, his offer to act as an SIS source in Iceland having been gratefully accepted. He would later receive a scholarship from the British Council to enable him to continue his academic career.

The final chapter in the *Arctic* story concerns a dastardly scheme, code-named ASSASSIN, which was dreamed up by Robertson, Foley, Milmo and Montagu in August 1942, just as the crew was being prepared for repatriation. ASSASSIN's objective was to utterly compromise Tome, the Dane who had been responsible for orchestrating the recruitment of Jonsson and Palsson by having COBWEB, GARBO and the released crew simultaneously reveal to the Abwehr that the consul had sold out to the Allies.

> COBWEB should send over the following message:
> I have learnt that a vessel called *Arctic* was seized here some time ago by the British. Friend I have made in Iceland Police tells me that ship being Government property is coming back soon with all of crew except skipper and radio man. He tells me that Consul at Vigo, Tome, had got the skipper and radio man to work for him and then had gone to British and sold them for large sum. British waited until *Arctic* sent radio message from here and then seized ship and took it and crew to England.
>
> Mr Milmo will arrange that some members of the crew should be told when they are being released that Tome betrayed the undertaking to the British.
>
> As soon as the men reach Glasgow, probably Monday next, GARBO shall write a letter saying that he has heard from his Glasgow agent the following startling story which he finds difficult to believe. Some Icelandic sailors were in Glasgow to take a ship called the *Arctic*, which has been in the Clyde for some time, back to Iceland. They were celebrating in a public house their being released from internment. They said they were all released except the skipper and radio man and that they were out for the blood of the man who had betrayed them who was their agent in Vigo whose name sounded like 'KUNE' but they were rather drunk and it was indistinct to hear.

Whether Tome survived ASSASSIN is unknown, but the Germans were not known to treat traitors leniently, as MI5 well knew, and the scheme would have been enough to discredit him in the eyes of the Abwehr. Additionally, pressure was applied to the Icelandic government to cease using Tome as a ship's agent in Vigo, a condition that Reykjavik accepted in return for the *Arctic*, which was not claimed by the Admiralty as a prize.

★ ★ ★

BEETLE was Petur Tomsen, landed by U-boat in September 1943. Thus, by the beginning of 1944, the Abwehr was dependent for information on just COBWEB and BEETLE, so this unsatisfactory situation was rectified by a veritable wave of espionage comprising no fewer than seven more spies.

The unexpected arrivals began on 17 April 1944 when a motor yacht crewed by two young Icelanders, Einar Sigvaldason and Larus Thorsteinsson, turned up on a two-masted 28-ton vessel off the island's north coast near the RAF camp at Raufarhöfn. They were brought ashore and when questioned by RAF personnel claimed to have escaped from Denmark through Sweden and Norway. They were then escorted to Reykjavik, where Sigvaldason introduced himself as having won an accordion playing competition in 1941, and described the circumstances of his escape from Kristiansund in the elderly, unseaworthy vessel.

On 2 May the two prisoners were escorted aboard the trawler *Lady Madeleine* for a voyage to Birkenhead and were transferred on 12 May to Camp 020 where, almost immediately, Thorsteinsson, a 26-year-old seaman who had contracted tuberculosis, confessed to his role as a Sicherheitsdienst spy on a mission to report meteorological data and stated that they had thrown both their German transmitters overboard before they landed. Sigvaldason promptly followed his lead and gave a detailed account of his recruitment in Denmark, where he had settled before the war, and his training at the SD's facility at Lehnitz in Prussia. Both also acknowledged having encountered a compatriot, Gudbrandur Hlidar, who would fall into MI5's hands in February the next year. They also identified his childhood friend, Sigurdur Juliusson, as a spy likely to be dropped into Iceland by parachute, unaware that he was already in custody, and Thorsteinsson named Pedur Tomsen as a German recruit he had heard about at the Icelandic Club in Copenhagen.

During the lengthy period of questioning that followed, both men corroborated each other in separate sessions and MI5 identified their SD handler as Helmuth Daufeldt, a familiar Abteilung VI figure based in Copenhagen.

Thorsteinsson's tuberculosis was treated in Brixton's hospital wing and he was transferred in July 1944 to Camp X at Peveril on the Isle of Man, MI5 being reluctant to risk having him infect others at Camp 020 or 020R. Another objective was to recruit him as a stool pigeon to extract further information from Pell Sigurdsson, who was believed to have been less than frank in his interrogation. They were accommodated in the same room at Peveril but Sigurdsson was so helpful to Thorsteinsson, by teaching him English, that he was not inclined to inform against him, as MI5 had intended.

This pair was followed on 25 April by Magnus Gudbjornsson and Sverir Matthiasson, two young Icelanders who had been living in Denmark in 1940, and had moved to work in Germany. Gudbjornsson had been employed as a broadcaster on Berlin Radio, while his companion had worked in a Hamburg printing business. During the spring of 1942 they were both recruited by the Abwehr with the offer of a passage home, and they underwent agent training in Copenhagen, Hamburg and Lubeck. They embarked in *U-289* in Bergen and landed on Iceland's north-east coast near Langanes after a voyage lasting ten days, but were quickly reported by a local farmer and arrested by the US occupation forces, who found two wireless transmitters. After a night under guard at Thorsforn they were escorted on to the *Erraid* and transferred to Reykjavik, where they embarked on the frigate HMS *Bullen* for a voyage to Liverpool, arriving on 1 May.

Once installed in Camp 020 the pair completed detailed statements in which they described their recruitment in May 1942 by Eduard Draude of the Abwehr's Eins Marine, based at the Hotel Cosmopolite in Copenhagen, a Kriegsmarine officer already identified by Ib Riis as his handler. Aspects of their wireless training in Hamburg in February 1943 were confirmed by ISOS in which they appeared as THORMATT and RUFU.

Aged 26, Gudbjornsson had been working in a cigarette factory in Hamburg in September 1941 when, as a virulent anti-Communist, he had volunteered to join the SS Panzer Division Wiking to fight on the Russian front. However, quickly disillusioned, he obtained a posting to Berlin, where he compiled and translated transcripts of shortwave radio bulletins. He was still in Berlin in May 1942 when he was contacted by Matthiasson, who invited him to return with him to Iceland where they believed conditions were better.

Under interrogation Matthiasson, the 32-year-old nephew of Iceland's Prime Minister Bjorn Thordarson, identified Gudbrandur Hlidar as the man who was to be their principal contact on the island, following his anticipated imminent arrival. They had been instructed to report on Allied activity in six named Iceland ports, an assignment that lent credence to the view that:

... these cases afford persuasive evidence that the enemy is anticipating an offensive of some magnitude to be launched from Iceland at some not far distant date. The fact that the Abwehr and the SD have hurriedly dispatched expeditions to this part of the globe suggests that this idea is not confined to the Intelligence Services, but may well be occupying the minds of the OKW itself.

Once safely established in Iceland, Gudbjornsson had been instructed to send an innocuous letter to Matthiasson's wife in Copenhagen, and this would be the signal for the Abwehr to open a radio link. Although this never happened, RSS reported in November 1944 that a message, numbered '11', had been intercepted:

> You are at present in danger. Hide everything incriminating and stop transmitting until 29/1. We shall continue to transmit as hitherto and occasionally send information. Only listen in when it is not dangerous to do so.

It was the fact that the Germans had invested six transmitters in the theatre, and had deployed assets of longstanding, that seemed so significant. 'Five of the ... seven agents were recruited for espionage purposes as far back as 1942, the other two being recruited the following year' and 'they have all been given extensive training', which suggested this was a serious commitment, reflecting a genuine anxiety.

Finally, on 30 April 1944, at the third attempt, U-289[4] dropped a trio of agents, two Icelanders, Hjalti Bjornsson and Sigurdur Juliusson, and a German, Ernst Fresenius, onto the Icelandic coast near Selvoganes, but they were apprehended on 5 May after they had been spotted by a search party of American troops who had been alerted to their suspicious behaviour by a local seal hunter. Once in custody, but still on the mountainside, Fresenius declared himself to be a German soldier and asserted that he had been a PoW in England during the previous war. Moments later, apparently shocked by this disclosure, Bjornsson revealed the hiding place of a transmitter and pedal-powered generator. He was questioned again by SIS's Harold Blyth and the CIC's Kenneth Haan in Reykjavik harbour aboard the *Erraid*, when he made a formal statement in which he acknowledged possession of $9,000 and described his mission. Aged 29, he had previously been employed as a cook on the merchantman SS *Lagarfoss*. He explained that the trio had been at liberty for a week, had provisions for another week, but had failed to make radio contact with the Abwehr despite numerous attempts because of poor atmospheric conditions.

All three were kept in American custody until 18 May when they were transferred on an anti-submarine trawler, HMS *Cape Mariato*, to Loch Ewe. They then went by train from Inverness to Camp 020, where the two younger men quickly abandoned their prepared cover story and, confronted with their confessions, Fresenius admitted to his espionage and gave directions to the site of a second buried transmitter. Ultimately he also provided details of his control sign (or security check) that would indicate his signals were made under duress and an attempt was made to establish contact with the enemy. At one point MI5 contemplated using one of Fresenius' two transmitters to request a pick-up for a return journey, and thereby lure a U-boat into a trap, but the idea was abandoned on the grounds that such a scheme would 'be doomed to failure'.

A convinced Nazi, Fresenius had been born in the Black Forest village of Alpirsbach in August 1887, studied theology at Giessen University, and had been wounded twice while serving with the 44th Infantry Regiment in the Battle of the Somme during the First World War. In August 1918 he had been taken prisoner by an Australian division, remaining a PoW in England until November 1919. After completing his university education he moved to Iceland in 1926 to study agriculture and acquired Icelandic citizenship in 1930, but eight years he later returned to Germany with his wife, Elisabet Fallen, and their four children.

In his statement Fresenius explained that he had been selected for the mission because he had farmed in Iceland for twelve years before the war, and had been recruited by an Abwehr representative, Dr Hellmuth Lotz, who knew of his background. He had been introduced to his two companions while attending an Abwehr radio course at the Schierensee Schloss near Kiel. The MI5 interrogators were particularly amused to learn that one of their instructors on a sabotage course in Norway had been a foreigner named Fritz, whom MI5 realised was actually Eddie Chapman. Fresenius soon dropped his cover story, that he and his subordinates had been engaged by a shipping institute to collect weather information, and explained that he had been ordered not to disclose German fears of an invasion in northern Europe.

Juliusson, aged 28, was a fisherman who had signed off his ship, the *Bruarfoss*, in Copenhagen and had shared lodgings with a circus performer whose weight-lifting act included carrying elephants. The three spies were kept in England until August 1945, when they were flown to Iceland from Hendon and returned to American custody in Iceland. Bjornsson and Juliusson were convicted of treason and sentenced to a year's imprisonment. Fresenius was sentenced to eight months' imprisonment and upon his release moved to Chile, where he was appointed director of the agricultural research institute at Osorno. He died in 1956.

Gudbjornsson, and Matthiasson were also sentenced to a year's imprisonment. Sigvaldason and Thorsteinsson received eight months, Hlidar five months, and Palsson three months. However, the court ruled that since all had spent longer than those sentences in detention in England, they would not be incarcerated.

★ ★ ★

BRUTUS was Roman Garby-Czerniawski, a Polish Air Force officer who had been captured by the Abwehr in Paris in 1942 while running the TUDOR network. Betrayed by his lover, Mathilde Carré, Garby-Czerniawski declared his true role to Kenneth Benton at the SIS station in Madrid in October 1942 after the Abwehr had arranged his escape from Fresnes. His supposed cooperation with the Germans was based on a threat to his mother in Poland and his brother, a PoW. His radio operator, code-named CHOPIN, was actually an MI5 technician. After the war Roman Garby-Czerniawski remained in London, was active in the government-in-exile, and wrote an account of his participation in the INTERALLIÉ network in Nazi-occupied France.[5]

★ ★ ★

ARTIST was Johannes Jebsen, an Abwehr officer based in Lisbon who had recruited his university friend Dusan Popov, and previously Petrie had referred to the problem he had presented (see Chapter 6). TRICYCLE had exercised considerable discretion in fending him off, but even he now suspected that ARTIST had come to realise that his network of Yugoslavs in London were probably under British control. An additional issue was his friendship in Lisbon with Hans Ruser's mother, a contact that had been frowned upon by the Gestapo, especially when all the defector's acquaintances were under scrutiny (see Chapter 8).

Jebsen was the only Abwehr officer to be an SIS agent and, having been run by SIS's Graham Maingot, he was abducted by his SD colleagues and returned to Germany in May 1944, accused of having embezzled Abwehr funds. His precise fate remains unknown, but it is thought that he was executed without casting any doubts on Popov, the source known to the Abwehr as IVAN.

* * *

MI5' knowledge of Wladyslaw Wilman began in May 1944 when he arrived in Lisbon and joined a group of fellow Polish refugees anxious to join the Allied forces in England. They were sent to Gibraltar, where Wilman took the opportunity to make a statement to the local Defence Security Officer. According to his version of events, he had been recruited by the Abwehr while worked as a forced labourer in a Hamburg aircraft factory in 1942. Having agreed to accept recruitment he had undergone various courses at training centres in Hamburg and Bremen, and received instructions for a mission to either Canada or Great Britain, where he was to report on preparations for D-Day. Realising his potential as a double-agent, the DSO had Wilman flown to England, and he arrived at Camp 020 on 19 May. However, the length of his interrogation precluded the chance of him fulfilling his espionage assignment, so he was released in June and found a job in an aircraft factory.

16

3 JULY 1944

JUNE 1944
A. <u>SPECIAL AGENTS</u>.
The outstanding event of the week has been the return of the agent ZIGZAG,
who was dropped by parachute on the night of the 28th/29th June. It will be
remembered that ZIGZAG made his first parachute landing in this country
under German orders in December 1942, and that he then worked under
our control as a sabotage agent. He returned to Lisbon on March 28th, 1943
and reported to his German masters. For his sabotage of the Hatfield works
(organised by us) and other services, he appears to have received rather
more than 100,000 marks as a bonus from the Germans. Since that date
he has been given an extended holiday in Norway, where he has indulged
in yachting and other recreations and has successfully withstood various
psychological and other tests, all of which have served to fortify German
belief in him. He has also paid three short visits to Berlin, the last in March
1944, but has had no opportunity to carry out his own proposal to assassinate
Hitler as a paragon. He describes Berlin as 'a complete shambles resembling
the ruins of Pompei', and the morale of the Germans as noticeably low. On
the other hand he stresses the growing French resentment against the British.
This view is founded on his observations made during his stay in Paris from
March to June of this year. His assignment on his present visit is not sabotage,
but straight intelligence, as follows:-

(1) To procure photographs or plans of our Asdic gear for spotting submarines.

(2) To ascertain details of the radio location system employed for the
detection of German planes, particularly as fitted to night fighters.

(3) To find out the effect of the P plane, places where they are landing and resultant damage.

(4) To ascertain the location of American Air Force stations, and corresponding towns in Germany to be attacked by planes leaving these aerodromes in England.

(5) To find out information about a new wireless frequency.
Reference 5: The Germans believe that we have discovered a new wireless frequency in which a new type of valve, square-shaped, plays an important part. They believe that this is likely to upset their Weapon No. 2 which, ZIGZAG says, is a radio controlled rocket. He was told that this valve was manufactured by a firm in Hammersmith. The names of the manufacturers would be sent to him by W/T later, and he was then to break into the factory and steal one of the valves.

2) As an appreciation of his work in the 'Front Line', GARBO, who is a Spaniard, has been awarded the Iron Cross (Second Class). As a further example of the Germans' appreciation of his work, the following are two messages which have been sent to him at the request of Berlin:

(1) 'I wish to stress in the clearest terms that your work over the last few weeks has made it possible for our Command to be completely forewarned and prepared and the message of Four would have influenced but little had it arrived three or four hours earlier.'

(2) 'Thus I reiterate to you, as responsible chief of the service, and to all your collaborators, our total recognition of your perfect and cherished work and I beg of you to continue with us in the supreme and decisive hours of the struggle for the future of Europe. Saludos.'

3) Another Special Agent, TATE, has also received an effusive message of encouragement for his work:
'Please, at this moment, make the most use of all connections and concentrate all energy. As the situation is at the moment, your messages about concentrations and movements (some especially signs of troops preparing for action) can be not only fabulously important, but can even decide the outcome of the war.'

The above messages indicate that our special agents are playing a successful, as well as an important part in passing to the Germans the cover and deception plans of SHAEF.

4) All our special agents with W/T communications have been asked to report on the effect of CROSSBOW on the morale of the people, the amount of damage it does and the number of people it kills. Two of our best agents have been asked to give details of the exact position where and the time at which the missiles land. It is suggested that this information is required by the operators of this weapon in order to enable them to take the necessary corrections in range and direction, It is known from Most Secret Sources that information on CROSSBOW is required so urgently that special arrangements have been made to pass reports from our agents as rapidly as possible from their Control Station to Arras. Arras is known to be the centre from which counter-measures against this country are directed.

5) It seems from all indications that the Germans have accepted the stories which we have told them about an intending attack on the Pas de Calais.

Messages in conformity with this Deception Plan were put over through our channels at the request of SHAEF. It seems pretty clear that the congratulatory messages, especially to GARBO, to some extent reflect the general military appreciation of the situation of the German High Command. It is known for a fact that the Germans intended at one time to move certain Divisions from the Pas de Calais area to Normandy but, in view of the possibility of a threat to the Pas de Calais area, these troops were, either stopped on their way to Normandy and recalled, or it was decided that they should not be moved at all. It is hoped that this threat may be kept going for as long as required for purposes.

B. SPIES.
Special arrangements were made for OVERLORD in order to ensure that any stay-behind spies captured in Normandy should be sent to this country for interrogation as quickly as possible. The Security Service also set up machinery so that any information derived from the agents could be sent back to the field with the utmost despatch in order to assist the Special Counter Intelligence units.

Two stay-behind agents have already been captured and sent back to this country. They have been intensively interrogated, and comprehensive reports of the cases were in the hands of 21st Army Group within seven days of our receiving the bodies.

2) The first stay-behind agent captured in Normandy and sent to this country for interrogation was Yves Guilcher @ GUILLAUME. His cover name of GUILLAUME and his German contacts have been well known to us in the past from Most Secret Sources. Guilcher was identified without difficulty as GUILLAUME when he was denounced to the British on their arrival in Bayeux. His mission was to report by wireless on unit and vehicle markings of Allied troops. Under interrogation he has stated that he never intended to carry out his mission, but the sincerity of this statement is extremely doubtful. He was, it is true, wounded in an air raid on the 2nd June, so that he would be unable to use his transmitting set for some time, but he made no effort to give himself up to the Allies on their arrival and after his arrest he at first denied the possession of a W/T set which he had buried. His general conduct is no more creditable since he has confessed that he has betrayed at least two French patriots to the Germans.

3) The other of these stay-behind agents is a Frenchwoman, Madeleine Bernard, aged 56 who, when the U.S. Forces entered Mestre near Isigny, asked to be put in touch with the Intelligence Authorities. Following a local interrogation she was brought to this country for further questioning, Bernard and her lover, one Poussin by name, have been working as double-agents on behalf of the French in France since 1941, Bernard performing the part of a courier carrying letters for the Germans between Marseilles and Dijon. More recently Bernard has been living with her daughter and grand-children on their farm in Normandy. In April of this year Bernard was asked by Poussin to play a further part, and was put by him in touch with Schneidar, a German Secret Service agent, who has been setting up an organisation of stay-behind agents to pass operational information to the enemy by W/T. Bernard was to find cover employment for such agents. The time was short, however, and this she was unable to do. In the course of her work for Schneidar, Bernard however came across a certain Durand whom she was able to identify to the US Authorities and whose W/T apparatus was found, though he himself had fled, when the US Forces entered Carentan.

4) The young Pole, Wilman, referred to in the last report, has now been fully interrogated. There is no reason to doubt his sincerity in asserting that he allowed himself to be recruited by the Germans as a means of escaping from occupied territory. [XXX]

C. SABOTAGE.

It was known from the interrogation of captured agents and Most Secret Sources that the German Sabotage Service was organising a network of saboteurs to work in the Rome area after its occupation by the Allies. Since the fall of Rome, an important saboteur belonging to Himmler's Secret Service has given himself up and supplied the names of forty saboteurs, and information on the positions of hidden dumps of sabotage equipment. One of these dumps was said to be in the German Embassy, which was therefore searched with the consent of the Swiss Legation. Arms, sabotage material, and a wireless transmitting set were found. An expert from this office has gone to Rome to examine these dumps and equipment. A study of the Rome organisation may provide information which will have application on the Western Front, where similar stay-behind organisations are known to exist.

D. TROTSKYISTS.

The four Trotskyists charged in connection with the Apprentices Strike at Newcastle whose arrest was mentioned in the report for April, were, on June 19th found guilty of aiding and abetting the commission of a strike, while Tearse, Lee and Haston[1] were found guilty of acting in furtherance of a strike. Tearse[2] and Lee[3] were sent to prison for a year, and Haston for six months. Mrs Ann Keen, who had already been imprisoned for thirteen days, was released.[4] In sentencing the three men, Mr Justice Cassels said that they were dangerous men and had sought to use the occasion of the boys' grievances in order to serve their own political ends. An appeal has been lodged on the question whether acts done prior to a strike can be acts in furtherance of a strike.

3rd July 1944

★ ★ ★

On 13 August 1944, as American troops of the US Army 4th Armoured Division entered Pré-en-Pail, 30-year-old Martial Durand, formerly a French navy mechanic, and 23-year-old electrician Robert Charrier approached them and offered information about the German Intelligence Service, claiming to be acting as double-agents planted on the enemy by the resistance. A wireless transmitter was quickly recovered from their room in the local Hotel La Croix Blanche and their version of events was largely accepted by the Counter-Intelligence Corps detachment. Nevertheless, both men were transferred by air on 12 September to Hendon for examination at Camp 020.

Even before the pair had arrived, Durand had been identified as an ISOS personality code-named CHEVALIER and known as MATELOT, a member of Abwehrtruppee 122 of Abwehrkommando 130, a stay-behind organisation based in Angers. He had also been denounced as a German spy by Mathilde Bernard, who had been at Camp 020 since 20 June 1944, and so was already on an Allied arrest list.

On 13 June Guy Liddell mentioned Bernard in a diary entry:

We have discussed with Trevor-Wilson the case of a Frenchwoman called Madeleine Bernarde, alias Gabrielle, alias Madeleine, who surrendered to the allied forces on or before 12 June at the bridgehead area. She claimed to be an agent of the French Deuxieme Bureau and mentioned the names of certain contacts in Marseilles. She says that she was recruited for the Germans as a double-cross agent by one [XXX] who was also a French double-cross agent. She claims to have carried letters from Marseilles to Dijon for one Dr Becker. She states that she was asked by one Schneider of St. Lo to set up a German stay-behind agent at Carentan who she believed to be there now. The French say that unless this woman is identical with one Madame Pellegrin of Antibes who was recruited by Poussin in the spring of 1942 in Marseilles they cannot identify her, although they know the names of other people with whom she claims to have been associated. The French have no special plans for this woman and it seems desirable that she should be got over here and thoroughly interrogated. Meanwhile, a stay-behind agent in Bayeux has been arrested on a denouncement by some other French citizen. He is to come here for interrogation.

Durand confirmed that, having been recruited as an agent in Nantes in December 1943, he had undergone three months' of wireless training, supervised by three German instructors. On the same course were eight other Frenchmen, whom he identified.

The problem for MI5 was deciding whether Durand and Charrier were sincere patriots or, more probably, mercenary opportunists who really had been prepared to serve the Nazi cause. However, in the absence of conclusive proof in ISOS, both men were returned to Paris in November 1944, leaving the question of Durand's complicity unresolved, even if the impression left by Petrie's brief summary was that Bertrand's denunciation had been justified.

As for the German officer named Schneidar, Petrie was probably referring to an Abwehr officer who adopted the alias Colonel Schneider to train and manage a stay-behind organisation in France. His address, 59 rue Sabline in

Carentan, was raided, as was his office, at 15 rue de Villedieu in Saint-Lô, but he was never caught. Reportedly he had confided to Durand that he had lived in France for twenty years before the war. He was also mentioned by Yves Guilcher, the other stay-behind agent referred to in Petrie's report.

The ISOS trail for Schneider showed him living in Paris at 9 rue de Loynes and as having adopted the alias Dr Schuster for a visit to San Sebastien in 1941 to send agents into Spain. In April 1942 he turned up as Haniel Schneider, holding a meeting in Madrid with an agent code-named BALLAFREG, and a month later he was referred to as 'Dr Schneider of Angers'. Later in the year he was in contact with the Abwehr in Tangiers, and in December he was connected to an agent in Tunis. He then dropped from sight in ISOS until May 1944, when he was linked to a stay-behind agent controlled by Kommando 130, Truppe 122. According to Section V's analysts, he had been employed by Abwehr II in Paris, based at 43 rue de Courcelles and the Grand Hotel Pavilion, 36 rue de l'Echiquier, and then by Abwehr IH in Angers. He was also mentioned by HARLEQUIN as a colleague from Dortmund who collected musical instruments and specialised in Arab agents, and by other agents, such as Van Eynde, as having been his principal instructor at the Château d'Ardannes, and Mathilde Bernard. Additionally, Section V analysts speculated that he might be the same Schneider who had been described by Frank Steiner in Brussels, and the German officer named Schneider spotted in the Hotel de Normandie, 35 rue de Normandie in Paris. Despite the accumulated evidence of Schneider's activities in Paris, at the Abwehr's headquarters at the Hotel Lutetia on the Boulevard Raspail, he was never traced.

Yves Guilcher was a 28-year-old former soldier who had joined the French infantry in 1934 and was denounced to the US 2nd Army by Guy Mercader, a local resistance leader. He had been demobilised in 1940 and since then had struggled to make a living as an itinerant salesman, peddling lavender water and then newspapers on the streets. A search of his lodgings on the first floor at 77 rue St Loup in Bayeux by the 19 Field Security Section revealed scraps of paper in the attic that, when reconstructed, indicated that a transmitter had been buried in the garden. Sure enough, a German-manufactured radio and a set of ciphers were dug up, but initially Guilcher denied all knowledge of them and was passed to 101 SCI. It was only on 16 June, when he was shipped by landing craft via Portsmouth to Camp 020, that he not only fully confessed, but named several other German spies with whom he had undergone radio training and revealed his book code system based on a copy of de Montgon's *Louis XIV*. Once MI5 had connected Guilcher with the ISOS personality code-named GUILLAUME, all the pieces began to fall into place.

Guilcher had shown up on a dozen ISOS intercepts between April and June 1944, all on the Paris–Wiesbaden channel, and had also been identified by two other stay-behind agents, Robert Charrier and Martial Durand, who had surrendered in Pré-en-Pail in August. When questioned at Camp 020, both had seen him at the SD training centre at 10 bis rue des Dervallieres in Nantes, where he had been known as 'Le Gangster' because of his unsavoury appearance and reputation. Even GUILLAUME's training transmissions, exchanged between Angers and his temporary location in Morlaix, had been intercepted and filed as ISOS traffic.

According to another Abwehr agent, Manual Roger, he and Guilcher had enlisted in the pro-Nazi Legion de Volonaires Francais to fight the Soviets and had served in Poland, where they had been recruited by the Abwehr. They had then been posted to Saint-Malô under the command of a Captain Bergeret, and underwent radio training at the Château d'Ardannes in Seiches. Both became members of Abwehrtruppe 122, details of which were disclosed after the capture of Adalbert Paulsen, their principal instructor. He also named Jacques Heuber, Marcel Baudrou and Roger Beccassion, who were all arrested.

Guilcher was also implicated by the seizure of documents at the SD office in Rennes, which included a list of local agents, together with their code names, call signs and home addresses. When confronted with the weight of evidence, Guilcher confessed but claimed that he had been injured during an Allied air raid in early June and prevented from using his right arm to transmit, insisting that he had never intended to assist the Germans, even though he had been paid 38,000 francs since his recruitment in 1942, with a promise of a further 30,000 at the conclusion of hostilities.

In his confession Guilcher recalled that while in Bayeux he had been summoned several times to Saint-Lô, where he had been lectured by a Dr Schneider on unit recognition for components of the British Army, in anticipation of his post-occupation mission. Gradually, each piece of the intelligence jigsaw puzzle was put in its proper place, with personalities and their movements matched to their appearances in the ISOS traffic by a team of skilled SIS analysts, among them Hugh Trevor Roper.

Although Guilcher himself was not of great significance, his case was the first of its kind in Normandy and served to illustrate how well prepared the Allies were for dealing with the known threat of a relatively sophisticated enemy stay-behind organisation. Having developed a system for identifying, detaining and questioning suspects, the Allies effectively eliminated the problem posed by the individual agents, and took their instructors and controllers into custody to complete the picture. Thus what could have represented a significant risk, with a military reporting network combined with saboteurs, was reduced to a very manageable challenge of scooping up those implicated. The resulting interrogations, supported by meticulous record-keeping and ISOS carding, gave the counter-intelligence staffs a huge advantage, and leverage.

Guilcher was returned to French custody on 21 June, and a damning Liquidation Report was completed on 11 July. Thereafter, administratively, Guilcher posed something of a bureaucratic problem as he was a French national, captured in France by American troops, and taken as a prisoner to England. SHAEF was anxious for his return to face a French military tribunal, and a group of other confessed enemy spies in a similar position, including Henri Mathieu, Henri Roger and a Corsican, Michel Scognamillo. Accordingly, as they were of no further use to MI5, they were returned to the custody of Martin Furnival Jones at 21 Army Group in Normandy by air from Northolt on 22 July.

By that time MI5 had acquired several other enemy agents, including Andrew Guy (alias d'Arnal), Roland Ball, Claud Lambert, Michel Girka and Gaston Piat, all of whom were used by SHAEF's intelligence staff to reconstruct the entire German espionage infrastructure.

★ ★ ★

The final item on Petrie's list was the conviction of four members of the Revolutionary Communist Party on two charges of furthering a strike following the Tyneside apprentices' dispute. However, Mr Justice Cassells' judgement was quickly overturned by the Court of Appeal, which ruled that the defendants' involvement had been before the stoppage had begun, so they had been charged with the wrong offence. Accordingly, the three remaining prisoners were freed, Keen having been released upon the verdict because of the time she had served on remand.

17

1 AUGUST 1944

As the Allied invasion forces made slower progress than had been planned in capturing their objectives and driving towards Paris, MI5 emphasised to the Prime Minister how the organisation had neutralised the activities of enemy stay-behind networks, again citing Yves Guilcher as an example, and then expanding on the deception role adopted by MI5's star performers, GARBO and TATE.

JULY 1944
A. SPIES.
The vast majority of spies arrested during July are individuals sent from the Normandy front for interrogation in this country. Some ten have been sent over and they fall into two main classes: those intended to stay behind as the Allies advance, communicating with their spy masters by W/T, and those who were sent through the lines to collect information, and then return to Axis-held territory. All branches of the German Intelligence Service are taking a hand in these ventures. The German military Intelligence Service directed the stay-behind agents, and Himmler's Secret Service sent agents through the lines to obtain information on political matters, such as the attitude of the population to the Allies. In addition to these two Services, certain para-military organisations have run agents through the lines to obtain technical military information. These last mentioned organisations are a new discovery, and it appears that the Germans have for some time been giving young Frenchmen military training as cover for their eventual despatch on short-term espionage missions when the Allies invaded France. As an example, shortly before the capture of Cherbourg, a party of such spies was taken by sea from St. Malo to Cherbourg, and from

there despatched to cross the American Sector and to return eventually to the Germans in the South.

This month's haul of spies contains members of all these organisations. All of these spies captured, save one, are French subjects, most of them young, and all of a very poor type. The chief advantage of having them sent to this country and interrogating them has been to discover the names and details of other men of similar character whom they denounce, either voluntarily or under interrogation. This has already borne fruit as four of these spies have been captured as a result of the interrogation of other individuals sent here.

Four spies captured last month, including Guilcher, mentioned in the last report, have been sent back to Normandy to be dealt with in an appropriate manner by an Allied court. It is anticipated that the majority of the others will be treated in the same way when we have finished with them here.

Besides these French spies, we have also received here an important German spy, who has been sent by the French in North Africa on a lease–lend basis. This man, Hans Scharf, has been working for the German Secret Service since early 1940. He went to South Africa with Robey Leibbrandt, the German ex-boxer and saboteur, who was arrested and sentenced by the South African authorities, but Scharf did not in the end accompany Leibbrandt on his mission after arrival in the Union. He has also carried out missions in Algeria and Tunisia, and was ultimately captured in North Africa, having been sent there by air from Italy and landed by parachute. He is in a position to supply a great deal of information regarding German espionage personnel and methods.

B. SPECIAL AGENTS.

1) Shortly after landing in Normandy, Most Secret Sources revealed three interesting appreciations of the work of Special Agent GARBO in implementation of the Allied deception plan.

(a) A message from Paris to Madrid in which certain tactical information that had been passed by GARBO was cited as having been described by Rundstedt as especially important.

(b) A message of congratulations from Himmler to GARBO's spy master in Madrid on the work of his organisation in England, and a request for further reconnaissance to ascertain in good time the destination of the groups of forces in South East England, and the notification of their embarkation.

(c) An appreciation of GARBO's reports in which he had built up the threat to the Pas de Calais area and listed the formations which would take part in this assault. This classified GARBO's reports as especially valuable, and said that they had been confirmed almost without exception. The request for information about British forces in the South East of England was repeated, and GARBO was asked to keep a watch on the formations assembled in Western Scottish ports.

GARBO was also asked to give urgent information regarding damage caused by CROSSBOW. In order to avoid compromising the case by inaccurate reports on CROSSBOW incidents and to comply with the SHAEF directives that all military information sent to the enemy by special means should be reduced to a minimum pending the embarkation of the FUSAG forces to the battle area, it was decided that GARBO should be notionally arrested whilst investigating and showing excessive curiosity in a bombed area. Immediately upon his arrest, his notional deputy took over the organisation, reporting first GARBO's detention, and later his release. Berlin, on hearing the news, described the loss of GARBO as 'particularly regrettable precisely at the present state of affairs'. They instructed Madrid to tell GARBO's deputy to stop transmitting for fourteen days, and to suspend all activities in investigating the effects of CROSSBOW. The Service was resumed after ten days under the auspices of GARBO's deputy, who is now handling not only W/T communication, but also the notional GARBO network. We were able, when we renewed contact, to pass over immediately the revised deception threat to the Pas de Calais area.

For the moment GARBO will content himself with writing secret ink letters giving details of the progress in the re-organisation of the network which includes the strengthening of the notional network already existing in Canada and its extension to India.

It appears from this experience that the Germans have complete trust and confidence in the ability of GARBO's notional deputy; indeed he is so well established that, should the necessity ever arise, the network could continue to operate with no great loss without GARBO, who is the only real character in the whole piece.

2) On July 15th TATE was asked whether the building of new transformer stations in connection with existing overland high tension lines was taking place in various parts of South-Eastern England, and, if so, what the new building looked like. On July 26th, not having answered the question, he was asked whether he had still found out anything about these buildings, and was instructed to send over 'even partial results'. These questions are thought to be connected with German theories regarding our possible counter-measures to V-2.

C. DIPLOMATIC.

1) There is evidence from Most Secret Sources that the German Secret Service still have easy and speedy access to the reports sent back from this country from the Spanish Embassy to the Spanish Foreign Office. This is illustrated very clearly in the case of the first report made by the Duke of Alba at the end of June on the effect of CROSSBOW. A verbatim copy of the despatch, which was a fair and objective account, was obtained by the Head of the German Counter-Espionage Section in Madrid within four days of its receipt there. Its contents were sent at once to Berlin.

2) Most Secret Sources reveal that the bull-fighter turned spy, Alcazar de Velasco, mentioned in previous reports, has had to flee from Spain, and is now taking refuge in Munich. Alcazar has recently been responsible for recruiting agents for the Japanese for despatch to the Americas. The principal reason for his expulsion was the exposure of one of his agents, Fernando Kobbe, the Spanish Consul in Vancouver. A protest was made to the Spanish Foreign Office on this case, causing them to investigate Alcazar, who, threatened with arrest, fled the country.

D. SABOTAGE.

Our representative has arrived in Rome to investigate sabotage equipment left behind by the German Sabotage Service for the use of post-occupational agents. The equipment discovered has proved to be of considerable interest. Our representative estimates that there must have been, or still are, fifty such dumps. One, which has been fully investigated, being hidden in the Emperor Caracalla's baths. He is shortly expected back in England, bringing with him a number of 'exhibits', knowledge of which may prove highly useful to those who may have to handle similar material coming to light in France.

1st August 1944

★ ★ ★

The reference to enemy spies planted in Cherbourg must have intrigued Churchill, even if no further details were provided. In fact, Petrie probably had in mind Alfred Gabas, a French former ship's wireless officer whose experience was a classic example of stay-behind espionage. Born in August 1909, he was an electrician by trade and completed his military service in the navy before joining the Paris Metro to work as a rolling stock and electrical inspector at the Gare du Nord. In 1939 he had been called up as a reservist and posted to an auxiliary minesweeper, the *Angele Marie*, based in Boulogne.

Having been evacuated from Dunkirk, Gabas had been placed aboard the SS *Moknes* in Southampton for repatriation to France but his ship was torpedoed in the Channel and the survivors were rescued and landed at Weymouth. Finally, in November 1940, he was repatriated to Toulon from Gourock at the second attempt and made his way home to his wife and three children in Paris. However, in June 1943 he was called up for compulsory labour in Germany and attempted to flee to Spain. He was caught at the border, imprisoned in Bordeaux, and then recruited by an Abwehr officer named Norberd. He took him to Paris, where he underwent two months of training, supervised by Sonderführer Stockmann, in an office at 32 rue de Varennes in preparation for his mission. Obligingly, Gabas identified five other agents who had attended the same courses in secret writing, enciphering and radio procedures.

When cross-examined, Gabas changed his story and admitted that he had been assigned a mission to Oran, and had been entrusted with a cover address in Madrid: Señora Lary de Badal, 44 Calle de Cartagena. His task was to cross into Spain from Perpignan and reach French North Africa posing as a refugee, but he was arrested by the Spanish police and in September 1943 interned at the Miranda del Ebro camp. In February 1944 he was allowed to return to San Sebastián, having been escorted through the frontier controls at Irun by German consulate staff. A second mission was prepared for him, but following the Allied invasion his Abwehr controller gave him a new objective, reporting from behind the enemy lines in Normandy under the alias André Dumont, accompanied by his second wife, Marcelle.

Having failed to reach Cherbourg, Gabas was arrested on 22 August by the American CIC in Saint-Pair-sur-Mer as he attended a rendezvous with another stay-behind spy, Juan Frutos, unaware that he was being run by an SCI as a double-agent code-named DRAGOMAN. Once in custody Gabas admitted his role and led his captors to the garden of his rented house, the Villa Mary-Lou, where he had buried his transmitter concealed inside a green wooden suitcase. He also admitted that he had intended to work in tandem with two other agents in Cherbourg, Frutos, alias John Eikens, who lived at 30 rue Victor Grignard, and Jean Senouque, at the Villa Philomele in Saint-Pair. Evidently Gabas never suspected that he had been betrayed by Frutos, a Portuguese interpreter employed by American Express who would be delivered to Camp 020 in August 1944, having been arrested by 104 SCI's Christopher Harmer and Neil MacDermot. Under interrogation, Frutos admitted that he had been recruited by the Abwehr's Johannes Bischoff in Bremen in 1936.

According to ISOS, dating back to September 1943, Gabas was an Abwehr agent code-named DESIRE and on 29 August 1944 Gabas was shipped from Arromanches to Shoreham and accommodated at Camp 020, where he provided his third and most comprehensive confession. He was returned to Paris from Southampton in November 1944.

Gabas was important partly because of his accumulated knowledge of Abwehr operations, procedures and personalities, but also because of his involvement in the very active DRAGOMAN double-agent case, one of six Abwehr transmitters controlled by SCI units. DRAGOMAN established his radio link in July 1944 and by the end of the war had exchanged some 200 messages without arousing the enemy's suspicion. Gabas also compromised an Abwehr agent in Le Havre who, code-named SKULL, was one of seven assets in that city managed by an energetic Abwehr officer, Richard Kaulen.

★ ★ ★

Angel Alcazar de Velasco was indeed well known to MI5, and had been the intermediary responsible for recommending the recruitment of Henri Chambard to the Japanese embassy in Madrid in April 1943. That episode, referred to in Petrie's earlier report, dated 3 April 1944 (see Chapter 13), showed that the Spaniard had shifted his attention from the Abwehr and developed a relationship with Tokyo.

★ ★ ★

The brevity of the passage mentioning Robey Leibbrandt, who had been sent on a mission to South Africa with Hans Scharf, deserved more detail. Leibbrandt was a former Empire Games heavyweight boxing champion who had attended the 1936 Olympic Games and met Adolf Hitler. In 1938, having worked as a boxing instructor at a police college in the Transvaal, and transferring to the railway police with the rank of lance-sergeant, he returned to Germany to train gymnasts, qualified as a glider pilot and joined the Wehrmacht.

In April 1941 Leibbrandt adopted the alias Walter Kempf and, accompanied by Scharf acting as radio operator under the alias Emil Dorner, sailed with a crew of five to South Africa aboard a 40-ton French yacht, the *Kyloe*. This was to be an epic voyage, from Paimpol in Brittany on the 20m, English-built vessel, to land Leibbrandt in June at Mitchell's Bay, 150 miles north of Cape Town. His mission was to establish contact with the pro-Nazi Ossewa Brandweg (OB) and assassinate General Smuts, but his plan went awry when in December he made a night visit to Bernard Gerling, an aide to the OB leader Hans van Rensberg, thereby inadvertently alerting the local police. A major manhunt followed, resulting in the capture of his German-manufactured wireless transmitter, which was found to contain Hungarian and American components. Leibbrandt himself narrowly escaped arrest several times, but was eventually apprehended at a road-block near Pretoria on 24 December 1941. In November 1942 he was convicted of treason and condemned to death. Smuts commuted the sentence in 1943 to life imprisonment, and he was amnestied in 1948. He later married, had five children, and died in 1966 in Bloemfontein.

Leibbrandt's 31-year-old companion Hans Scharf was actually Hans Schneider, an Abwehr officer originally from Alsace-Lorraine who had joined the Brandenburger Lehr Regiment as a corporal in November 1939 before being transferred to the Abwehr II headquarters in Paris. He had been captured on 4 December 1943 by the French in Port Say after he had parachuted into Algeria on an intelligence collection mission and had tried to flee to Spanish Sahara posing as a Spanish Jew named Jaime Toledo.

When questioned by his French captors, led by Paul Paillole, Scharf volunteered the identities of fifty-eight German intelligence personnel and their agents, and disclosed details of his previous assignments. He described how he had been employed to promote Breton separatists in PoW camps before sailing to South Africa with Robbey Leibbrandt in March 1942. In August 1943, following assignments in France, Scharf was sent to Montpellier to prepare for a mission to either Tunisia or Algeria, dressed as an Arab, that ended at the second attempt. He was incarcerated at the Caserne de Vieux Château for seven months before arrangements could be made for his interrogation in England.

After his arrival by air at RAF Lyneham from Algiers Scharf was cross-examined at Camp 020 on his role in an aborted mission to North Africa with Charles Bedaux and, as anticipated, proved to be a mine of information, so much so that he remained in England for seven months before he was returned to French custody. Camp 020's commandant, Robin Stephens, would have preferred to keep him permanently as a research resource, remarking in August 1944 in his Liquidation Report, 'Personally, I would like to add him to the Ambulatory Library at Ham.'

Before he was questioned, MI5 drew up the customary ISOS schedule, which detailed his known activities between September 1941 and July 1943. This was the template against which Scharf's answers were compared, and he turned out to be truthful, not least because he feared French retribution if it was discovered that he was not a German, but a French collaborator from Kreuttingen in Lorraine. Furthermore, it was alleged that he had deserted from the French army while serving on the Maginot Line in November 1939.

Our first record of Scharf is in November, 1941, when he was in the Rio de Oro working under PILA, the head of the Cisneros station. He was officially an Abt. II agent under the direction of Kurt Haller, a member of Abt. II, Paris, but his work in Cisneros was also of interest to Waag and Huebner, heads of the Eins Heer and Eins Marine in the Paris Astleitstelle, which controlled the Cisneros station. It is probable that Scharf's career with the Abwehr started much earlier than this, however, since he was at some time condemned to life imprisonment by the French, presumably for espionage.

Scharf appears to have been able to establish good contacts in French West Africa, and to obtain information from Port Etienne. He was also able to perform the useful service of getting into direct touch with French Emirs without the assistance of the Spanish. In January and February of 1942 he was engaged in organising the WIND expedition. This was an Eins Heer project and involved sending a man, most probably a Frenchman, in the guise of a soldier along the West African coast through the Gambia and Sierra Leone to Liberia.

5,000 pesetas was sanctioned to pay for the expedition, which was run entirely independently of the Spanish. The money was brought over from Madrid by an official of the Cisneros station known as Mendez. The agent was presumably to make his reports by wireless, as after he had started out, Scharf was to go to the Spanish frontier with a W/T set, presumably for the agent's use. The organisation of this and other missions was considered sufficiently important for a proposal to be made that Wang and Huebner should visit Cisneros for discussions in March 1942. It was eventually decided, however, that the visit was not possible, and instructions were given that Scharf should go over to Madrid by military plane for discussions, to take place either there or in Paris. The WIND expedition was eventually ready in May, 1942, and on 2nd May the agent was due to leave by mail packet for La Aguena. He had a relative in Port Etienne who was a French officer.

Other expeditions with which Scharf was also probably concerned were the FISCH expedition and the HEKA undertakings. The FISCH expedition was an Eins Marine undertaking which involved sending a boat across to the South American coast. This also was organised quite independently of the local Spaniards. The Heka undertakings were probably small forays into the interior of French West Africa from the borders of Rio de Oro, and were probably organised with the collaboration of the Spaniards. There were probably also other projects for voyages along the coast of West Africa.

Scharf's work was considered very valuable by PILA, who during January and February, 1942, sent urgent requests to Paris that Scharf might be allowed to stay at Cisneros as he was essential for the development of the work of the stelle. He was entirely responsible for the organisation of the Wind undertaking, and his successor did not know the agents and contact men whom he met on the coast. In order to prevent Haller from writing to Scharf and instructing him to return to Paris, PILA asked the Paris station not to send on any mail to Scharf unless they knew the contents. He was therefore very indignant when a private letter reached Scharf from Haller through a certain 'Neno' informing him that he had been awarded the Iron Cross 2nd class, and that he had only been seconded to Cisneros to relieve Mendez. Haller had been pointing out for a long time that Scharf was due for leave, and eventually it was agreed that he should take his leave following his visit to Paris to discuss the WIND enterprise. PILA pointed out, however, that he still had to complete four weeks' disciplinary punishment, and asked that this should be cancelled before he went on leave in recognition of his excellent work. PILA emphasised that it was essential that Scharf should be available after his leave as he was to be head of a coastal transmitting station which it was planned to set up and which would be vital for the work in West Africa. The project involved living in the desert for some time with two Arabs, and Paris was asked to provide Scharf with funds to buy sufficient equipment for this. A tent was to be delivered at a place called Avoninti and a six-wheeled lorry was also made available for him.

He had, however, to negotiate for tyres when he was in Paris. The enterprise, which was to start before the spring, would not leave from Cisneros for reasons of cover.

Scharf eventually arrived in Madrid on 13 March 1942, and went via Hendaye to Paris on 19 Match 1942. There he was to report to the station master and would be met by one of the Paris officials. While he was in Paris he discussed the various projects afoot in Cisneros, and also the equipping of fishing smacks with W/T sets. It became clear that he and PILA did not always see eye to eye over these arrangements, and finally it was proposed that PILA should visit Madrid so that the differences could be cleared up.

There is no indication of what Scharf was doing between March, 1942 and August, 1943 when he was concerned in an enterprise based on Italy. He was to have been dropped by a machine from the Gartenfeld squadron, but the aeroplane which was to have been used was brought down and the crew taken prisoner by the British. The operation had therefore to be postponed until another plane became available.

Naturally, MI5 was anxious to extract from Scharf every detail of his mission with Leibbrandt to South Africa, but was hesitant to challenge him with details that might compromise ISOS. Accordingly, on 9 August 1944 Blanshard Stamp asked his French opposite number, Commandant André Bonnefous, for an assurance that Scharf would be executed upon his return to Algiers:

> Scharf is to be returned to North Africa on 23rd August. If we were sure he was then to be executed we could conduct our interrogation rather more freely than would be the case if Scharf is to mix with other prisoners on his return. There are certain matters of delicacy on which he might become aware during the course of the interrogation which we are anxious to safeguard. Could you therefore find out from Algiers how he is to be dealt with when he returns there.

However, while Bonnefous considered MI5's request, it was decided that Scharf was too valuable to return as agreed, and a delay was sought:

> This man is proving himself a mine of information and we feel both here and at Camp 020 that he would be a very valuable acquisition for reference purposes if we could retain him for, say, a further three months. As an example of the sort of information Scharf can provide I would refer you to the Camp 020 report dated 11 August 1944, four copies of which went to the War Room. This shows how valuable Scharf may be in identifying stay-behind agents. Further, he has displayed a formidable and perhaps unique knowledge of the activities and organisation of the Abwehr in Paris, and it might be very convenient indeed to have him on hand when we start to receive the products of the comb out of the city in the not too distant future.

One reason why MI5 was so interested in Scharf was his willingness to disclose information that he had not mentioned when questioned by the French in Oran, and his participation in a mission involving Charles Bedaux was one such topic, recalling that he had been called to Paris in 1942 where:

> ... he reported to Ledenburg as instructed, and the latter outlined to him the proposed mission. He was, it seemed, to travel to Algeria with an agent

in the German pay by name of Bedaux, for whom he was to act as wireless operator, transmitting all items of information which Bedaux wished to send to his chiefs in Paris. Bedaux, he was told, was identical with the well-known man of that name who acquired United States citizenship and became chief of the concern known as 'Bedaux Undertakings Incorporated' in America. He had also acquired fame by lending his home in Paris for the marriage of HRH the Duke of Windsor to Mrs Simpson.[1]

The mission was being undertaken ostensibly for the purpose of surveying a projected pipe line which was to convey vegetable oil from French West Africa to Algeria, and it had received the blessing of de Brinon and other members of the Vichy Cabinet, who were affording Bedaux all possible assistance. The Germans for their part, however, wished to make use of this admirable cover for the purpose of obtaining military information, and the Hotel Lutetia officials had decided to send two Abwehr W/T operators with the expedition who could carry out the necessary Secret Service work. Scharf unfortunately never learned the precise nature of the secret information which was to be obtained, though he suspected that it was to be, to a certain extent, economic as well as military.

After the plan had been briefly outlined, Hauptmann von Ledenburg took Scharf to a private hotel at 53 Avenue Hoche, which had formerly been the property of the well-known Greek financier, Sir Basil Zaharoff, and there introduced him to Bedaux. The discussion was now carried on in French, though Bedaux occasionally conversed with Ledenburg in what seemed to Scharf to be perfect English. Scharf was now told that the expedition was to be split up into two groups. The first of these, under the command of Bedaux himself, was to cover the territory bordering the projected railway line from Colomb-Bechar to Cao in the French Sudan, while the second, under the leadership of a colonel whose name Scharf never learned, was to operate along the route Colomb-Bechar, via Tibosti to Cao. The party was to consist of some fifteen to twenty men, and as they were to travel as much as possible in cars and lorries, the Germans had been approached with applications for the necessary petrol and tyres.

Bedaux was scheduled to set out for North Africa at the beginning of November 1942 and he, Scharf, and GEORGES (the second W/T operator) and [Jean] Caudron, a technical expert, duly alerted Paris for Lyons at the time arranged, where they were to catch the plane which was to take them to Algiers. On arrival in Lyons, they found that they had three days to wait, so Bedaux obtained accommodation for himself at the Carlton Hotel, while Scharf put up at the Grand Nouvel Hotel. Before the time fixed for the departure of the expedition, however, Scharf was unexpectedly recalled to Paris, where Gastl informed him that he would be unable to accompany Bedaux as Hauptmann Burkhardt of the Hotel Lutetia had a more important mission for him. He heard later on Burckhardt and Caudron caught the plane arranged, whilst GEORGES the V-Mann followed them by sea from Marseilles. The remaining members of the expedition were, of course, already in North Africa.

Before leaving the subject of the Bedaux mission, it should be pointed out that Scharf was instructed to operate under the cover name of André L'Huillier, and given a code based on a French novel by Pierre Benoit. This code was operated by means of a grid, but unfortunately Scharf is unable to remember the name of the particular novel which he was to use with it. His instructor was Unteroffizier Fitzentum of the Funkstelle at the Hotel Lutetia.

When pressed for more details, Scharf revealed further information about the Frenchman known to him as GEORGES:

… the W/T operator who accompanied Bedaux to Algeria, and who is still known to be working for the German Secret Service. When first introducing this man to Scharf, von Ledenburg mentioned that he had formerly been established with his wife in a villa on the coast of Normandy or Brittany, where he had set up a wireless transmitter for communication with the Paris Stelle. Considerably later, during 1943, the same von Ledenburg, who had in the meantime been transferred from Gruppe III to Gruppe I, told Scharf that GEORGES had returned safely via Spain after having satisfactorily carried out his duties for Bedaux, and that he had reestablished himself in his villa with a view to remaining as a W/T agent behind the Allied lines in the event of invasion of the continent. In the circumstances, therefore, it is desirable that this export agent be located at the earliest possible opportunity, and arrested.

MI5 would eventually receive help from Carl Eitel to identify GEORGES as Georges Aubry, whom he had employed as an agent in Brest operating under the code name CARLOS. Aubry somehow made a miraculous escape from

Algiers and returned to Paris, where he was welcomed with some scepticism by the Abwehr. Bedaux was not so lucky, and was arrested when American troops entered Algiers, to be kept in custody until December 1943 when he was shipped to Florida.

The issue of Bedaux's loyalties would become moot following his suicide by an overdose of deliberately hoarded sleeping tablets in February 1944, but the evidence was collected anyway as Liddell was anxious to tie up all the loose ends. As well as testimony from Scharf, who had been rejected for the task by Bedaux, MI5 gathered other witnesses, including Josef Graf von Ledebur-Wicheln, an Austrian aristocrat and member of the Paris Abstelle who was later appointed aide to Colonel Georg Hansen in Berlin and in 1944 defected to the British embassy in Madrid. The fact that Bedaux had himself insisted on being accompanied by two Abwehr wireless operators was itself a significant indicator of the intelligence dimension to his mission. It also shed light on his relationship with senior Abwehr personnel, such as Kapitan Erich Pfeiffer[2] and his chief, Major Alexander Waag, who had selected and assigned the appropriate personnel. Waag, who was Admiral Canaris's nephew, became the second most senior figure in the Paris Abstelle, under Colonel Friedrich Rudolf who headed the Abwehr across the whole of France throughout the occupation. These were indeed friends in high places, but such contacts would leave him defenceless when a federal grand jury was convened in February 1944 to bring charges of treason and trading with the enemy.

When in January 1945 the time came for Scharf to be returned to the French, Helenus Milmo recommended that the authorities should be informed of the assistance he had rendered:

> It seems the French Military Court is anxious to lauch proceedings against Scharf, and if this is so I think that whilst it would probably be unwise to make any positive recommendation we should draw the attention of the French to the fact that this man has given a very great deal of assistance to us voluntarily whilst he has been over here, and that this might be taken into account in mitigation of the offences of which he will doubtless be found guilty.

When finally Scharf was ready to go back to Algiers, his flight from RAF Lyneham was delayed by bad weather for a few days, and he was held in the cells at Wootton Bassett police station until 5 February, much to the discomfort of the Chief Constable of Devizes. Upon his arrival Scharf was charged with treason and sentenced to death on 14 March by a military tribunal.

★ ★ ★

Unwittingly, the Spanish consul in Vancouver, Fernando Kobbe, would bring about the downfall of that most assiduous German spy, Alcazar de Velasco. Even before his arrival in Canada, Kobbe, who was a widower, formerly married to a German woman, had been compromised by Japanese decrypts that suggested he had been recruited as a Japanese spy, perhaps by his mistress, Marichu Amenza. Initially, some consideration was given by Peter Wilson of SIS's Section V to making a pitch in the hope of turning Kobbe into a double-agent, but it was decided that such a move might compromise another double-agent, ASPIRIN.

There were other complications, too. With MI5, SIS, British Security Coordination, FBI and RCMP interests to be consulted, Guy Liddell and Section V were anxious to protect certain very secret aspects of the investigations into Alcazar de Velasco, Luis Calvo and del Pozo, which had involved the highly sensitive TRIPLEX source, and an agent inside the Spanish embassy in London, PEPPERMINT. Additionally, there was anxiety about the codebooks that Kobbe had carried to the United States on the SS *Marques de Commilas* that had been surreptitiously inspected in Trinidad.

While en poste Kobbe was subject to the most intense surveillance by the RCMP, encouraged by MI5's liaison officer in Montreal, Cyril Mills, who had a further advantage in his investigation of the diplomat. One of his sources, actually managed by the FBI's Special Agent John Williams, and code-named ASPIRIN, was a Spanish journalist, José Aladrin, who was in contact with Kobbe, code-named FISHERMAN, using secret writing since October 1942. In August 1943 ASPIRIN returned to Madrid in an effort to be recruited by the Japanese, and he was the source of an incriminating letter, sent through the regular mail, which contained $1,000 and a Japanese code concealed in secret writing. Naturally the RCMP copied the contents, and this and other items, including a microfilm sent from an unknown contact, became the basis of an official protest to the Spanish Foregn ministry from the British ambassador, Sir Samuel Hoare, in January 1944 complaining about the employment of Spanish diplomats as Japanese agents.

Rather unexpectedly, the Spanish government reacted swiftly to Hoare by recalling Kobbe to face a judicial tribunal in Madrid. Accordingly, he sailed back to Europe from New Orleans on the SS *Megalles*, accompanied by his daughter, Beatrix, in February 1944.

18

AUGUST 1944, UNDATED

With the invasion troops firmly established in France, MI5's monthly report concentrated not on the role of the double-agents engaged in deception, but on a scheme for BRUTUS upon his return to Paris, and on updating the Prime Minister on the activities of TRICYCLE and his brother DREADNOUGHT, and on DRAGONFLY who had narrowly avoided being compromised by the British traitor Oswald Job.

AUGUST 1944
A. SPECIAL AGENTS.
1) BRUTUS.
This agent has continued to play an important part in putting across the cover plan of SHAEF. A completely new possibility has however been opened up since we have just learnt that the Germans have been persuaded to deposit a wireless transmitter for him in Paris, should he be able to get to France.

It is hoped to recover this set in the near future, and we shall then be in a position to offer to SHAEF a channel of the highest possible grade at the centre of operations.

2) TRICYCLE.
This agent's elder brother, DREADNOUGHT, who has been operating against the Germans in Yugoslavia for the past three years and has helped to recruit for us four more special agents, recently escaped from Yugoslavia owing to the attentions of the Gestapo. He is now in this country, and has given us a great deal of information. In particular he has confirmed that

as late at the end of July, the Germans appeared to have no suspicions that TRICYCLE was controlled.

3) <u>DRAGONFLY</u>.

An unexpected development in this case which was long thought to be dead shows how slow on the uptake the Germans are in realising when their agents are compromised. A spy of British nationality, Job, was arrested in this country and hanged on March 16th last. He had as one of his missions to this country, to deliver jewellery at an address supplied by DRAGONFLY. At the time of Job's execution it was felt that the Germans could not fail to realise that this implicated DRAGONFLY, but they have now succeeded in making a payment of £1,000 in favour of DRAGONFLY.

This indication that they still trust him is confirmed from Most Secret Sources. Unfortunately the present confusion in the German Secret Service makes it doubtful whether we can take advantage of this trust to open up the case again.

B. <u>SPIES</u>.

The energies of our special interrogation centre have been almost exclusively devoted in the last month to investigating some nineteen enemy agents taken in the field, and sent back to this country. The qualities of these agents is considerably higher than in the case of those taken during the first month of the operations in France, no less then twelve of the new arrivals were to direct wireless sets, and several of them had long been in the service of the German Intelligence.

The interrogation of Hans Scharf, referred to in last month's summary, has been completed with particularly satisfactory results. Owing to his extensive knowledge of the German Intelligence Organisation in Paris, he is, by agreement with the French, being kept in this country for a further period for 'reference'.

C. <u>SABOTAGE</u>.

It has now become apparent that the German Secret Service planned their greatest sabotage effort of the war in Italy. By August 1st, 1944 about fifty saboteurs had been caught, including two Italian Communists, and an Italian Intelligence Service agent, who had deliberately penetrated the German Organisation. The Germans left sabotage agents behind in towns captured by the Allies, and arranged for others to cross the lines and reach Rome and other towns in small groups. The sabotage equipment was usually left buried

in, or near, ruins in Rome. One such dump, however, was discovered in the
German Embassy to the Quirinal. In this case the explosive had been buried
for a considerable time and was in such a dangerous condition that a serious
explosion occurred when it was discovered.[1]

An officer of the Security Service has just returned from a visit to Paris,
where large hauls have been made of German sabotage material, besides
documents, a detailed examination of which seems likely to yield results that
may be of considerable future value.

Director-General

★ ★ ★

This report, among all the others, is quite unusual since it appears from a
memo left in the file dated 8 August 1944 that it was also read by the Foreign
Secretary, Anthony Eden, and his Permanent Under-Secretary, Sir Alexander
Cadogan. Their reaction is not recorded, but they were probably both surprised
to see the extent of MI5's involvement overseas, such as the visits to Rome and
Paris by MI5's sabotage expert, Victor Rothschild, and the extent of its double-
agent operations, mentioning four different cases. While SIS had played a part
in TRICYCLE and his brother DREADNOUGHT, who had been brought
to England under SIS's sponsorship, the references to DRAGONFLY and
BRUTUS may have been a revelation.

19

5 OCTOBER 1944

This report appears quite different to Petrie's other submissions, and may have been written by a different hand. It takes a reflective, somewhat self-congratulatory view of MI5's adversarial relationship with the Abwehr, and highlights two past milestones in the conflict. The first was an outline of how the Germans had sought to influence British public opinion through such subversive groups as the Anglo-German Fellowship and The Link, organisations which had attracted some political support from such controversial figures as Admiral Sir Barry Domvile and Captain Archibald Ramsay MP, both regarded as right-wing extremists. In 1940 MI5's Max Knight had successfully penetrated The Link with several agents and Ramsay, though still with a seat in Parliament, was detained at Brixton.

The other major German pre-war objective was access to British manufacturing data, as a means to monitoring the government's policy of rearmament, and this had been accomplished through a commercial front, Benrath Machine Tools. Through this entity the Germans were able to keep an eye on the speed and scale of industrial mobilisation without having to engage in conventional espionage.

MI5's strategy of confronting and closing down perceived enemy activity had led B Division to one of the Abwehr's few assets in England, Arthur Owens, code-named JOHNNIE. A Welsh businessman with a battery business, Owens had been recruited by the Abwehr in 1936, but MI5 had been monitoring his illicit correspondence to a compromised cover address in Belgium so he was detained on the very first day of the war. This intervention led Owens to reveal the existence of a wireless transmitter, and, code-named SNOW, he began transmitting daily weather reports under MI5's control. Clearly trusted by the Abwehr's branch in Hamburg, Owens provided carefully crafted information, such as identification data and home addresses, for subsequent agents who were dropped into the country by parachute, and promptly taken into custody. This, as the report suggests, was the foundation of what became the hugely successful and profitable double-cross system.[1] As the anonymous author explains, most of the spies infiltrated into the United Kingdom during the 'invasion summer' of 1940 were quickly neutralised, leaving MUTT and JEFF, who landed on the Banffshire coast in April 1941.[2]

SEPTEMBER 1944

The main objective of enemy intelligence is shifting more and more away from the United Kingdom and towards the Armies in the field, though there have been indications recently that the enemy still hopes to increase the efficiency of his supposed spy service in this country. At this stage therefore it may be of interest to review in bare outline the development of German espionage activities in this country since the period immediately preceding the war.

From about 1936 onwards the German Intelligence machine in this country was mainly directed towards persuading people here that Germany's expansionist aim on the continent were no concern of ours and in no sense a menace to British security. To this purpose they employed a variety of organisations directed by the Foreign Branch of the Nazi Party. The Party itself had a headquarters in London with provincial branches, and through its outer constellation, which included such organisations as the Anglo-German Fellowship and the Link, endeavoured to recruit a body of opinion favourably disposed towards Germany. On the higher diplomatic level, the Ribbentrop Bureau was engaged in similar activities.

The Germans seem to have been confident right to the last moment that their propaganda through these agencies would be successful in keeping us out of the war, but to reinforce this opinion they thought it expedient to obtain an accurate picture of our industrial mobilisation capacity and so to assess whether in fact we were in a position to engage in active hostilities. The method was simple. They relied largely on German agencies in this country engaged in the supply of machine tools both to Government Ordnance factories and to other factories which were concerned in our re-armament programme.

In Manchester they established a German agency called Benrath Machine Tools representing some thirteen machine tool firms in Germany. As British firms could not give delivery under a year to eighteen months, the business went to Benrath, who were offering delivery in three months.

It was essential, therefore, for Benrath to be informed about the design of the article to be manufactured and the number that it was expected to produce per month. Worse than this, it was apparently found necessary for German mechanics to be employed in setting up the machines and in servicing them from month to month. It was therefore not surprising that when a delegation from the German Ministry of War was allowed to visit this country in 1936 it was joined in the Midlands by the head of Benrath's, who subsequently returned to London with the party and spent the night with them before they returned to Germany. So easy in fact did the Germans find it to acquire information about our inclination and capacity to make war that they omitted to lay the foundation of any underground organisation in this country capable of coming into operation after the outbreak of war. The few agents, or potential agents, left behind were dealt with by the arrests made in September 1939 and during the late summer of 1940. There remained only one active agent who, under our control, established wireless communication with the enemy and ultimately became the corner stone of the intelligence organisation which the Security Service built in this country on behalf of the Germans. More important still, a study of his wireless procedure and observation of his control station led to the discrimination by the Radio Security Service of the wide network of enemy Secret Service communications.

It seems probable that the Germans never seriously considered the invasion of this country until they reached the Channel Ports. If this were so, it might account for the period of comparative inactivity during the early months of the war and for the hastily improvised adventures in the early autumn of 1940 onwards involving the arrival by parachute and rubber boat of a number of agents, both badly equipped and ill-instructed. Their apprehension in a matter of a few hours presented little difficulty in a country which at that moment was vigilant and thoroughly spy-conscious. One party which arrived in Scotland by rubber boat, waded ashore and went to the nearest railway station, where they asked for tickets to London. This unusual request aroused the booking clerk to scrutinise the travellers more closely, and struck by their bedraggled appearance and their poor English, he informed the station-master. The local policeman was summoned and arriving on his bicycle, soon established that all the documents carried by these spies were out of order. Such was the calibre of the first batch of spies who operated during what may be called the period of illegal entry. In the eyes of the Germans all failed except two, whose services were recruited for our double-agent network.

After the enemy's invasion project had been abandoned, methods improved, and a policy of legal entry was adopted. Spies began to arrive in the guise of refugees wishing to join the Allied Forces and as seamen sailing between this country and the Iberian Peninsula. In some cases, the Germans would penetrate our escape organisations on the Continent and so insert an agent into a bona-fide party of refugees. To meet this situation arrangements were made by which the Security Control Officer at the Port sent certain categories of aliens and listed suspects to a special interrogation centre in London where their cases could be gone into in greater detail, and at this establishment an information index was built up by which the stories of all refugees could be compared and closely checked, It has been possible in this way to track down a large number of spies, totally unaided by information from other sources. Where a confession is obtained or strong suspicion exists, the alien is sent to our special spy camp, for detailed interrogation. The information obtained at these two camps has given not only a complete picture of the German Intelligence organisation, its personnel and methods, but also an immense amount of data about conditions in Occupied Territory which has been passed to the Services concerned.

As a further insurance against penetration the double-agent network was built up on a large scale and reached the point where virtually the whole of the supposed German Intelligence Organisation in this country was under the control of the Security Service. This controlled organisation reached a point of such complexity that, through a series of elaborate cross-checks, it provided almost irrefutable proof that the Germans had not succeeded in building up any other espionage organisation for work in this country. This knowledge enabled the Security Service to state to the military authorities its firm conviction that in the period preceding the Second Front, there were no channels working from this country to the Germans which could jeopardise the operation.

In addition to this a very close watch has all along been maintained on the activities of neutral and Allied diplomats in the United Kingdom, as it was known that information which they sent out to their capitals was in certain cases passed on to the enemy.

Through the feeding of accurate, though unimportant, information to the enemy, the position of the controlled organisation was maintained up to the opening of the Second Front, when in conjunction with Service wireless deception units it was used to implement the Controller's plan of major deception. Proof is available not only that the reports of our controlled agents backed by the appropriate wireless signals were accepted by the Headquarters of the German Intelligence Service in Berlin, but that the German strategy in the field was based upon them. A German map captured in Italy on May 15th 1944 shows the false disposition of our units in this country precisely as they were reported by us to the enemy, while practical events and the conversations between Hitler and his generals which have recently been published, show that the threat to the Pas-de-Calais caused Rommel to delay committing the full weight of his armour until the bridgehead had been sufficiently established to enable us to repel his attacks.

Another function which has been discharged by the Security Service during the period preceding and immediately following Overlord has been the preparation of the counter-espionage intelligence policy and instruction for the Armies invading Europe. Not only, however, have we supplied written instructions and information, but we have also held training courses for British and American officers about to undertake counter-espionage work in the field, and have supplied as many as eighty officers from the Security Service itself to act as key personnel in this organisation. These are at present undertaking investigation work, the control of special agents in the field and the interrogation of members of the German Secret Service captured on the Continent. Our special interrogation centre in this country is, moreover, undertaking the detailed examination of such captured agents as are thought sufficiently interesting to be brought back to the United Kingdom. The intelligence thus obtained is immediately distributed to the armies in the field.

The duties of the Security Service are being further extended to the training of officers for counter intelligence work in Germany itself after the cessation of hostilities. These officers, who again include members of the Security Service, are being incorporated in the Control Commission.

5 October 1944

★ ★ ★

Churchill was very interested to see evidence of the success of the Allied deception schemes and demanded to inspect an enemy map captured in Italy just before D-Day, which had been marked with the German assessment of the Allied order-of-battle in Great Britain. He also wanted other proof, and Dick White suggested the transcripts of conversations exchanged between senior enemy commanders on and immediately after D-Day.

The Prime Minister, when reading the last Monthly Report on the activities of the Security Service, asked to see certain conversations between German Generals, showing the success of the Deception Plan and the consequent retention of troops in other parts of France which might have been brought into action against our troops in Normandy.

Records of these conversations have been found in the Telephone Journal of the German Seventh Army, which was captured by the Polish Armoured Division. The following two extracts, taken from the SHAEF Weekly Intelligence Summary of the 9th September 1944, are the most significant:-

6 June 1944

1655 hrs. Chief of Staff reports situation to Chief of Staff Western Command.

Chief of Staff, Western Command (RUNDSTEDT's H.Q.) emphasizes the desire of Supreme Command (HITLER) to have the enemy in the bridgehead annihilated by the evening of 6 June, since there exists a danger of additional sea and airborne landings for support. ... The beachhead in CALVADOS must be cleaned up by NOT later than to-night.

9 June 1944

1530 hrs. Conversation of Field Marshal ROMMEL in Army Hq. with the Commanding General and Chief of Staff.

The Chief of Staff expresses the opinion that the enemy, because of the increased resistance SOUTH of CHERBOURG, will commit more airborne troops in order to take possession of CHERBOURG rapidly.

Field Marshal ROMMEL does NOT share this opinion, since the Supreme Command expects a large landing on the Channel Coast within the next few days, and therefore the enemy will NOT have more airborne troops available.

20

3 NOVEMBER 1944

MI5's very brief report for October 1944, completed in early November, confined itself to three enemy prisoners, all examples of intelligence personnel who disclosed valuable information after their capture in newly liberated areas, and four double-agents, LIPSTICK, BRONX, SNIPER and ROVER.

The three German captives were Carl Eitel, arrested by the Americans in Nancy, Fritz Lorenz,[1] who was seized in Namur, and Peter Schagen, an Abwehr defector in Madrid.

OCTOBER 1944

Out of the rabble of spies who are being rounded up in the field during October, twelve have been of sufficient interest to be sent home to this country for closer examination at our special interrogation centre. These have included several members of Himmler's Secret Service, who have been able to supply us with a considerable amount of information, both about the organisation of this service in France and Belgium, and about individual agents whom the enemy proposed to leave behind after his retreat.

One of these spies, Carl Eitel, is an old hand at the job. His name figured in the American spy trial of 1938 as a contact of agents working on German liners travelling from Europe to the USA. At the fall of France he was in Brittany and remained there working for the Germans till 1943, when he was sent by his masters on a mission to Lisbon. He there made contact with the Americans, who took him on as a special agent. In May 1944 he returned to Germany and was not heard of till he was arrested in Nancy after Americans had captured the town. At that time he pretended that he was still genuinely working for the Americans, but he was sent to this country in order that his story could be taken more fully and it rapidly became apparent that he had consistently lied, and that at the time of his capture by the Allies, was in fact still working for the Germans. His subsequent interrogation has provided a mass of interesting Intelligence, and has also revealed the fact that his career with the German Secret Service goes back even further than was supposed.

A second spy of interest, Werner Lorenz, is a man of quite a different type. His main interests are politics and propaganda, and after joining the Ribbentrop Bureau in 1934, he became a close friend of Ribbentrop and frequently acted as his personal courier to this country when Ribbentrop was Ambassador here. In 1940, on Ribbentrop's advice, he joined Himmler's Secret Service, and carried out a number of missions for it, mainly political in character. He was in Paris at the time of his capture by the Allies, and deserted to them shortly after.[2] He has been able to provide us with much useful information about various secret German political organisations about which little was known from other sources.

A third agent, Peter Schagen, was an important organiser of preparations for sabotage behind the lines after the German retreat. During the campaign in France this man escaped to Spain. There he got in touch with the Americans. From his information we have learnt much about the policy and methods in sabotage behind the Allied lines. It is clear that they intend to use long term methods, leaving sabotage material hidden so that agents can, at a much later date, be sent over to find and make use of it. Their first object will be to destroy important Allied material and their second to cause political trouble by the sudden outbreak of sabotage all over the country which might be attributed to the Communists, the FFI, the British or any other group which the Germans wished to discredit.

Just before the fall of Paris the Security Service sent over an expert to take the necessary counter-measures against the German sabotage threat. This officer has examined the headquarters of the German Sabotage Service which was captured in the Château de Rocquiemcourt, near Paris. In this château there were found not only large quantities of sabotage material, but also files giving details of the organisation and lists of agents with whom material had been deposited. From this it was learned that the Germans have concealed nearly a thousand small dumps of bombs and sabotage equipment throughout France.

One development of interest has taken place recently in connection with our special agents. The Germans have suddenly attempted to revive some cases which were thought to be completely dead. They have, for instance, recently revived contact with an agent, LIPSTICK, who had ceased to communicate with them for more than six months. Another agent, BRONX, who had sent material of a very low grade, has now been asked to pay a personal visit to the Peninsula. A third, SNIPER, has now been promised two wireless transmitters. A fourth agent, ROVER, whose letters to the Germans had not been answered for some months, has suddenly received a wireless message and has been able to establish contact with the Germans. A possible explanation of this revival of this activity is the influence of Himmler who for some months seems to have been surveying and revitalizing many parts of the German Security Service.

3rd November 1944   Director General

★ ★ ★

The case of Peter Schagen is especially interesting as he was an Abwehr II defector who turned up unexpectedly at the US embassy in Madrid hoping to make his way to the United States with his 23-year-old French mistress, Jeanette Bertremieux. In fact, she had made the first approach to the Americans, through the US military attaché, without Schagen's knowledge. Initially she had met a Lieutenant-Colonel Clark, but had been rebuffed, so she then talked to a Lieutenant-Colonel Hoffman, who was more receptive and introduced Schagen to the military attaché, Colonel Sharp, and to a member of the British embassy calling himself 'Mr Simpson'. By negotiation it was agreed that Schagen would be taken to the British consulate in Seville before travelling to Gibraltar, and that a letter would be mailed from Barcelona, addressed to Jeanette, that he had flown back to Germany. In exchange, Sharp promised to have her returned safely to her parents' home in France.

Unknown to them, Schagen was a familiar figure to the analysts studying the ISOS traffic, who recognised him as the leader of a stay-behind sabotage organisation based in southern France.

Schagen was flown to Hendon from Gibraltar and delivered to Camp 020 on 2 October 1944 for detailed interrogation. He proved entirely cooperative, his statements having been compared to numerous ISOS references. He was then returned to the custody of OSS's X-2 branch in London in November 1944 and was flown to France, where he helped find and uncover nineteen Abwehr arms caches hidden in anticipation of a stay-behind sabotage campaign. However, this development caused dismay in the US, where G-2 expressed concern that Schagen had not been delivered to Washington DC, where he was due to be questioned by the FBI about his knowledge of pre-war Nazi activities in Brazil, where he had lived until the outbreak of war.

★ ★ ★

Born in 1900 and employed from August 1928 as a wine waiter on the *Bremen* and other Norddeutscher Lloyd transatlantic liners, Carl Eitel was recruited by the Abwehr's Erich Pfeiffer in Bremen in 1934. His role as a courier was compromised in 1938 in the Karl Schluter espionage case when he was named in court by the FBI as a German spy. Consequently Eitel was put on the Abwehr's reserve list, occasionally acting as a cut-out for Jean Frutos in Cherbourg, but in 1939 he was sent to Genoa to recruit seamen working for the American Export line ships SS *Washington* and *Manhattan* as agents. This episode was of intense interested to the FBI, who pursued three of them, Johann Kassner, Fred Ehrich and Karl Elwert, based on his testimony. In June 1940 he was posted to Brest, equipped with a wireless transmitter.

In July 1943 Eitel was transferred to Lisbon to work as a seafront recruiter under Hans Bendixen, and was recruited in November under the code name SPEARHEAD by an OSS X-2 case officer using the alias Charlie Grey. In May 1944 he was recalled to Berlin for a mission to Vienna to assist in the repatriation to Egypt of Joseph Farrag, the purser off the liner *Zamzam*, and then was sent on another assignment to Saint-Jean-de-Luz, to organise stay-behind networks along France's north-east coast, which was interrupted by his arrest in Nancy.

MI5's assessment of the uncritical attitude adopted by OSS when Eitel turned up in Lisbon is scarcely concealed:

> Early in 1944 Eitel, who was cautious enough to conceal not only his early espionage history but many of its most recent and compromising chapters, contacted the American Intelligence representatives in Lisbon with the offer of his services; he was ready to betray his masters of ten years' standing while admitting only to five to reinsure his European future through American favour. The offer was accepted. Eitel supplied information on the Abwehr in general and its Lisbon personalities in particular; and he was used by his new contacts to 'feed' false information, directly and indirectly, to his full-time masters.

Eitel was arrested in Nancy in September 1944 by the French, who handed him over to the US 3rd Army CIC at Chalons-sur-Marne. It ran him as a source until he was passed to Camp 020 in October 1944. Somewhat belatedly, and under intensive interrogation, Eitel was matched to an ISOS personality, code-named CARLOS, an analysis that showed he had lied constantly about the extent of his lengthy service for the Abwehr. He remained at Ham until July 1945, when he was delivered to CSDIC at Diest.

The FBI concluded that Eitel had 'unlimited information of infinite value' regarding German espionage in the United States, but one of the priorities was to learn whether he had been responsible, after he had been recruited by OSS, for the betrayal of Juan Frutos, code-named DRAGOMAN. Certainly Eitel had identified Frutos as a German spy to the Americans, who had arrested him on 8 July at his home at 10 Avenue Aristide Briand as one of three Abwehr stay-behind agents active in Cherbourg. But had he then informed the Germans that OSS had run Frutos as a double-agent against them? According to his ISOS traffic, he had remained in radio contact with Wiesbaden until 20 July. Truly, Eitel was one of the slipperiest customers ever in the espionage business, apparently loyal only to himself, but the challenge was to assess the accuracy of his stories. For example, to prove his bona fides, he claimed to have conveyed two important items of information to 'Colonel Grey':

> The Portuguese consul in Dakar, a German spy, reported to the German embassy Lisbon that an Allied convoy of 60 ships, troops, materiel and naval escort was sailing on a certain date. This was wirelessed to Berlin by the embassy and a reply received that U-boats would handle. Subject reported to Colonel Grey who confirmed a week later that sailing postponed convoy saved. (March 1944)
>
> A Russian woman, agent of British Intelligence, was a double-agent in the employ of the Germans. She was flown to London from Lisbon by British in April 1944 and on return gave full report to Germans. Subject reported matter to Colonel Grey, latter presumably to British who confirmed.

Both messages were extremely important, and the latter appeared to incriminate TREASURE, who exactly fitted the description given, and the date coincided with her most recent visit to Lisbon. Had she really given the Abwehr a 'full report' of her role of an MI5 double-agent? If so, she had been in a position to compromise much else besides to Buecking, a known IM personality in the Portugal KO. A search of the files revealed confirmation:

> Early in March the British Secret Service sent to Lisbon a Russian woman who got in touch with Buecking, whom she had known previously. She gave Buecking the name of the Chief of the British Secret Service in Lisbon (name not given in our message). Since then she has returned to London and is corresponding with Buecking.

TREASURE's MI5 file showed that she arrived in Lisbon on 3 March 1944, and after her return to London, immediately after her lunch with Emil Kliemann on 22 March, she remained active for MI5 over a further six months, until December 1944. She had been approved for participation in the FORTITUDE deception, reporting on her radio that there were not many troops to be seen in south-west England, thereby supporting the fiction of a concentration of Allied forces in the south-east. However, if TREASURE was compromised, her signals would be reinterpreted, and doubtless Kliemann's other agent, DRAGONFLY would also come under suspicion.

When pressed further, Eiten recalled more about his meeting on 22 April 1944 with Buecking, who had been drinking whisky in his chief's apartment in Lisbon, and told him about:

> ... his recent meeting with a Russian woman in Lisbon, whom he had known before the war. She was working for the British Intelligence service now, and he had met her in the street by chance. She had told him that her British chief in England, whom she named, had sent her to contact a certain person in Lisbon; she had given him the name and address. Through her he had learned a considerable amount about the British Secret Service. She was a dark, good-looking girl but he was afraid he could not mention any names ... She had left Lisbon with the undertaking to keep in touch by mail. Eitel did not dare to question him more closely and Buecking went on to tell his agent that he would never make good in the Abwehr unless he got a really worthwhile contact like this woman.
>
> At a meeting a few days later with Colonel Grey, Eitel reported in outline his recent chat with Buecking, stressing his reference to the Russian woman agent.

When checks were made with OSS X-2 in Lisbon, MI5 received confirmation that the name 'Charlie Grey' was an alias used with low-level agents, and that in fact Eiten had been handled by an OSS cut-out named Silverberg.

MI5 finally concluded that Eitel's only real contribution to the Allied cause was an intelligence questionnaire that he claimed had been entrusted to him as a microphotograph in August for delivery from Bremen to the Abwehr office in Saint-Jean-de-Luz, for distribution to the key agents run from Madrid, among them Hans Grimm. However, Eitel's role as a courier had only lasted as far as his journey to Nancy, where he had gone to ground to await the Allies.

The questionnaire, evidently assembled by Eins Marine in Berlin, showed the Kriegsmarine's priorities at a moment when the U-boat fleet was under severe pressure from RAF Coastal Command and Royal Navy destroyers apparently taking advantage of new technology especially in the Bay of Biscay as submarines transitted into the Atlantic.

Subject: <u>Location Method Above Water</u>
    Find out the following:
1) The enemy's most usual Radio Location apparatus, where and with what special objectives used; land, nautical and air equipment.
2) The development and trial of radio location apparatus. The enemy plane. The trend of development.
3) The names of the inventors, the designers, who at present direct development.
4) The names and sites of the manufacturers. Where are the laboratories, experimental and testing centres.
5) As precise as possible a possible a description of the apparatus; and the range.
6) The instructions for the manipulation of the apparatus, and the methods used for measurement.
7) The frequencies used by the enemy, his achievement and progress, especially in the region of 1 cm to 3 cm.
8) The enemy's jamming and misleading apparatus, description of how and where operated.
9) What wireless observation apparatus the enemy uses, description of how and where installed, the frequency bands engaged, the D.F. methods the effectiveness of the apparatus.
10) The apparatus and procedure for the distinction between his own and enemy location apparatus.
11) The instructions about enemy jammers on land, on board ship and in the air.
12) The apparatus and procedure, which are used for artillery fire.
13) The equipment of long-range recce aircraft and fighter bombers with search gear.
14) The instructions about optical D.F. sets which are worked with ultra-red or possibly with ultra-violet beams; where and with what special objectives they are used – especially nautical and air apparatus 'h.w.'
15) As precise a description as possible of the apparatus, source of light, effect required, lens construction, angle of vision, the kind of filters used.
16) The range of the apparatus, the effect of weather (thick fog).
17) The instructions for thermo D.F. sets and their operation, especially against U-boats.

Subject: <u>The Enemy's Underwater Location Against Submerged U-Boats</u>
The methods in respect of acoustic underwater location certainly consist on the one hand of Asdic location (Asdic apparatus, sound impulsion producer (Schallimpulseaseuger) with the receiver for eventual returning echoes) and on the other hand sound direction-finding (single listening for U-boat noises through listening apparatus).

a) Are there yet other acoustic under water direction finders and methods?
b) How long have these methods been in operation?
c) As precise as possibly a description of these methods and of apparatus or gear which is necessary for their application.
d) On what are these installed, ships, aircraft, U-boats?
e) How is the prospect of success of these methods judged?
f) By what firms is the apparatus supplied?
g) Do any research and development centres still engage in the investigation of acoustic underwater problems or study the further development of acoustic apparatus already in use, including Asdic and listening apparatus?
h) What improvements are expected from the innovations?
2) Has the enemy also a method for the location of submerged U-boats, which is not on an acoustic basis (sound measurement) but on an electric or magnetic basis?
3) Is this apparatus already in use or is it still in the research or testing stage?
4) Describe as precisely as possible such apparatus and in addition the method of use.
5) What researchers, discoverers, are taking, or have taken part in this development?
6) What institutions or firms are engaged in the development and manufacture of the apparatus respectively?
7) What importance is attached to this method, first in research work, secondly in actual practice (reports from the personnel who use it, and so on)?
8) What carriers are or will be used, ships, aircraft, U-boats?
9) Sound buoys.
10) What must be aimed at with such buoys?
11) When, where and how are they operated?
12) Account of the sound producing apparatus.
13) Describe as precisely as possible the quality of the noise made (pitch, timbre, volume, secondary noises produced etc.)
14) Are several kinds of noises used?

15)   The duration of the noise made, can interruptions (pauses) be made?

16)   What firms are employed in the manufacture of this buoy?

17)   Do there exist owing to the nature of the sound any possible confusion between a sound buoy and any acoustic means of location?

Underwater Location

a) Will ships sailing alone or in convoy send out into the water alternating currents of very low frequency (under 1 hz)? In case such a procedure exists it is urgent to ascertain what the enemy has in view. The most precise details of the procedure is very much desired.

b) What is known about 'the 'Transient' procedure: does the same apply to U- boat location?

c) Is an electric or acoustic method of underwater location with audible frequencies involved?

d) What is known about the Asdic method of the American (ultra sonorous) location? What frequencies? Is it doubly effective? Does a visual indicator exist? How does this appear?

2) Ultra Red Location

a) Are the screens (Bildwandler) cooled? What means of cooling are used?

b) Up to what wave-lengths etc. up to what smallest differences of temperature respectively, is the observation apparatus for heat rays practicable?

c) Are there sensitive screens in stock (Warmebild-wandler)?

d) What other light converting beams will be used for thermo D.F. sets? What sensitivity have they, up to what wavelengths do these photo cells work?

e) How does the location apparatus work? Which apparently locates U-boats underwater with ultra violet rays; does this apparatus work by television (Abtastung)?

f) Have Anglo-Americans ultra red filters which let through no visible beam?

g) Can Anglo-Americans locate from aircraft a submerged U-boat by means of a strong searchlight (Scheinwerfer)? As many details as possible about it.

h) What ranges are reached with thermal D.F. sets or screens (Bildwardler) against surfaced and submerged travelling U-boats?

i) Do Anglo-Americans use beams of waves long enough to penetrate thick fog?

j) Does the apparatus for the location of the U-boat work with fixed or variable waves?

a) Thermo-sensitive screen (warmebildwandler); Down to how low a temperature can the objects be seen through this apparatus?

b) The most detailed technical information above all about the electric control and the technical composition of those particular parts, through which boat is transformed into light.

c) Are the images formed by reflection which have been observed on aeroplanes and protective units on the front side of the glass or the side opposite to that from which the light emanates.

d) Often, red discs on protective units will be observed from U-boats; such discs apparently alter their shape to crescents when they revolve. Moreover, it has been observed that a bluish-white light lies over the red light. It might be presumed that it was a question of ultra-red reflectors (scheinwerfer) whose filters were not good enough to absorb completely the visible light. As far as we can tell good ultra red filters are known which allow no visible light through are known to the enemy, it may therefore be presumed that insofar as these red discs are concerned, it is a question of secondary apparitions caused by a process which has nothing whatever to do with ultra red.

e) It may probably be presumed that the red discs in conjunction with bluish-white light are concerned with ultra violet beams.

3) <u>Radio Location</u>

a) On what waves below 1m do the English and American radio location apparatus work when they are used in movement? More especially, is something known about radio location apparatus in the wave sphere 12 − 25 cm.

b) What is known concerning image reproduction and image analysis retrospectively in respect of panorama apparatus i.e. apparatus with automatic aerial rotation and visual indicator.

c) What are the working waves of this Panoramic apparatus and which ones are used from aeroplanes against U-boats.

    (i) Is something known about a radio-location development in wave sphere 1cm − 5cm.

    (ii) Are the installations already in manufacture?

d) Is anything know about the suitability of panoramic location, e.g. 3 cm.

e) Is something known about the possibilities of producing single radio location sets, especially taking into consideration the change of requirements to new types.

f) What radio location observation receivers does the enemy possess?
  (i) Wave sphere
  (ii) Detector or W/T valves and down to which wavelengths are detectors or W/T valves made use of.

g) Details about short transmissions and their possibilities of direction finding.

h) Do the Anglo–Americans make use of the in itself inconsiderable beam of the German receiver for location finding.

i) When can the 9mm and the 25mm developments respectively of the Americans be expected to reach finality? When may the use of these wavelengths at the front be expected? Will those waves be used against U-boats? Will they be used from the air and/or from ships? What advantages are there as opposed to the 3 cm apparatus? What detectors will be used by this apparatus? How will the W/T aerials appear? Is it a question of panoramic apparatus? What turning velocity has the W/T aerials?

k) What wavelengths of the shortest kind are the USA laboratories studying from the long range point of view?

4) Mine Location

a) Can the enemy detect anchored mines locate barriers by means of underwater listening apparatus? In case there is such a method, have successful results already been obtained? Details about such methods are very desirable. Are our enemies thereby enabled to circumvent such barriers?

b) Is it possible to locate mines lying on the ground? Has the enemy evolved methods to this end? What are the conditions present if success is to be achieved? What influences are of importance and what difficulties have emerged?

c) Can the enemy detect anchored or ground mines from the air, and how?

5) U-boat Combat

From previous reports there is the possibility that the enemy is using torpedoes in the U-boat combat which automatically steer towards a boat after they have been launched from the U-boat chasers or the anti–U-boat aircraft. All obtainable details about this, sketches etc., are urgently desired especially a clarification of the following questions:

a) Size, weight, shape, external markings?

b) The manufacturer? Since when in use? To an increasing extent? In what waters? How many in comparison with depth charges? Only from aeroplanes?

c) Preparations before use?

d) Size of the charge? For what range is it effective?

e) The position on the aircraft? The number per aircraft?

f) The height from which and the direction in which it is launched? The permissible deflection angle between the direction in which it is fired and the direction in which the target is travelling? Time of the course? The extent of the course? Spread? Straight or zigzag?

g) How long after the U-boat has dived can it be used? Are prior location and ascertainment of the depth necessary? By what methods? How precise?

h) Are they effective against stationary targets? At what distance? At what depth?

i) Where must the destination be encountered (stern, midships, or bow)?

When it steers itself acoustically
a) Without wire or by wire?
b) How is the course observed? The track of the bubbles?
c) Is the depth also regulated?
d) How deep?

Ignition. Contact of distant ignition.
In case of distant ignition, at what distance? Magnetic? Electric? Acoustic? What happens if the torpedo does not hit its target? If the U-boat causes noises or detonations to be made with the object of producing a disturbance? If the U-boat stops?

There is no indication of how valuable this document was regarded by the Admiralty, but quite obviously it provided clues to U-boat vulnerabilities and showed German concerns about the Leigh Light, carried by Coastal Command to mount night attacks by illuminating surface targets, and radar. Direction-finding was also a preoccupation, with the enemy convinced that the Allies had made some scientific breakthroughs in the field of beam technology. In reality, of course, cryptanalysis was playing a major, unsuspected role in betraying the exact location of submarines.

★ ★ ★

Fritz Lorenz, who was captured by the Belgian police and handed over to the US Army in Namur as the Allies advanced towards Belgium, was an SD officer, journalist and broadcaster who had worked for Joachim von Ribbentrop and his Dienstelle.

Born in Cuxhaven in 1913 and destined for the merchant marine, Lorenz had gone to sea as a cadet and during seven years aboard various ships, including the training vessel *Bremen*, had became fluent in French and German.

His linguistic skills had attracted the attention of a German passenger on the Norddeutscher Lloyd steamer *Stuttgart*, who had recommended him to Ribbentrop. In 1935 Ribbentrop employed him as a press officer and used him in London as a confidential courier, carrying the weekly diplomatic pouch to Berlin. Lorenz was called up for national service in September 1939 with the 19th Minesweeper Flotilla in Kiel and then Hennsburg, but in January 1940 was posted to the Reich Security Agency's Amt VIF, responsible for France, Belgium, Holland and Switzerland, and sent on a mission to Paris, adopting the role of an Italian shoe salesman, Giovanni Laini, who had travelled through Switzerland. Established in the French capital, he had negotiated the sale of 300,000 pairs of shoes, at 120 francs each, to a corrupt official at the War Ministry.

While in Milan acquiring samples, Lorenz boasted at a party that he seen the transcript of a telephone conversation conducted on the evening of 30 April between the French premier Paul Reynaud and Neville Chamberlain in which a French plan to invade the Balkans from Syria was alleged to have been discussed. News of this reached Berlin, and the drunken invention was published as fact by the *Volkischer Beobachter* on 7 May.

After the German occupation of Paris Lorenz joined the staff of the SD chief, Dr Helmut Knochen, and was sent on various assignments to southern France to trace the political exile Dr Fritz Thyssen, and certain German Jewish refugees. However, after a disagreement with Knochen he was transferred to Berlin, where he participated in foreign language radio broadcasts before he was sent with the Waffen SS to Russia as a war reporter. There he was a witness to numerous atrocities committed by the Allgemeine SS Division, including the murder of 5,000 Jews at Mariupol in the Ukraine. Among the crimes he described was the execution of 10,000 Russian PoWs by the Adolf Hitler SS Panzer Division.

In 1942 Ribbentrop engineered Lorenz's removal from the Eastern front and entrusted him with a delicate mission to Madrid, where he was to investigate rumours about the behaviour of Maria von Günther, the wife of the German ambassador, Eberhard von Stohrer. Upon his arrival in Spain in May he reported to the head of the SD, Hauptsturmführer Pfisterer, and worked with the SD's embassy informant, Erich Gardemann, but cleared Frau von Stohrer of misconduct.

Once completed, Lorenz was sent to Trieste to supervise propaganda broadcasts for Radio Littoral Adriatico, and in April 1944 transferred to Paris to edit war reporting. As the Allies approached, following D-Day, Lorenz's unit was evacuated to Chaumont–Gistoux, near Brussels, and he decided to desert. As he was found in civilian clothes, and had been an SD agent of long standing, he was not treated as a PoW but as an enemy spy and, after his arrest in September, was sent for interrogation to Camp 020, where he arrived on 1 October and was judged to be a man of exceptional ability with a very good memory for detail.

Lorenz willingly disclosed a huge amount about the Ribbentrop Dienstelle, the composition of the RHSA, the many SD personalities he had encountered, and described the Foreign Ministry's highly secret cipher organisation, the Reichsforschungamt, led by a Professor Diettmar.

In April 1945 he was nearly released to the Political Warfare Executive as a contributor to German language programmes that were transmitted as part of a black propaganda campaign intended to undermine enemy morale, but Tom Sefton Delmer changed his mind. Lorenz remained at Camp 020 until the end of August 1945, when he was flown from Hendon accompanied by Alfred Naujocks, Ernst Kaltenbrunner and Wilhelm Kuebart to Nuremburg, where they were handed over to US Army custody to be questioned about war crimes by John Waldron, the US chief prosecutor.

The reason for PWE's change of heart appears to have been a reluctance to take on new 'talent' in the closing stages of the war in Europe, but there was also a lingering doubt avout Lorenz's motives. He claimed that he had intended to make his way back to Paris and surrender to the Allies, but some suspected that he had hoped to lie low for a period and then quietly return home. In those circumstances there remained an element of risk in giving him his liberty at Woburn, and MI5 was not prepared to guarantee that Lorenz was fully and genuinely committed to the Allied cause. In these circumstances, and with an official request to hear his testimony regarding atrocities on the Russian front, the expedient adopted by MI5 was to turn him over to the Americans.

★ ★ ★

BRONX was Elvira Chaudoir, the daughter of the Peruvian ambassador in Vichy. She was well connected in London social circles and communicated with the enemy via secret writing, having been recruited by the Abwehr in October 1942. She played a significant role in the D-Day deception scheme intended to draw attention to Bordeaux as a possible site for an Allied landing in 1944, and continued to send letters containing secret writing under the supervision of MI5's Hugh Astor, until the end of hostilities.

21

12 DECEMBER 1944

MI5's twentieth monthly report introduced a double-agent GELATINE, but concentrated on two Abwehr agents in the Netherlands, Cornelis Verloop and Antonie Damen, who under interrogation compromised a third, Christiaan Lindemanns, a man hitherto considered a hero of the resistance. Also captured and questioned was a Sicherheitsdienst officer, Alfred Naujocks, who would acquire considerable notoriety, and a Russian, Elie Golenko, was had been employed by the Abwehr in Paris.

NOVEMBER 1944

An interesting case has recently arisen which indicates with what skill the Germans had succeeded in penetrating resistance movements and Allied escape organisations. A Dutch subject named Cornelis Verloop was sent by the German Secret Service through the Allied lines in Holland to make contact with another agent, Antonie Damen, who had, in fact, already fallen into our hands and under interrogation had denounced Verloop as a German spy. The latter was arrested and, when questioned, produced the somewhat startling statement that a man named Chris Lindemanns (known in Dutch circles as KING KONG) who had been appointed by Prince Bernhard as liaison officer with the Dutch Forces of the Interior, was also a German spy. Lindemanns was in his turn arrested and despatched for treatment at our special interrogation centre in England. He has now admitted that he has worked for the Germans since the spring of this year and was particularly active in naming an escape route from Holland through Paris.

From the knowledge gained in this work he denounced some forty Allied agents and members of the Dutch Resistance, who were as a result arrested by the Germans. He was in Antwerp when the Allied force arrived, and then obtained his post on Prince Bernhard's staff. In the middle of September he crossed the enemy lines on behalf of the Allies and went to Eindhoven, where he contacted members of the Dutch Resistance Movement. After his return he was engaged in seeing off Allied agents who were to carry out missions behind the German lines. He has now admitted that, when in Eindhoven, he betrayed to the Germans the names of those directing the enterprise which he was carrying out for the Allies. He has denied giving operational information to the Germans, but there is reason to believe from Most Secret Sources that, before the arrival of the Allies in Brussels, he in fact passed to the enemy operational information which he had obtained from Resistance leaders. Verloop, Damen and Lindemanns have provided us with a very considerable amount of information about the organisation and personnel of the German Secret Service in Holland.

Another recent capture, Alfred Naujocks, a German spy, was arrested while trying to cross the Allied lines. He claimed to be an emissary of an Austrian underground movement but, from his interrogation, it appeared that he had a long history with the German Secret Service and was a personal friend of Heydrich. He has admitted that he was entrusted with three important missions. The first was to kill Otto Strasser in Prague in 1934, in which he failed; the second, given him by Heydrich, was to liquidate a secret W/T transmitter broadcasting anti-Hitler propaganda in Czechoslovakia in 1938; in this case he succeeded in murdering the operator. The third was in August 1939 when he took a considerable part in the creation of Polish frontier incidents.

According to his story, prisoners in concentration camps were murdered. These bodies were dressed in Polish uniform, riddled with bullets and then placed in German frontier villages to provide evidence that the Poles had raided German territory.

On their entry into Paris, the Americans discovered a former Tsarist Intelligence Officer called Elie Golenko who had since shortly before the war been engaged in intercepting Russian radio telephony. Before the collapse of France he did this work for the French, but, on the fall of France, he continued and handed the results to the Germans. In spite of this admission he made a not unfavourable impression on his American interrogators, who brought him to London for examination on technical matters and lodged him at Claridge's. Golenko's activities as interceptor of Russian traffic were known to us from Most Secret Sources and, after his arrival in this country, further evidence of the same kind was discovered which showed that he had also reported on Gaullist activities to the Germans. Golenko maintained that the Germans had wanted to take him with them when they evacuated Paris, but that he had eluded them. Most Secret Sources showed, however, that the Germans deliberately left him behind to perform a mission for them after the entry of the Allies. They prepared to leave a large sum of money for him and throughout September tried to make contact with him by wireless without success. In view of his failure to tell us essential parts of the truth, Golenko has, with the consent of the Americans, been arrested and transferred to our special interrogation centre.

The Germans have continued their efforts to revive the activities of controlled spies in this country who have for some time been inactive and have re-opened contact with GELATINE, whom they have neglected for eight months.

She has been told amongst other things to report on discord between British and Americans and on certain British factories. The Germans claim to have hidden two wireless sets in Belgium for the use of two spies controlled by us. As soon as their exact position is known it is hoped to operate them to continue the policy of deception.

The German Sabotage Service is now taking to assassination on a larger scale. Three German agents have been arrested who admit that their mission was to murder German spies who were left behind in France and were believed to have gone over to the Allies. Another agent has been given the job of assassinating a French Deputy.

The German Sabotage Organisation has been detected in Greece using a new disguise for its material. At the end of October twenty cardboard boxes were found among captured enemy ammunition labelled 'Swedish Red Cross', the contents being described as American dehydrated food and vegetables. In fact, each box contained about 100 lbs of high explosive. There is no evidence to show that the Swedish Red Cross in any way connived at this deceit.

12 December 1944

★ ★ ★

The brevity of MI5's reference to Cornelis Verloop did little justice to a professional spy who had certainly worked for the German intelligence services in France, Belgium and the Netherlands. According to his version, after his arrest in Holland on 2 October 1944, he had been a private detective and a member of the French Foreign Legion, but had abandoned the Allied cause after he had been detained by the Germans in Loos.

Originally from The Hague, Verloop was transferred to Camp 020 in November 1944 and under interrogation told an astonishing story that began in April 1942 when he was recruited by the Abwehr IIIF as a low-level penetration agent based in Lille, posing as a *resistant* and denouncing members of Allied escape organisations in northern France. Among his victims was a Black Watch officer named Colson, a Polish colonel and a suspected member of the French Deuxieme Bureau. Colson later turned out to be Sergeant Harold Cole, a British deserter who would later be turned by the Abwehr and employed as an *agent provocateur*. He was shot dead in Paris in 1944 while attempting to evade arrest.[1]

In February 1944 Verloop was transferred to Brussels, where his assignment was to follow a collaborator, Christiaan Lindemanns, who headed a resistance network in Holland, and expose anyone who came into contact with him.

In May 1944 Verloop married a Dutch woman in Amsterdam and bought a cafe, but still remained active on behalf of the Abwehr until, in October 1944, he was arrested as he tried to cross the Allied lines near Breda. After being questioned at Turnhout, on 11 November 1944 he was sent to Camp 020, where he made a detailed confession which served to incriminate Lindemanns, the celebrated resistance leader and supposed Dutch patriot known as KING KONG because of his enormous size.

Verloop was flown back from Croydon to Brussels for prosecution at the end of the following month but was later released from prison. Meanwhile Lindemanns, who was arrested on 28 October, was imprisoned at St Gilles prison in Brussels for five days and then transferred to Camp 020. Over a period of two weeks Lindemanns, a former wrestler, confessed to having been recruited by the Abwehr as an informer in May 1944 and admitted having betrayed members of the resistance and a British officer to his German controllers. According to one estimate, he bore direct responsibility for the arrest of 247 of his compatriots. He was returned to Holland in December 1944, but in July 1946 Lindemanns committed suicide with an overdose in Scheveningen prison's hospital wing after he had been tried for treason and condemned to death.

After his death there was considerable speculation that Lindemanns, who supposedly had gained advance knowledge of the Allied assault on Arnhem, might have betrayed the plan to his enemy contacts, and this was the version peddled by a former Dutch intelligence officer, Oreste Pinto, in his 1952 autobiography *Spycatcher*.

In reality Lindemann's Abwehr recruiter was Herman Giskes, who would also be interrogated at Camp 020 where he confirmed that Lindemanns had not mentioned any Allied plans relating to the Arnhem landings code-named MARKET GARDEN.

Another Camp 020 inmate was Alfred Naujocks, an engineering graduate of Kiel University, the city where he had been born in 1911, who was arrested in France by the US Army in October 1944. Under interrogation Naujocks stated that he had joined the SS as a driver in 1941, and recalled having been sent with an SD colleague, Werner Goettsch, to Prague on a mission to assassinate the German politician Otto Strasser. He had failed on that occasion but in 1939 he had been entrusted with the task of fabricating the scene on the Polish frontier at Gleiwitz that would become Germany's stage-managed bogus pretext for invasion. Two months later he was on the Dutch border to participate in the abduction of two hapless SIS officers, Major Richard Stevens and Sigismund Payne Best, who thought they were attending a rendezvous with a senior Luftwaffe officer who was scheming against the Nazis. Best and Stevens survived the war in a concentration camp.[2]

Promoted by Heydrich, Naujocks conducted various counter-espionage and counter-black market investigations in Copenhagen and Brussels, but after some disagreement with his sponsor was posted to the 1st SS Panzer Division in Russia, where he was wounded. He re-joined the SD and was arrested by the US Army in France in October 1944.

After his interrogation Naujocks was returned to Germany in September 1945 to be prosecuted by the Nuremberg tribunal, and sentenced to four years' imprisonment. He later escaped from detention, settled in Hamburg, where he granted an interview to the journalist Gunter Peis, and died in April 1966. Peis published his biography, *The Man who Started the War*, in 1960.[3]

★ ★ ★

One of the really fascinating cases mentioned by Petrie in this report is that of Colonel Elie Golenko, a 65-year-old former Russian officer, chief of counter-espionage in the 6th Imperial Army and playwright, who fell into American hands soon after the liberation of Paris. His personal history is quite extraordinary, and can be pieced together from his MI5 personal file, which records that he was found by an SCI unit and this gave him the code name LOTUS. When news of his appearance reached London in November, there was excitement at the Radio Intelligence Section, and Stuart Hampshire drafted a brief report for MI5's John Stephenson on what was known of his activities when they had been picked up by intercept operators and circulated as ISK and PAIR decrypts:

This man is almost certainly identical with an agent who has been known from PAIR since 1942. In February of that year RSS heard a W/T link working between Stuttgart and Paris whom they eventually numbered 3/84 though it was originally identified by the reference 0/140. This link was read by GC&CS and messages sent over it were published in PAIR until 15 September 942. These messages showed that there was an agent in PARIS signing as G or GXE (e.g., 3/8413.6.1942 and 22.7.1942, ISOS 34603 and 3431&) who was forwarding to his controlling officers in Stuttgart the texts (translated into French) of alleged conversations between various official bodies in the USSR. It was subsequently agreed that since the conversations appeared to be genuine, the agent in question must therefore have been intercepting Russian R/T links. (eg, 3/84, 3 September 1942, ISOS. 37851). At the same time it seemed almost certain that the intercepted messages were sent 'en clair' and that the agent's expertise lay in his knowledge of Russian rather than in his cryptographic skill. Very few messages were heard passing to this agent from his controllers, but there were enough to show that he was administered by Ast I Stuttgart (eg, the references to Schultze, in 3/84, 17-2M-2 and 26 February1942, ISOS 22374 and 23139), so by September 1942 it was the accepted doctrine that there was an agent at work in Paris intercepting Russian R/T traffic and translating it into French before forwarding the result with his comments to Ast Stuttgart on 3/84.

At this point the publication of the messages passed on 3/84 as PAIR was suspended, though RSS continued to hear the service, and GC&CS continued to be able to read it; some time later GC&CS ceased to be able to read it and the messages were filed at RSS. This seems to have been the position from June 1943 but the exact date will be available at GC&CS. In February 1944, as a result of the merging of agent traffics in France in RSS's group 17, the reference number of this link was changed from 3/84 to 17/128. This was the situation until the end of September 1944 when, after a month of fruitless calling by Stuttgart without any reply being made from the agent in Paris, RSS suspended their watch. It is clear from these facts that for the period September 1942 to June 1943 there are solved messages which may throw further light on the case; doubtless these will be readily available to you.

It had always been assumed that the distribution of these messages within the Abwehr followed more generous lines. The publication of the messages passed by Stuttgart to Berlin on 2/49 during August and September 1944 gave force to this belief. Thus on 8 August 1944 Stuttgart forwarded to Berlin a message which it described as having been sent by an agent R.4927 by W/T from Paris on the previous day. This message was then quoted in French and followed strictly the pattern of G's messages of 1942 which had appeared on 3/84. It was marked to Mil. Amt B for passing to the teleprint station HXWX (known to be Warsaw) for information (see ISK.112488).

The inference was that G and R.4927 were one and the same. Further messages showed that R.4927 was highly valued by Stuttgart, that he was in receipt of assignments from Mil. Amt C-R (Operational intelligence East, Russian department), and that he was employed, presumably as a cover, on the staff of the German Army news-sheet *Soldat in Westen*. (See 2/49, 11.8.1944, 18.9,1944, 28.9.1944. and 30 September 1944 ISK.112167, 117560, 118650 and 118061).

There seems, then, to be sufficient information to establish whether Golenko is in fact the same as the PAIR character G or GXE @ R.4927. But apart from the historical interest of the identification, we are anxious to know whether Golenko can throw light on any similar activities in Eastern Europe by other White Russians and in particular whether General Turkul was or is concerned.

Initial interviews with Golenko revealed his unusual background. After the revolution he moved to France and became editor of *Radio Nice et Mediterranee*. He also wrote *L'Institut Catholique et le Cardinal Bauirillart* and founded *L'Ami de Livre*. As an amateur radio technician he had monitored Russian conversations on Russian radio-telephone links to keep himself well informed on events in the Soviet Union, and when war had broken out in 1939 the French government employed him in the same capacity at an intercept site at Rennes. After the armistice he moved back to Paris and installed his apparatus in the rue Reaumur under the sponsorship of three German officers. Evidently his product was considered sufficiently highly valued to merit a direct teleprinter link to Hitler's headquarters, and when the Soviets introduced a scrambler, Golenko assisted German engineers in the construction of a device to descramble the traffic. However, as the Allies approached Paris in July 1944 the Germans departed and Golenko went into hiding, adopting the name Gobelin, until he could make contact with the American Signal Corps and offer his services.

An OSS officer, Captain Ben Welles, escorted Golenko to London in November 1944, flying from Paris to Bovingdon, and accommodated him in room 607 at Claridge's until he underwent interrogation by MI5, resulting in this summary:

1. Golenko is a former Procureur Militaire in the Russian Imperial Army who was counterespionage chief of the 6th Army in Helsingfors until the Russian Revolution. He was then asked by the White Russian general, Denikin, to raise a volunteer army, in which Golenko served as Procureur Militaire. At the end of Denikin's campaign he was for a short time commander of the fortress of Sebastopol and finally embarked before the Russian advance on a Greek vessel. On his arrival in Athens he spent some six months creating a Greek secret police against Communism, and then went on to Constantinople, where there was a large White Russian colony.

2. He stayed here until early 1922, working as teacher and secretary to a White Russian refugee committee. Then, on the invitation of Cardinal Gaspari, he went to the Vatican to advise a Catholic Mission about to leave for Russia to investigate the famine there. After some four months in the Vatican he went on to Rome and covered the Genoa Conference, attended by leading Allied statesmen, as a journalist, specialising in Bolshevik questions. He was arrested by the Italian police because of his facial resemblance to a White Russian terrorist who was believed to be contemplating an attempt on the Bolshevik delegation. There was at first some question of handing him over to the Bolsheviks, but he managed to obtain his release and returned to Constantinople, where he stayed until the end of 1922.

3. As counter espionage chief in Helsingfors he had suppressed anti-French and anti-Poincare press propaganda and drawn up new legislation regulating the press. For these services rendered Poincare invited him to Paris and arranged for him to enter the Idris bar — it was then possible for foreign lawyers to practise there. This seemed not very lucrative, so that instead Golenko worked as an expert consultant on company law, and later as journalist and playwright. From about 1927 to about 1930 he edited the periodical *Radio Nice et Mediterranae*. In 1931 he became president of the association L'Ami du l'Avre, a Catholic literary society with some anti-Bolshevist tendencies. From 1936 onwards he was a prominent official of the Dispensaires Parisiens de Nuit, a chain of poor peoples' dispensaries launched under the patronage of Mme. Albert Lebrun, wife of the last president of the Third Republic. Through this lady he made the acquaintance of leading politicians, among them Georges Bonnet, French Foreign Secretary at the outbreak of war.

4. From 1926 onwards Golenko had studied the technical side of radio. From about 1935 when Russia set up a radio telephone network, he had, for his own edification, listened in to conversations over this network.

5. He affirms that whilst he was engaged on this pursuit before the war he received no propositions from the French or any foreign government to act as their agent by monitoring Russian radio telephone conversations. He thinks most governments were unaware of the possibilities of such monitoring, and says that he himself had discovered it only by accident.

6. About five days after the outbreak of war, however, he was asked by Georges Bonnet, French Foreign Secretary, to monitor these conversations on behalf of the French Government. Thereafter his work was passed direct to the French Foreign Office. He had one assistant, whose name he cannot remember.

7. Bonnet had become interested in Golenko's monitoring system after the failure of his negotiations, together with the British, for the conclusion of a pact with Russia. From this failure Bonnet had retained a violent distrust of the Russian Government.

8. In September 1939 Golenko's department was sent to Rennes and worked here until the Germans arrived in June 1940. On the very day of their arrival two German staff officers came to Golenko's flat, where all his apparatus was installed. He was ordered to stay in the flat and guarded there by two Gestapo men. He was told that he must continue his work on behalf of the Germans, but for the time being must wait for the arrival of a German officer from Paris, who would give him orders. This official did not, however, arrive.

9. Some two weeks later Golenko was therefore taken by his Gestapo guards to the Hotel Majestic, Paris, where, in an office on the second or third floor, he saw a Major Betticher (phonetic), aged about 45. This man was not a radio specialist, but apparently a counter espionage official. He later transferred to Room No. 15, Hotel Lutetia, Paris.

10. Betticher let Golenko know that the Germans had a very exact and detailed file on Golenko's activities containing full reports on his arrest of a German espionage network in Helsingfors in 1916. Betticher then told Golenko that he must consider himself under German orders and must

start work as soon as he received instructions from Berlin. Meanwhile he was to return to Rennes.

11. Golenko says that this proposal was made courteously, but that he could not do otherwise than accept; in view of his anti-German work in the last war the Germans would otherwise have had no compunction in deporting him to Germany.

12. Later in the interrogation Golenko said that, although an exile, he still regarded himself as Russian and was intensely interested in conditions in his homeland, Russia; that he was very violently anti-Soviet; and that his monitoring work offered him a unique chance of keeping in touch with conditions in Russia. He was therefore very happy to carry on with this monitoring. The question that his information benefited the Germans does not seem to have weighed with him in the slightest degree.

13. After another fortnight at Rennes Golenko returned to Paris, this time with his apparatus. He was installed on the 8th floor of the *Paris-Soir* offices, 37 rue du Louvre, Paris, where his apparatus was installed and where he was given three German officers as assistant monitors.

14. The first of these was Walter Wolf, who he had already met in Rennes. Wolff is aged 30/32 about 1m.72 tall, medium build, brown hair, not a German type, very well educated and intelligent.

15. Of the other two officers, Leutnant Koenig, Christian name unknown, aged 30/35, was rather tall, strong, of sporting appearance, a very blond Swedish type; 30/35, tall, thin, fair, with a long fencing scar on his cheek. All three spoke very good Russian.

16. He was also given two capable radio technicians Sonderführer Fahrenkampf, aged 30/35 and Sonderführer Miller, aged about 26. Another technician, name beginning with E, attended occasionally.

17. Once installed at this address, Golenko was forbidden to live elsewhere. His French foreigner's identity card, docunent No 1 above, was taken from him and in exchange he was given a German document showing that he was employed by 'Radio-Abteilung'.

18. About October 1940 a Colonel von Scholte (aged 30/35, height about 1m. 75, strong very handsome German type resembling Ribbentrop, conceited) arrived from Berlin and announced himself as Golenko's chief. Golenko's colleagues told him that Schulte looked after radio intelligence for German GHQ. Schulte thereafter paid visits of three or four days to Paris at least once a month.

19. Golenko started work for the Germans about October 1940. The results of his monitoring service he translated into French, since he does not know German. They were at once transmitted in morse by Fahrenkampf and Miller transcribed into a complicated cipher. Later the technician Miller, an anti-Nazi with whom Golenko became friendly, let him take a copy of this cipher, which Golenko now has in his papers and produced at the interrogation. He states that it is valid until the end of this year.

20. Golenko claims that not all the information he had was passed to the Germans. Some of it he kept for himself, meaning to incorporate it in a book to be written after the war. He did not pass this information to any other intelligence service.

21. On the outbreak of war between Russia and Germany the Russian Government confiscated all receiving sets in Russia, and broadcast through loud speakers installed in official institutions throughout the USSR. Radio telephone conversations by the public, which had hitherto been allowed, were banned and the network confined to official business. These official conversations were scrambled by an apparatus known as the Vertuschka. For about two months this apparatus made Golenko's monitoring system useless.

22. About a week after the scrambling had been reported to Berlin a wireless specialist, Colonel Hertz or Hoertz, arrived in Paris with a suite of technicians, took (gramophone) records of many Russian radio telephone conversations and reported to Berlin. The Russian scrambler was not at first very efficient, so that some two months later the Germans built a de-scrambler, which was installed in Golenko's department and which allowed him to listen in as before. Once this de-scrambler was installed, Golenko's staff was kept extremely busy monitoring official conversations. Because of this the Germans requisitioned new premises at 100 rue Reaumur, to which they transferred all Golenko's offices and apparatus. Golenko was given two rooms for his private use here and forbidden to lodge elsewhere. He moved here at about the end of 1941.

23. 'About two years ago', i.e. some time in late 1942, Golenko conceived the idea of getting into touch with the British Intelligence Service. This idea he traces to his association in Constantinople about 1920 with two British officers, Colonel Maxwell and Captain Hankin, or Henkin, who had occasionally consulted him on Soviet questions.

24. He did not know how to get into touch with the British Intelligence, but learned through a *Paris-Soir* journalist that a bar at 23 rue Caromartin, Paris was frequented by Allied and de Gaullist agents. He began to frequent this bar, and once heard there two men talking English quietly. He struck up an acquaintance with one of them, Merchant, who said that he was American and on the point of leaving Paris. He promised, however, to introduce Golenko to a member of his organisation. Merchant disappeared and Golenko never met Merchant's colleague. He made no other attempts to contact an Allied organisation.

25. Merchant incidentally told Golenko to contact the Americans or the British Army when they entered Paris.

26. Golenko did not finally give up hope of seeing Merchant again for about six months, During this time there was some question of sending his whole department, and him with it, to Berlin. He had no wish to go to Berlin, both because he feared German vengeance for his anti-German work as counter-espionage chief in the last war and because he had his home, his literary activities and his mistress in France. Also he does not speak German.

27. Accordingly, early in 1943 he got a false identity card in the name of Gobelin for 2,000 francs from a man, name unknown, introduced to him by the *Paris-Soir* journalist Gerard de Beecker, about 45, of 6 rue Vavin, Paris, He kept this in reserve until a favourable opportunity should arise for him to go into hiding.

28. Golenko explains that it was difficult to make very serious efforts to contact Allied organisations because he was watched. His subordinate, Lt Wolf had apparently been detailed to report on his activities. Thus, although Golenko could go out alone, Wolf continually asked him what he had been doing. Early in 1944 Wolf was transferred to the Propagandastaffel in the Champs Elysees and later sent to the (? Eastern) front. Thereafter Golenko was watched by Hauptmann Benter aged about 50, and his sonderführer

Hermann who lived on the same floor as Golenko and were employed by the German military press bureau publishing the papers *Soldat im Weston, Waoht am Canal* and *Naohtriohten Blatt* at 100 rue Reaumur,

29. As another example of the surveillance, Golenko says that after a visit to his rooms by a Mlle Simone Guybout, who is 28, and her friend, Mlle Andre Zenar, aged about 25, Colonel Schulte, whilst dining with Golenko a few days later asked him why he had left these girls alone in a room containing his technical apparatus.

30. Mlle Simone Guybout, of 64 bis rue Dulong. Paris 17eme, had been Golenko's private secretary when he was president of *L'Amie du Livre*. She was a journalist and playwright, and later Golenko's mistress. She often visited him at 100 rue Reaumur and he actually taught her to transmit morse on the apparatus there. No other person was near at the time and her visits did not arouse suspicion because she was known to be his secretary-mistress.

31. Mlle Zenar was a nurse in a German hospital at or near Boulogne. At the end of June 1944 she visited Paris and Mlle Guybout commented on the money she was spending. Mlle Zenar then admitted that 'for years' she had been a member of the Intelligence Service and tried to recruit Mile. Guybout, who, however, has 'a horror of politics' and therefore refused. Mlle Guybout told Golenko this after Mile. Zenar had returned to Boulogne. Golenko does not appear to have bothered to use her as a means of contacting the 'Intelligence Service'.

32. For two or three months before August 1944 Golenko's work had lessened, since there was less radio telephone traffic in Russia. The last transmission made from his office was on 5 August 1944.

33. On 6 August 1944 (he is sure of this date) his apparatus was removed by German soldiers who, however, overlooked a transmitter-receiver left behind in case his regular apparatus should break down.

34. On 5 August 1944 Golenko, who had been told that his apparatus was to be removed the next day; and who guessed that the Germans were preparing to evacuate Paris and that he would shortly have a chance of going into hiding, booked a room under his name Gobelin at a hotel, name unknown, situated at 1 Place de la Sorbonne, Paris. From 5 August 1944 onwards he

slept in this room and returned to his office in the morning. There was no danger because night work had ceased and nobody would therefore call for him during the night. Benter and Hermann, who were nominally supposed to keep an eye on him, were too busy preparing the evacuation of their press bureau to do so. At that time it was tentatively arranged that Golenko was to leave for Germany with Benter when the press bureau was evacuated. No date had been fixed for this departure.

35. On 12 August Colonel von Schulte visited Golenko for the last time, telling him that he, Golenko, was to be transferred to Germany. He gave him back his French foreigner's identity card, document No. 1 above, and took away his German identity document showing him to be employed by Radio Abteilung. He gave him in addition a foreigner's passport showing his nationality as Russian, plus a paper which authorised Golenko to receive lifts by all types of military transport, into Germany.

36. Golenko continued sleeping at his hotel and returning to his office each morning until 15 August 1944, when Benter told him that they were to leave for Germany the following day, 16 August 1944. By this time all Golenko's subordinates and assistants had left but the Germans apparently continued to trust him and he noticed no surveillance.

37. On 15 August 1944 Golenko removed from his office copies of the telegrams, containing the results of his monitoring, which had been transmitted to Germany (his office records were to be evacuated to Germany by Benter). He also removed the transmitter–receiver set left by Hertz, intending to hand all these over to the Allies when they reached Paris.

38. On 16 August 44 he returned his German passport and the pass allowing him to use military transport, as a precaution should he be arrested by the FFI.

39. On 17 August 1944 street fighting in Paris began and a few days later rumour had it that the Senate building was mined and was to be blown up. This building was too near his hotel for safety and he moved to the Hotel Studio Meuble at 73 rue Nicolau, Paris 16eme. This building was subsequently requisitioned by the American Red Cross and Golenko then moved to a furnished room at 1o rue Louis David, Paris. Only his mistress knew his address. He left his hotel only for meals.

40. As soon as the American Army arrived it set up its HQ at 2 Avenue de l'Opera, under General Rogers. Golenko, after various unavailing attempts to get into touch with the Americans, approached a friend whom he knew to be on good terms with them. This was Clavelier, aged about 40, of 35 rue Marboeuf, Paris, director of the 'Rival' (?) perfume works. This man introduced him to the journalist Riesner, an American, who introduced him to the American Secret Service on the second floor of 2 Avenue de l'Opera.

41. Here Golenko saw a Colonel, who introduced him to three other colonels. To them Golenko communicated his telegrams, the German cipher and gave them his transmitter-receiver. The US authorities retained the transmitter, and Golenko has the receiver with him now in London.

42. The only persons who know that Golenko is in possession of this German cipher are (a) the American authorities, and (b) the British authorities through the undersigned. No private person in Paris or London, not even his mistress, knows of this.

43. Golenko stayed at his room in the rue Louis David until 31 October 1944, when he was arrested by the French. Before this he had been followed by a man whom he had seen in the German Major Betticher's offices, but had shaken him off.

44. Golenko believes he was arrested by the French because his mistress stayed with him for one night and had registered with the landlord or hotel keeper under her real name. Her hotel 'fiche' had been noticed by the Police, who knew of her connections with Golenko and knew that Golenko had been working for the Germans in some capacity. Accordingly when they saw that she had ostensibly been staying with a Mr. Gobelin they rightly assumed that Golenko was using this false identity and arrested him.

45. Golenko was interrogated by a police inspector at the Prefecture annexe, 11 rue des Ursins, Paris. He was asked what had been his work for the Germans, but was careful to say only that he listened to 'Russian broadcasts' – as anybody with a suitable apparatus could have done; he did not mention radio telephony because he was frightened that his information would find its way through the police to Soviet agents, who would thereupon take a most inconvenient interest in him. It was useless to deny having worked for

the Germans on radio matters, for the French knew that aerials and other wireless apparatus had been installed at his old German-occupied address.

46. Golenko told the police that he worked under compulsion for the Germans, got away from them at the first opportunity, and did not attempt escape before for fear of reprisals on his family.

47. Golenko states that the French Police seemed to wish to liquidate him, firstly because he was a White Russian and the French Police was full of Communist sympathisers, secondly because of Golenko's relations with politicians of the old regime, and thirdly because, as a foreigner whom nobody would worry about, he would be a suitable scapegoat for the treason trials being held in deference to French public opinion.

48. His mistress was arrested for a time, Golenko says to prevent her spreading news of his own arrest. Golenko, however, got a clandestine message through to his daughter, who got the Americans to intervene and obtain his release. He is, however, only under provisional liberty and liable to re-arrest at any time for using a false identity and for collaboration.

49. Golenko was released after one week, i.e. about 7 November 1944. He returned for a time to the rue Louis David and about five days before his departure on 18 November 1944 went to the Hotel California, 19 rue de Berry, under American auspices.

50. He left for this country on 18 November 1944, but does not know why he has been brought here.

SPECIAL POINTS

51. It seems to be true that Golenko was requisitioned, together with his apparatus, by the Germans in 1940, and did not himself make efforts to enter their employ. On the other hand there is no doubt that he was very happy to continue the work started for the French under German auspices, both because the work interested him and because by doing it he realised his dearest ambition, viz. anti-Soviet activity.

52. The above report follows closely Golenko's previous statement to the Americans.

53. There is a slight discrepancy with the RIS report, which mentions a message sent by W/T from Paris on 7 March 1944. Golenko says his last transmission from Paris was on 5 August 1944. The discrepancy does not appear important.

54. The same report, however, states, that Germany had been calling Golenko in Paris, without result, for about a month, i.e. until the end of September 1944. This implies that Germany had not intended to evacuate Golenko to Berlin as he says and had left him the means of communication between Paris and Germany. This means was presumably the transmitter-receiver mentioned by Golenko.

55. On the other hand Golenko's account of how he went into hiding rings true. It is very possible that the disorganisation of the German administration, even early in August 1944, was enough to render safe what would normally have been a risky procedure – sleeping out and returning to his office each morning.

56. Para. 3 of the same report says that Golenko was employed, presumably as a cover, on the staff of a German Army news sheet, *Soldat im Westen*. Golenko denies this.

57. An interesting detail is that Golenko appears to be the father-in-law of the German agent, Feygune (EPS. 15,013), who himself accepted a mission because of his anti-Russian opinions.

CONCLUSIONS

58. It appears that Golenko's main interest is to continue the work he has done successfully for the Germans and the French. Doubtless he will do it loyally so long as he is kept out of the way of the enemy. On the other hand he is rabidly anti-Soviet and an exceptionally versatile, intelligent and sharp individual. From that point of view he may be very dangerous. There is no doubt that he would work for any employer so long as his anti-Soviet opinions wore served.

59. The only doubtful point in his story is raised by para. 2 of the RIS report, which states that a month of fruitless calling was made by Germany, but that no reply was received from the agent in Paris. This implies that Golenko was left in Paris with the knowledge and approval of the Germans, with whom he was expected to communicate by W/T.

60. When his future employment is discussed the wisdom of allowing him the use of transmitting apparatus should be most carefully considered.

Golenko was moved from Claridge's to a mews house in Belgravia and placed under MI5 surveillance until he could be moved to Camp 020. There he was challenged on his version of his work for the enemy, unaware that Herbert Hart had accumulated a significant dossier on a personality on the Paris–Stuttgart circuit code-named GUSTAV listing the activities since March 1942. MI5 concluded that Golenko had lied concerning his post-occupation mission, for he had received a substantial amount of money. Furthermore, the very fact that his controller continued to transmit to him for the entire month of September 1944 was a sure indication that a reply was expected from behind the Allied lines.

Most Secret Sources show that this man has been an agent of Ast Stuttgart working in Paris since early in 1942. His principal, but by no means only, task was to intercept Russian radio telephony links and send to Stuttgart the results of his interception, sometimes worked up with a commentary. These intercepts were translated into French before they were forwarded with Golenko's comments to Ast Stuttgart. This activity seems to have been going on from early in 1942 till at least 7th August, 1944, when the agent sent by W/T from Paris a report about Russian arrangements for sending aviation petrol to the front, based on intercepts of Russian communications from Baku.

Most Secret Sources show that Golenko was regarded as an extremely valuable agent, both by Ast Stuttgart and Berlin HQ, though he was described in a report from Ast Stuttgart on 2nd March 1943 as having recently been judged reliable. Apart from this interception of Russian traffic, Golenko was engaged in the following activities at least:

(a) on 7 January 1944 he provided a report of a conversation of two journalists who had connections with Gaulliste military circles, relating to the Allied landings expected in France, giving as places the following points:

    1 between St. Raphael and Nice,
    2 Saulac,
    3 Arcachon,
    4 places unspecified in Brittany and further North.

(b) in April 1944, he seems to have got into contact with some British agent in Paris and this fact was communicated to Ast Stuttgart, who requested instruction. The inference is that in making contact with this British agent Golenko was acting on behalf of the Germans.

In June 1944 Golenko was asking urgently to be provided with a revolver. Attempts were made by his masters in Paris to provide this.

In July, 1944, Ast Stuttgart instructed Paris to give Golenko 20,000 French francs to pay for an operation on his daughter.

The most important evidence from Most Secret Sources relates to the Germans' intentions with regard to Golenko after the occupation of Paris. This evidence, which flatly contradicts his assertions that he was ordered back to Germany but had eluded the Germans, may be summarised as follows:-

(a) The last transmission known to us of Russian intercepts by Golenko was made on August 7th, 1944.

(b) On 9th August, 1944 Berlin HQ inquired from Stuttgart whether Golenko could send reports on industry and production, and an affirmative answer was given from Paris on 11th August.

(c) On 10th August Paris informed Stuttgart that certain agents in Paris, among them Golenko, needed sums of money to carry on after occupation, if Paris were occupied. Stuttgart replied on 11th that they had asked Berlin to provide a million francs and meanwhile ordered Paris to pay out to Golenko some money then available in Paris.

(d) On 16th August, Stuttgart was considering where its Paris network should go in the event of the Allies' occupying the city, and suggested Brussels. Stuttgart also added that this might be done possibly by arrangement through Golenko and other agents.

(e) On 18th September, Stuttgart were making enquiries as to what had happened to Golenko and were attempting to get into contact in Paris with the offices of the newspaper Soldatim Westen, where according to Stuttgart Golenko was employed. On 28th September, Stuttgart had still failed to find Golenko, and described his dropping out as very disturbing.

It appears from RSS evidence that Stuttgart, throughout September 1944 was calling Golenko in Paris without any reply.

Golenko, of course, had absolutely no idea that the British had been monitoring his traffic and were therefore in a position to know where he had been less than candid about his Nazi collaboration, and that he had concealed the true nature of his stay-behind mission. In fact the cryptographic evidence amounted to 309 messages exchanged between 17 September 1942 and 29 June 1943, and 110 messages sent between May and September 1942 concerning R.4927, which was GUSTAV's alternative. The fact that Golenko had an 'R' prefix was significant because the Germans referred to stay-behind networks as RICHARD and assigned the membership R numbers.

When Golenko was arrested by two Special Branch detectives he was staying with Norman Holmes Pearson, a senior OSS X-2 officer, and MI5 concluded that the most expedient solution to the problem of his continued detention was to release him into American custody so he could be taken to the United States. Nevertheless, MI5 remained determined to extract the truth from Golenko, and was suspicious that his pre-war 'hobby' had involved an intensive study of sixty Soviet stations, and his denial of any knowledge of German or such notorious White Russian intriguers such as Generals Vlassov and Anton Turkul unconvincing. Traces in MI5's Registry identified Betticher as Major Bohrer of Abwehr IIIC, Miller as Müller, and von Schulte as an Abwehr officer dismissed for embezzlement.

Ultimately OSS was persuaded of Golenko's duplicity, and he remained in Camp 020, unaware of the weight of incontrovertible evidence against him.

★ ★ ★

Born in April 1914 in The Hague, Antonie Damen was arrested in Weeyr at the end of September 1944 by an SCI unit attached to the US 82nd Airborne Division, detained at St Gilles prison, and then on 12 October flown to Northolt for transfer to Camp 020 for interrogation. Damen attracted considerable attention from MI5 because in his role as an Abwehr III penetration agent he had been deployed to insinuate himself into MI9 escape lines and into SOE's resistance networks. Evidently he had performed these tasks with great efficiency, and his evidence would be of the very considerable interest to those organisations, which were still largely unaware of the scale of the German success in investigating, and even controlling, the Allied circuits.

In his confession Damen described how he had been recruited in September 1941 for a mission to report on Allied shipping from Lourenço Marques but then was briefed for a different assignment in Montevideo. He had undergone a training course in Hamburg and, having failed to obtain a visa for Uruguay, was told in April 1942 his new destination would be the Dutch East Indies. Instead, following the Japanese occupation of the region, he was transferred to Abteilung III with the task of penetrating the Dutch resistance movement. This was of particular relevance to MI5 because several suspects had been detected while attempting to reach England along well-established escape lines. That some of the 'underground railroads' should have been compromised in this way would have severe ramifications, as would Damen's assertion that the Dutch government-in-exile was riddled with German sources, among them the former police chief François van 't Sant who, incidentally, had long been regarded as a loyal SIS asset. Yet, according to Damen, van t'Sant was really an important German agent.

Before the war Damen had completed his compulsory military service in the Royal Netherlands Navy and then had worked as an engineer officer on several ships in the Far East. He had married a German woman, Wilhelmina, but his ship, the *Nantau Panjung*, had been sunk by the battlecruiser *Admiral Scheer* in February 1941 while on a voyage from Durban to Singapore. He was placed aboard the *Ermland* as a PoW and disembarked seven weeks later at Bordeaux. During his subsequent internment at Stalag Xb at Sandbostel he had been employed as an interpreter by the Germans to communicate with Javanese seamen, and then was recruited by the Abwehr and released from captivity.

In January 1943 he took German nationality and later was sent to Utrecht to attend a wireless course and be trained as a stay-behind agent. At the time of his arrest he had been attempting to cross the Allied lines on a mission to report on the Allied airborne landings in Arnhem. His testimony, combined with his colleague Cornelis Verloop, led to the exposure of Christiaan Lindemanns, described by Helenus Milmo as 'one of the most important captures of the war'. They also incriminated several other Abwehr penetration agents who had insinuated themselves into SOE's trust, among them Nicolaas de Wilde, Suzanne Marteau[4] and a mysterious figure known only as Arnaud, who were all still active, and the notorious George van Vliet, who had been responsible for betraying dozens of French, Dutch and Belgian patriots, as well as numerous escaping Allied airmen.

Damen's statements caused consternation. 'Arnaud' was actually Richard Christmann, a German from Alsace who had served pre-war in the French Foreign Legion and was an accomplished Abwehr agent who made a very plausible French refugee.[5] It was Christmann who had wreaked havoc when he gained access to the PROSPER network in France, bringing SOE's F Section to the point of collapse. Similarly, van Vliet was Mattis Ridderhof, another skilled and experienced Abwehr *agent provocateur*.[6]

In September 1943 Damen had impersonated a member of the resistance and had been passed down the famous VIC escape line from Paris to Perpignan, compromising everyone he had encountered. Named after its founder, Victor Gerson, the VIC line was a chain of safe houses stretching from Paris to Barcelona managed by Jews, which made the organisation extremely vulnerable.

When in November 1944 SOE's John Delaforce was informed by MI5's Mark Johnstone of the scale of the treachery uncovered, he was aghast, but also slightly defensive, insisting that apart from three identified traitors, Hendrikus

Knoppens,[7] Kas de Graaf and Nicholaas Celosse,[8] the only SOE agents who had returned to England had been dispatched by SOE in the first place, and any refugees recruited for missions back to the Continent had been provided and vetted by the government-in-exile. Clearly Johnstone did not regard this as much of a guarantee of integrity.

A pre-war Royal Netherlands Air Force wireless technician, Knoppens had arrived in England in September 1943, having travelled along the VIC line from Brussels with help from Arnaud. When in November 1944 Arnaud's true identity was unmasked, MI5 investigated Knoppens, who was about to go on a mission, but concluded that he had not been a conscious spy. This view would later be contradicted by Hermann Giskes, but in the meantime Knoppens was promoted within the Dutch intelligence service.

Kas de Graaf, accompanied by his fellow food inspector Celosse, had used the VIC line in November 1943, travelling from Paris where they had been entertained by Christiaan Lindemanns. However, de Graaf was considered so compromised (but not initially an espionage suspect) that he was given a senior Dutch Intelligence staff post, while Celosse returned to Holland in March 1944 but was arrested two months later and shot. De Graaf would later interview Lindemanns and clear him of suspicion.

Damen demonstrated an encyclopedic knowledge of Dutch Nazis and other collaborators who were employed by the Germans. If he was to believed, and Blanshard Stamp concluded that he was 'essentially unreliable but on the other hand he is in the position in which he has probably discovered which side his bread is buttered and is likely to wish to give us as much information as he can and would be unlikely to pass wholly unreliable information', then the implications for SOE were grave indeed. More of their escape routes had been compromised, and from a much earlier period, than had been contemplated hitherto. Specifically, Damen recalled the circumstances in which Arnaud had arranged in early June 1943 for Knoppens, code-named SERGEANT, to travel to England. This had been requested by a respected Dutch resistance leader and air force officer, Colonel Leonardus Koppert, who had vouched for Knoppens and communicated with London over two different radio circuits, one of which was run by an SOE agent code-named FRANS.

In reality, FRANS and his three companions had been arrested upon their arrival in Holland, and the Germans had substituted Damen as FRANS for their supposed escape to the Pyrenees. In the event, the Germans had skilfully manipulated both wireless circuits, arrested everyone involved in the escape line, and sent Knoppens to England on a mission to penetrate SOE.

Damen represented the first account, from the enemy's perspective, of one of the most damaging German counter-intelligence operations of the war. By September 1944 both SOE and SIS realised that virtually all Allied resistance organisations in the Netherlands had been severely compromised, but Damen's knowledge proved that the damage inflicted was far greater than anyone in London had imagined. The magnitude of the disaster would be spelled out by Guy Liddell in January 1944, although even he was far from certain about how many Germans had penetrated the VIC line, and had not yet grasped Damen in the role of ANTON and a possibly notional 'Nicolaas de Wilde':

I have read Blanshard Stamp's note on the activities of Abwehr IIIF The Hague, against SOE. It is purely factual, and worded in moderate terms but is an appalling indictment of SOE methods and intelligence.

The story began in June 1942 when a certain JOHANNES[9] and a radio operator were dropped in Holland. JOHANNES had been sent to contact the Orde Dienst, an indigenous loyalist organisation. He was to tell its leaders that he had come on a joint Dutch–British mission and was to disclose to them the plan for Holland which had been worked out. He was to obtain their comments on the plan and emphasise that the Dutch government in London had approved it in principle and expected it to be accepted in substance. After introducing himself to the leaders of the OD, JOHANNES was to make contact with its various sub-groups operating throughout the country. He would report back to London, who would send out a trained organiser and instructors to the groups as and when JOHANNES reported they were ready to receive them. For the purpose of carrying out this mission JOHANNES had to organise reception committees, weapons and supplies and for the additional personnel which were to be sent. The indications are that JOHANNES never operated except under the control of the Germans or that he was certainly under control in November if not in August of that year. SOE were informed on a set which was obviously under control that JOHANNES had been arrested on 8 November 1942. It is astonishing that this arrest did not indicate to SOE that it was quite hopeless to continue the undertaking if the chief organiser with all the plans was under German control. To act upon the assumption that a captured agent has not been broken is to court not only mortal peril for those concerned but disaster to the whole enterprise.

After 8 November 1942 the part assigned to JOHANNES by the Abwehr was carried out in the name of KALE, his successor who had been sent out from this country as his number two.[10] Upwards of twenty-five receptions were arranged over KALE's radio set and no less than ten wireless operators were despatched from this country. As SOE had failed to get back JOHANNES owing to his arrest, KALE was asked to send to England some other person thoroughly well informed about the progress of the secret organisation. In the face of this requirement the Abwehr determined to go through all the motions of supplying such a person. On the one hand this would serve the purpose of allaying any suspicion which might be felt in London and on the other hand SOE should be made to disclose the method by which agents could be evacuated from Europe. On 14 March 1944 SOE was therefore informed that KALE would send his chief assistant who was called ANTON. The Germans were asked for particulars about ANTON and gave his name as Nicolaas de Wilde of a certain address at The Hague. Damen, who we subsequently captured, was in fact the occupant of the address and on instructions from the Abwehr was to say, if anyone called, that de Wilde was away and would return in a few days.[11] When SOE decided to arrange for ANTON's evacuation through Belgium and Holland, someone was found by the Germans to fill this part and he left Holland about 12 May 1943 and travelled to Paris. The spurious ANTON was accompanied by a certain Arnaud who has been an Abwehr IIIF agent since 1940 and who we also know was recruited by SOE as a *passeur* of theirs. In Paris ANTON and Arnaud made contact with another SOE agent, MARCEL.[12] As soon as they sat down in the café with MARCEL three German soldiers came in and started to examine the cards of those at the back of the café. ANTON got up and walked out. Arnaud said 'They have arrested ANTON'. MARCEL looked out and saw ANTON crossing the road with a man in civilian clothes. Such was the account given by MARCEL when he arrived in this country of ANTON's disappearance. A great deal of trouble was taken to decide whether ANTON had been arrested because he had been followed or whether it was sheer bad luck as the result of a snap check for identity cards. A great deal of trouble was also taken to stress the dangers which would fall upon the organisation as a result of this arrest, regard being had to the fact that ANTON, according to MARCEL, had been carrying compromising papers. It never occurred to anyone that ANTON was nothing but a German agent and that Arnaud was lying when he said that ANTON had been arrested. Arnaud's stock inevitably rose in the eyes of London and MARCEL was sent back to the continent to fall into the enemy's hands. The problem raised of SOE's request for the sending to England of a man who was well acquainted with the secret army had been answered by the Abwehr with striking success.

Liddell's version of the Paris café rendezvous, which had taken place on 9 June, was flawed, for he even then had not appreciated that ANTON was Damen and he had been accompanied by Arnaud to meet an SOE agent code-named GLAZIER. This account had been supplied by GLAZIER when he reached London in July, who had added that he had been told the next day by Arnaud that ANTON had been arrested. The story could not be verified because soon afterwards GLAZIER, code-named MARCEL, who was Jack Agazarian, returned to France on the night of 22/23 July and was captured. Liddell then completed the saga:

> SOE then requested the field to send another man who had full knowledge of the secret army and the reply came back that a man in close touch with the Orde Dienst would be sent. Instead of choosing a fictitious individual or someone who might by chance be known as a German agent here they chose a man against whom nothing adverse was known in London, who was in fact a bona-fide patriot. This man was Knoppens. He had been approached at the end of 1942 or the beginning of 1943 by the IIIF agent van Vliet. Knoppens had been doing resistance work and had been in contact with a certain Colonel Koppert when van Vliet, representing himself as a member of the resistance, asked him if he might use Knoppens' address as a letter-box. Thereafter Knoppens continued to see van Vliet regularly until he finally left Holland. Van Vliet gave himself an excellent build-up and got thoroughly into the confidence of Knoppens. On 20 June 1943 he asked Knoppens if he would travel to England and return with instructions for the resistance organisations. As Knoppens understood it the idea was that several resistance movements needed coordination and central direction and official recognition and support from London. This could best be obtained by sending an emissary from Holland and securing his return as a liaison officer with London credentials. Knoppens went via Paris, where he stayed some weeks and was finally brought out by SOE channels over the Pyrenees to Spain. For the purpose of facilitating Knoppens' mission he was provided with documents purporting to come from resistance circles. These included a note to the Dutch and British authorities concerned suggesting the desirability of establishing an escape route over which important Dutch intellectuals, industrialists and officials in Holland who without themselves acting in a rash manner had assisted in the sabotage of the German war effort, might be got out of Holland. When Knoppens arrived here there were certain discrepancies in his story and that which had been put over on the German-controlled wireless from Holland, and when the investigation

was still proceedng information which had been in the possession of SIS for many months but which had not been distributed by them, was brought to our notice. This showed that van Vliet, if not a German agent, was at least highly suspect. We came to the conclusion that Knoppens had been planted by SOE on van Vliet and that the wireless agent in Holland was under control. Arnaud however, escaped suspicion and the suggestion that the SOE escape route from Paris onwards might have been blown was not accepted. According to KALE, who was supposed still to be in charge of SOE's activties in Holland, one STEAK,[13] recruited in the field, had taken ANTON's place as second in command, ANTON having been reported as arrested when attempting to reach this country. SOE were determined to get STEAK over here. He was also told to bring two other agents with him. The Germans had all these people interned and were placed in the position of having either to make excuses for the failure of the SOE field officers to bring out the four men or to announce the arrest of these people in circumstances which would inevitably suggest that the SOE organisation had been blown. They decided to create four substitutes for the four SOE agents. They were taken to Paris where they met the fourth man. There they were handed over to Arnaud with instructions to find out by what route they would be evacuated from France. Arnaud handed them over to a member of the VIC espionage organisation and they were accepted for what they pretended to be. The last stage of the journey was in a lorry across the frontier. Before they reached this point two of them jumped off. A little later the third jumped off and hailed a car belonging to the Feldgendarmerie, showing his papers. He made this car follow the lorry and in due course his partner was arrested. The four German agents returned to Paris and made their report to Arnaud. Subsequently SOE was informed by a member of the VIC organisation that the four agents had been arrested while attempting to escape in the Pyrenees. This was accepted as sufficient explanation. As van Vliet was under some suspicion the Germans decided to make strenuous efforts to build him up. It so happened that the SOE agent APOLLO[14] was dropped in Belgium with BRUTUS[15] on 18 October 1943 with instructions to use the route taken by Knoppens in reverse and to go to Holland. APOLLO reached his contact addresses in Brussels, the house of a certain Madame Mertins, and was there visited by van Vliet. The latter successfully played the part of a patriot and assisted his return to this country. APOLLO gave a tolerably good account of van Vliet upon his arrival back here. The night after APOLLO was dropped a Lieutenant John Hurst, an American airman, made a forced landing in Holland.[17] Hurst, by devious means, was put on to van Vliet, who facilitated his escape. This story was also regarded as a reassuring incident in proof of van Vliet's bona-fides. In August 1943 two of the captured SOE agents CHIVE and SPROUT[18] escaped. They reached this country in February 1944 and at some stage the Germans became aware of this. They almost immediately closed the traffic by a message on all lines addressed to the two SOE officers by what in fact were their correct names, thanking them for their long mutual cooperation and promising them that if they came to the continent they would be received with the same care as their agents. Had the whole of the wireless traffic been under review in the light of all the known facts; trick questions been put to the agents; had each mishap been examined with a view to appreciating its possible implications on the position of themselves and the organisation as a whole; had each returning agent been meticulously questioned not because he was suspect but with a view to obtaining all possible information from him; above all, had a record been kept which set out in chronological order all the known facts regarding the enterprise and the sources from which such facts were known, a record which would have been readily available for consultation in considering all the above matters; had all this been done there is very little doubt that the SOE organisation in Holland would not have met the fate that overcame it.

Liddell's damning analysis would be borne out by further evidence, including the interrogaton at Camp 020 of Hermann Giskes, the Abwehr officer who had masterminded the *Englandspiel* operation code-named NORDPOL. The statistics that emerged were chilling. Dozens of Dutch patriots had collaborated with the enemy, opening some seventeen radio channels to London, and many more had perished in concentration camps.

Much of the debacle could be traced back to 23 May 1943 when three agents, Anton Mink (POLO), Laurens Punt (SQUASH) and Oscar de Brey (CROQUEY), had been dropped straight into the enemy's hands. All would be executed, but not before Damen had made his contribution by impersonating one of them. All three would perish at Mauthausen, together with Jambroes.

SOE headquarters finally realised the gravity of the situation in November 1943 when CHIVE and SPROUT, both *Englandspiel* victims, escaped from their incarceration in Haaren and reached Switzerland to send a warning to London. The grim news, that virtually every SOE network had been under the enemy's control for the past year, prompted a furious reaction. Bomber Command, which had taken over the RAF Special Duties squadrons in August, immediately suspended all SOE flights across Western Europe on 30 November, having found an explanation for its heavy losses. Although the ban would soon be lifted on everywhere except Denmark, Poland and Holland, the RAF losses over the latter ensured the prohibition would continue.

On 13 December the Joint Intelligence Committee chairman, Bill Cavendish-Bentinck, and the JIC secretary, Denis Capel-Dunn, assembled an informal board of enquiry to review SOE's situation. Liddell attended, together with Geoffrey Wethered and Victor Rothschild, but the only SOE officers present were the organisation's security officer, John Senter, and Eric Mockler-Ferryman, in charge of Western European operations. However, neither man was in the room when SIS presented its evidence, which was highly critical of SOE's security in Holland and Belgium, nor saw the JIC's draft report that recommended 'closer integration' between SIS and SOE. The JIC's verdict went, in Churchill's absence, to Clement Attlee, who declared the position 'highly disturbing'.

Churchill would learn from SOE's chief, Lord Selborne, on 12 January 1944, that his organisation had suffered severe hostile penetration and acknowledged that SOE 'knew about the penetration'. Selborne argued for SOE's independence, and his view prevailed, but the catastrophe would cast a long shadow over Anglo-Dutch relations. It is doubtful that the Prime Minister was ever fully briefed on what had really happened.

The RAF resumed parachute flights to Holland in late March 1944, and on 1 April the Abwehr, recognising that the game was up, sent N Section's leadership a message gloating over their 'long and successful cooperation'. This was the final proof of the enemy's interference, and meant that in the weeks before D-Day the Dutch resistance was in no position to play any significant role to assist the Allies. Indeed, during the vital last weeks of May 1944 Dutch patriots were short of weapons, with no radio link to London. Furthermore, the only SOE wireless operator known to be at liberty, Jan Steman, who had been dropped on 31 March, was without his transmitter as it had been stolen from its hiding place where he had buried it upon arrival.

* * *

Code-named GELATINE by MI5, Friedle Gaertner was an Austrian living in London was already known to the Germans as a Nazi sympathiser who had been a frequent visitor to Joachim von Ribbentrop's embassy in London before the war. In reality she had acted as an *agent provocateur* for the Security Service, identifying other contacts who were suspected of disloyalty. This had enabled MI5 to arrest and intern a large number of potentially dangerous enemy aliens on the outbreak of war. Code-named GELATINE because her case officer Bill Luke thought her 'a jolly little thing', she was to become a key double-agent, supplying the Abwehr with political gossip. She was in an especially good position to do this because her equally beautiful sister, Lisel, had married Ian Menzies, whose elder brother Stewart was SIS's Chief. The Abwehr believed it maintained contact with Friedle through Dusan Popov who, of course, was himself another double-agent.

22

6 JANUARY 1945

Petrie's last report of 1944, read by Churchill on 12 January, and marked 'Good', would deal with the Allied preoccupations of the time, being, perhaps predictably, the enemy's preparations for the liberation of German-occupied territory made by the combined forces of the Sicherheitsdienst and the Abwehr and, rather surprisingly, a very British case of anarchy.

DECEMBER 1944
THE GERMAN STAY-BEHIND ORGANISATION IN BELGIUM
Since entering Belgium the Allies have captured upwards of a hundred agents, among whom were many intended to act as spies or saboteurs in Belgium after the German withdrawal. Some of these stay-behind agents have been brought back from the field to our interrogation centre (Camp 020) for more detailed and expert examination than is possible in the field, and on their evidence combined with information from the field and from Most Secret Sources, it has been possible to estimate the character and the degree of danger now presented to Allied security by the stay-behind plans of the two organisations concerned, namely the Abwehr or espionage section of the High Command, and the Sicherheitsdienst (SD) or Himmler's special spy service.

THE SD
Before the Allied entry into Belgium, our knowledge of the SD stay-behind plan was exiguous, amounting to little more than the fact that there was an office in Brussels which had for a time been training stay-behind agents in wireless. Within a few days of the fall of Brussels, four of the principal agents of this organisation surrendered themselves. Three more were arrested, one

as a collaborator, one on the basis of captured police records, and one on a denunciation. Finally, two Belgians, Pierre Sweerts and Arthur Garitte, who had deliberately established themselves as highly placed officers of the SD came over to us with a mass of information.

From those sources we soon obtained a comprehensive picture of the SD's plans. We learnt that the order to lay down a stay-behind organisation had been given by Himmler's Head Office in Berlin in the summer of 1943 and that the task was entrusted to two officers who, from our evidence, appear to have been remarkably efficient. Their scheme was to place a W/T agent in ten towns in Belgium, each with instructions to transmit some military information, but above all to report signs of discontent, the fate of the collaborator parties, the relation between the Allied forces and the local populations – in fact any information which might assist Himmler's plans for promoting disorder in Allied occupied Belgium. The insufficiency of the Brussels office of the SD was seen principally in their selection of known collaborators as suitable stay-behind agents and their employment in that capacity of former members of the Belgian underground who had been tortured into acceptance of their mission, or had agreed to work for the Germans as the price of a reprieve from the death sentence. This policy resulted in the defections mentioned above. Farther, the Brussels office was grossly insecure and its secrets exposed to penetration by resolute characters such as Sweerts. Indeed, the only efficient aspect of the SD's plans was the W/T training of the agents. On the sabotage side the SD's plans were to establish some ten dumps and ten saboteurs, but it was not until November that we were fully informed of these and we owe our insight into this part of the SD scheme to the fortunate capture of a line-crosser sent back into Belgium by the SD. This man had studied the appropriate files in Himmler's office in Berlin and was able to give us a full account of the sabotage scheme, of which to that date we had only known some fragments.

Our conclusion is, therefore, that the SD stay-behind organisation has been effectively smashed by the capture or defections of most of its agents, and the discovery of its main sabotage dumps, though the recent discovery of a further stay-behind agent acting as a liaison officer between the Canadian Forces and the Belgian Resistance Movement, emphasises the need for care. In the main, however, it will be difficult for the Germans to regain contact with such agents, and a far greater danger is constituted by the possible insertion of new agents trained in the SD's special school as saboteurs, terrorists and experts in the art of disruption. It is known, incidentally, that some SD agents have specific instructions to cause disturbances in such a way that the blame for them will fall on Left Wing elements.

THE ABWEHR

The Abwehr stay-behind plans present a more complicated problem since they have been longer in preparation (they were begun as early as 1941), a number of separate offices had a hand in then. The position is further complicated by the substitution in the spring of 1944 of mobile control centres for these stay-behind agents. Further, we have captured no officer of a status equivalent to that of the SD officer Sweerts. Against these disadvantages we had, for some time before our entry into Belgium, a considerable amount of information about the Abwehr stay-behind plans, both from Most Secret Sources and free agents who had already been interrogated by us, and we now have drawn the conclusion that the ambitious Abwehr schemes have not really fulfilled the German hopes and do not constitute a serious danger to Allied security. Of the fifty agents identified in advance we have only captured twenty, but there is strong reason to believe that most of the remainder are already interned, or have abandoned their mission. The principal evidence for this is the fact known from Most Secret Sources that the only agents who have reported to the Germans from Belgium during the last few weeks are those under our control. Moreover, the extraordinary policy adopted by the Germans of selecting well-known members of collaborator movements as stay-behind agents has led to the arrest and internment of many agents on the grounds that they were collaborators long before they were identified as spies. Further, a remarkably high proportion of the agents captured had already destroyed their wireless sets, or clearly abandoned their mission before they fell into our hands. The principal remaining danger is forced by Abwehr informants who had been deliberately planted in Resistance Movements and may perhaps be still undetected.

On the sabotage side we knew that the Abwehr had long planned a ring of sabotage agents in Western Flanders and we consider that this ring has been effectively smashed by the surrender of the W/T operator and principal agent of the group, together with eight supporting members. Nearly all of these were members of the Devlag, or the Flemish SS, and would probably have been arrested as collaborators; none of them appear to have had any intention of working for the Germans after our occupation. There is, however, one further sabotage ring planned by the Abwehr office at Münster, the existence of which is known to us from other captured agents, but of which we have so far not caught any representative. The evidence, however, suggests that the speed of our advance into Belgium took the Germans by surprise before their sabotage plans were concocted, and before their agents were properly placed. No act of German, or German-inspired sabotage, is known to have been committed in Belgium since the entry of the Allies.

Our conclusion is therefore that, though there may be individual W/T agents and saboteurs at large, the stay-behind organisation has been largely smashed. Many agents may still be identified among those interned as collaborators. As in the case of the SD, the further uncovering of the stay-behind organisation is of far less importance than the capture of new agents which the Abwehr is preparing to send as line-crossers and parachutists into Belgium, partly with the object of regaining contact with members of the stay-behind organisation.

We have communicated the results of our survey to 21 Army Group, who agree with our conclusions and are in fact devoting the greater part of their resources to the hunt for line-crossers and parachutists, of which activities they have reported a considerable recrudescence.

ACTIVITIES OF ANARCHISTS IN THE UK

The anarchist paper, War Commentary, has been publishing during the last six months a series of articles dealing with mutinies in the British Armed Forces. The articles dealt with past events and were not specifically addressed to members of the Armed Forces. At the end of November, however, the Security Service learned that a roneoed circular was in existence, urging serving soldiers to join discussion groups in the Army as these discussion groups might form the basis for future soldiers' councils. It further stated that an article would shortly appear in War Commentary on soldiers' and workers' councils, and that one of the most important questions was the action of soldiers' councils in a revolutionary situation. Articles on the subject appeared in the next and subsequent issues of War Commentary.

As a result of searches carried out by the Special Branch of the Metropolitan Police, copies of this circular were found on the premises of Freedom Press, the publishers of War Commentary, and at the house of a leading anarchist, together with an address list of men in the Armed Forces and a considerable amount of correspondence from the Armed Forces. Snap kit inspections have revealed that the roneoed circular was in fact distributed to members of the Armed Forces, and the case will be submitted to the Director of Public Prosecutions.

6th January 1945

* * *

Paul Sweerts was a Belgian SD agent who crossed the Allied lines on 10 September 1944 near Antwerp, gave himself up to the 53rd Infantry Division and declared that he had been recruited in The Hague. He was questioned initially by the 103 SCI before being incarcerated at St Gilles prison in Brussels, and transferred to Camp 020 for interrogation on 24 September 1944. Under interrogation Sweerts explained that he was a Belgian army officer who had been wounded during the German invasion in 1940. Upon his return home at St Josse in Brussels he tried to organise a resistance group but, anticipating his imminent arrest, volunteered to join the Waffen SS in May 1941. His motive, so he claimed, was to acquire information that would assist the Allies. While on leave in Brussels in December 1941 Sweerts was approached for recruitment by the SD and this process was completed in December 1942 and he was given his first assignment, to manage four Belgian agents. In June 1943 he was sent to Berlin for training and attended a radio course at Wannsee with Ramon Gamotha, a spy who would be a key figure in German subversion in the Middle East. Sweerts was then selected for a mission to Iran and given further agent training at Lehnitz, but when the operation, code-named NORMA, was cancelled in February 1944 he was posted to The Hague with the rank of obersturmführer.

Sweerts' truly encyclopedic knowledge of the SD proved to be of exceptional value and he supplied details about dozens of SD agents and personnel. Where it was possible to corroborate his story the information turned out to be genuine but the decision was taken not to accept his offer to return across the lines as a double-agent. Instead he was kept in England, where he was the source of some embarrassment as the Belgian authorities indicated their intention in January 1945 to prosecute him if he was released. Although he insisted that his motive for joining the SS had been noble, there were only three people who could confirm his story, and two were dead, while the third had been arrested by the Gestapo. The expedient solution was to release him from custody in February 1945 to fly to Belgium from Northolt to join a counter-intelligence unit, SCI 106 in the Netherlands, where he also worked as an interrogator. However, in November 1946 he was sentenced to death *in absentia*, and in March 1947 he was arrested by the Dutch police in Haarlem on a charge of smuggling contraband and possession of forged papers. On that occasion he was released, but in May 1951 he was arrested in Brussels and allowed to appeal his death sentence.

The information supplied by Sweerts proved extraordinarily valuable and extended far beyond his own direct experience in Europe, In particular, he shed new light on the SD's machinations in the Middle East and filled in many of the gaps in British knowledge of the enemy's plans that, hitherto, had depended on ISOS and double-agents, among them BLACKGUARD, an Iranian in Istanbul, formerly employed as a broadcaster by Radio Berlin.

At the end of October 1944 the DSO in Tehran, Alan Roger, expressed his views on Sweerts' contribution:

We find the information given by Sweerts extremely interesting, not only from the point of view of German intelligence activities, but also as giving us further light on Soviet agents and methods.

First, about the NORMA expedition. This connects up with the interrogation reports of the Mayr troupe reported in our Counter-Intelligence Summaries and also with the recent interrogation of Pierre de Letay and Hamadi Ben Slata in Syria. The school in Wannsee at which Sweerts trained was obviously the Havel Institute, full details of which are given in Appendix C to our Counter-Intelligence Summary No 24 of 11th May 1944. (Sweerts spells many of the German names he gives in the French way e.g. Afel for Havel).

According to Hamadi Ben Slata, Wannsee was the administrative centre of the other SD schools and was in W/T communication with the Lehnitz school at which Slata, Letay and Sweerts all trained. Skorzeny, who was in charge of the administration of the NORMA expedition, had, according to Kurt Piwnkal of the ANTON expedition, been OC of the special company at Oranienburg described in Appendix A to our Counter-Intelligence Summary No 26 of 7th June 1944. The technical personnel of the NORMA expedition also seem to have been drawn from old members of the Oranienburg company, for the wireless expert, Rabbe, is obviously the promoted SS Rottenftlhrer Raabe who appears as personality No 54 in the above quoted Appendix on Oranienburg, while it is very probable that the first and second unknown W/T operators also appear in the same list. Possibly they are identical with SS Rottenftlhrer Arkuszewski, SS Rottenftlhrer Müller or SS Unterscharftlhrer Stadler, who all went to Wannsee with Raabe. For further information about Skorzeny's connection with Schellenberg and the ANTON expedition see paras 84–88 of the interrogation report on Homayun Fahzad given in Appendix B to our Counter-Intelligence Summary No 25 of 28th May 1944. SS Unterscharftthrer Groking is obviously the Groening, who, along with Otto

Schwerdt, was offered to Mayr by the SD as a saboteur. (see message No 76 on page 3 of Appendix P to our Counter-Intelligence Summary No 11 of 20th September 1943).

As regards SS Untersturmführer Steich, this is obviously Theodor Staisch, who accompanied Gamotha on his journey through Persia. Staisch was born on 29th March 1911 in Cologne, the son of Franz and Rosalia Staisch. He came to Persia via Russia in 1931 travelling on German Passport No 8198 issued in Cologne on 31st July 1931 and while here worked for Siemens. He is almost certainly identical with a small unfriendly-looking civilian described by Letay in connection with Gamotha's proposed expedition.

We have had several reports that Gamotha intended returning to Mazandaran and have therefore kept a close eye on some of his old acquaintances here for any sign of his reappearance. So far there is no indication that the expedition has been sent, though we are at present investigating a report of four Germans who are supposed to have been at large in the Veramin area thirty miles south-east of Tehran and may have been connected with a plane reported in that vicinity. So far, however, we have found out nothing concrete and certainly nothing to connect these reported Germans with Gamotha. We are very much inclined to agree with Sweerts that Roman Gamotha may be a Russian agent. The following are our reasons for thinking so:

(a) Gamotha, according to Mayr and others, attempted to win over Dashnaks and other groups hostile to the USSR during the period between his arrival in Persia and the entry of Allied troops. Among others, he saw the Dashnak leader, Varos Babayan, who disappeared at the end of 1941 and was almost certainly taken by the Russians. Gamotha's name figured prominently as the leader of German agents in Persia given in the pamphlet dropped by Russian planes when Red Army troops entered the country. It is thus fairly obvious that he was one of the people they were most interested in getting hold of in August 1941.

(b) Gamotha escaped from the German Summer Legation with two other Germans in a car driven by Mahmoud Khosrovi in the direction of Semnan. Khosrovi also helped Mohammed Hussein Hissam-Vaziri to escape, when we asked for Vaziri's arrest in 1942, and we had several reports that the latter was hiding in Semnan in the winter of 1942–3. We were able to discover in June of last year that Mahmoud Khosrovi was engaged with Lt Col Hissam-Vaziri, Mohammed Hussein's father, in a deal over the very car in which Gamotha escaped the day before the event took place. This was reported in section 2 of our Counter-Intelligence Summary No. 3 of 14th June 1943.

The car was left abandoned on the Semnan road and brought back to the Tehran Prefecture of Police, where it was robbed of its parts. It was decided to auction the remains in June 1943 and the Chief of the Political Police, Colonel Sharif, asked for the dossier on the case before giving the necessary orders. This was not to be found. After an energetic search through the files of the Prefecture and Ministry of the Interior it was eventually located and the part played by Lt Col Vaziri, then head of the Police Personnel Department, came to light. The Soviet Security Officer has since admitted that both father and son Vaziri are and were Soviet agents. Finally, a source who was in touch with Mahmoud Khosrovi in 1942 reported the latter as saying that Gamotha had been seen in Semnan in the uniform of a Soviet officer.

We always thought it curious that, while we were able to keep track of the movements of Franz Mayr through some of his Tehran contacts, we never really knew where Gamotha was, though we had several reports that he was in Mazandaran. It later transpired that Mayr was also unable to get in touch with him, although he thought that an intermediary of Gamotha once contacted Ahmed Namdar, who did not realise the significance of the password previously arranged between Gamotha and Mayr and therefore failed to bring about a meeting between the two. It now seems as if the Soviet security authorities deliberately tried to put us off the track of both Gamotha and Staisch. In March 1943 they told us they had reason to believe that Nikolaus Ausberg, Peter Josef Pogatschnig and Ludwig or Alois Staisch, all interned in Australia, had been German agents in North Persia and asked for them to be interrogated. The reference to Ausberg may have been to put us off Theodor Staisch. Again, In May 1943 they asked us if we had any information about a French officer called Gamotha who travelled to Turkey on a French passport with a Turkish visa issued by the Turkish embassy in Tehran. The stupid nature of this request is obvious in view of the fact that the Soviets and ourselves had been searching for Gamotha since 1941. Finally, when the question of the control of the northern frontier was discussed in the summer of this year, Maximov, the Russian ambassador, counterattacked about our control of the western frontier alleging that we had allowed Gamotha to escape that way. Gamotha himself broadcast from Berlin only a very vague account of his journey through North Persia and it would seem that both he and the Russians did what they could to deceive us as to what really happened. These rumours about Germans in the Veramin area may well be another part of this deception plan, for one report of a strange aircraft has been brought by Captain Salari, a one-time collaborator of Mayr and now a known Russian agent.

BLACKGUARD reported that on August 1st last Gamotha was to leave Vienna by air for Istanbul under a false name in order to contact Vaziri there. BLACKGUARD gathered that the latter was a member of the SD and closely connected with Gamotha. It will be remembered that Vaziri left Istanbul on 27th February 1944 ostensibly for Switzerland and returned on 5th May from Vienna. It would seem very probable that he went to Vienna in the first place to contact Gamotha there.

When the above points are considered in the light of Sweerts' statements that Gamotha believed Germany would lose the war and that Gamotha told him to mention his case should he, Sweerts, ever come into contact with the Allies, then it seems fairly certain that Sweerts' belief that Gamotha is a Soviet agent is justified.

What seems to have happened was something like this: Lt Col Nissam-Vaziri was like the Cavam-es-Sultansh and other German Fifth Columnists in that during the period of the war prior to the German attack on Russia he worked for both the Russians and Germans (he was an agent of Schulze). After the entry of Allied troops into Persia he continued his connection with the Russians, although his son, while German arms seemed to be successful, concentrated more on the German connection. Lt Col Vaziri, through his influence with the police, probably arranged for Gamotha, Staisch and one other German to escape from the German Summer Legation, got Mahmoud Khosrovi to tell them half-way to Semnan that they were in danger and that the car must be abandoned, and agreed previously with the Russians as to the spot where this would take place so that the party could be kidnapped. They were then probably taken to a Russian camp in North Persia, interrogated, broken down and recruited as Soviet agents. The attempt to contact Mayr might have been made by the Russians, using Gamotha's code. The Russians were out, however, for bigger game than the German Fifth Column in Persia and decided to use Gamotha as a superior BLACKGUARD to penetrate the highest circles of the Third Reich. Staisch and Gamotha were sent to Turkey, but the third German of the party for some reason or other did not accompany them. This was probably the German who Gamotha said was killed trying to escape.

Having launched off Gamotha and Staisch on their career of duplicity, the Russians then turned to Vaziri. They could get into touch with him both through his father and also through contacts revealed by Gamotha under interrogation. With the changed war situation Vaziri was probably willing to take up his old Russian connections through his father again. Major Mohamed Alai probably cooperated with Vaziri in making the change over and possibly also Hussein Keyhari, for Vaziri seems to have had a violent quarrel with Mayr and then been taken by Alai and Keyhari to the North, whether this was all pre-arranged with the Russians or Vaziri was let out of Alai's house by the latter later is not known. However, Vaziri was sent by the Russians to Turkey and later to Vienna (probably with the Khalilnias) with instructions to get in touch with Gamotha and work jointly with him for the Soviets.

The Vaziri–Gamotha case shows that the Russians have been bold, ambitious and to a certain extent ingenious. Their great mistake has been to try and keep it all secret from us, for they are now getting into difficulties with controlling the numerous agents whom they had to employ, six of whom are to be brought to trial in connection with the Vaziri passport forgery case. It is interesting to speculate on which Russians in Persia have been running the cases. There is evidence to show that the ambassador, Maximov, may be at the head of the Soviet organisation. HM Ambassador remarked the other day on the way Maximov seemed able to give instructions to the local Red Army commander and added that he would not be surprised if Maximov were a high-ranking member of the Party. Maximov's references to Gamotha's escape show that at least he was in the know over something, while the Swedish counsellor yesterday expressed his surprise that he had been told by his Soviet opposite number that he would have to discuss questions relating to the repatriation of Bulgars with the Soviet ambassador himself and not, as would be more normal, with Maximov who is usually the one to deal with such matters and is generally regarded as the Soviet SIS representative in Tehran. We shall go through our records and see if there are any other signs of Maximov playing a part in Soviet Intelligence Service activities. If Sweerts is correct about Gamotha being intimate with Schellenberg and Himmler, not to mention the interviews with Hitler and Kaltenbrunner, then of course he could be an extremely valuable agent for the Russians. But the question immediately arises as to whether he is playing straight with the Russians and whether, even if he is doing so now, he will continue to do so after the war, should the Russians demand his freedom. He would obviously be invaluable to the Nazis for the penetration of the Soviet Intelligence Service either now or later, should the party go underground. By checking on Gamotha's other contacts in Berlin it may be possible to find Germans he has recruited for the Russians and who are in the same position as himself.

One thing of local importance is that almost all the loose ends of the German Fifth Column in Persia have now been tied up; those which we thought were still loose are now known to be tied to the Russians.

Clearly Ramon Gamotha and Franz Mayr were key figures in the Nazi plans for Iran, and Mayr would be mentioned in MI5's sixth report prepared for the Prime Minister. Evidently Sweerts came to know Gamotha quite well, and formed a high opinion of his capabilities:

The head of Amp VIc and the organiser of the NORMA enterprise. He was educated at the Marie Therese College in Vienna, then at the University which he left with a degree in Political Science and Journalism. Stayed in Austria on behalf of the Nazi party.

He was a member of the Waffen SS before the war, was recalled from France in 1940 and sent to Russia, from where he travelled to Teheran on a journalistic (SD) mission, was interned in a Russian concentration camp in 1941, escaped in company with Staisch and a third person who was killed in the attempt. After many adventures, he reached the Turkish frontier. They were interned in Turkey, finally released and returned to Germany. He reported his adventures to Schellenberg, Kaltenbrunner, Himmler and Hitler. On Hitler's order he was promoted to Hauptsturmführer and received the Iron Cross, 1st Class.

Gamotha told Sweerts this story, but he also heard it from various members of Amt VI and the account of his adventures appeared in several Viennese newspapers. After Sweerts had gained his confidence, he told him that the NORMA expedition was merely bluff and that he had no intention of going to Persia, because German prestige was so low owing to the failure of the Russian campaign. All the same, he succeeded in obtaining vast quantities of money from the SD for equipment, etc. which he later sold in Vienna. He proposed to Sweerts one day that he would give him 100,000 Reichmarks if he could smuggle Jews into Switzerland. Sweerts states that he had plenty of money and also many sources of money in Austria, including a printing works. Gamotha always told Sweerts that if he came into contact with the Allies, he was to mention Gamotha's name. About the beginning of 1944 he married the wife of one of his friends, an old fiancee of his own. In confidence, he told Sweerts that he believed Germany would lose the war and gave Sweerts to understand that he was putting money aside for such a contingency. Sweerts thinks it quite possible that Gamotha is a Russian agent, as he could not have escaped from Russia so easily otherwise.

The friendship between Gamotha and Staisch could be explained in the same way. To sum up, Gamotha is very intelligent, very fond of money and power, and on very good terms with Schellenberg and Himmler.

The significance of Alan Rogers' observations lies in part in his belief that the Soviets had succeeded in recruiting Gamotha while he was their prisoner, and this places a very different complexion on events in Iran. Reportedly Gamotha was arrested by the Soviets in Vienna in April 1945 and later the following month was working for the NKVD with a former SD Amt VI (Ausland) officer, Dr Wilhelm Hoettl.

This extraordinary story was mentioned in the report alongside that of Arthur Garitte, code-named MEADOW, a Flemish nationalist operated by the Belgian Sûreté as a double-agent against the Abwehr from 1939. A writer by profession, MEADOW revealed himself in 1944 to have been part of a German stay-behind network in Brussels and was interrogated at Camp 020, having been denounced as an SD agent by Sweerts. While he was detained Garitte was also identified by two other former SD agents, René Delhaye and André de Smidt, as having been on the Nazi payroll over a much longer period than he had initially admitted. All three were held until the end of the war and then handed over to the Belgian authorities.

★ ★ ★

The issue of anarchist subversion in the armed forces, as manifested by *War Commentary*'s preparations for the introduction of soldiers' councils and other such innovations, intended to undermine military discipline. *War Commentary* had begun as a fortnightly publication, *Stalin and the World*, during the Spanish Civil War, which was retitled *Revolt!* in 1938. Upon the outbreak of the Second World War there was a further tranformation, under the editorial leadership of an Italian, Vero Recchioni, who changed his name to Vernon Richards.[1]

The group of pacifists and anarchists who backed *War Commentary* bought a printers, Express Printers, in 1942, but they were all under varying degrees of surveillance, and in November 1944 the homes of Richards' wife Marie-Louise Berneri, John Hewetson and Philip Sansom were raided by Special Branch detectives investigating an attempt to 'endeavour to seduce from their duty persons in His Majesty's Service and to cause among such persons disaffection likely to lead to breaches of their duty'. Richards, Hewetson and Sansom were arrested in February 1945 and tried at the Old Bailey the following month.

The prosecution, led by the attorney-general, was partly presented by an MI5 officer, John Maude, and became quite a *cause célèbre*, with evidence produced about literature seized from the kitbags of various soldiers, among them Privates Taylor, Pontin, McDonald, and Colin Ward. The three men were convicted of incitement, but Berneri was acquitted on the grounds that a wife legally cannot conspire with her husband, and she continued to edit *War Commentary* during his imprisonment.

23

19 FEBRUARY 1945

The first MI5 monthly report for 1945, and seen by Churchill on 3 March, reflected the organisation's satisfaction in laying out the evidence that the Germans, apparently content with their agents in England, and completely unaware that they were, without exception, under British control, were no longer interested in sending further spies but instead were concentrating on the development of stay-behind networks.

JANUARY 1945
SPIES EXPECTED.
There is no evidence to show that the Germans have succeeded in sending any agents to this country, but it is known from Most Secret Sources that they are planning to despatch one who is probably intended to cross the lines on the Western Front and make his way to this country. Details available about his are meagre, but the Field has been warned to be on the watch for him.

SPECIAL AGENTS.
GARBO's sub-agent in Canada has now been equipped with a wireless transmitter with which he has established direct communication with his masters in Madrid.

TATE and ROVER have been successfully supplying misleading information about the fall of V-l and V-2, and there is some reason to believe that their messages are having an effect on the places where these missiles are falling. TATE has also been used at the Admiralty for Naval deception with great success.

SABOTAGE.

A case of sabotage aboard HM *LST 368* was reported on the 30th January, and subsequently investigated by the Security Service. It was found that sand had been put into the gearbox. There was no clue whatsoever to indicate the guilty individual, but after extensive interrogation a confession was extracted from a stoker, Albert Bliss, that he had committed the act. The investigator's suspicions were aroused by Bliss's unsatisfactory answers under interrogation and were confirmed by an examination of the dirt under Bliss's nails, which was found to contain particles of sand for which he could not account. Bliss has been tried by Court Martial and sentenced to twelve months with hard labour. His motive for doing this sabotage was that he was worried about his wife and wished to delay the sailing of the ship.

SPECIAL INTERROGATION CENTRE.

A survey of the activities at our special Interrogation Centre during the year 1944 shows a considerable change in the type of work performed. Before the invasion of the Continent the spies interrogated there were mainly people with espionage missions against this country, or agents picked up at the various control points throughout the Empire. Since D-Day, however, this type of arrival has become much rarer and the majority of cases studied have been agents detected in the Field and sent back for special and more detailed study by our interrogators. During the year 116 persons have been interrogated, of which 71 have been sent to us from SHAEF. Of the remaining 45 derived from other sources, only 14 were admitted after D-Day.

During the whole year only 13 agents were taken into the camp who had missions directed against the United Kingdom, and these included one who was already under our control. This number is surprisingly small, for it was expected that before the invasion of the Continent the Germans would take every possible effort to send agents to this country. It is worth noticing, moreover, that of the 13 agents just mentioned only 3 had assignments directly connected with invasion preparations. In this second half of 1944 there is no known case of the enemy sending an agent with a mission to the United Kingdom.

Several reasons may be suggested for this change in German methods. The most obvious is the fact that the Germans are now probably less interested in activities in this country than previously, and are concentrating more on espionage against the liberated countries. A second and perhaps equally important reason, however, is the satisfaction which the enemy appears to have felt about his espionage organisation in this country, which is in fact under our control. Two other factors probably also contributed. The first is the ban imposed early in 1944 on the travel to the United Kingdom of recruits for the Allied forces, which is known to have been one of the most profitable channels from the German point of view.

The second is the liberation of Southern France which closed another channel, namely the Franco–Spanish frontier, over which the Germans habitually sent their agents.

The Interrogation Centre has, however, continued to serve an important function in interrogating agents who have supplied us with extensive information about the organisation and activities of the German Secret Service, much of this should prove of value during the period of occupation.

Of the cases reaching us from sources other than SHAEF, several have been of considerable interest. In the early Spring the American authorities in Iceland sent us 7 agents who had landed illegally there, and whose arrival suggested that the Germans were expecting an invasion launched from Iceland against Norway.[1] It is quite clear that the American authorities would not have been able to obtain from those men the information extracted from them by our interrogators, who have a far more extensive background against which to work.

AFHQ have also supplied certain agents, including one of particular importance, namely an Italian called Manfredi de Blasis. The AFHQ interrogators failed to extract from him the information which was, however, soon obtained when he underwent more experienced examination in this country.

Of the cases received from the Western Front it is notable that by far the greater part come from 21st Army Group. This is due to the fact that the Belgian and Dutch authorities have little means of investigating cases and are prepared to hand over almost any agent to us, whereas the French have a well-trained body of interrogators and are somewhat jealous of their right to deal with spies on their own territory. We have, however, arranged for the French to 'lend' us for limited periods important agents arrested by them, when there is reason to think that we should be able to obtain more information from them than was got by their captors.

19 February 1945

★ ★ ★

Petrie had drawn attention to the case of Baron Philippe Manfredi de Blasis, one of the war's most unusual examples of espionage, who arrived at Prestwick from Marrakesh in January 1944.

Manfredi de Blasis was recruited by the Sicherheitsdienst to operate behind the Allied lines in southern Italy in August 1943 and was compromised, even before his departure on a mission to Cerignola, by signals intelligence, together with some fifty other SD agents. However, after his arrest in Bari in October 1943 he was so convincing that both his SIS case officer and his CSDIC interrogator became persuaded of his innocence, to the point that the accuracy of the original source came into question, asserting that 'it was psychologically impossible for this man to be a German spy'. Accordingly, under SIS's sponsorship he was sent to Camp 020, where he shared a cell with Andrés Bonzo. After just three weeks in detention he admitted having been recruited by an embassy attaché, Koehler, to undertake an assignment for the SD that included sheltering at least one saboteur on the large agricultural estate he inherited from his mother.

Born in Rome in 1906 to an aristocratic landowning family, Manfredi de Blasis graduated from Rome University with a law degree and in 1937 married an older Finnish divorcee, Anna von Winter. She would later meet, and boast of her friendship with, Heinrich Himmler, whom she met early in 1943 in a Berchtesgaden hotel where she was undergoing medical treatment. She would later be exposed as a German spy, although her husband was unaware of her espionage role. He was released from Camp 020 and repatriated, with Alfredo Manna, in August 1945.

★ ★ ★

GARBO's sub-agent in Canada was Agent FIVE, code-named MOONBEAM by MI5 and designated V-Mann 274 by the Abwehr, who was notionally based in Ottawa. According to GARBO, MOONBEAM was a Venezuelan named Carlos who had been living in Aberdeen, and brother of Agent THREE, code-named BENEDICT, supposedly a wealthy, recent graduate of Glasgow University named Pedro. Initially, MOONBEAM had intended to return to Venezuela, where he hoped to establish a U-boat refueling base near his home in Camana, on the Caribbean coast, a proposal that the Abwehr had not encouraged. GARBO had invented FIVE before his arrival in England in an attempt to discover if the Kriegsmarine possessed servicing facilities for submarines in the Caribbean. He tried the same ploy, probing about agents in Northern Ireland, before formally recruiting FIVE as a sub-agent in June 1942, under MI5's sponsorship.

Having been trained by his brother who had formally enrolled him in June 1942, MOONBEAM successfully undertook missions as a full-time, paid agent to South Wales, and even to the closed military area of the Isle of Wight, an achievement considered very impressive that led to an offer to visit Northern Ireland, which was not pursued. Instead, in response to a questionnaire, he went to Brighton to report on the deployment of Canadian troops in the area.

In the summer of 1943 MOONBEAM reached Montreal legitimately, or so the narrative went, and he began communicating in secret writing to a cover address in Scotland. Then he acquired a 350-watt radio transmitter and recruited his cousin CON, a resident of Buffalo, New York. In reality, his role was played by MI5's liaison officer with the RCMP, Cyril Mills, while he supposedly found a job as a commercial traveller in Toronto.

When Agent FOUR, code-named CHAMILUS, allegedly a Gibraltarian employed as a NAAFI waiter in a US Army canteen in Chislehurst, deserted in June 1944 he hid in a remote farmhouse in South Wales, but managed to flee the country in October 1944 when he travelled to Canada as a steward and became MOONBEAM's radio operator, opening a direct link to Madrid in February 1945 with his 350-watt apparatus, which allegedly he had smuggled into Canada. His transatlantic passage had been facilitated by a seaman, Agent SEVEN, code-named Stanley, who provided him with papers that allowed him to be employed as a steward. SEVEN, known as Stanley, appeared in Madrid's ISOS traffic as V-Mann 1245.

FOUR, known as Fred, had been recruited by GARBO in May 1942 to report on military activity on England's east coast but after three months had moved to Soho, where he had bought a wireless transmitter on the black market. When his lodgings were bombed out he moved to the Whitelands Hotel in Putney, which was being used as a refugee centre for Gibraltarians. In the ISOS traffic FOUR appeared as V-Mann 377.

MI5's brief summary of GARBO's activities fell far short of explaining what happened to him later in 1944 when, in August, the Section V officer in Madrid, Jack Ivens, was approached by a Spaniard, Roberto Buenaga. He claimed to be a friend of Friedrich Knappe-Ratey, a senior member of Kuhlenthal's staff at the Madrid embassy, with an offer to sell the name and address of the Abwehr's star spy in London who, he alleged, communicated with Madrid by wireless. Ivens interviewed Buenaga and was persuaded that he probably could compromise GARBO, and immediately reported the crisis to London. Meanwhile, he stalled Buenaga by insisting he required instructions before proceeding to agree his terms.

MI5's ingenious solution was for GARBO to tell Kuhlenthal that his courier had learned of Buenaga's treachery, and he was therefore disappearing to the Welsh hideout that previously had accommodated his sub-agent FOUR when he had gone on the run. In his absence Pedro would run the network from Glasgow, and MI5's hope was that Buenaga would be silenced before he could make a return visit to Ivens. However, Kuhlenthal responded to GARBO with a reassurance that Buenaga knew nothing to endanger him.

As it turned out, Kuhlenthal was wrong, and when Buenaga kept his appointment with Ivens he gave GARBO's correct name and address, and even supplied Aracelli's home address in Burgos. Accordingly, GARBO notionally moved to Wales, where he maintained contact with both the Abwehr and his network. Through this expedient Kuhlenthal retained his absolute confidence in GARBO, and MI5 gave every sign of being in pursuit of the fugitive Spaniard, including a formal protest by the Foreign Office in December addressed to the Spanish government about Knappe-Ratey's undiplomatic behaviour, accompanied by a demand to interrogate him.

★ ★ ★

ROVER was a Polish naval officer who reached England in May 1944 after many adventures. Before the war he had been a professional boxer and a baker, and had worked on the railways, before joining the navy in early 1939. He had fought as an infantryman and, having been made a PoW, was sent to a forced labour camp where, in June 1942, he accepted an offer of recruitment from the Abwehr.

When ROVER arrived in Madrid he revealed his mission, and surrendered his transmitter, code, secret ink and cover address, making him an excellent candidate for a double-agent. He also revealed that his mission was to gain a job in an aircraft factory and collect technical information about new designs. Indeed, the Germans had invested so much time in training ROVER that MI5 concluded that he was regarded as a valuable asset.

However, upon his arrival in London, when he followed his instructions to mail his readiness to begin transmitting, there was no reply to his signal and the decision was taken to return him to the Polish navy. Almost as soon as the arrangements were made, the Abwehr commenced transmitting, and on 1 October an RSS operator named Reason was substituted. Unfortunately, Reason fell ill and died, so a second operator was introduced with the claim that ROVER had been injured in a road accident and had been hospitalised, as an explanation for his change in style. This explanation was accepted, and ROVER's transmitter remained active until the end of hostilities.

24

5 MARCH 1945

At this late stage in the war MI5's counter-espionage role was diminishing, and Petrie's report reflected the necessity to screen released PoWs, investigate allegations of collaboration and build prosecution cases against renegades.

FEBRUARY 1945

1. <u>TRIALS OF RENEGADES</u>.

The first two cases have occurred of renegades being brought to trial in this country. One was a civilian, Gerald Hewitt, the other a Private in the Gloucester Regiment, James Robert Styles.

Hewitt was tried at the Central Criminal Court on March 5th and was sentenced to twelve years' penal servitude under Defence Regulation 2 A. He had lived in Paris since 1931 and went to the South of France when that city was occupied by the enemy. From 1942 onwards he undertook propaganda work for the Germans in return for which he was allowed to go to Paris with his mother. He was paid at a rate of between 20,000 and 25,000 francs a month for writing propaganda articles and for broadcasting in French in the guise of 'Mr Smith, an Englishman, interned in France, who has asked permission to come to the microphone'. His task was to inflame French opinion against the United Nations. When the liberation of Paris was near, Hewitt was taken by the Germans to Belfort en route for Germany, but he left them and took refuge in Switzerland. From there he was expelled, and was arrested by the FFI on arriving in France. The case was investigated in detail by the Security Service Liaison Section attached to SHAEF, and a report prepared which led to his trial and conviction.

In passing sentence Mr. Justice Macnaghten said: 'When you thought that your native land and your adopted country were bound to fall you treated with Germany. You sold yourself and the country of your adoption to the enemy. Then the scene changed. Paris was about to be liberated, and a liberated Paris was no place for you, so you went away to Germany. I have no doubt you were genuine in distrusting the Germans, so you went to Switzerland, but Switzerland did not want you, and you chose to fall into the hands of the Allies rather than into the hands of the Germans. You have been assisting the cause of the enemy.

'It is impossible to measure or even estimate what assistance you were to the enemy and what harm you did to your compatriots and friends. Public Justice requires that offences such as yours must be punished.'

Styles was captured in France in 1940, and throughout the time that he was a prisoner of war in Germany, adverse reports on him were received by the Military Authorities. At the end of 1943 he reached Sweden and was ultimately brought to this country. Over 200 repatriated prisoners of war were interviewed by officers of the Security Service, and statements were taken from them which established beyond doubt that Styles had acted as a stool pigeon while prisoner of war. Some of the prisoners were able to give conclusive evidence that Styles had disclosed to the enemy the plans of men intending to escape from prisoner of war camps, and had thus frustrated their projects. Styles has been tried by General Court Martial and convicted of voluntarily aiding the enemy. For reasons of security the trial was held in camera. Sentence will be promulgated in due course.

2. SABOTAGE.

A further instance has occurred of malicious damage to a ship carried out by a man anxious to avoid leaving this country. The damage occurred in the engine room of HMS *Harrier*, a Fleet Mine Sweeper Flotilla tender, which was found flooded to a depth of three feet. The cause was the deliberate opening of the inlet and outlet valves of the starboard circulator. A board of enquiry was unsuccessful in tracing the culprit and a special officer was sent by the Security Service to investigate the cause. After lengthy enquiry and interrogation this officer obtained an admission from a member of the crew, Victor Cladingboel, a stoker, that he had flooded the engine room in an attempt to delay the sailing of the ship. Cladingboel stated that while rockets were falling on London, he was worried about his wife who was living alone with their young child. He was tried by Court Martial, sentenced to three months' imprisonment, and dismissed the Service.

3. <u>SPECIAL AGENTS</u>.

TATE and ROVER have continued to supply misleading information about the fall of V-2 and it is now possible to conclude with some certainty that the shift to the north-east of London of the mean point of impact of V-2 is due to reports from Special Agents. The renewed use of V-1 was foreshadowed by a message sent to TATE a week before the event.

Most Secret Sources show that the Germans, who had promised to pay £2,000 to BRUTUS, have entrusted this arrangement to an agent in Spain who has for long represented that he has sub-agents in this country, though in fact they almost certainly do not exist. It is hoped that the failure to carry out this transaction may serve to discredit the agent.[1]

5th March 1945

ADDENDUM

Since the last sentence of para. 1 was written, sentence on Styles has been promulgated. He has been awarded 7 years' imprisonment.

★ ★ ★

Compared to Petrie's other monthly report, this example is quite brief, and for the first time raises the unpalatable issue of British renegades, of whom there were mercifully few.

In March 1945 the first renegade, Gerald Percy Sandys Hewitt, was sentenced to twelve years' imprisonment. Although British, he had lived in France since 1931, had contributed articles to the British Union of Fascists' journal *Action*, and had been associated with the Action Française movement. His crime had been broadcasting between 1942 and 1944 for Dr Goebbels' ministry of propaganda from Paris and Berlin. He was arrested in France in September 1944 after he had been deported from Switzerland, where he had attempted to take refuge as the Reich collapsed.

By January 1946 MI5 had obtained convictions against twenty-two suspects, with Liddell reporting that 'large numbers of other cases have been submitted by the Judge Advocate-General and a considerable number are under investigation'.

Petrie's other topic, the V-1 and V-2 attacks, had far more potential for political controversy, and directly involved MI5, which was proposed as the instrument by which Sir Findlater Stewart's Security Executive in July 1944 would recommend adoption of a policy to use double-agents to mislead the enemy about where the rockets were landing. The objective was to save an estimated four thousand lives, but the situation was complicated by OSTRO's uncontrolled bogus reporting that London had been flattened. His messages dated 17 and 18 June claimed:

> Whitehall, College Street nr Parliament (Big Ben) completely destroyed. Heavy devastation with very high numbers of dead between Limehouse and West India Docks. Also devastation in East India Docks. Extensive destruction at Bromley gasworks by River Lea. Gigantic blaze here. Serious damage to houses at Greenwich, Clapham, Earls Court. Large goods depot and hall burnt out. Direct hit on East Croydon Station. Eye-witnesses report many dead.

Specifically GARBO, TATE and ROVER were tasked by their handlers to supply further details and thereby presented MI5 with an opportunity to suggest that the rockets were overshooting their target area, thereby encouraging the Germans who, because of Allied air superiority, had no means of substantiating the reports, to reduce their range. Stewart was also conscious that GARBO in particular had a key role in the FORTITUDE D-Day deception campaign, and it was vital not to undermine his credibility. But the Home Secretary, Herbert Morrison, a former leader of the London County Council, was outraged at the prospect of his constituents in Lambeth being sacrificed for the benefit of more wealthy residents north of the Thames, and persuaded the War Cabinet, in Churchill's absence, to ban the scheme, which had initiated the discussion with a paper circulated on 24 July that acknowledged Morrison's Ministry of Home Security:

> … does not accept these arguments. They are not satisfied that any substantial saving of life would be effected, even if the deception was completely successful, and they express themselves as very doubtful about the possibility of achieving success.

Or, as Dr Reg Jones recalled, 'the attempt to keep the aiming-point short was an effort by government officials and others in Westminster, Belgravia and Mayfair to keep the bombs off themselves at the expense of the proletariat in South London'. When informed of the position taken by the Home Secretary by MI5's Charles Cholmondeley, acting as a liaison with the Air Ministry, Jones had been appalled.

The Cabinet debated the issue on 27 July and the minutes noted that 'the general sense of the War Cabinet was that it would be a serious matter to assume any direct degree of responsibility for action which would affect the areas against which flying bombs were aimed'. Accordingly the Chiefs of Staff were directed to 'create confusion in his mind and present him with an inaccurate picture' but not to authorise Stewart's scheme, declaring that 'the draft of any instructions to be issued on this matter should be submitted to the Prime Minister for approval before issue'. This response, regarded as unsatisfactory by the CROSSBOW Committee chairman Duncan Sandys and Churchill's scientific adviser, Lord Cherwell, advocated that 'instead of attempting vaguely to confuse the enemy a positive deception plan should be adopted'. Two days later, on 4 August, Morrison reacted:

> I hope you will not decide in favour of it without reference to the War Cabinet as a whole. Apart altogether from the gravity of the responsibility, if what was being done should ever come out, there might be most serious political consequences.

In the light of Morrison's continued opposition, the issue came before the Cabinet on 15 August, when Attlee chaired the meeting while Churchill was in Naples for a two-day conference with Marshal Tito at Villa Rivalta. However, the conclusion of the deliberations on what was termed the CROSSBOW deception plan, as conveyed to Sir Findlater, was curiously ambiguous:

> It was agreed that your object should be to ensure that there is no deterioration in the position and that the enemy does not shift the pattern of bombs towards the north-west. With this in view you should continue to convey to the enemy information which will confirm his belief that he has no need to lengthen his range. You are also at liberty, within limits, to take such steps as you may judge safe to intensify this belief.

Stewart seems not to have declared any reversal of policy, for his deputy John Drew told the XX Committee on 17 August that he had been instructed 'to prevent the enemy from moving his aim towards the north-west and, to a slight extent, to attempt to induce him to move it towards the south-east'. Meanwhile, of course, the advancing Allies were occupying the V-1 launch sites, making the salvo fired on 30/31 August the last from northern France.[2]

In any event, the whole matter became somewhat academic six months later, on 27 March, when the last two V-2s to reach England detonated in Stepney and then Orpington, Kent, killing 145 civilians. Two days later the final V-1 exploded harmlessly in a field near Letchworth, Hertfordshire. Earlier in the month, the 444 Training and Experimental Battery and the 485 Mobile

Artillery Detachment had stepped up the offensive to launch an average of thirteen V-2s a day, but then they were forced to withdraw across the Rhine, placing all targets in England out of range.

Since 8 September, when the second phase of the missile attack had commenced, exactly as ARTIST had warned TRICYCLE, 517 V-2s had hit London, out of a total of 1,054 launched. Unlike the fixed V-1 doodlebug ramps constructed by Flak Regiment 155(W) in western Holland at Delft, Ypenburg and Vlaardingen, which provided the RAF with relatively easy targets after they had been identified by aerial reconnaissance, the V-2s were fired from mobile launch vehicles located first in Wassenaar and then in The Hague's densely populated city centre. The three catapults only fired 274 flying bombs, and of that number thirty-four penetrated the British defences, and just fifteen reached the capital.

Whereas the V-1 deception campaign, though controversial, had been quite simple to convey to the enemy, MI5 being confident that the enemy had no method of double-checking their agent reports, it was clear that the V-2 ballistic missile was much easier to link to specific points of impact. This meant great care had to be taken to switch the timing of specific incidents, but this was achieved with sufficient success for the Germans to shorten the V-2s' range by a rate of 2 miles a week between 20 January and 17 February 1945, terminating in Kent, although the enemy was aiming for Trafalgar Square.[3]

The whole question of V-weapon deception had raised uncomfortable issues for government scientists, agent case officers, politicians and strategists to ponder, and, although emerging relatively late in the war, was passed by the Chiefs of Staff and the War Cabinet to the Prime Minister. Hitherto, Churchill had been informed about espionage investigations, double-agent operations, subversion and MI5's counter-intelligence activities, but had not been called upon to express an opinion or stand in judgement on a particular dilemma, but the CROSSBOW proposal had put him in a difficult position, requiring him to balance the competing interests of protecting valued double-agents against the protests of the Home Secretary, whose views were supported by the Minister for Production, Oliver Lyttleton, the Tory MP for Aldershot. If the challenge was daunting, we will probably never know as no record survives of how Churchill dealt with it. Presumably he made his views known, which emboldened MI5 to ignore Morrison, save the lives of thousands of Londoners and enhance the standing of the vulnerable double-agents in whom so much had been invested.

25

MARCH AND APRIL 1945, UNDATED

A week after Hitler's death, and on the very day General Jodl signed the instrument of Germany's unconditional surrender, MI5's Director-General completed a rather short summary covering events over the previous two months, concentrating on two individuals, an Icelandic spy, Gudbrandur Hlidar, and Hermann Rainer, who was thought to be knowledgeable about any SD-sponsored post-occupation resistance. The other topic covered was the threat posed to military discipline by the anarchists who published *War Commentary*, among them John Olday.

MARCH AND APRIL 1945

During the past two months a number of enemy agents have been sent for examination at our special interrogation centre. They include one of purely academic interest, and one of current importance. The former, an Icelandic subject, Gudbrandur Hlidar, was passing through this country on his way to Ireland but, owing to the difficulties which the German Secret Service had found in sending him here and their incompetence in organisation, the mission which he had to fulfil was already twelve months out of date. The more serious character is Untersturmführer Hermann Rainer who was apprehended and sent to us by 21st Army Group on the basis of previous information that he was a member of an important German resistance organisation. Rainer has been persuaded to talk not without some difficulty and has revealed much of interest of German plans and organisation for partisan resistance and sabotage behind the Allied lines. His most interesting item of information, however, is his identification of a group of spies who have not yet been captured, and who, according to his statements, were to be dropped by parachute in the Aachen area with the assignment of murdering the mayor of that town. At the time that Rainer gave this information we believe that he had no means of knowing that the mayor of Aachen had actually been murdered. Full details of Rainer's identification of the alleged culprits were at once cabled to the field.

An officer of the German Intelligence Service who was captured last month revealed under interrogation that a Frenchman named Lagall was a German spy who had been sent to this country. Lagall had in fact arrived here over two years ago and had been detained by the Security Service since his arrival, although there was no conclusive evidence that he was a German spy. The story which he told, however, of his escape from France was so unconvincing that even without more tangible evidence we felt justified in keeping him under restraint for the duration of the war. The new evidence which has now reached us shows that our suspicions were amply justified. Lagall has recently been deported to France where he is being dealt with by the French authorities.

The Security Service has had under observation for some considerable time past the activities of the 'Freedom From Anarchists', a group of people with headquarters in London and a branch in Bristol. They are the publishers of the fortnightly paper *War Commentary* and have been carrying on their activities at an office and bookshop in Belsize Road, Swiss Cottage, a studio in Camden Town, and premises in Whitechapel occupied by a firm known as Express Printers, who print the paper.

The persons most actively engaged in the management of the Freedom Press were a Vernon Richards and his wife, both of Italian extraction with anarchist family connections; Dr John Hamilton, a qualified medical practitioner, who has served a sentence of imprisonment for refusing to be medically examined for military service; and John Olday (or Oldag) the illegitimate son of a German woman, who is technically a British/German dual national, but who was educated and has lived mostly in Germany. This man produced chiefly scurrilous anti-war cartoons with subversive captions.

The members of the group, while condemning out-and-out almost all the forms and appearances of any system of government, are bitterly opposed to warfare in general and the present war in particular and to the existence of Armed Forces and the discipline necessary to maintain them. Broadly speaking, the line of policy in *War Commentary* was to write up and to dilate on military and naval mutinies such as those in the Russian and German navies in the last war; and this whole teaching was calculated, and indeed designed to undermine the determination, loyalty, morale and discipline of readers in the forces. During 1944, however, there were clear indications of a

more positive policy and on increased boldness in asserting it, accompanied
by a greater following in the Forces. A most important development was
the issue by the Freedom Press of a circular letter dated 28 October 1944 to
members of the Forces drawing their attention to a forthcoming series of
articles in *War Commentary* on 'Soldiers' and Workers' Councils'. Three of
these, with the usual flavouring of revelations and mutinies, advocated the
formation of such councils in the British Forces, who are also advised to
'Hold on to your arms'.

Search of the Freedom Press and the results of a number of snap kit
inspections confirmed the impression that a sustained attack was being
made on the loyalty of the Forces and it was achieving some degree of
success. Richards and his wife, Dr Hewetson and one Philip Sansom were
accordingly prosecuted under the Defence Regulation 29A (seducing
persons from duty and causing disaffection), and last week the three men
were sentenced by Mr Justice Birkett at the Old Bailey to be imprisoned for
nine calendar months, the woman being acquitted.

The sentences perhaps do not adequately indicate the pernicious and
even dangerous nature of the propaganda so sedulously conducted by these
people, for an over-all study of it leaves no shadow of doubt that what they
were aiming at was to incite the Armed Forces to violence and mutiny.
On this point it is pertinent to record that Olday, who was not put on trial as
he is already in prison, has been sentenced to twelve months' imprisonment
for using false identity papers. Though the Freedom Press Anarchists are
not a large body, they are obviously one whose teachings under certain
circumstances might be productive of the gravest consequences.

7 May 1945   Director-General

★ ★ ★

Hermann Rainer provided a mass of information to MI5, and named a French
refugee, Lagall, as one of his agents. This individual in fact had been interned
since his arrival in England in August 1943, having been exfiltrated across the
Channel by a resistance organisation in Carantec headed by Ernest Sibiril,
using his boat, the *Pourquoi Pas*. Under examination at the London Reception
Centre, Lagall had raised suspicions, but when ISOS later revealed that the
Breton route had been penetrated by the Germans, Herbert Hart had argued
that the compromise had occurred long after Lagall, and a few hundred other
escapees, had benefited from the route, which suggested perhaps that he had

not been responsible for the leak. However, Stamp and Milmo had disagreed, and Lagall had been detained until his true loyalties could be ascertained. Ernest, Louise and Leon Sibiril finally reached England in October 1943 on another boat, the *Shark*, which had been built in eleven days for the purpose.

★ ★ ★

Gudbrandur Hlidar was a 30-year-old veterinary student, the son of an Icelandic member of parliament, who had been studying in Copenhagen since 1935. He had been mentioned as an Abwehr recruiter by Einar Sigvaldason and Larus Thorsteinsson, and he had also been incriminated by the German spy, Ernst Fresenius. Accordingly, when he applied in Stockholm for a transit visa to return to Iceland via Scotland in October 1944, it was granted. After various delays he finally reached Prestwick on 12 February 1945 and was transferred initially to the London Reception Centre at the Oratory School so as to give him the opportunity to offer an innocent explanation for the accumulated evidence against him. He failed to do so and accordingly was moved to Camp 020 on 2 March.

Having initially failed to mention his Abwehr connections, Hlidar was challenged about his contacts with Dr Hellmuth Lotz, and then confessed to his espionage mission, claiming that Lotz had pressured him on the grounds that his father had been Germany's vice consul in Akureyri. He admitted visiting Lotz's country home at Klein Kiesow and discussing issues of the repatriation of Icelandic students from occupied Denmark. He also acknowledged that upon his return to Copenhagen he had received training in secret writing, and had been given a cover address of an Otto Kaiser in Gothenburg. Of course, MI5's interrogators had the benefit of checking Hlidar's version with several other Icelandic detainees, which led to further admissions, including the nature of the military information he had been instructed to collect, and the fact that he was to provide money and assistance to other Abwehr agents who approached him for support once he was established in Iceland. Specifically, he was to pay 1,000 kronen to Ib Riis. He also conceded that he had introduced five other compatriots to Lotz, who had sworn him to secrecy. All on the list were known to MI5, including Pall Sigurdsson, who had been an inmate of Camp 020 before he was sent to the Isle of Man. The payment to COBWEB was also potentially significant, as it suggested the Abwehr's continuing confidence in their source.

Buster Milmo concluded that Hlidar would have been an important German spy if he had undertaken his assignment as planned in 1944, but by the time he reached Scotland, with the war almost over, he had become an irrelevance. He was deported to Iceland by air from Hendon on 2 August 1945, accompanied by seven of his compatriots.

★ ★ ★

John Olday, also known as Arthur Oldag, was an author, cartoonist and political extremist very familiar to MI5. His wife, Hilde Meisel, a member of Militant Socialist International, was a Hungarian Jewess born in Vienna, known to Special Branch.[1] She was employed by the BBC to compose German language talks, and had published *How to Conquer Hitler* under the name Hilda Monte. They had married in September 1938 and lived in a top floor flat in Greek Street, Soho. According to Scotland Yard, Oldag's British passport had been issued in Hamburg in April 1937, and he had been interviewed in September 1939 upon his return to London from Geneva. On that occasion he claimed to have been born in London in 1905 but to have lived in Hamburg when his mother moved to the United States, and was reported to have asserted the need for 'IRA action' against the Nazi regime in Germany. When questioned he described himself as the illegitimate son of a German woman who had taken him as a child back to Germany. There he had been brought up by grandparents in Kiel and Hamburg, and later, when working as a journalist on the *Anzeiger*, had joined the Young Communist League.[1] He also claimed to be a member of a small nameless terrorist group based in Paris that had access to explosives and intended to mount a bombing campaign across Germany:

> ... the sole object of which would appear to be the destruction, by means of sabotage, of points of military importance in Germany. The principal of this group, he stated, was a German named Karl GROEHL or FRIEDBERG of 7 rue Barrault, Paris XIII, which address is also the headquarters of the organisation.

In 1937 he had moved to London and found a job as a cartoonist on *Everybodies Weekly*, lodging in Victoria with a poet, Rose Fyleman. He had also adopted the pen-name John Olday to publish *Kingdom of Rags*,[2] a collection of anti-Nazi cartoons. According to his MI5 file, Olday was considered for recruitment by SIS for some undisclosed purpose, but he was rejected as being unstable and indiscreet.

Oldag was described as possessing 'a superior intellect and education', and in July 1941 joined the Pioneer Corps, prompting MI5's Mark Johnstone in November to send his commanding officer a discreet warning about his political extremism and his potential for spreading subversion. However, Olday was highly regarded in his unit, at least until March 1943 when he was registered as a deserter. In August 1943 he was reported by the police for having created a booklet of caricatures entitled *The March to Death*, which was published by the Freedom Press, and F Division reopened its investigation of him. According to Max Knight, Oldag's wife had been a Trotskyite, but recently had abandoned both the cause and her husband and had moved in with a Communist, Baron Hellmut von Rauschenplat.[3] His agent reported that Olday's booklet was being sold by the Peace Pledge Union, a group of pacifists closely monitored by MI5's F Division. Another informant suggested Olday was being sheltered by the Chinese in Soho, as he had demonstrated a particular affinity for that community.

Olday was eventually arrested by the police in 1944 on a charge of carrying false identity papers, and upon his release was sentenced by the army to two years' imprisonment for desertion. In 1946 he resumed his activism for the anarchist movement, and thereafter made frequent contributions to the *Anarchist* fortnightly journal.

26

11 JUNE 1945

MI5's last report of the war to the Prime Minister was dated June 1945 and concentrated exclusively on those British turncoat soldiers who had been recruited into the Legion of St George, a Waffen SS infantry unit, supposedly to fight on the Russian front, but in fact which never really left their barracks in Dresden for lack of numbers. MI5's response to the issue had been the creation of a special section of four Scotland Yard detectives, designated B4(a) and then SLB3, and led by Donald Fish and Reg Spooner, to investigate each case and assemble the evidence for submission to the Director of Public Prosecutions. As a first step, in November 1933 Len Burt and Jim Skardon opened an office in Paris.

During the course of the war a total of fifty-four British and Empire soldiers joined the Free Corps, but there were never more than twenty-seven in the unit at any one time. John Amery was tried and executed in December 1945, but the other participants received prison sentences of up to fifteen years. MI9 was particularly well-informed about the Free Corps' membership as Quartermaster-Sergeant John H.O. Brown of the Royal Artillery, who had been in contact with its personnel, had also been reporting to London. After his return to England in 1945 Brown was decorated with the Distinguished Conduct Medal, an award that caused some surprise among the British prisoners of war with whom he had shared the previous four years. They remembered him as having often expressed pro-German sympathies and had been regarded as more likely to face a court martial when he was back in England than be the recipient of a medal. The secret of Brown's true role was finally revealed at the Old Bailey trial of Walter Purdy, a renegade Briton who was convicted of broadcasting propaganda for the Nazis. Both he and Tom Cooper, a leading recruiter for the British Free Corps, were sentenced to death after Brown had given damning testimony for the prosecution.

Educated at Cambridge and a man of deep religious beliefs, Brown had attended a course of MI9 lectures to prepare him for the possibility of capture. He memorised a simple code to use in his correspondence home and was taught to indicate the existence of a secret message by writing the date in a particular way and by underlining his signature. Scrutiny of the letters upon their arrival in London by British censors enabled those with secret messages to be diverted to MI9, where they were decoded.

Brown had been captured in France at the end of May 1940 with a dozen survivors of his battery, a remnant of the British Expeditionary Force. His first camp was Lamsdorf but he volunteered for a work camp at Blechhammer in Upper Silesia, where he gathered information and conveyed it to MI9. Later, masquerading as a Nazi sympathiser, he switched to Berlin where he was approved for a special camp, Genshagen, which from June 1943 accommodated potential members of the British Free Corps. Brown was eventually liberated by American troops in April 1945 but was kept in custody as a suspected traitor until MI9 could confirm his credentials. Upon his release he was flown home for a lengthy debriefing by MI5's Len Burt.[1]

William Joyce, who broadcast on German radio, was convicted of treason and hanged at Wandsworth in January 1946, while his colleague, Norman Baillie-Stewart, escaped a death sentence by pleading guilty to a lesser charge and receiving a sentence of five years' imprisonment. Purdy and another BFC volunteer, Thomas Cooper, had their death sentences commuted to life terms.

MAY 1945
BRITISH RENEGADES

During the war the Security Service received information about the conduct of British subjects who were in Germany or in the occupied territories, and who had in one form or another taken service with the enemy. Some of these persons were notorious, such as William Joyce,[2] Norman Baillie-Stewart[3] and John Amery,[4] whose activities were reported in the Press, while others, although the subject of intelligence reports, were not, and indeed are not, well known to the public in this country.

It was necessary that the Allied forces should be warned in advance as to who the renegades were, otherwise there would be danger of the renegades being accepted as loyal British subjects and even being given employment, a situation which would have involved grave security risks.

Before D–Day therefore, Supreme Headquarters Allied Expeditionary
Forces were furnished with the names of those British subjects who were
known to have assisted the enemy, or who were suspected on good grounds
of so doing. The list of these names has become known as the Warning List
of Renegade British Subjects, and the names upon it have been circulated
by SHAEF to Army Groups. Similar information was given to Allied Force
Headquarters in Italy and to Consular posts who were likely to have to deal
with British subjects seeking to leave the Continent.

As a result of a discussion between the various authorities concerned,
SHAEF were requested to arrange, in the more serious cases, for the
detention of the persons concerned until enquiries could be made on the
Continent into their activities with a view to their being reported to the
Director of Public Prosecutions. In the less serious cases detention was
not asked for but advice was given against the employment of the person
concerned by any Allied Institution until the case had been investigated. In
December 1944, at the request of SHAEF, the Security Service sent over
to Paris a Liaison Section in order to advise on matters concerning British
renegades, and where necessary to make enquiries and collect evidence as
to their activities. This section now consists of four officers, two of whom
are experienced police officers from New Scotland Yard, who are attached
to the Security Service.

There are at present on the Warning List the names of 95 British subjects,
and of these 40 have so far been located, Reports have already been made
to the Director of Public Prosecutions regarding a number of those persons
located, and investigations as to the activities of the remainder are in progress.
Cases hitherto unknown to us have also to be examined.

The British subjects who took service with the enemy were employed
either as broadcasters, or writers of propaganda for broadcasting, or for use
in the Press.

The Germans did, however, seek to form a British unit to serve with the
German Army. This was first known as the 'Legion of St George' and later
as the 'British Free Corps'. Their efforts in this direction proved a failure as,
according to our information, the total number of recruits never amounted
to more than sixty. For the most part these recruits came from members
of the Services detained in prisoner-of-war camps though a few civilian
recruits were obtained. All were assured that they would only be used to fight
against Bolshevism. Each person who is known, or who may be discovered,
to have joined the British Free Corps is the subject of enquiries which are
now proceeding. Many of those so far interviewed state that they joined the

Corps in order to sabotage its activities, or with a view to escaping from the enemy. Each case is being studied and when the enquiries are complete a report will be submitted to the proper authorities.

The collection of evidence in all these cases will take time, involving as it does the examination of broadcasting times and the archives of German broadcasting establishments, the search for documents concerning the British Free Corps and the general organisation of the German effort to relieve British subjects from their allegiance. Progress has already been made and with the cessation of hostilities the task will become easier.

The nature of the charge to be preferred against a renegade is a matter for decision by the legal authorities in each case. It is understood that in the more serious cases a charge of either treason or treachery will be preferred, while in other cases Defence Regulations will be invoked.

The Security Service officers are working in close and constant touch with the Director of Public Prosecutions.

11th June 1945

★ ★ ★

By the end of the inquiries conducted by SLB3 every allegation of collaboration with the enemy had been investigated and almost all were resolved, the exception being an SOE officer, Ronald Seth, whose behaviour after his capture while on a sabotage mission in Estonia on Operation BLUNDERHEAD in 1942 led to accusations that he had acted as a stool pigeon in a PoW camp, and had allowed himself to be recruited by the Sicherheitsdienst. Despite many interrogations and much conflicting evidence, no charges were ever brought against Seth who successfully lobbied the government for his back-pay. He later gave a version of his adventures in his autobiography, *A Spy Has No Friends*.[5]

27

HARLEQUIN

During the period of MI5 reporting to the Prime Minister, two special reports were compiled at his request, the first on the defector Richard Wurmann, the second on GARBO. The first MI5 dossier on a specific case, generated at Churchill's request, concerned HARLEQUIN, the Abwehr prisoner captured in North Africa who had become a walking encyclopædia on the German Intelligence apparatus.

THE HARLEQUIN CASE
HARLEQUIN is a German officer who was captured by British troops in North Africa in November, 1942, when endeavouring to make his escape onto Tunisia. Whilst purporting to be a member of the German Armistice Commission, HARLEQUIN was in fact the Leiter of the Abwehrstelle at Algiers and was known to us as such.

Technically an American prisoner, be was brought to the UK where he was turned round to a point where, convinced of the inevitability of a German defeat, he placed in our hands a written offer of his services, subject only to the reservation that he should not be compelled to take up arms against the German forces. He has supplied a wealth of intelligence, much of which is subject to check, though this fact is unknown to him. He has also been used in a consultative capacity and has contributed helpful and informative comments on cases submitted to him.

HISTORY
HARLEQIN was commissioned in the German Army in April 1914, and served with distinction in the war 1914–1918, being wounded on five

occasions and being twice decorated, once with the Hohenzollern EK 1,[1] and once with the Verdienstkreuz for bravery in the field. On leaving the Army he became a chartered accountant, and in 1933 became a member of the Nazi Party when the Stahlhelm, of which he was a member, was incorporated in the Party. In 1937 he was recalled to the Reserve and the following year was transferred to the Abwehr. From the outbreak of war until May of 1940 he was stationed at Cologne, and during the Battle of France was engaged upon the interrogation of British Prisoners of War. After Dunkirk he was sent to Biarritz to organise an Abwehrstelle and remained there until November of 1941. During this period his principal duty appears to have been the surreptitious slipping of German Secret Service agents and personnel across the Franco–Spanish frontier, with the assistance and collaboration of the Spanish authorities. In December 1941 he was transferred to Berlin, where he worked until March 1942. From Berlin he went to Paris and remained there for two months, after which he was transferred to Algiers as Head of the local Abwehrstelle.

REASONS FOR CO-OPERATION

HARLEQUIN is a doubly disappointed and disillusioned man. His early hopes and expectations of a military career culminating in his becoming a general staff officer were shattered by the defeat of German arms in 1918. Like many others of the Prussian officer class, to which he belongs, he disapproved of much that the Nazi regime represents, but he saw in its rise to power the agency through which Germany could shake off the shackles of Versailles and achieve her aggressive ambitions. It was on this basis that he was prepared to, and did, support the new Party. With the failure of the German summer offensive on the Eastern front in 1942 to achieve decisive victory, he realised that the war was lost. Lacking the moral courage to face internment and the bitterness of defeat for the second time he found it consistent with his none-too-rigid conscience to convince himself that it was in the interests of humanity in general, and the German people in particular, that the termination of the war should be accelerated, and, aided by our inducements, decided to do what he could to assist this end. So far he has played well by us and it is anticipated that provided we hold to our side of the bargain he will continue to do so. Moreover, the letter which he has written and which is referred to above puts him completely in our power; and he is fully aware of that fact.

It would not be possible to do more in this note than to indicate topics upon which HARLEQUIN has provided intelligence, and to set out by way of illustration some of the more interesting items which he has recounted. He has supplied important information upon the following subjects inter alia:

Organisation and Personnel of the Abwehr
Abwehr Agents employed by, or otherwise known to HARLEQUIN
Abwehr System of Recruiting, Training and Running Agents
Abwehr Terminology
Pre-War Activities of the Abwehr vis a vis the UK
Relations between the Abwehr (High Command Intelligence Service, Controlled by Canaris) and the Sicherheitsdienst (Party Intelligence Service Controlled by Himmler and including the Gestapo)

The following are examples of detailed intelligence supplied by HARLEQUIN:-

FAILURE OF THE GERMAN SUMMER OFFENSIVE ON THE EASTERN FRONT, 1942

In April of 1942 at the Hotel des Ambassadeurs, Paris, a conference of all Abwehr officers in France was addressed by a general, the chief of foreign Armies Section of the German Intelligence. The lecturer gave a very lucid and convincing account of the situation on all the fronts, and came to the following conclusion – 'The great offensive which Germany is going to start against Russia in the summer must lead to the decisive annihilation of the Russian Army. If this result is not achieved then, in view of the growing discrepancy between German and Allied arms production, the war must be considered as lost.' HARLEQUIN states that when the German summer offensive failed to bring about the annihilation of the Russian armies, every single officer of the Abwehr was convinced, as was HARLEQUIN, that Germany had lost the war.

SECURITY OF BRITISH ARMY W/T SIGNALS

The UK is badly covered by the Abwehr and according to HARLEQUIN the best information from and about the UK is obtained from wireless monitoring service, which apparently intercepts and deciphers Army signals W/T traffic. HARLEQUIN has seen the periodical results of this traffic and states that it upset him considerably by showing him how useless was the Abwehr Intelligence product when compared with that of this splendid intercept service, as a result of which, he alleges, everything is known about the distribution and battle order of the troops in England, their numbers and etc. He saw similar results compiled from intercept signals in the Western desert.

BRITISH EMBASSY IN MADRID

Admiral Canaris has a number of very special and trusted agents who work direct to him. Amongst them is Prince Maximillan von Hohenlohe, who was Lord Runciman's host during the Czechoslovakian negotiations prior to Munich. This man is used for matters necessitating penetration into high diplomatic or social circles abroad. In February, 1941, Hohenlohe, on the instructions of Canaris himself, took steps to have the Prince's villa at Biarritz derequisitioned in order that the Prince might take up his residence there. The Prince later confided to HARLEQUIN that he had gone to Madrid to see Sir Samuel Hoare, who had asked him if he would be prepared to act as intermediary between the British and German Governments for certain proposals which might be forwarded. Whether Prince von Hohenlohe went to Madrid by invitation or at Canaris's instigation HARLEQUIN does not know, but he is certain that Canaris knew in advance of the proposed meeting. Hohenlohe agreed to Sir Samuel Hoare's request and Sir Samuel saw him off at the station and told him 'You will be hearing from me sometime in April, 1941, and I want to have your promise that, no matter where you are, as soon as you receive a telegram from me you will come to Madrid at once.'

To this proposition he assented but heard nothing more from Sir Samuel Hoare, and the Germans thought that this was because the British Government had advance knowledge of the impending attack upon Russia.

PASSING OF AGENTS OVER FRANCO–SPANISH FRONTIER

HARLEQUIN arranged with the Spanish Consul at Bayonne for facilities for helping agents across the frontier. These facilities were on a basis of reciprocation, i.e. HARLEQUIN agreed to persons being passed into occupied France at the request of the Consul in exchange for facilities granted by the latter for the entry of German agents into Spain. In addition, the Spanish frontier Control had orders from above to pass well-known German personalities – HARLEQUIN himself would come into this category – without question and also anyone accompanying them and their servants. Thus the Germans were able to pass in the guise of a chauffeur or servant any agent to whom they did not wish attention to be directed.

BEDAUX

HARLEQUIN had strong reason for suspecting that this notorious American citizen had links with the Abwehr, although he was definitely not working as an agent of HARLEQUIN himself. Well knowing HARLEQUIN to be an Abwehr officer, Bedaux had deliberately supplied him with information picked up in the household of Mr Murphy, the American Consul General. Further, when he had failed to enlist the support of the French General Juin in connection with a commercial enterprise in which he was interested. Bedaux got the German Armistice Commission to communicate with Wiesbaden in order that pressure should be put upon Vichy to compel Juin to give him the assistance which he required. In November of 1942 Bedaux was receiving preferential treatment in North Africa from both the Vichy authorities and the Germans. In a conversation with HARLEQUIN, Bedaux stated that he knew Admiral Canaris, and displayed an acquaintanceship with other German notabilities including the Leiter of the Paris Abwehrstelle.

He claimed to HARLEQUIN that he had been granted German nationality and the rank of Sonderfuehrer (B), the equivalent of Major, in the German Wehrmacht. HARLEQUIN does not reject the possibility that Bedaux may be one of Admiral Canaris's special agents.

★ ★ ★

The French businessman Charles Bedaux was controversial before the war because of his apparent sympathy for the Nazi cause, and of course for his friendship with the Duke and Duchess of Windsor, to whom he had lent his house, the Château de Candé, for their wedding in June 1937. He had also arranged their honeymoon in Germany and their meeting with Adolf Hitler. Although he was arrested in Algeria by the US Army in January 1943, little was known about the extent of his collaboration until the Abwehr prisoner Richard Wurmann, code-named HARLEQUIN, supplied a detailed, first-hand account, which resulted in an MI5 report prepared in May 1944 in anticipation of the interrogation of Hans Scharf,[2] who had actually participated in what had become known as the Bedaux mission:

The history of Charles Bedaux from the time of the collapse of France is one of out and out collaboration. As early as 1937 he is known to have stated that he believed in the social superiority of the Nazi system over that of the Democracies. His attitude in 1940, when he supported the reorganisation of France on Axis lines, is therefore hardly surprising. He associated with all the leading members of the Vichy Government, and is also alleged to have been in contact with Otto Abetz, the German ambassador in Paris. He was afforded full facilities for travel between the occupied and free zones of France and priority passages in aircraft. He was further in charge of the organisation building the Trans-Saharan railway, and visited North Africa every two or three months.

In the autumn of 1941 it is known from ISOS that Bedaux visited high Abwehr officials in Berlin. This visit was carried out at the request of the German embassy in Paris, and apparently with the full knowledge and backing of Oberst Rudolf, Leiter Ast Paris. The precise purpose of this journey is not clear from the ISOS traces, but according to Bedaux's own statement it was to discuss the preservation of oil refineries in the Persian Gulf. A certain Dr Bensmann of Nest Bremen also travelled to Berlin to partake in these conferences, and Bedaux was introduced at the same time to a Professor Endrou of Berlin.

A short while after these meetings took place, ISOS shows that Bensmann journeyed to Paris to discuss the 'Caudron affair'. This is presumably a reference to the manager of the French Bedaux Co. who has also been mentioned by Scharf.[3]

Between this time and September 1942 Bedaux busied himself with a scheme to build a pipe line from the Niger river, in Central Africa, to Colomb Bechar in northern Africa, This pipeline was to be used to bring water through the desert, thus assisting in the construction of the Trans-Saharan pipeline, and it was also to carry peanut oil from the Mossi country for shipment to Marseilles where it would be refined into edible products.

Bedaux stated that he sold the idea of the pipe line to the French authorities on the theory that it would unite French Colonial Africa and avoid dissidence on the part of the African peoples. This was not without considerable effort and took some time to ratify. The acquiring of German approval was, however, considerably more difficult, though it was eventually secured. To obtain the necessary support for his mission Bedaux enlisted the help of many highly placed French and German officials, amongst them Pierre Laval and the Militarbefehlshaber Stulpnagel. In spite of this considerable influence in governing circles, Bedaux was arrested on 24 September 1942 together with all other male American citizens between the ages of 16 and 65, and interned at Compiègne. He secured an early release, however, and succeeded in completing his plans and setting out for Algiers on 27 October 1942.

At this stage there is a further relevant trace in MSS and a detailed account of his activities has been given by HARLEQUIN, who was at that time attached as an Abwehr officer to the Verbindungkommando, a detachment of the German armistice commission in North Africa.

ISOS shows that on 7 November 1942 Oberst Rudolf was informed of the various difficulties Bedaux was encountering with the French military authorities, who were proposing to supply him with less powerful wireless sets than those which it had been agreed he should have. Scharf is referred to in this message by his @ d'Huillier, and it is evident that he was to have been one of the W/T operators attached to the mission.

In support of this, HARLEQUIN states that at the beginning of November 1942 Scharf presented himself at the headquarters of the Verbidungskommando with a certificate from the Vichy Government bearing the stamp of the German military commander in Paris, which informed all French authorities in North Africa that they were to give all possible help and protection to Bedaux in his undertaking. Bedaux explained that this undertaking consisted of investigating and developing the possibilities of extracting vegetable oils from plants growing in those parts of French Africa which still belonged to the Vichy Government, and also the transport of these oils to the coast of French North Africa with, as far as possible, the aid of the Trans-Saharan railway, which was still under construction, The expedition consisted of a dozen or half a dozen people, some of whom had already arrived in Algeria and the rest (presumably including Scharf), were still expected.

These persons were to be left behind at different points along the route taken by the expedition, from where they would separately take up their work of investigation. They were to have wireless communication with each other and with a coastal station, eventually Algiers. (It is here, presumably, that Scharf was to figure and the inference appears to be that the Abwehr regarded Bedaux's undertaking as affording ample opportunity for the establishment of a reporting service, in an area which was of particular interest at the time and which in ordinary circumstances it would be difficult to penetrate).

Bedaux apparently told HARLEQUIN that the Abwehr was interested in his organisation, and mentioned that he knew Admiral Canaris and Oberst Rudolf, and claimed for himself the membership of the German Wehrmacht as a Sonderführer.

HARLEQUIN declared that he was sceptical of all this and states that he was far from convinced that Bedaux was seriously considering placing his expedition in the service of the Abwehr. He is inclined to believe that if

Bedaux did do so, it was only either to get himself out of internment, or to gain the support of the German military commander in bringing pressure to bear on the French authorities to make them assist him in the matter of lorries and motor fuel for the expedition. HARLEQUIN's arguments are based on the following facts:

Bedaux arrived in Algeria without wireless sets. These would have been essential for the use of the expedition by the Abwehr. Furthermore if the objective, from an Abwehr point of view, was the obtaining of information from the frontier areas occupied by de Gaulle or the Allies, any sets which were to be used would have had to be of considerable strength. These, however, would have aroused the suspicions of the Deuxieme Bureau officials working at entry and customs control points, who were on good terms with the de Gaullists. Bedaux appeared to have no idea how to obtain sets which would have been suitable for Abwehr work or how to get them through the customs. The Oberkommando was openly mistrustful and would only supply him with French military sets of short range and with incompetent operators. HARLEQUIN therefore, on his own initiative, tried to have suitable sets despatched by courier plane and also sent a similar suggestion by wireless to Ast Paris. He received no reply to any of these requests however and therefore remained forever in doubt as to the authenticity of Bedaux.

Bedaux with his exceptional intelligence and experience should have foreseen these difficulties and, considering the seriousness of his project, should have endeavoured to dispose of them before landing. This could easily have been done with the help of the Abwehrstellen in Algiers, Oran or Casablanca. These Stellen could have supplied suitable W/T sets, with the necessary camouflage, and also could have acted as relay stations for the further transmission of messages.

HARLEQUN's final impression was, therefore, that Bedaux succeeded in interesting the Abwehr in his scheme, whilst cleverly avoiding any close ties, and that he never proposed placing the expedition in the service of the Abwehr or acting himself as a German agent. Furthermore, none of the other members of the mission in Algiers knew anything about his relations with the Abwehr, though more staff, amongst them Abwehr agents, were supposed to be arriving later.

This memorandum, drafted by MI5's Jean Leslie, was intended as a summary for Scharf's interrogator so the gaps in the chronology could be filled in. However, although Scharf proved entirely cooperative, Bedaux took a drug overdose while in the FBI's custody in Miami and died in February 1944.

28

GARBO

MI5 prepared a report for the Prime Minister on the GARBO double-agent case, arguably the most important and successful of its kind ever, and the original draft was cut by some unknown hand, perhaps Anthony Blunt, so a slightly abbreviated version could be presented in late 1944. The two excisions are marked [ ].

[If confidence is 'a plant of slow growth in an aged bosom', its development in the suspicious minds of the German Secret Service is even slower and more hazardous. Usually in the early days of double-agents we were compelled to tend and nurture this delicate plant: we allay the suspicions of the Germans with apparently candid and forthright messages; we assuage their appetite with true and easily verifiable information; only gradually and at length do we sometimes create in them a robust faith in their agent. The case of GARBO among all double-agent cases, is unique in that he himself, rejected by our officials abroad and playing a lone hand, imposed himself upon the Germans and himself successfully performed the difficult operation of creating and establishing his own trusty and trusted espionage agency. He came therefore to us a fully-fledged double-agent, with all his growing pains over – we had only to operate and develop the system which he had already built up.]

GARBO is a Catalan industrialist, equally hostile to Communism and Fascism. During the civil war he was compelled to hide, remaining inured in one house for a period of two years. When the World War started it occurred to his inventive mind that he might obtain employment as a British agent in either Germany or Italy. His offer was rejected in January 1941 and he therefore conceived the bolder project of offering himself to the

Germans with a view to double-crossing them. Once recruited by them, his value to the British, so he argued, would be sensibly increased. The event was ultimately to justify his expectations. He was well received, by the Germans in the Embassy in Madrid, and after characteristically lengthy and involved negotiations, he persuaded them that he could contrive to be sent by the Spaniards on a mission to England. To this end he forged a Spanish diplomatic document and departed from Madrid in July, 1941, with a questionnaire, secret ink, money, cover addresses and the German blessing, notionally en route for England.

But for nine months he did not go to England at all. Instead he remained in Lisbon, whence he edited long and colourful letters to his German friends, supposedly written in England, conveyed by courier to Portugal for posting and containing his espionage reports on the British Isles. He worked with indifferent tools; a Blue Guide, a map of England, an out-of-date railway time-table formed his stock-in-trade, supplemented by the meagre gleanings of Portuguese bookstalls. But fiction, when governed as in this case by a vivid and correct imagination, is more easily credible than truth, and it was not long before the Germans came to trust his reports and to appreciate them highly. Moreover, GARBO played his cards with masterly skill, when his railway time-table told him that some line was important, owing to the amount of traffic passing along it, he would defend that line with newly erected wire and pill-boxes, cunningly camouflaged; when the Germans asked him to find out if armoured units had been observed moving south in Herts and Beds, he did not forget a little later to report just such units passing southward through Guildford. To assist him he created three sub-agents, who reported to him from the West Country, from Glasgow and from Liverpool. Since he always reported what the Germans expected to hear, and since much of his information was startlingly near to the truth, he was more and more readily believed.

None the less, GARBO's existence was precarious in the extreme. He had so little knowledge of English ways and English habits that he remained permanently poised on the edge of a precipice, over which some blunder or other must, as it seemed, soon impel him. He could, for example, not convert pence into shillings or shillings into pounds, and so the early expense accounts of his sub-agents present a problem to students of the curious; again, he knew almost no English names, and so his post-box in Lisbon carried the all-British legend 'Mr. Smith-Jones'. But such trifling difficulties as these did not unduly alarm him. Once his correspondence was in full swing he made further attempts to offer his services to the British authorities only to experience again the cold rebuffs of officialdom. But his wife did succeed, in December 1941 in getting into touch with an American Assistant Attaché, and in February 1942 some account of GARBO's activities percolated to this country.[1] At about the same time secret sources revealed that the Germans were making elaborate preparations to intercept a large convoy which was supposed to have left Liverpool for Malta. We later established the fact that GARBO was the sole inventor and begetter of this convoy and thus responsible for a vast expenditure of useless labour on the part of the enemy.

It became clear to us at this stage that GARBO was more fitted to be a worthy collaborator than an unconscious competitor. In April 1942, therefore, he was smuggled across to England and continued from this country the work which he had notionally already performed from here since July of the preceding year. [His wife followed him in June, and indeed it was necessary that she should, for she was about to become the mother of a second child. Had she met any of her German patrons almost a year after her husband was supposed to have left for England, they would hardly have retained their confidence in both GARBO and his wife.]

Since GARBO's arrival in England the case has developed enormously and he now has an active and well-distributed team of imaginary assistants, some of whom write direct to the Germans, though all receive the answers, orders and questionnaires through the head of the organisation. Among the three original sub-agents there has been one casualty. When Operation TORCH was pending it seemed that Agent No 2, who lived in Liverpool and from whom GARBO had received notice of his Malta convoy, was in a position to see more than was desirable. Accordingly he became afflicted with a lingering malady and ceased to send in his reports.[2] Much perturbed, GARBO hurried north and from there informed the Germans that the poor man had died. An obituary notice inserted by us in the *Liverpool Daily Post* was duly conveyed to the Germans, who expressed their profound sympathy with the widow. The other two sub-agents of this original creation remain, and to these four more have been added – a Gibraltarian waiter; a brother of Agent No. 3 who is now to go to Canada; an FSP who was sent to North Africa and has written from there some ten letters to GARBO for transmission to the enemy; and a seaman whose main use has been to arrange notionally for such documents and espionage material to be conveyed to Lisbon as have in fact travelled in the SIS bag.

[Unfortunately the officer who acted as scribe for the FSP has been killed in a flying accident and, as it is a practical impossibility to forge secret writing, it appears that this sub-agent must needs come to an untimely and lamented end.

The time of Agent No. 4 is chiefly occupied with a plan based on the creation of a very large underground depot for small arms and a complete system of underground communications. These are supposed to extend from the Chislehurst Caves and to connect through the London Underground Railway system to the main railway lines and the centres of our war industry. From the movements within the depot the agent will in due course deduce an imminent operation; the Germans will be invited to sabotage the communications, and it is hoped that they will believe themselves to have been responsible for its collapse. Alternatively they could be persuaded, by news of the depot, to regard a cover plan on the south-east coast as a real operation.]

The communications between GARBO's spy ring and the Germans have been established in various ways. The imaginary airman-courier of the early days still continues, but more and more GARBO tends to send his letters with their secret ink writing by air mail. In addition he has, since March of this year, been operating a wireless set for more urgent messages. The purchase of this set was arranged through Agent No. 4, who also recruited an amateur operator who is featured as a Communist and is supposed to be working for people whom he believes to be Spanish Reds. He is in fact, needless to say, one of our own operators.[3] The purchase of the set gave GARBO the excuse to demand a safe cipher since the messages must be handed to the operator already enciphered. The Germans showed their trust by sending over the identical cipher then in use between certain German Secret Service stations. Later these services changed over to a superior cipher, reputed to be unbreakable, and the Germans have now decided to entrust GARBO with a cipher based on the one newly introduced. This is not only remarkable evidence of confidence, but may also, quite possibly, provide a means of breaking the unbreakable.

The finance of the case has also presented some novel and interesting features. It is always difficult for the enemy to pay their agents, since the transfer of large sums of money may well direct attention to the recipient. GARBO himself is, in Teutonic eyes, a high-souled idealist who works for motives of political conviction, but none the less he and his family must live and his subagents must be paid. Fortunately we have made contact with some Spanish fruit merchants who desire to get rid of sterling in return for pesetas in Madrid. The consequent transaction has worked to admiration. We receive sterling in London, the Spaniards receive pesetas paid into their account in Madrid, the Germans pay the pesetas and everyone is happy. So far we have received for GARBO about £8,000 from the Germans, the major portion in the manner described.

The GARBO spy system may therefore be said to be working smoothly and efficiently. He has certain useful though notional contacts, especially a friend in the Ministry of Information, his sub-agents provide him and the Germans lavishly with reports, he himself can pass information by letter, courier or wireless. Some estimate of the volume of the work entailed can be made by considering that he and his assistants have already written upwards of 250 secret ink letters and received 53 letters with questionnaires. Over and above this, he has since March been communicating by wireless. Apart from the work done by those of our officers who forge the letters of the sub-agents and from the work of the case officer, who spends his entire time in controlling, organising and developing the case, living GARBO's life and thinking GARBO's thoughts, GARBO himself works on an average from six to eight hours a day drafting secret letters, enciphering, composing cover texts, writing them and planning for the future. Fortunately he has a facile and lurid style, great ingenuity and a passionate and quixotic zeal for his task. This last quality has indeed caused an outburst of jealousy on the part of his wife, who, considering herself neglected, was with difficulty persuaded not to ruin the whole undertaking by a public disclosure.

Such in brief outline is the GARBO case. It will be noticed that he has already fulfilled many or most of the functions which we expect our double-agents to perform. The size of his organisation and the volume of the traffic prevent the Germans from seeking to establish other agents (whom we might not control); the system used for his wireless messages should assist materially in the breaking of German ciphers; through him we are enabled to send such credible misinformation as we wish to the other side, and we have ample evidence from secret sources that our messages are eagerly awaited and implicitly believed. We conceal what we would have concealed, we expose what we would have the Germans known from the questionnaires, we gain valuable Intelligence information of enemy intentions; finally we are in a position to give verisimilitude to deception and cover plans – and this, as we pass more and more to the offensive, puts a weapon of the highest value into our hands. In fact GARBO could, if mistakes are not made, and if his credit is not recklessly expended, hold almost unlimited potentialities for good, especially in the sphere of deception. There seems no reason why his undertakings should not only continue but be developed to an even higher pitch of beneficent activity.

Although the GARBO story is now well documented and established, there are two aspects to it that have been overlooked hitherto. Firstly, there is the death in an air accident of the FSP officer who had been assigned the task of writing in secret ink from North Africa, an unanticipated setback that highlighted the impossibility of replacing a source whose handwriting had become very familiar to the enemy. Secondly the incentive to bring GARBO's wife, Aracelli, over to London was her pregnancy. She could hardly remain in Portugal, with the very real risk of encountering an Abwehr officer, and claim not to have seen her husband for the best part of a year. However reluctant MI5 might have been to sponsor her travel, such an expedient was absolutely required if the deception was to be continued.

The GARBO story may have been 'well documented', but Churchill was never told the agent's true identity, and was not even informed of his existence until June 1943, more than a year after his arrival in England in April 1942. While GARBO himself only understood his role as a double-agent, and as a conduit of misinformation in a deception campaign, the Prime Minister was indoctrinated into his significance as a cryptographic 'crib' into enemy cipher systems. Some of GARBO's traffic was repeated on the Abwehr's Madrid–Berlin Enigma circuit. And he had been entrusted with the very latest hand cipher, which the Radio Security Service had previously assessed as extremely challenging.

GARBO's status as MI5's star double-agent was not immediately obvious when he was first mentioned in the Third Report in June 1943 (Chapter 3), and then again in the fourth (Chapter 4) but as the case developed he made more appearances in Chapters 7, 10, 15, 16, 17 and 23. In October 1943 GARBO was the chosen instrument in a campaign designed to force the enemy to find new cover addresses in Lisbon, having been presented with evidence that a dozen had been compromised by tighter controls imposed by the British postal censorship authorities. This particular scheme was intended to harass the local Abwehr station and served to close down almost all the enemy's postal routes until December 1944.

Coincidentally, a Portuguese man, José Dias de Silva, turned up at the Lisbon embassy and explained to SIS that his home in the rua Antonio Pereira Carrilho was being used by the Abwehr as a cover address. He stated that he had been recruited by a friend, Antonio de Souza Lopez, who had also persuaded his girlfriend, Maria Estrella, to receive letters from England. Both the other addresses, rua Castillo 31 and rua José Falcao 22/1, were already well known to MI5, which concluded that all three addresses were compromised, and that news of de Silva's disclosures would certainly reach the Germans. However, the consolation was that GARBO's letters were virtually untraceable, in that they bore fictitious return addresses and were written on the purloined stationery of various London hotels. Thus the Germans could be confident that any British investigation of the letters would fail to expose the spymaster known to them as ALARIC, so MI5 took the opportunity to make very public enquiries at all GARBO's addresses, including a visit in October 1943 to Odette da Conceição at her home at rua Teofilo Braga 59. She was already known as the principal contact for GARBO's courier, but when interviewed she flatly denied her role as a 'cut-out'. Nevertheless her reaction was monitored on an ISOS decrypt, which prompted a substantial reaction from the Abwehr.

Nearly all Lisbon addresses have been interrogated with regard to the origin of letters. This appears to be a general measure all over the country. In accordance with instructions addresses have replied satisfactorily. Nevertheless no more letters have arrived. Our representative has left for Lisbon.

An inspection was conducted by an Abwehr officer dispatched from Berlin to review the collapse, and he recommended two significant changes that were introduced immediately. One was the permanent termination of all air mail correspondence with England, which meant total reliance on radio and couriers, and the second was the replacement of secret writing with micro-photography. In total, twenty-three Abwehr cover addresses in Lisbon were closed down, representing a major setback for the enemy.

In the New Year of 1944 MI5 reported that GARBO had been advised to seek accommodation outside the capital, in anticipation of the CROSSBOW secret weapon offensive.

In May 1944 (Chapter 15) GARBO was mentioned as having been assigned the task of identifying the Allied invasion headquarters, and in June referred to his recent German decoration as a reward for his information, and to his role in SHAEF's deception campaign that had succeeded in preventing reinforcements from being sent to Normandy. The next month, Chapter 17, there was much to say about GARBO. Firstly, ISOS intercepts addressed to Madrid showed that Field Marshal Gerd von Rundstaedt and Heinrich Himmler separately had expressed their warm approval of his reporting and, strategically more importantly, an acceptance of the concept of a further invasion in the Pas-de-Calais. Although GARBO himself was unaware of these accolades, he fully understood the problem presented by the Abwehr's demand that he should report on damage inflicted by the V-1 flying bomb offensive. To avoid this task MI5 choreographed an elaborate charade in which it was alleged that GARBO had been arrested by the London police for showing too much interest in V-1 bomb-sites, thereby creating an entirely artificial crisis that required his organisation to suspend operations at a particularly vital moment. This expedient had two objectives: one was to persuade Aracelli that her husband really was at risk of detention, and the other was to suggest to the Abwehr that GARBO's (entirely notional) deputy Pedro, based in Glasgow, could fulfil his duties during his temporary absence. ISOS revealed that the Germans were alarmed by this unwelcome development and withdrew the request for what was regarded in London as rather too sensitive CROSSBOW data that really could assist the enemy.

The main storyline of the GARBO drama contained many sub-plots, some of them unplanned, and one such was the loss in an air accident of Pilot Officer Martin Grimaldi, the FSP officer attached to MI5's B1(b) who had masqueraded as SIX, a South African posted to Algiers as a linguist soon after the TORCH landings, who was virulently anti-Communist. Known as Dick, his distinctive handwriting had become familiar to his German controller in Madrid, so when he was killed on 3 July in an air accident flying from Tiree to RAF Machrihanish at the end of his week's leave in June, a similar excuse was found for his alleged demise in North Africa.

The youngest of four brothers, sons of a vicar in east Devon who all joined the RAF, Martin Grimaldi had transferred to MI5 on the recommendation of a family friend, Charles Cholmondeley, a B Division officer. He had spent his leave with his eldest brother, Dr C.E. Grimaldi, who was serving as a medical officer on Tiree.

On 4 July Guy Liddell confided to his diary that:

T.A. Robertson tells me that young Grimaldi has been killed in an air accident. He was visiting his brother in the Outer Hebrides and the plane on which he returned has not been heard of. This is a real tragedy for us since, apart from being a nice little chap, he was doing very valuable work in B1(b).

Grimaldi had been a passenger on a Fokker XXII aircraft that experienced an engine fire and crashed into the sea, killing the crew of five and all twenty passengers.

SIX's first letter containing secret writing, supposedly posted in Algiers, had been relayed to Lisbon in January 1943 and had been well received, even though the content had taken six weeks to reach its destination. This very convenient time lapse, of course, had been exploited by MI5 to make it appear that at the time of its composition the letter had included some high-level, accurate information. Supposedly ten such letters had been mailed to GARBO's bank in London, who had deleted various incriminating items, such as the signature, addressee and the name of the Field Censorship official who had approved the innocuous content. Then GARBO had inserted the letter in the binding of a book, which had been passed to a seaman courier for posting in Lisbon to an Abwehr cover address in Madrid. In reality, the letter had been fabricated in London and then delivered in the SIS bag to Portugal, where the package was placed in the mail on a date that coincided with the arrival of a ship from England, thereby supporting the false narrative.

In July 1943 GARBO reported that SIX's mistress, Dorothy, had informed him that her lover had been killed in an air crash while travelling to his new posting. All his kit had also been destroyed, thus eliminating the risk that his supply of secret ink might have been discovered amongst his belongings and raised suspicions. Accordingly, both MI5 and the Abwehr closed their files on 'Dick'.

As GARBO grew in stature, the risks attached to him escalated, as became evident when ARTIST opened negotiations with SIS and hinted that he could make his defection more attractive by compromising the Abwehr's best agent in England. Fortunately, on that occasion the crisis dissipated when, in April 1944, ARTIST had been abducted by the Gestapo and thrown into a concentration camp accused of embezzlement, his captors apparently unaware of his contacts with the British.

A not dissimilar development occurred at the end of July 1944 when a very senior Abwehr officer, the Graf Josef von Ledebur, approached SIS in Madrid to negotiate his defection and was accommodated in an embassy safe house. Once again, his offered 'meal-ticket' was information about the Abwehr's agents in London, mentioning specifically a Yugoslav who communicated to Karl Kuhlenthal by wireless. To complicate the matter, Ledebur was connected to Dr Otto John, a Lufthansa lawyer who had been implicated in the failed 20 July plot and had escaped to Lisbon, where he was in touch with SIS. Study of ISOS revealed that Berlin was particularly excited about the prospect of Ledebur's treason and had suggested his credibility somehow be undermined by pretending he was in possession of false information.

Aged 44, Ledebur was the third son of a wealthy landowner whose American wife, Gladys Olcott, divorced him in Vienna in 1943. His own engineering business had prospered and in 1929 he had been introduced by his younger brother, Frederick, to Charles Bedaux in Palm Springs, California. In August 1936, as a veteran of the first conflict, Ledebur was called up by the 11th Cavalry and was posted to Stockerau, near Vienna. In 1939, when his bicycle platoon was attached to the 45th Infantry Division, he participated in the Polish campaign. In 1940 his unit was then transferred to France and, based at Saint-Quentin, he took a few days' leave in September at the Ritz Hotel in Paris, where he encountered Bedaux. He saw him again later in the year, but returned to his regiment, which was transferred to the Russian front, and he was wounded there in March 1942. When he had recovered from dysentery and an injured hand he was ordered to Paris, where Bedaux had arranged for his appointment as a liaison officer. Accordingly, he was installed as Bedaux's ADC on the authority of Erich Pfeiffer and acted as a link between the Abwehr and a senior Bedaux executive, Alexandra Ter Hart, who was a Dutch Jew who had moved to France. Ledebur did not formally join the Abwehr until December 1942, a month after Bedaux's departure for Algiers, and at that point he moved into the Royal Monceau Hotel in Paris and worked at the Abwehr's headquarters in the Lutetia.

Ledebur cultivated several of his Paris contacts as potential sources of information and gained a reputation for being able negotiate the release of internees. In March 1943 Pfeiffer sent him on a mission to Madrid to assist his agent Bastide penetrate de Gaulle's organisation in Spain. When he returned to Paris later in the month he had accomplished little but found that the Abwehr had taken possession of the Bedaux commercial empire. By July Ledebur was in Berlin, on a new assignment to assist Colonel Hansen, who demanded a report on corruption within the Paris Abstelle. He also travelled to Madrid for the second time, to stay with Max von Hohenlohe in Zarauz, who confided that he had been in touch with OSS's Allen Dulles in Switzerland. Upon his return, via the south of France, he found a new posting in September to the Abwehr headquarters in Berlin, where he was employed as Hansen's aide and sent for ten days to the OKW to learn its intelligence requirements.

His initial interviews with the British were arranged through an Italian intermediary, Count Mario Pinci, a Bank of Indo-China director who was identified by Ledebur as one of his sources, together with a French mining engineer, Pierre Bastide. In them Ledebur claimed to have proved his anti-Nazi credentials by assisting the escape from France of an SOE agent, the lawyer Michel Brault, who confirmed his story. The very first contact, made by mutual acquaintances in Madrid in June, was with MI9's Michael Cresswell, who received a short verbal report on the Wehrmacht and deteriorating conditions in Germany and agreed to a further discreet meeting when Ledebur returned to Spain.

Ledebur was encouraged to defect by the news, conveyed personally by Dr John, that he and Hansen had been deeply involved in the plot to assassinate Hitler. Indeed, Hansen had actually handed the explosives to

Count Klaus von Stauffenberg, having removed them from the Abwehr's own stores. Apparently unaware of Hansen's complicity, and his subsequent execution, Ledebur realised that he could not return, as ordered, to Berlin. Upon his arrival in Madrid on 27 July he had reported to the KO, where he had been handed a personal message requiring him to fly back immediately. In the circumstances, Ledebur opted to switch sides.

The sheer drama of Ledebur's dilemma is plain. He had been incriminated in a scheme that had gone terribly wrong, and suspects were being recalled. Some, like John, had fled the country, and in his case he had established a link with the British in Lisbon. Quite obviously, for Ledebur to obey orders would mean certain death, even though he had not been one of the plotters, yet he appeared hesitant about defection, even if his funds and choices were limited. However, Ledebur's proposal alarmed GARBO's case officer, Tommy Harris, who sent a minute to Tommy Robertson on 7 August:

> The Germans in Madrid have expressed concern to Berlin on discovering that Ledebur is contemplating going over to the British in case he is in the possession of information which might lead to the British discovering the network of the Special Agent, GARBO. In the event that this risk is non-existent they propose that they should pass mis-information to the British through him with the collaboration of a confidant of Ledebur who continues to remain loyal to the Germans. This presupposes that Ledebur is to remain in Madrid in touch with both the Germans and the British.
>
> Berlin's replies are obscure. They appear to be making up their minds. They wish Madrid to stall. Meanwhile Madrid is to endeavour to discredit Ledebur in our eyes.
>
> It would seem, in wishing to discredit Ledebur that they do not know in Berlin how much he may know about the GARBO network; that they wish to stall for time may indicate that they are preparing a plan to have him kidnapped by the Gestapo.
>
> Should we, meanwhile, arrange for him to be facilitated in his escape from Spain we will, in all probability, be left in uncertainty as to whether or not the true activities of GARBO are in the process of being discovered by Berlin.
>
> We would then be open to two courses of action, either to close down the GARBO network or to continue as before. If we continue and they have reached the decision that Ledebur must have disclosed the GARBO organisation to us then they are left with no alternative other than to believe that GARBO has all along been a controlled agent. If we close

down the GARBO case when, in German calculations Ledebur could not possibly have known anything about his case, they might arrive at the same conclusion.

Since Otto John and Ledebur are friends and they each know the others story we can, for all purposes, consider that they must be treated alike.

If the enemy is able to assess GARBO as having been controlled since he has been operating in the UK, the following would be the repercussion:

(i) The cover plan for future operations would be blown.

(ii) The Special Agents, BRUTUS and TATE, would be blown.

(iii) The Germans would discover that our military operations are co-ordinated with operational deception plans backed by wireless cover and implemented by Special Agents.

(iv) From the cover plan the enemy would learn the true nature of our operations now in progress.

If, in these circumstances, it is considered essential to evacuate these two men on account of the danger of compromise to HM Embassy, Madrid and that if they were now abandoned by us a dangerous situation would be created, I would recommend that the following plan be put into operation in order to safeguard operations and the future running of Special Agents.

I propose that immediately prior to the evacuation of the two men, GARBO, acting in his notional capacity of an employee in the Spanish Department of the Ministry of Information, should send over a message on the following lines:-

'My chief called me urgently to the Ministry requesting that I submit earliest possible drafts for propaganda campaign against Spain to be put out on BBC Broadcasts within next 18 hours on following subject: Oil supplies were restored to Spain on condition that 200 German Secret Service agents listed in a note handed by British Embassy to Spanish Foreign Office were expelled. This has not been done and wolfram agreement has not been fulfilled by Spaniards. Now two German agents, one an Austrian who has worked for years for the German Secret Service, the other a member of the Lufthansa who was a prominent member of organisation who plotted assassination of the Führer, have offered to betray their countries to the British. They are both in Madrid and are shortly to be evacuated to Gibraltar. On arrival there they have promised to tell the truth about German organisation in Spain, how they work with the Spaniards, to give details about wolfram exports, and give information about the anti-Hitler party in Germany. British intend to make great propaganda of these traitors implying that this is further indication of Germany's disintegration. If the Spanish information proves interesting it will be used as excuse to reimpose oil sanctions and bring pressure on Spain to expel Germans. It is essential to take immediate action before the escape of these traitors materialises and they reach British soil. At time of discussing the matter with me they were, according to my chief, both in Madrid.'

On the arrival of Ledebur and John in Gibraltar it would then become necessary to broadcast on the Overseas Service the announcement that two German Intelligence Officers had escaped to British territory with valuable information for the Allies. The Broadcast would report this incident as a further indication of Germany's disintegration.

After a lapse of a few days during which time the two men will be interrogated, the Foreign Office should direct HM Ambassador in Madrid to present a note to the Spanish Foreign Office disclosing the names of the two Germans who had come over to the British. Evidence should be produced to show that the German spy master, Karl Kuhlenthal, had not been expelled from Madrid in accordance with the undertaking of the recent agreement in which his name appeared on the list of Germans which was supplied to the Spanish Government.

A request should be made that in view of the fact that information had come to light through the interrogation of Ledebur, to show that Karl Kuhlenthal was controlling by wireless from Madrid an espionage W//T service in the UK run by an unidentified Jugoslav (this information was in fact given by Ledebur to SIS's representative in Madrid). HM Government would request the Spanish Government that in view of this information which had come to light and the non-fulfilment of their part of the agreement, that Kuhlenthal should be interrogated by British authorities under Spanish supervision with regard to his hostile acts against this country whilst on Spanish territory. This prior to his deportation from Spain, which would also be requested.

Meanwhile, GARBO would be in constant touch with the Ministry of Information learning developments. Discovering that this protest was about to be made he would notify his masters to warn Karl Kuhlenthal, unaware that they were one and the same person:

There is abundant evidence to show that Kuhlenthal and his superiors in Berlin believe GARBO to be in a position to get hold of most secret information through the MoI. There is every possibility that this story will be believed and acted upon. Kuhlenthal would no doubt leave Spain on GARBO's recommendation and continue to operate him from German soil. His removal from Madrid might be very advantageous at the present time when numerous deserters may be expected to approach us.

There is every likelihood that we will see sufficient reaction on RSS if the above plan is put into operation to be able to measure the extent of the success or failure of the plan.

Past experience has shown that whenever we have taken the initiative in the running of the GARBO case we have achieved a success and I consider that failure to do so at this critical juncture would, at the best, result in:

(a) The notional arrest of GARBO.

(b) A wireless silence imposed on GARBO's Agent No.3 on instructions from the Germans.

After much discussion, and pressure from the ambassador, Sam Hoare, who was keen to be rid of a potential diplomatic embarrassment, Ledebur was delivered to Gibraltar when, on 21 November, he was flown to Hurn by a BOAC Constellation, carrying travel papers identifying him as a Mr Johnson:

The main reason for bringing Ledebur to this country was on account of the anxiety which HM Ambassador there expressed at his continued presence in an Allied safe-house which was thought might become most embarrassing to Allied interests. Ledebur may, however, be a useful informant. It is known from the case of Hans Scharf that Ledebur has been in contact with the Abwehr over a considerable period and it is known from this and other sources that he has particular knowledge of the Bedaux mission which is of interest to B1(b). It is also possible that Ledebur may have more information than had been previously supposed regarding Abwehr activities and personalities generally.

Upon his arrival at Camp 020 on 30 November Ledebur gave a harrowing account of the circumstances of his defection, which was included in the standard interim report:

On the following day Ledebur lunched with Otto John and Bernhard Rohe, and all three spoke of their uncertain situation and the possibility of going over to the British. John was still unwilling to commit himself openly in favour of such a decision. After Rohe retired to return to his work at the W/T station, Ledebur took John to a cafe and demanded of him what he knew about Hansen, for John had stated that he had flown to Berlin shortly before July 20th and had returned only a few days ago.

John now broke down completely in tears. He confessed to Ledebur that Hansen was no longer alive; that Count Stauffenburg, to whom Hansen had personally handed the explosives to be used in the attempt on Hitler's life, was also dead; also that he, John, had also been deeply implicated in the plot. The revelation stunned Ledeber, who suddenly realised how deeply he must himself be compromised through his close contact with Hansen ('It is the only grudge that I have against Hansen; he never told me, and left me walking around with a noose around my neck of which I was not even conscious').

John refused Ledebur's offer to be put in contact with the British, stating that he was already in touch with them, though he would not name any person. The same evening, on seeing his own British contact, Ledebur disclosed the information which he had obtained from John; and on another occasion he brought from Tertsch's home the radio set which he was to have delivered to Rohe; it had been obtained through Major Podansky, Chef 1 Nachrichten, on orders from Hansen.

As he wished still to save his friends in France, Lebedur told his contact that he intended to continue his 'play' with Berlin: he sent messages announcing, first his reluctance to leave, then his 'decision' to return to France around August 15th. The reaction was violent; he was ordered to come back at once, obtaining plane reservations through the Air Attaché, Major Schartz. Ledebur called on Schartz and urged him to make a reservation for August 7th.

As he was now in daily touch with the Allied organisation, Ledebur tried to save his friends in France as long as possible: through Bastide he sent to Alexandra Ter Hart, through the French Resistance channel, a message warning her that OLIVIER [Ledebur] would not be returning, and asking her to destroy his files.

He was still living at the home of Ekkehard Tersch [the assistant press secretary who lived at Calle Malaga 10], who was quite unaware of the crisis through which he was passing, when Kurt von Rohrscheid 'phoned one morning to enquire whether Ledebur had read the day's papers, which announced the execution of Hansen for his share in the plot against Hitler. Ledebur replied that he had been very surprised to read it. Rohrscheid invited, rather than ordered, him to his office, and Ledebur agreed to call.

He found Rohe first, and asked him to wait outside the III offices, promising to signal to him in the event of danger, for Rohe was now well aware of his double game and apparently a party to it.

On his arrival Rohrscheid asked him directly whether he had been involved with Hansen in the plot. Ledebur replied truthfully that he had not. Rohrscheid turned away, scratched his head, and murmured that had he been in Berlin he would almost certainly have been 'in it'. Reverting quickly to his official duties, he demanded to know what Ledebur proposed to do, was he going to return? Ledebur said that there was no reason why he should not do so; he had relatives in Germany and he would leave on the 7th.

Satisfied with the reply, Rohrscheid called a secretary and dictated a radio message to Berlin stating that Ledebur had called on him on his own initiative; he had the impression that Ledebur was not involved in the plot, and that he would return to Germany on August 7th.

Shortly after the encounter, Ledebur left Tertsch's house and was taken by the British into hiding, when he learned that the Gestapo and the Spanish police were already on his track. After several weeks' isolation in Madrid, Ledebur was finally transferred to the UK.

Ledebur exceeded all expectations by demonstrating his impressive knowledge of the German intelligence apparatus and its personalities. In particular, he identified three of his own agents, and mentioned two spies in England, one code-named KILLIAN:

In the autumn of 1942 Kapitan Erich Pfeiffer, at that, time Loiter III, Ast Paris, gave Ledebur a 'otiminungsbericht' to read; it dealt with general conditions in Britain, and asked Ledebur to give him an opinion as to its value. It covered the food shortages, shipping difficulties, and Kriegsmuedigkeit (war-weariness).

When Ledebur enquired the author's name, Pfeiffer told him that he had obtained it from Oberst Rudolf, and that it had come from Eins Luft. The agent, KILLIAN, belonged to Colonel Garthe, l/L, and was run by Major Kliemann. Pfieffer added that Eins Luft were 'very proud of this bird, who occasionally gave a peep which was really worth reading', though the present report was 'journalistic nonsense'. Not long before KILLIAN had supplied a three line radio report about port movements in Plymouth which was worth very much more than this ten-page story, which had arrived in secret writing via Portugal.

Pfeiffer could not, or would not, tell Ledebur the identity of KILLIAN. According to Ledebur he was the 'show agent' of Alst Frankreich and at that time they had no other agent in the UK reporting regularly by W/T.

Ledebur heard later through Helge von Bülow, who helped him at the Bedaux office in Paris before re-joining Eins Luft, that KILLIAN was a Scandinavian who knew England well from before the war, and that he had been won over and trained by Major Kliemann, alias Kielburg. The latter had only managed to keep his job thanks to KILLIAN's industry.

He had sent no news since the spring of 1944, and it was believed at the Hotel Lutetia that he had been 'turned around' by the British. When D-Day arrived, adds Ledebur, Alst Frankreich had not a single W/T agent in the British Isles.

Another spy in England he heard about was described as a Yugoslav diplomat, and was almost certainly TRICYCLE:

Ledebur first heard of this agent at Zossen on 5th June 1944, when Colonel Karl-Heinz Engelhorn told him that the most valuable reports on England for the last six months had been received through Kuhlenthal of KO Spain, who had 'a most valuable agent in the UK'.

When Ledebur asked to see the latest reports, he was referred to von Bohlen IH/West. The latter refused to produce copies of the original reports or to commit himself beyond stating that the agent was Yugoslav with very good connections; but he declared that the Allied invasion must be imminent, as the reports from the agent during the last few weeks had stated that 'the landing operations had reached a stage where one could already call them the prelude to the coming sea-invasion'.

As jealousy plays a big part in the different sections, and he was curious to learn about the agent, Ledebur spoke to Kapitan Humpert, I/M Zossen, about the esteem and reputation which Kuhlenthal enjoyed with the High Chiefs owing to the success of his agent. Humpert burst out laughing and said that the source of Kuhlenthal's information was much contested; he could only say that the agent was an active diplomat of the Yugoslavian Government, working in London but going regularly each quarter of the year to Lisbon and Madrid; he was Kuhlenthal's most expensive agent, costing £400 every month already for two years. (It was suggested by officers of the KO in Madrid, that Kuhlenthal was splitting the monthly allowance 'between his and the diplomat's pocket').

Humpert referred Ledebur to Kapitan Mueller, recently returned from an Abwehr post in Seville, for additional information. Mueller could add little, except to belittle Kuhlenthal's activities in Spain; but he confirmed that the agent frequently visited Lisbon and stated that the reports were not exclusively transmitted by radio, but were more often sent in secret writing.

Later, in Paris, Ledebur tried to find out more about the agent from Kapitan Call, but the latter also disliked Kuhlenthal and was not disposed to talk about the source of his information.

Ledebur adds: 'When I entered the KO in Madrid on 26th July, 1944 Kuhlenthal passed through the room where I was waiting for the money. I said hello and asked what his valuable friend in London was now saying, after the landing had happened. He blushed ostensibly and answered with embarrassment: "But nevertheless I was right with my landing prediction." When I saw Colonel von Rohrscheidt he happened to mention that the latest reports received from London through H/I were very interesting, about the damage in London through V-I.

Ledebur also gave a profile of Prince von Hohenlohe, who had previously been mentioned by HARLEQUIN (Chapter 27):

Descended from Austrian branch which resided in Bohemia for more than a century; in 1925 married wealthy Spanish–Mexican heiress, Yturbe.

Took over family estate at Rottenhaus with money given him by his wife to provide for his parents, sisters, brothers. Before Franco regime, lived most of time at Rottenhaus, Czechoslovakia. About 15 years ago became citizen of Principality of Lichtenstein. Now behaves like a Spanish grandee; one of his daughters married to titled Spaniard.

Every year during war he goes to France, Germany, Czechoslovakia and Switzerland, having business interests everywhere. Three years ago became representative of Skoda Works for Western Europe; as manager for France appointed Dr Mueler, who came from Cologne and might be the twin brother of Dr. Goebbels. As Skoda manager in Spain has Reinhold Spitzi.[4]

Close relations with Allied embassies in Madrid and Berne.

His brother, one of twins, nicknamed 'Zwauserl' who belonged to one of Jewish Brigades of Waffen SS, with headquarters in rue Galilee, but whose position was not very secure, as he had quarreled with his Obergruppenführer and nearly been dismissed. Max Hohenlohe, disgusted that brother should be working for such a disreputable service, approached Ledebur in spring of 1944 with request that he obtain position for him with Abwehr. Ledebur obtained such a bad impression of the man, enormously fat, with spectacles; of distinctly Jewish appearance, that he never pursued the matter.

As well as drafting a lengthy account of his work for the Abwehr, detailing all his activities and contacts, he described the Madrid KO's operations, and confirmed that it had identified a Colonel Wren as the local SIS representative, and Jack Ivens as his 'gangster'. This was certainly accurate in respect of Section V's Ivens. His final report amounted to eighty-six pages of narrative, with a further 100 pages of appendices, 'every word of which was of value', according to Helenus Milmo.

Ledebur remained at Camp 020 until October 1945, when he was flown to the British zone in Austria. He later moved to Argentina. He married again in 1954, had two children and died in Buenos Aires in December 1963.

POSTSCRIPT

Early in 1944 Guy Liddell reflected on how MI5 had performed during the previous twelve months:

Buster Milmo has made out his analysis of Camp 020 cases for the year 1943. The total number of cases held on 31 December 1943 was 120 as against 90 on the same date in 1942, and 54 on the same date in 1941. 67 were admitted in 1943, 18 released, 7 transferred and two prosecuted. Of those admitted in 1943, 54 proved to be spies as against 43 in the previous year. Of the above 54, there were 39 cases in which there were identifiable traces on ISOS (an increase from 55.8 to 72.2 per cent over the previous year). There were 21 cases in which the capture of the agent was attributable to ISOS, an increase from 35 per cent to 38.9 per cent. There were 15 cases for which there was no identifiable trace on ISOS at all, a decrease from 44.2 per cent to 27.8 per cent. Of the total of 54, 30 were captured abroad, as against 14 in the previous year, and 24 in the UK as against 29 in the previous year. Out of the total of 24 apprehended in the UK, only 22 were intended to operate in this country. Of these, ISOS showed traces of 16, and three were captured on account of ISOS. 16 gave themselves up or were double-agents *ab initio*. Of the three whose capture was attributable to ISOS, Rogerio de Menezes would certainly have been otherwise detected, Huysmans would almost certainly have been detected, while [Raymond] Lalou's fate would have been problematical. Among those who came to this country de Graaf, Oswald Job and Steiner are really the only three that we can claim to have captured single-handedly.

Liddell did not repeat this statistical exercise at the end of 1944, or at the conclusion of hostilities, but if he had done so, it is likely that the influence of ISOS, which continued to grow in volume, would have escalated proportionately. Certainly the source proved invaluable for the SCI units that accompanied the liberation forces across Europe, and quickly neutralised the threat from the enemy's stay-behind networks, which were scooped up before they could become operational. Several of the organisers, such as Colonel Schneider, were caught, their circuits rapidly decapitated, and their agents, such as Mathilde Bernard and Yves Guilcher, cooperated fully to tie up any loose ends and ensure that the investigation of the Abwehr's plans for post-occupation sabotage was comprehensive.

It might have been anticipated, given MI5's skill in the management of double-agents, that the Director-General would concentrate on the work undertaken by Tommy Robertson's B1(a) section, which accounted for twenty-three double-agents mentioned in the reports, but it is striking that he kept a balance between them and the spies executed in London (Job, Neukermans and Vanhove); the defectors (Wurmann, Zech-Nantwich, Schagen and Ruser); the neutral diplomats (de Menezes, Alcazar de Velasco, Hellmuth and Kobbe); the Soviet spies (Springhall, Uren, Sheehan and Milne); and the adversary (Kliemann, Mayr, Baumann, Schneider, Scharf and Naujocks). Similarly, Petrie did not dwell on MI5's counter-subversion role beyond some pointed remarks about Communists (Springhall, Robson, Tearse, Lee and Haston) and scarcely mentioned the more routine security aspects of sabotage and indiscretion.

In terms of geographical coverage, the reports extended to South Africa (Leibbrandt), Lourenço Marques (Manna), Mombasa (Batos), Havana (Jude and Urzaiz), Vancouver (Kobbe), Buenos Aires (Hoppe, Perez and Leiro), Iceland (Tomsen, LAND SPIDER and COBWEB), Cairo (Mayr), and served to highlight MI5's global reach and the importance of its overseas bases in Gibraltar (Bonzo, Botana, Muñoz, Buetto and Cordon Cuerca) and Trinidad (Balleta, Blay, Chambard, Pacheco, Laski and Liehr). Indeed, MI5 proved to be particularly adept at disrupting the Axis transatlantic courier route (Baticon and Oliveiro) and the Ybarra line wireless operators (Beltrán-Leiro and Ruiz). Combined together, these examples of espionage illustrated how an ISOS lead could result in an arrest far from the British Isles, and conclude in a revealing confession at Camp 020. As a model for integrated counter-intelligence, it was a seamless classic, even if the cryptographic foundation had shifted from being MI5's creature to SIS.[1]

The spies described to the Prime Minister who had been sent on missions to Great Britain ranged from the parachute arrivals (BASKET, Hansen, TATE and ZIGZAG); the French and Belgian pilots (FIDO, FATHER, SNIPER, Fraval and Creteur); and the false refugees (Hlidar, Job, Wilman and Wijckaert).

Although Churchill would never have known it, a couple of the cases generated considerable inter-agency tension between MI5 and SIS (Polo and HAMLET) and between MI5 and SOE (Aben and Knoppens), and over the appearance of captured radio transmitters as supplied to MUTT and JEFF. He also would not have known that several of the cases mentioned with such optimism and certainty did not always end with the desired results. For example, Knut Brodersen, whose arrival in England was anticipated in March 1944 (Chapter 13), turned out to be a candidate for execution in a Treachery Act prosecution, but the controversial circumstances of how his confession was taken meant that the proceedings went no further than the magistrates' court. In a similar case, where the trajectory turned out to be rather different to the one predicted by Petrie's report, Juan Polo duped SIS into sending him to Gibraltar, thereby compromising MI9's secret sea route from Seville. That blunder meant Polo had to be kept in isolation in England for the remainder of the war.

It may have come as something of a surprise to Churchill that, towards the end of the war, MI5 played such a significant role with SHAEF in scooping up the British renegades who had collaborated with the Nazis, participating in the SCI units that tracked down the enemy's stay-behind networks, and detaining members of the Abwehr. Camp 020 had proved so successful that CSDIC established a facility on the Continent at Diest's citadel in Belgium before transferring the staff in June 1945 to a former spa resort at Bad Nenndorf in Germany.

One aspect of what might be termed the intelligence war, rather overlooked by historians, is the scale of defection from the German intelligence services beginning around mid-1943 when members of the Abwehr and SD effectively jumped ship. This may be partly because they were in a better position than most of their compatriots to see through the pervasive Nazi propaganda, and their better access, particularly in Lisbon, Madrid and Stockholm, to international opinion and foreign news reports. Staff based in the neutral capitals also had greater opportunities to make contact with their adversaries, and the time to negotiate terms.

In coming to a final assessment of the reports' value, one is bound to be struck by the very comprehensive nature of ISOS, which gave MI5 (and SIS) a huge advantage in dealing with such a large and well-organised opponent. Although it has become fashionable in recent times to denigrate the Abwehr, and portray the senior staff as corrupt and venal, the reports give a good idea of how much was known about its various branches. Individual personalities were 'carded' and their movements, tracked through ISOS, monitored as they moved from post to post. What was accomplished is even more impressive when one considers that virtually all personnel, operational and administrative, routinely adopted aliases and used code names in their communications. Although the quality of individual agents was sometimes poor, the staff personnel were generally well-educated, multilingual and often with a peacetime legal or police background.

Particularly striking, as emerges from the foregoing, is the frequency with which some names reappeared. MI5 was a comparatively tiny organisation, and the cases mentioned in the Prime Minister's reports revolved around just a few personalities: Herbert Hart managing ISOS, with Buster Milmo and Blanshard Stamp undertaking the analysis and answering to 'DB' Guy Liddell, who relied heavily on Tommy Robertson, Dick White and Anthony Blunt. For SIS it is Kim Philby and Felix Cowgill who emerge as the dominant counter-intelligence sages, especially when the enemy spies surfaced in Iberia. This handful of officers, supported behind the scenes by dozens of cryptanalysts, linguists, Section V staff overseas, DSOs at Gibraltar and Trinidad, and Security Control Officers at the British ports, interdicted Nazi infiltrators and transformed often fleeting, vague references in the ISOS traffic to specific suspects who required close investigation. These counter-espionage operations, encapsulated in Camp 020's distinctive reports known as 'yellow perils', amounted to another side of the double-agent coin, B1(a)'s team of case officers who skilfully manipulated dozens of controlled enemy agents.

Pitted against these resourceful young men, usually drawn for wartime intelligence duties only from the law and from academia, were the Abwehr's Abstellen in the espionage front line in Iberia and Scandinavia. Once again, the same personalities recur, with Emil Kliemann and Karl Kuhlenthal appearing prominently in cases originating in Paris and Madrid, respectively.

Any reader, even knowing that the Prime Minister's staff would not have access to the reports, cannot but be impressed by the level of trust shown in Churchill, especially in respect of the acutely sensitive cryptographic dimension. A good example is the reference to a new cipher system such as the hitherto impenetrable triple transposition code delivered to assist a double-agent's communications, which proved of great assistance to the cryptanalysts who, very likely, would not have been able to read the traffic without the crib. Yet Churchill was regarded as notoriously indiscreet and occasionally impetuous to the point of recklessness. He was always known to be fascinated by the inside track offered by intelligence, and Stewart Menzies was a familiar visitor delivering his distinctive buff coloured box containing selected intercept summaries and raw decrypts. The paradox is that although Churchill proved the past master of exploiting SIGINT, he exercised unusual discretion when he supervised the compilation of his magnum opus, *The Second World War*, published in six volumes between 1948 and 1954, which made no reference to double-agents, wireless intercepts or even FORTITUDE. Although Churchill had wanted to include mention of ULTRA and its influence on the conflict, the Cabinet Secretary Sir Edward Bridges, and 'C', Sir Stewart Menzies, had prevailed upon him to refrain from disclosure on the grounds that the techniques employed were still operational. Reluctantly, Churchill acquiesced, so we have no way of knowing the Prime Minister's attitude to the MI5 case histories on which he had been briefed.

Details of the XX Committee would not be released until 1972 when its former chairman, J.C. Masterman, received Cabinet Office permission to publish a slightly censored account of his own post-hostilities report on MI5's double-agent operations compiled in 1945.[2] The approved version made no mention of ISOS, and nor did Fred Winterbotham's *The Ultra Secret*, which was released two years later.[3] Actually, the role played by ISK and ISOS in wartime counter-espionage, and the degree of integration between the Radio Security Service and MI5 would remain under wraps until 1981.[4] Sir Michael Howard's official history of strategic deception would not be released until September 1981[5] and Roger Hesketh's *Fortitude* would have to wait until November 2000.[6] Given Whitehall's instinctive reticence, it is not surprising that the Prime Minister's monthly reports would have to wait until after 2000 to be passed to The National Archives at Kew.[7]

ESPIONAGE CASES

Franciscus Aben	A Dutch sea captain arrested in January 1944; he was detained at Camp 020 until 1946. He was imprisoned in the Netherlands for ten years. KV6/52.
Angel Alcazar de Velasco	A Spanish journalist, and press attaché at the London embassy, recruited by the Abwehr. KV2/3535; KV2/3536; KV2/3537; KV2/3538; KV2/3540; KV2/3541.
Fernando Lipkau Balleta	A Mexican recruited by the Abwehr; he was arrested in Trinidad in May 1943 and transferred to Camp 020. KV 2/2460.
Joaquin Baticon	A Y barra Line ship steward recruited in Buenos Aires who acted as an Abwehr courier; he was arrested at Trinidad in March 1943, transferred to New York and then detained in Camp 020. KV 2/2111.
Basil Batos	A Greek journalist and Abwehr spy; he was detained in Mombasa in January 1942 and incarcerated at Camp 020. KV2/1715.
Friedrich Baumann	The alias of Wolfgang Blaum, an Abwehr officer in charge of sabotage, based in Madrid between 1941 and 1945 who was captured and interrogated in 1945. KV2/1976.
Charles Bedaux	A French collaborator, Bedaux was arrested in North Africa and taken to Florida where he committed suicide in February 1944.
Diego Beltrán-Leiro	A wireless operator working on a Spanish merchant ship *Monte Monjuich* sailing to Buenos Aires, he was arrested on December 1943 and detained at Camp 020. KV 2/1939.
Madeleine Bernard	A French stay-behind agent arrested in Calvados in June 1944; she remained at Camp 020 for just five days.
Hans Bertrand	Belgian pilot and Abwehr agent code-named SNIPER by MI5.

Hjalti Bjornsson	An Icelandic spy for the Abwehr, landed by U-boat on Iceland in April 1944 with Ernst Fresenius and Sigardur Juliusson. He was arrested and interrogated at Camp 020, where he remained until he was deported from Hendon in August 1945. KV2/3009.
Baron Manfredi de Blasis	A suspected SD stay-behind agent in Italy, he was detained at Camp 020 in February 1944. KV2/1940.
Andrés Bonzo	An Italian spy arrested at Gibraltar on his return from a mission to Argentina. KV2/2702.
Manuel Serna Botana	An Abwehr suspect in Gibraltar; arrested in May 1943.
Juan Brandes	An Abwehr officer based in Lisbon suspected of fabricating information from an imaginary network of Swiss spies. KV 2/3295.
Knut Brodersen	An Abwehr agent infiltrated into England from Spain, Brodersen was detained at Camp 020. KV 2/547; KV2/548; KV 2/549; KV 2/550; KV2/551.
Edouardo Buetto	An Abwehr suspect in Gibraltar, Buetto was arrested in May 1943.
Umberto Campini	The Italian consul in Lorenço Marques, Campini was also the local representative of the Italian intelligence service. FO371/1739597.
Comte Gabriel de Chaffault	An Abwehr spy suspect, de Chaffault was detained in Gibraltar in August 1943 and transferred to Camp 020. He was returned to France in 1945 and was sentenced in February 1946 to five years' imprisonment for collaboration. KV 2/2634.
Henri Gravet Chambard	A Japanese agent, Chambard was arrested in Trinidad in November 1943. KV 2/2305.
William Craven	A British renegade arrested and convicted in 1945. KV 2/486; KV 2/487; KV 2/488
Jean Creteur	A Belgian pilot and Abwehr spy incriminated by SNIPER.
Luis Cordon Cuenca	Abwehr saboteur arrested in Gibraltar in June 1943, tried in August, and executed in January 1944. KV 2/2114. His uncle, Augusto Cuenca, was also considered a German spy based in Gibraltar and his MI5 file is at KV2/1950.
Antonie Damen	A Dutch suspect and Abwehr agent. KV 2/134; KV 2/135; KV 2/136; KV 2/137; KV 2/138.
Martial Durand	A member of an Abwehr stay-behind organisation in Carentan in August 1944, Durand was interrogated at Camp 020 and then returned to Paris. KV 2/218.
Carl Eitel	Linked to a 1938 espionage case in the United States as a steward aboard the *Bremen* acting as a contact for Hamburg-Amerika Line couriers involved in the Günther Rumrich prosecution. KV 2/382; KV 2/383; KV 2/384; KV 2/385.

Hans Fanto	Real name of an SIS double-agent code-named PUPPET. He operated in London and reported via HAMLET in Portugal.
Georges Feyguine	A French fighter pilot and naval officer, Feyguine declared his recruitment by the Abwehr when he reached Gibraltar in June 1943. He was eventually interned at Camp X on the Isle of Man. His father-in-law was Colonel Elie Golenko.
Jean Fraval	French pilot sent to England to steal an aircraft in 1943; he was detained at Camp 020 until he was returned to France in May 1945. KV 2/2446; KV 2/2447; KV 2/2448.
Ernst Fresenius	A German who had acquired Icelandic citizenship, Fresenius was arrested after having been landed by U-boat in Iceland in April 1944. He was arrested and interrogated at Camp 020, where he remained until he was deported by air from Hendon in August 1945. KV2/3009; KV2/3010.
Alfred Gabas	A French former naval officer recruited by the Abwehr as a stay-behind spy in Cherbourg, he was captured in 1944 and interrogated at Camp 020. KV2/210.
Manuel Perez Garcia	A Spanish security officer attached to the embassy in Buenos Aires, Perez was detained in Trinidad and transferred to Camp 020. He was repatriated in 1945. KV2/2443.
Arthur Garitte	A Belgian SD agent alias Wanstein who defected in September 1944 and was detained at Camp 020.
Johannes de Graaf	A Canadian recruited by the Abwehr, de Graaf was detained at Camp 020 when he arrived in England. KV 2/125.
Ben Greene	A Quaker detained having been denounced in 1940 by an MI5 informant. LCO 2/1454.
Magnus Gudbjornsson	An Icelandic spy arrested upon his arrival in April 1944. He was detained at Camp 020 and deported from Hendon in August 1945. KV2/123.
Yves Guilcher	A French stay-behind agent in Bayeux arrested in June 1944 and sent to Camp 020. KV2/211; KV2/212; KV2/213.
Elie Gwozdawo-Golenko	A White Russian employed as an intercept operator by the Abwehr in Paris. Detained in London and sent to Camp 020 in November 1944; KV 2/315; KV 2/316; KV 2/317.
Nikolay Hansen	A Norwegian miner and Abwehr agent who parachuted into Scotland in September 1943 and was detained at Camp 020. KV2/1936.

Jock Haston	A former CPGB member, he split the Party to organise a Trotskyite rival, the Revolutionary Communist Party, in 1934. He died in 1986.
Osmar Hellmuth	An Argentine SD agent of German origin, he was arrested in Trinidad on the *Cabo de Hornos* on 29 October 1943, flown to Bermuda and then taken by HMS *Ajax* to Plymouth. He was detained at Camp 020. KV 2/1722; KV 2/1723; KV 2/1724.
Gerald Hewitt	A British renegade convicted of treason in 1946 after he had broadcast for the Nazis. He was sentenced to twelve years' imprisonment. K2/427; HO45/24474.
Gudbrandur Hlidar	An Icelander arrested at Prestwick in February 1945 having arrived from Stockholm. He was detained at Camp 020 and admitted to having acted as a talent-spotter for the Abwehr. He was deported from Hendon in August 1945 and died in 1997. KV 2/214; KV 2/215; KV 2/216.
Prince Max von Hohenlohe	An influential Abwehr agent in Spain, he died in 1968 at the age of 71.
Ernesto Hoppe	An Argentine recruited by the Abwehr in Holland in 1936, Hoppe was arrested in Gibraltar while travelling to Buenos Aires and detained at Camp 020. KV 2/2636.
Jean Huysmans	A Belgian Abwehr agent arrested in Lisbon in May 1943, deported and detained at Camp 020, where he became the librarian. KV 2/295.
Waldemar Janowsky	An Abwehr double-agent arrested in November 1942 in Canada, he was code-named WATCHDOG and was later transferred to Camp 020.
Joseph Janssens	A Belgian Abwehr agent, he was arrested in Portugal in 1943, deported to England and detained at Camp 020. KV 2/1934.
Oswald Job	A British refugee and Abwehr agent, he was arrested in London, convicted and hanged at Pentonville in March 1944; KV 2/501; KV 2/51; KV 2/52.
Leon Jude	A pre-war Sabena pilot, Jude was a Belgian recruited by the Abwehr in 1940 for a mission to the United States. He was arrested in 1942, incriminated by SNIPER and detained at Camp 020R until 1945, when he was deported to Belgium. KV 2/375.
Sigardur Juliusson	An Icelandic spy for the Abwehr landed by U-boat on Iceland in April 1944 with Ernst Fresenius and Hjalti Bjornsson. He was arrested and interrogated at Camp 020, where he remained until he was deported from Hendon in August 1945. KV2/3009.

Emil Kliemann	An Abwehr officer based in Paris and interrogated in September 1944. KV 2/278.
Fernando Kobbe	The Spanish consul in Vancouver in 1943, he was suspected of being a Japanese spy. KV 2/637; KV2/638.
Johann Koessler	An Austrian Jewish businessman in Lisbon and MI5 double-agent code-named HAMLET.
Lagall	A Frenchman arrested in London in January 1945 and detained. Later identified as an Abwehr agent by Hermann Rainer, he was deported to France. See Guy Liddell's *Diary* entry for 6 August 1943.
Hans Laski	A German spy bound for Argentina. Laski was intercepted at Trinidad in March 1943 and detained at Camp 020.
Josef von Ledebur-Wicheln	A senior Abwehr officer in Paris and later aide to Colonel Georg Hansen, the Graf von Ledebur defected to the British embassy in Madrid in 1944. KV2/159.
Robey Leibbrandt	A South African Abwehr assassin arrested in Pretoria in December 1941 and imprisoned. KV 2/924.
Oscar Liehr	An Argentine arrested in Trinidad in June 1943, he was detained at Camp 020. KV 2/2112; KV 2/2113; FO 1093/258.
Christiaan Lindemanns	Dutch resistance leader code-named KING KONG and an Abwehr spy. He was arrested in November 1944, detained at Camp 020, but committed suicide in 1946. KV 2/233 – KV 2/237.
Fritz Lorenz	A member of Ribbentrop Bureau, war correspondent and SD officer captured in France, Lorenz was interrogated at Camp 020 in October 1944 and then employed by PWE in March 1945 to broadcast propaganda. GFM 33/93/87/2; KV2/310.
Alfredo Manna	An Italian intelligence officer under Stefano News Agency cover in Lourenço Marques, he was lured to Swaziland by Anna Levy, abducted by SIS to South Africa and transferred to Camp 020. KV 2/1107; KV 2/1108.
Sverir Matthiason	An Icelandic spy arrested upon his arrival in April 1944. He was detained at Camp 020 and deported from Hendon in August 1945. KV2/122.
Franz Mayr	Abwehr officer arrested in Tehran in August 1943. KV 2/1477; KV2/1479; KV 2/1480; KV 2/1482; KV 2/1483.
Rogerio de Menezes	Portuguese diplomat at the embassy in London and Abwehr spy arrested in February 1943. Condemned to death in April 1943 but sentence commuted. FO 1093/256; PCOM 9/993.

Ray Milne	An SIS secretary, née Mundell, in contact with the CPGB's Douglas Springhall. Mrs Milne was dismissed but never charged.
Alfred Naujocks	An SD officer arrested in October 1944 in France and detained at Camp 020. KV 2/280.
Pierre Neukermans	A Belgian pilot and Abwehr spy, Neukermans was arrested in London in February 1944 and executed in June 1944. KV 2/53.
José Olivera	A radio operator on a Spanish ship sailing from Buenos Aires, he was arrested by a Dutch patrol vessel and transferred to Camp 020 in November 1943. KV 2/1938.
José Pacheco	A Cuban dancer and Abwehr spy, he was arrested in Trinidad while en route to Cuba in March 1943 and detained at Camp 020. KV 2/296; KV 2/297.
Jens Palsson	The radio operator of the *Arctic*, an Icelandic trawler, Palsson was arrested in Reykjavik in 1942 and interrogated at Camp 020. He was deported from Hendon in August 1945. KV2/1147.
Louis de la Panouse	The son of the former French military attaché in London, General de la Panouse, he was suspected of clandestine correspondence with Violet Trefusis.
Antonio Pastor	The London University professor of Spanish. He was an MI5 contact but considered by the Abwehr as a possible future agent.
José Polo	A Spaniard recruited by the Abwehr in Kiel, he was arrested in Gibraltar in January 1943; he was detained at Camp 020. He was deported to Spain in 1945. KV 2/1943; KV2/1944.
Poussin	The French lover of Mathilde Bertrand.
Hermann Rainer	An SD officer who deserted to the Allies while on a sabotage mission in France in 1945; he was detained at Camp 020. Under the alias Ernest Hermann Reinsberg he acquired British citizenship in July 1947. HO 334/184/29244.
Robert Robson	A senior CPGB figure as London District Organiser and member of the Control Commission, he was under MI5 surveillance from 1922 to his death in 1951. A recruiter for the International Brigade during the Spanish Civil War, he was convicted of handling stolen goods in 1931. KV 2/1177; KV 2/1179.
Joaquin Ruiz	Arrested aboard the *Cabo de Hornos* in Trinidad in August 1943, he was an Abwehr courier and was detained at Camp 020. He was deported to Spain in 1945. KV 2/1716; KV 2/1717; KV 2/1718.

Hans Ruser	An Abwehr defector previously based in Lisbon, code-named JUNIOR by MI5 and ARTHUR by SIS; he was detained briefly at Camp 020 after he had been exfiltrated from Madrid in November 1943.
Peter Schagen	An Abwehr II saboteur in France in a 1944 stay-behind organisation, he defected to the Americans in Madrid, but was detained at Camp 020 in October 1944 and deported to France. KV 2/161.
Hans Scharf	An Abwehr officer actually named Schneider, captured by the French in Algeria in December 1943 and transferred to Camp 020 in July 1944. KV 2/207; KV2/208; KV2/209.
Nathalie Sergueiev	MI5 double-agent code-named TREASURE but known to the Abwehr as TRAMP. KV 2/466.
Olive Sheehan	Air Ministry clerk and Soviet spy, convicted in London in 1943 with Douglas Springhall. KV 2/1596; KV 2/1598.
Sibart	French espionage suspect.
Einar Sigvaldason	An Abwehr agent landed by U-boat on Iceland on 17 April 1944 with Larus Thorsteinsson. He was arrested and interrogated at Camp 020 before being interned on the Isle of Man. He was deported from Hendon in August 1945. KV2/121; KV2/122; KV2/123.
Douglas Springhall	The CPGB National Organiser and a Soviet spy convicted of espionage in London in 1943, Springhall was in contact with Ormond Uren, Olive Sheehan and Ray Milne. KV 2/1597.
Frank Steiner	A Belgian journalist and Abwehr agent, he was arrested in April 1943 upon his arrival from Lisbon and detained at Camp 020. He was flown back to Belgium in February 1945 and executed. KV 2/1165.
Pierre Sweerts	A Belgian SD agent, he gave himself up to the Allies in Holland in September 1944 and was detained at Camp 020. He later joined an intelligence unit. KV 2/230.
Larus Thorsteinsson	An Abwehr agent landed by U-boat on Iceland on 17 April 1944 with Einar Sigvaldason. He was arrested and interrogated at Camp 020 but moved to the Brompton Hospital for treatment in May 1944 before being transferred to Brixton. Both men were deported in August 1945. KV2/121; KV2/122; KV2/123.

Justin Tocabens	A Frenchman recruited by the Abwehr who operated a wireless in Barcelona. He surrendered to the Free French and was interrogated at Camp 020 in July 1944, but was flown back to Algiers in August.
Petur Tomsen	An Icelander landed by U-boat from Norway, Tomsen adopted the alias Jens Fridrikson and was sent to Camp 020 in September 1943. He was recruited as a double-agent, code-named BEETLE.
Violet Trefusis	Virginia Woolf's lesbian lover, Violet Trefusis was the daughter of Alice Keppel, the mistress of King Edward VII. She was married to Denys Trefusis and broadcast on the Free French radio station *La Voix de la France Libre* during the war.
Ormond Uren	SOE officer convicted of passing secrets to Douglas Springhall. KV 2/1596; KV2/1597; KV 2/1698.
Guzman Urzaiz	A Spanish banker, he was arrested in Trinidad in October 1843 when returning from an Abwehr mission to Cuba. KV 2/3288.
Joseph Vanhove	Belgian waiter and Abwehr agent, he was arrested upon arrival from Sweden in February 1944, detained at Camp 020 and executed. KV 2/54.
Cornelis Verloop	A Dutch private detective and Abwehr agent, he was arrested in October 1944 and detained at Camp 020. KV 2/139.
Hilaire Westerlinck	A Belgian ship's doctor, code-named THE WEASEL by MI5, arrested upon arrival in England in May 1942 and incarcerated at Camp 020. His wife was jailed at Holloway. KV 2/2444.
Guy Wijckaert	A young Belgian refugee who declared some of his Abwehr connections to the Belgian consul in Barcelona; he was detained at Camp 020 in December 1943.
Wladyslaw Wilman	A young Polish Abwehr agent, he arrived as a refugee in Gibraltar in May 1944 and was detained at Camp 020. He was released in June 1944 to work in an aircraft factory, having missed the opportunity to become a double-agent.

APPENDIX 2

MI5 DOUBLE-AGENTS

ARTIST	Abwehr officer Johnny Jebsen, based in Lisbon and responsible for handling his old friend Dusan Popov, was abducted by the Gestapo in April 1944.
BASKET	Originally from Athlone, Joseph Lenihan surrendered to the police in Northern Ireland in July 1941. His Home Office file, HO 45/23803, is closed.
BEETLE	An Icelander, Petur Tomsen was landed by U-boat in September 1943. He died in 1988.
BRONX	Elvira Chaudoir, neé de la Fuentes, was the socialite daughter of a Peruvian diplomat in Vichy.
BRUTUS	Roman Garby-Czeriawski, a Polish army officer who supposedly escaped from German custody in Paris.
COLOMBINE	Waffen SS defector Obersturmführer Hans Walter Zech-Nenntwich.
DREADNOUGHT	Ivo Popov, brother of Dusan Popov, code-named TRICYCLE.
FATHER	A famous French pilot, Captain Pierre Arend, who arrived in England in June 1941.
FIDO	A French pilot, Roger Grosjean, who arrived in England in July 1943 from Lisbon.
FREAK	A Yugoslav aristocrat, the Marquis Fano de Bona, an old friend of Dusan Popov's.
GARBO	The Spanish double-agent and master-spy Juan Pujol, who fabricated his reports to the Abwehr in Madrid for nine months while in Portugal, but operated from London from April 1942 until the end of the war. KV2/4213.
GELATINE	The Austrian Friedle Gaertner, whose sister, Lisel, was married to Ian Menzies.
HAMLET	Dr Johann Koessler, a Jewish businessman, former Austrian cavalry officer and double-agent recruited in 1941 in Lisbon by MULLET. He ran an imaginary network in England consisting of PUPPET and some notional agents until 1944, and died in Brussels in March 1947. KV2/325.

HARLEQUIN	An Abwehr defector, Richard Wurmann was captured in North Africa and brought to London in January 1943.
JEFF	The Norwegian agent Tor Glad who arrived in Scotland with MUTT in April 1941.
JOSEF	A Russian seaman, Powitzkow, active between August 1942 and December 1944 against the Japanese in Lisbon. KV2/2272.
LIPSTICK	The Catalan activist Josef Terradelas who arrived in London in November 1942.
METEOR	A Yugoslav pilot, Eugn Sostaric was recruited by his friend Dusan Popov.
MULLET	A British businessman, Ronald A. Thornton, based in Belgium and linked to HAMLET, who asked him to approach SIS on his behalf. KV2 326; KV 2/328.
MUTT	The Anglo–Norwegian John Moe was landed by a Luftwaffe seaplane off the coast of Scotland in April 1941 on a sabotage mission. Accompanied by JEFF, Moe immediately surrendered to the police and acted as a double-agent until 1944, when he joined the Norwegian Army.
PUPPET	Code name for Hans Fanto, linked to MULLET and HAMLET, who notionally sent him to England as his business agent. KV 2/327; KV2/329.
ROVER	A Polish naval officer who arrived in England in May 1944. His wireless transmitter remained active until the end of hostilities.
SNIPER	A Belgian pilot, Hans Bertrand, who reached England in November 1943.
TATE	The Danish parachute spy Wulf Schmidt, alias Harry Williamson, was arrested in Cambridgeshire in September 1940. He worked as a double-agent until the end of hostilities, and remained in England afterwards.
THE WEASEL	A Belgian ship's physician, Dr Hilaire Westerlinck, from the liner *Thysville*, who landed in England with his wife in May 1942.
THE WORM	A Yugoslav, Stefan Zeiss, from Belgrade, recruited by Ivo Popov.
TREASURE	The French journalist Lily Sergueiev, known to the Abwehr as TRAMP, who arrived in London in November 1943. KV 2/466.
TRICYCLE	The Yugoslav playboy Dusan Popov, known to the Abwehr as IVAN. KV 2/848.
ZIGZAG	The British safe-cracker Eddie Chapman, known to the Abwehr as FRITZCHEN. KV 2/458.

NOTES

Introduction

1   TRIPLEX was a joint MI5-SIS clandestine operation that copied the content of certain diplomatic pouches sent to Lisbon, Madrid and Stockholm from their London missions. The project was managed by Anthony Blunt for MI5 and David Boyle for SIS.

1   First Report, 2 April 1943

1   No German saboteurs were ever landed in Palestine by U-boat, although in August 1942 an Abwehr courier, Jawad Hamadi, had been dispatched on *U-372*, but the submarine was sunk off Haifa.

2   Charles O. Boyd was a South African student arrested in Scotland in November 1942 soon after his arrival from France. He had been compromised by ISOS, which revealed that he had been trained for an Abwehr mission to South Africa. He was interrogated at Camp 020, where he tried to commit suicide by slashing his wrists, and was imprisoned for the remainder of the war at Dartmoor. The suggestion that he be run as a double-agent was vetoed by Prime Minister Jan Smuts. KV 2/1158.

3   Gastao de Freitas, formerly employed by the Marconi Company in Lisbon, was a wireless operator on the *Gil Eannes* at the end of June 1942, when he was recruited by a German agent named Schmidt to make radio reports of his sightings of Allied shipping in the Atlantic. Compromised by ISOS, he was detained on 1 November 1942 by a destroyer, HMS *Oribi*, and taken to Gibraltar for transfer to Camp 020. After some initial resistance, de Freitas confessed to having broadcast encrypted reports of Allied shipping for enemy U-boats and was detained until the end of the war, when he was deported to Portugal. KV 2/2947.

4   Manoel Mesquita dos Santos was a Portuguese journalist who left Lisbon at the end of April on a mission to Lourenço Marques. However, the ship returning him to Lisbon in October 1942 put in at Freetown, where he was arrested and transferred to Camp 020. KV 2/2108.

5   Ernesto Simoes was arrested soon after his arrival at Poole from Lisbon at the end of July 1943, having been betrayed by ISOS that indicated he had been recruited in May and given a training course in secret writing by a well-known Abwehr figure, Kuno Weltzien. A well-travelled 31-year-old Portuguese aeronautical technician recruited by the Ministry of Labour, he was placed under surveillance by MI5 B6 watchers, and given discreet help to obtain a job at the Percival Aircraft factory in Luton, where he lodged with one of the other employees. He wrote a single

letter to a German cover address in Lisbon, Lucia Gonzales, rua Jardin do Regador 29, 40, and apart from seducing his landlady, Mrs Gibbs of 27 Alton Road, made no attempt to engage in espionage, even when he was encouraged to do so by an MI5 *agent provocateur* code-named EGGS who was fluent in Spanish and worked at the Napier factory assembling Sabre aero engines. Simoes did, however, receive a reply to his letter, concealing a message instructing him to use a new cover address in Lisbon: Maria da Conceição de Almeida, rua Astor Isadore 13–10. The decision to liquidate the case was taken because of the fear that he had found a method of communicating with the Abwehr undetected, and the general lack of progress over a period of three months' surveillance.

Simoes was arrested on 16 November 1943, questioned at Luton police station, where he made a partial confession, and then was transferred to Camp 020 for interrogation by Tommy Harris of B1(g). He signed a comprehensive confession in March 1943 and remained at Camp 020R, at Huntercombe Place, until June 1945, and was deported from Hurn to Lisbon by air in September 1945. KV 2/294.

2   Second Report, 2 May 1943

1   Johann (Julius) Hagemann was interrogated in Belgium at the end of the war. KV 2/32992.
2   Werner Unversagt was interrogated by MI5 at the end of the war. KV2/90; KV2/91.
3   OSTRO was Paul Fidrmuc, a Czech suspected of fabricating his information.

3   Third Report, 1 June 1943

1   Frank Duquesne was a German spy arrested by the FBI in New York in June 1941 and sentenced to eighteen years' imprisonment. The prosecutions resulted in nineteen pleas of guilty and a total of thirty-two convictions but several of the couriers employed on Nord Deutsche-Amerika liners evaded capture because they were out of the jurisdiction. KV 2/1956.
2   Compromised by ISOS, Juan Lecube was arrested at Trinidad while on a voyage to Panama and reached Camp 020 in October 1942. In spite of the weight of evidence against him, including the formulae for secret ink, he never confessed and was transferred to Huntercombe. In December 1944 he was moved to Dartmoor, and was deported to Spain in August 1945. KV 2/1456.
3   After his dismissal from MI5 Hooper was employed by Shell Oil in The Hague and retired aged 54 to run a translation business. He died at Epe in 2001.

4   Fourth Report, 2 July 1943

1   Joe Garber had fought in Spain with the 15th International Brigade and then spent two years employed by the Servicio de Investigacion Militar.
2   For Oliver Green's MI5 file, see KV 2/2204.

5   Fifth Report, 1 September 1943

1   The Italian sabotage offensive on Gibraltar was described by Marshall Pugh in *Frogman: Commander Crabb's Story* (New York: Scribner, 1956) and the 1958 film *The Silent Enemy*.

2   Popov eventually published an account of his wartime adventures, *Spy Counter Spy*, in which he changed the names of the members of his network, and in December 1980 Ivo Popov died at home outside Nassau. Eight months later, on 10 August 1981, Popov died at his home, formerly the bishop's palace in Opio.

3   Harry Williamson's own account may be found in *Seven Spies Who Changed the World* (London: Secker & Warburg, 1991).

4   A Foreign Office cipher clerk, Captain John King was convicted of Soviet espionage in October 1939 and sentenced to ten years' imprisonment. KV 2/815.

5   Dr Alan Nunn May was convicted of Soviet espionage in May 1946 and was sentenced to ten years' imprisonment. He was released in 1952 and died in January 2003. KV 2/2209–2226; 2563–2564.

6   Sixth Report

1   For the internal histories of CICI see WO 208/3088, and SIME KV4/223.

2   See also the account by Grosjean's son in the *International Journal of Intelligence and Counterintelligence* (Vol. 18, No. 2, February 2005).

3   For Frank Ryan's MI5 file, see KV 2/1291.

4   Hermann Goetz had been sentenced in London to four years' imprisonment in March 1936 for espionage. He parachuted into County Meath in May 1940 and was arrested in Dublin seventeen months later. He took his own life in May 1947 shortly before he was due to be repatriated.

7   Seventh Report, 1 November 1943

1   See also *Camp 020: MI5 and the Nazi Spies* edited by Oliver Hoare (London: Public Record Office, 2000).

2   Ken Crosby, unpublished autobiography, *Crosby's Luck*.

3   A Type VII submarine attached to the 6th Flotilla, the *U-252* was on her first patrol when Ib Riis was delivered to Iceland from Norway but was sunk on 14 April 1942 by HMS *Stork* and *Vetch* during an attack on Convoy OG 82.

4   The *U-279* was sunk on 4 October 1943 during a depth-charge attack by a Coastal Command Liberator off the coast of Iceland.

8   Eighth Report, 1 December 1943

1   *Secret Service Rendered* by Lily Sergueiev (London: William Kimber, 1968). Her MI5 file documents the murder of her sister, the Countess Moussia Sauty de Chalon, by a Belgian mechanic, Leon Murant, near Asniere-sur-Seine in northern France in September 1945.

9   Ninth Report, 1 January 1944

1   The two German submarines that did reach Argentina were the *U-530*, which surrendered in in Mar del Plata, and the *U-977* a month later.

2   Malcolm Muggeridge described some of his warime experiences in Mozambique in his autobiography, *Chronicles of Wasted Time* (London: Collins, 1972).

10 Tenth Report, 1 February 1944

1   GARBO released his autobiography *GARBO*, by Juan Pujol with Nigel West (London: Weidenfeld & Nicolson, 1985). See also *GARBO: The Spy Who Saved D-Day* (London: Public Record Office, 2000); *Agent Garbo* by Stephan Talty (New York: Houghton Mifflin, 2012); *The Spy with 29 Names* by Jason Webster (London: Chatto & Windus, 2014).
2   The condemned spy was Oswald Job.
3   The 'recently arrived' SD spy in Italy was probably Mandredo de Blasis.
4   The Yugoslav naval officer was most probably Eugn Sostaric, code-named METEOR, and introduced previously in the second report.
5   One of the two returned double-agents was TRICYCLE.
6   An oblique reference to Ernesto Hoppe as the character who had been instructed to deliver cash and valuables to Argentina by U-boat. Oddly, his case had already been covered in the Ninth Report.
7   Kenneth Rose. *Elusive Rothschild* (London: Weidenfeld & Nicolson, 1981).

11 Ninth Report, 7 March 1944

1   Louis de Bray was captured on 26 September 1944 and interrogated at Camp 020. His MI5 file is at KV2/120.

12 Churchill Intervenes

1   Sir Walter Citrine was General Secretary of the Trades Union Congress for twenty years, and a director of the *Daily Herald* until 1946.

13 3 April 1944

1   G.W. was MI5's code name for Gwylym Williams. See *SNOW* by Madoc Roberts (London: Biteback, 2014).
2   Vera Erikson had landed near Portgordon in Scotland in September 1940. She was detained for the remainder of the war and was interrogated by Klop Ustinov. See *Klop: Britain's Most Ingenious Spy* by Peter Day (London: Biteback, 2014).
3   Justin Tocabens was interrogated at Camp 020 in July 1944. He had been employed by Werner Unversagt to pay Joseph Vanhove's salary to his wife.
4   Waldberg and Meier were hanged at Wandsworth in August 1941.

15 3 June 1944

1   The assault on Tito's headquarters at Drvar in Croatia on 25 May 1944, code-named ROSSELSPRING, by the 500th SS Parachute Battalion failed. The Abwehr had exploited signals intelligence to locate Tito, but could not find the cave in which he and his staff had been living. The Germans withdrew after suffering heavy losses.
2   Saetrang's fellow passengers Stefansen and Elverstadt were transferred to Glasgow on the *Leopoldville*, and detained for two months before being released.
3   In 1991 Ib Riis's memoirs, *British Spy in Iceland*, were published in Icelandic.

4 Fresenius was uncertain whether the U-boat was the *U-287* or *U-289* but identified the commander as Alexander Kellwig. This mission, while attached to the 3rd Flotilla at Bergen, was *U-289*'s first and last. It was sunk on a second patrol on 31 May 1933 by HMS *Milne* off Jan Mayen Island.

5 *The Big Network* by Roman Garby-Czerniawski (London: George Ronald, 1961).

16 3 July 1944

1 Having broken with the CPGB in 1934, Jack Haston became a founder member of the Trotskyite Workers International League and moved to Ireland with the Delta group when he feared the organisation would be banned. As he returned he was imprisoned for travelling on false papers. He later campaigned in South Africa, was a parliamentary candidate in the 1945 Neath by-election and joined the Labour Party in 1950. He was employed as a lecturer for the National Council of Labour Colleges and died in 1986 aged 73.

2 Roy Tearse was the Industrial Organiser for the Trotskyite Revolutionary Communist Party on Tyneside and his party's influence on the shipyard apprentices was discussed in Cabinet on 3 April 1944 (CAB 65/41). His 1944 conspiracy conviction was quashed on appeal. He retained his commitment to the Trotskyite cause and in 1971 formed a secretive faction, the Discussion Group. He died in October 1986. ASS 34/104/2.

3 Heaton Lee radicalised the divorcée Anne Keen while on a voyage from South Africa to England in 1935.

4 Born Angel Ryan, the daughter of a Hampshire vicar, Anne Keen emigrated to Cape Town with her family but returned to England in 1935 and two years later, having been radicalised by Heaton Lee, became secretary of the Workers Internnational League. She remained an active Trotskyite, joined the Labour Party and died in London in December 2001 aged 86.

17 1 August 1944

1 Bedaux's home, lent to the Duke of Windsor, was the Château de Candé in Touraine, just south of Tours.

2 Erich Pfieffer had been implicated, with Dr Ignatz Griebl, in the 1936 Günther Rumrich espionage case in New York. On that occasion Pfieffer had eluded the FBI and escaped to Germany.

18 August 1944, undated

1 For an account of 30 Commando's entry into the German embassy in Rome and the destruction of the sabotage cache, see *Gentle Johnny Ramensky* by Robert Jeffery (London: Black & White, 2011).

19 5 October 1944

1 See also *SNOW* by Madoc Roberts (London: Biteback, 2013).

2 See also *John Moe: Double Agent* by Jan Moen (Edinburgh: Mainstream, 1986).

20 3 November 1944

1   Mistakenly identified in the MI5 report as 'Werner' Lorenz, he was actually Fritz Wilhelm Lorenz. In his diary entry for 24 November 1944 Guy Liddell also referred to him as 'Werner Lorenz'.

2   Lorenz was arrested in Namur, not Paris.

21 12 December 1944

1   See *The Strange Case of Traitor Sergeant Harold Cole* by Brendan Murphy (London: Macdonald, 1987).

2   See *The Venlo Incident* by S.P. Best (London: Hutchinson, 1950).

3   See *The Mirror of Deception* by Gunter Peis(London: Weidenfeld & Nicolson, 1976).

4   Suzanne Marteau was identified by Verloop and Damen as an 18-year-old girl from Mons who had been coerced by van Vliet. Her brother had been deported as a forced labourer and she pretended to assist an escape line from Brussels to Paris via Erquelinnes and Jeumont. MI5 received reports that she trafficked in tobacco and drugs.

5   For Richard Christmann's MI5 file see KV2/946.

6   For Ridderhof's MI5 file see KV2/1170.

7   For Knoppens' MI5 file see KV6/38. In his *SOE in the Low Countries* (London: St Ermin's, 2001) M.R.D. Foot erroneously stated that 'senior Abwehr agents exonerated him just after the war' (p. 181).

8   For Celosses' SOE file see HS9/284/3.

9   JOHANNES was Professor George Jambroes. In fact he and his wireless operator had been arrested by the Germans at his drop-zone upon arrival.

10 KALE was K.W. Beukema Toe Water, who was arrested in September 1942 and executed at Mauthausenin in September 1944.

11 The address was Charlotte de Bourbonsatraat 229. According to Damen, de Wilde was a 40-old pre-war Dutch policeman and Nazi Party member from Groesbeek who joined Abt III in 1943 under Willi Kup. Supposedly an expert forger, Damen was allegedly told by his American captors that de Wilde had been arrested on 19 September 1944 at Nijmegen but sent by accident to England as a PoW.

12 MARCEL was Jack Agazarian, a key member of the PROSPER *reseau*. He was arrested soon after his return to Paris in July 1943 and was executed at Flossenburg in March 1945.

13 STEAK was an entirely notional agent supposedly recruited in the field.

14 APOLLO was J.D. van Schelle, who returned to England in December 1943.

15 BRUTUS was Johan Gruen (not to be confused with MI5's double-agent Roman Garby-Czerniawski) who was arrested in January 1944 and released in April 1945.

16 Madame Mertins was actually Mrs Mertens, proprietor of the Hotel Leopold II at 5 rue de Croisards in Brussels.

17 The navigator of a USAAF B-17 bomber shot down over Holland in October 1943, John Hurst supplied a detailed account of his experiences along the VIC line, unaware he had been under German sponsorship throughout his journey to Spain.

18 CHIVE was Johan Ubbink, who escaped to Bern in November 1943, where
    he contacted London to raise the alarm. SPROUT was his companion, Pieter
    Dourlein, whom the Germans tried to discredit when he attempted to warn
    SOE about NORDPOL.

22 6 January 1945

1   *War Commentary* was published by Vernon Richards, whose father Emilio Recchioni
    was involved in a plot to assassinate Benito Mussolini in 1931. Richards was
    convicted at the Old Bailey of incitement and was sentenced in April 1945 to nine
    months' imprisonment. After his release he continued to manage the Freedom Press,
    publishing anarchist material. He died in Hadleigh, Suffolk, in 2001. His co-editor,
    Philip Sansom, was also editor of the *Sewing Machine Times* and died in October 1999.

23 19 February 1945

1   The seven spies in Iceland had been captured in April 1944. They were: Einar
    Sigvaldason; Larus Thorsteinsson; Magnus Gudbjornsson; Sverrir Matthiasson;
    Ernst Fresenius; Sigurdur Juliusson; and Hjalti Bjornsson. See Chapter 15.
    Evidence that the Germans expected an invasion on the Norwegian coast may
    be deduced from the scale of the garrison, amounting to eleven divisions and five
    brigades, totaling 350,000 troops. In addition there were twenty-seven U-boats
    based at Bergen, Narvik, Trondheim, Hammerfest and Kirkenes.

24 5 March 1945

1   The agent in Spain was almost certainly the fabricator OSTRO.
2   Ewen Montagu, the Naval Intelligence Division representative on the XX
    Committee, recalled in *Beyond Top Secret U* (New York: Coward, McCann, 1977)
    that 'Churchill was away at a conference and the decision was based on the
    cowardly principle that no one was entitled to decide that A should die rather
    than B, and the scheme was vetoed. At this point Sir Findlater Stewart revealed his
    great courage. After his briefing by John Drew he was convinced that the Germans
    valued several of our agents highly and would accept their reports' (p. 159).
3   See *The Double Cross System of the War of 1939–1945* by J.C. Materman (London:
    Pimlico, 1995) p. 181. After the war Flak Regiment 155's commanding officer,
    Max Wachtel, confirmed that he had relied on agent reports rather than the data
    transmitted by equipment fitted to some of the V-1s.

25 March and April 1945, undated

1   John Olday was arrested on a charge of incitement, having printed a circular
    letter addressed to troops on a press established in Philip Sansom's studio.
    KV 2/3599; KV 2/3597; KV 2/3588.
2   *Kingdom of Rags* (London: Jarrolds, 1939)
3   Helmut von Rauschenplat was employed by the Political Warfare Executive. See
    his MI5 file, KV6/106.

26 11 June 1945

1 See *In Durance Vile* by John Brown (London: Robert Hale, 1981).
2 For William Joyce's biography, see *Haw-Haw* by Nigel Farndale (London: Macmillan, 2005).
3 Norman Baillie-Stewart was convicted of espionage for the Germans in March 1933 and sentenced to three years' imprisonment. His autobiography is *Officer in the Tower* (London: Leslie Frewin, 1967).
4 For John Amery's biography, see *Patriot Traitors* by Adrian Weale (London: Viking, 2001).
5 *A Spy Has No Friends* (London: Andre Deutsch. 1952). For Seth's SOE file, see HS9/1345. For his MI5 file, see KV2/378.

27 HARLEQUIN

1 Eiserne Kreuz First Class.
2 See Hans Scharf, Chapter 17.
3 The Caudron Affair was a reference to Bedaux's director of his French companies, Jean Caudron.

28 GARBO

1 Aracelli Pujol contacted the assistant US naval attaché, Theodore Rousseau Jr, Born in Freeport, Long Island, Rousseau was a distinguished art historian who was educated at Eton and the Sorbonne. His post-war career was at New York's Metropolitan Museum of Art, and he died in December 1973, aged 61.
2 The Swiss agent was William Gerbers.
3 The W/T operator was Charles Haines.
4 Reinhard Spitzy released an autobiography, *How We Squandered the Reich* (London: Michael Russell, 1997).

Postscript

1 Having created the organisation in the first place, MI5 failed to retain the Radio Security Service, which became SIS's Radio Intelligence Section in May 1941.
2 *The Double Cross System in the War of 1939–1945* by J.C. Masterman (New Haven, Conn: Yale, 1972).
3 *The Ultra Secret* by F.W. Winterbotham (London: Weidenfeld & Nicolson, 1974).
4 *MI5: British Security Service Operations 1909–45* by Nigel West (London: Bodley Head, 1981).
5 *Strategic Deception in Wotld War II* by Michael Howard (London: HMSO, 1981). KV4/83.
6 *FORTITUDE: The D-Day Deception Campaign* by Roger Hesketh (London: St Ermin's Press, 1999).
7 See National Archives file KV4/83.

INDEX